E.C. DRURY: AGRARIAN IDEALIST

In a fiercely fought provincial election in 1919, a new political movement came to power in Ontario. The victorious party was the United Farmers of Ontario. Its leader, Ernest Charles Drury (1878—1968), became the province's eighth premier.

Idealistic agrarian reformer, staunch temperance man, free-trade advocate, Simcoe County 'yeoman,' and progressive populist, Drury was a man of the people and of the land, inevitably tagged the Farmer Premier. In this biography, Charles M. Johnston follows the career of Drury through agrarian activism and partisan politics, and explores the personal and ideological forces that directed him.

Drury began his career in the farm movement as leader of the Dominion Grange and Farmers' Alliance. He went on to act as the driving force behind the Canadian Council of Agriculture, and then co-founded the UFO in 1913. Activist though he was, Drury as premier sought no dramatic departures from established political procedures. When others of his party did, notably J.J. Morrison and W.C. Good, Drury disavowed their class-consciousness and their formula of group government. Instead he advocated the creation of a people's party, based on what he called Broadening Out–an appeal to all citizens, regardless of class, occupation, or political stripe, who were seen to share the farmer's desire for a more humane, moral, and progressive society in the wake of the First World War.

The question of Broadening Out was a controversial one within agrarian ranks, and it led to dissension among the leaders. This weakening of the party combined with the shrewd tactics of Howard Ferguson's Tories to bring about the Drury government's downfall in 1923. During its four years in power it had enacted some solid social welfare legislation, but its defeat was resounding. With it came the effective end of Drury's political career.

Johnston offers a revealing study of a brief chapter in Ontario history and of the man whose principles and ideals shaped it.

CHARLES M. JOHNSTON is Professor of History at McMaster University. He is the author of The Valley of the Six Nations, Brant County: A History, and the two volumes of the history of McMaster University, *The Toronto Years and The Early Years in Hamilton.*

Premier E.C. Drury: a studio portrait taken in August 1922

CHARLES M. JOHNSTON

E.C. Drury:
Agrarian Idealist

Published by University of Toronto Press
Toronto   Buffalo   London
for The Ontario Historical Studies Series

ISBN 978–0–8020–3432–8 (cloth)
ISBN 978–1–4875–9208–0 (paper)

Canadian Cataloguing in Publication Data
Johnston, Charles M., 1926–
    E.C. Drury: agrarian idealist
    (Ontario historical studies series, ISSN 0380–9188)
    Includes index.
    ISBN 978–0–8020–3432–8 (bound)   ISBN 978–1–4875–9208–0 (pbk.)
    1. Drury, E.C. (Ernest Charles), 1878–1968.
    2. Prime ministers – Ontario – Biography.
    3. Ontario – Politics and government – 1905–1919.*
    4. United Farmers of Ontario.   I. Title.   II. Series.
    FC3073.1.D78J65 1986   971.3'03'0924   c86–094468–9
    F1058.D78J65 1986

PICTURE CREDITS
All photographs have been provided by the Drury family with the following
exceptions:
Ministry of Agriculture, Guelph: Charles Drury
Archival Collections, University of Guelph Library: Ontario Agricultural College;
    graduating class OAC 1900
Ontario Archives: first United Farmers of Ontario cabinet; W.E. Raney; Peter Smith;
    Frank Biggs; Beniah Bowman; Manning Doherty on steps of legislature; Premier
    Drury in 1922

This book has been published with funds provided by the Government of Ontario
through the Ministry of Citizenship and Culture.

Contents

The Ontario Historical Studies Series

For many years the principal theme in English-Canadian historical writing has been the emergence and the consolidation of the Canadian nation. This theme has been developed in uneasy awareness of the persistence and importance of regional interests and identities, but because of the central role of Ontario in the growth of Canada, Ontario has not been seen as a region. Almost unconsciously, historians have equated the history of the province with that of the nation and have depicted the interests of other regions as obstacles to the unity and welfare of Canada.

The creation of the province of Ontario in 1867 was the visible embodiment of a formidable reality, the existence at the core of the new nation of a powerful if disjointed society whose traditions and characteristics differed in many respects from those of the other British North American colonies. The intervening century has not witnessed the assimilation of Ontario to the other regions in Canada; on the contrary it has become a more clearly articulated entity. Within the formal geographical and institutional framework defined so assiduously by Ontario's political leaders, an increasingly intricate web of economic and social interests has been woven and shaped by the dynamic interplay between Toronto and its hinterland. The character of this regional community has been formed in the tension between a rapid adaptation to the processes of modernization and in-dustrialization in modern Western society and a reluctance to modify or discard traditional attitudes and values. Not surprisingly, the Ontario outlook is a compound of aggressiveness, conservatism, and the conviction that its values should be the model for the rest of Canada.

From the outset the objective of the Board of Trustees of the Ontario Historical Studies Series has been to describe and analyse the historical development of Ontario as a distinct region within Canada. The series as planned will include some thirty volumes covering many aspects of the life and work of the province from its original establishment in 1791 as Upper Canada to our own time. Among these will be biographies of several premiers, numerous works on the growth of the provincial economy, educational institutions, minority groups, and the arts, and a synthesis of the history of Ontario, based upon the contributions of the biographies and thematic studies.

In planning this project, the Editors and the Board have endeavoured to maintain a reasonable balance between different kinds and areas of historical research, and to appoint authors ready to ask new questions about the past and to answer them in accordance with the canons of contemporary scholarship. Nine biographical studies have been included, if only because through biography the past comes alive most readily for the general reader as well as the historian. The historian must be sensitive to today's concerns and standards as he engages in the imaginative recreation of the interplay between human beings and circumstances in time. He should seek to be the mediator between the dead and the living, but in the end the humanity and the artistry of his account will determine the extent of its usefulness.

This biography of Ernest Charles Drury is the eleventh volume in the Series to be published. It depicts the life and times of the first and only Farmer-Labour premier of Ontario, whose administration has been described as 'an unforgettable interlude' in the political history of the province. Drury and his colleagues were committed to 'the creation in some way of a new order of things,' but when they were driven from power in 1923 many of their hopes and aspirations were still largely unfulfilled. We believe that this study illuminates the ideals and the objectives of E.C. Drury and his movement, and that it will deepen our understanding of an important aspect of the political and social development of twentieth-century Ontario.

The Editors and the Board of Trustees are grateful to Charles Johnston for undertaking this task.

Goldwin French
Peter Oliver
Jeanne Beck
Maurice Careless, Chairman of the Board of Trustees

Toronto
18 August 1986

Preface

The published memoirs of Ernest Charles Drury, Simcoe County native and eighth prime minister of the province of Ontario, carry the simple title *Farmer Premier*. On the face of it any other would have been absurd. His rural background, agricultural pursuits, professional training, and protracted labours on behalf of the farm movement in Canada make the title a particularly apt one. Co-founder of the United Farmers of Ontario, leader of the Dominion Grange and Farmers' Association, and a moving spirit behind the organization of the Canadian Council of Agriculture – these were the highlights of Drury's career as an agrarian activist. To clinch matters, he was called upon in the wake of the Ontario election of 1919 to head the so-called Farmers' Government after UFO candidates had startled the community by winning the largest block of seats in the legislature. No other leader in Ontario's political experience had been placed in the position of forming a government that did not draw its support from either of the old-line parties. No other leader had come to the task with so little formal political training.

However, E.C. Drury was not the first, nor certainly the last, 'son of the soil' to occupy the premier's office at Queen's Park. Others also brought a rural view of the cosmos to their understanding of the challenges of government in Ontario. It should be borne in mind as well that agrarian activist though he was, Drury sought no dramatic departures from the established procedures of Ontario politics. From the very outset he worked assiduously toward what he dubbed 'Broadening Out.' Without jettisoning the party system as such, he would urge his legislative followers to reach out to other citizens, urbanite and non-urbanite alike, who were seen to share his desire to fashion a more humane, moral, and progressive society in Ontario.

Drury did not seek to restructure the Ontario parliamentary system so much as to launder it, hang it out morally to dry, and make it more presentable and responsive to the community. And for him community embraced people and interests drawn from every walk of life and from every political quarter who

were nonetheless united in a common desire to cleanse society of the imperfec-
tions that had been allowed to accumulate in Ontario's unhappy political past.
But for the radicals in the farm movement, this attempt to create a so-called
people's party would merely end up duplicating the evils of the thoroughly
detested party system and do nothing to ease the full-blown political crisis that
all were agreed was facing the province and the country at large. They urged
instead a system of group government whereby democratically elected occupational or class blocs would collaborate or compete in a restructured legislature.
Only this departure, they argued, would undo the 'plutocratic interests' that had
long manipulated the political process in Ontario. In the end the struggle between
group government's champions and Broadening Out's supporters would help to
dig the Farmer Government's grave in 1923.

At the same time, Drury's passionate dedication to the rural ethic made him
less than credible in the eyes of many an urban voter. His article of secular faith
that 'the farm is the bulwark of the land ... , the simplest, truest, and sweetest
social life of the nation' would command little respect in those circles that equated
the city with the blessings of modernization and the delights of civilization. The
more Drury railed against urbanization and its supposed evils, the more remote
he was perceived to be from the mainstream of progress.

Yet the fact remains that the bugbears of the Ontario farm movement – rural
depopulation and its concomitant, the lure of the city – were for Drury and the
UFO very real dangers to the world they were anxious to preserve. Nor was it
just a case of Drury's overlooking the countryside's shortcomings and blaming
the city dweller for all its woes. He clearly realized early on that life on the
concession lines must be made more palatable, stimulating, and rewarding,
through educational reforms and advances in agriculture, if farmers' offspring
were to stay content with life down on the farm.

On the other hand, one must concede Drury's preoccupation, indeed obsession,
with free trade as a cure-all for the nation's varied ailments. If only protection
could be done away with, he thundered over the years, the whole of society
would be immeasurably improved and a new and more liberal age ushered in.
The crusade for free trade ranked with prohibition as an all-embracing panacea
for Canada's ills. And throughout, Drury left few in doubt about his almost
pathological dislike of the selfish businessman who fattened on the benefits
conferred by high tariffs. This was a species of economic man that symbolized
for Drury the cynical, unethical, and corruptive attitudes and practices that were
polluting the Canadian market place. Yet, in spite of all this, he was no simple
Luddite out to dismantle the economic structure of Ontario, even though some
critics of his Hydro policy might have been excused if they thought so.

Similarly, Drury was not other-worldly when he gave expression to his religious commitment. He spurned the anti-intellectualism and the sectarian nostrums
of the fundamentalist just as forcefully as he lampooned the sophisticated com-
plexities of theological debate. For him religion constituted a personal endeavour

to live by the golden rule of a 'simple functional Christianity' that would be sensitive to the needs of his fellow man and responsive to the problems of his society. At times admittedly he affected a smugness and a moral arrogance that were unwarranted by inconsistencies in his own behaviour and that laid him open to legitimate charges of being stuffily self-righteous. For the most part he shrugged off such recriminations as he went happily about the task of reminding his and subsequent generations where their flaws and faults resided.

This, then, in part was the Ernest Charles Drury who was invited to form Ontario's government in the fall of 1919. For all his lack of formal political and parliamentary experience, he came to the task reasonably well equipped. Years spent actively in varied and exacting branches of the Canadian farm movement, his own family's taste for politics, both local and provincial, and his enviable gifts as an orator, debater, administrator, and spokesman gave him formidable weapons with which to wage what he considered to be the good fight at Queen's Park after 1919.

A special vote of thanks is owed to the editors of the Ontario Historical Studies Series, Goldwin French, Peter Oliver, and Jeanne Beck, who were perceptive and sympathetic guides and constructive critics of the work as it progressed. And when it did not progress, because of other commitments, their forbearance was nothing short of remarkable.

The work of research was eased immeasurably by the cheerful exertions of a host of archivists and librarians, all the way from the Public Archives of Canada and the Archives of Ontario to a variety of local repositories and the collections that flourish on university campuses in this province. I had a particularly happy and productive association with Peter Moran and his colleague, Su Murdoch, at the Simcoe County Archives. The annual spring excursions that my wife and I undertook to their picturesquely situated treasure trove will always be memorable. Ed Phelps of Western's Regional Collection demonstrated his inimitable informality and unfailing ingenuity when he sought out and put at my disposal vital documents and theses. The same kind of co-operation and expertise marked the response of archival staffs at other institutions, which included the universities of Guelph, Queen's, Toronto, McMaster, Waterloo, and Brock. In the early stages of the research I received commendable assistance from Michael Woods, a former student, and I am happy to acknowledge that assistance in these pages.

And then there were the people who uncomplainingly took time out to be interviewed or to answer questions. Topping the list is the Drury family. Harold Drury and his wife Marion gave unstintingly of their time and hospitality, and allowed me to examine family letters that had to do with their father's later writings. On one occasion, Harold's sisters, Beth and Mabel, attended a gathering at the home farm in Crown Hill and shared with me colourful reminiscences and reflections. In turn Varley and Margaret Drury invited my wife and me to their Southampton home and told us what they remembered of Ontario's farmer premier. R.O. Biggs of Waterloo, the son of F.C. Biggs, Drury's highways minister, provided a number of welcome insights, and Robert Nixon, MPP, followed suit with recollections of his father's political career as Drury's lieutenant. Similarly Beth Good Latzer, the daughter of W.C. Good, graciously augmented what was known about her father's relationship with Drury. Allan Ironside of Orillia and Pete McGarvey of Toronto, both unabashed Drury admirers, added substantially to my understanding of the closing stages of his long life. They also supplied documentary items and tape recordings of his speeches.

Drury's former subordinates during his years as sheriff at the Simcoe County Court House in Barrie made informative contributions of their own. Amelia Whalen and Greta Harradine, respectively at the time of writing senior deputy local registrar and supervisor of court reporters, joined forces at their interview with John Murphy, who fondly recalled Drury's penchant for political discussion. Leonard Harmon, long active in the Ontario co-operative movement, was good enough to put me in touch with people in the farming community, such as Lloyd Cumming and Hunter Russell of the Barrie area, who enlightened me on Drury's accomplishments as a farmer and rural spokesman. Mr Harmon also furnished an entrée to UFO documentation and other relevant materials in the library of the United Co-operatives of Ontario. Kenneth Kidd, archaeologist emeritus of the Royal Ontario Museum, kindly filled me in on Drury's efforts to recapture the province's Indian past. And one summer day the office staff of Collingwood Terminals good-naturedly spared an hour from a busy schedule to ferret out records of those early times when Drury was actively involved with the firm.

I enjoyed my conversations with my friend and former student, Jim Greenlee of Memorial University, who patiently and stimulatingly responded to my attempts to sort out the problems inherent in this project, particularly when they impinged on his current interest – Sir Robert Falconer and the University of Toronto. I also appreciated the editorial suggestions and formidable typing skills of his wife Joanne, who prepared the manuscript for the editors. A McMaster friend and colleague, Tom Willey, generously bolstered my morale in the dark moments of unproductivity. Finally, the sharp eye, shrewd judgment, and editorial talents of Diane Mew rescued the manuscript from many an infelicitous statement and confusing passage. To all these people I owe an imposing debt of gratitude.

The financial assistance afforded by the Social Sciences and Humanities Research Council is also gratefully acknowledged. Their timely award of a leave fellowship enabled me to complete the bulk of the task. As in the past, McMaster University provided encouragement and financial aid, along with congenial surroundings in which to work.

I am, as always, enormously indebted to my wife, Lorna. Her unflagging cheerfulness and interest in the undertaking, together with her eagerness to help with varied research chores, made the labour of preparation much less arduous than it would otherwise have been. Since I have already dedicated one of my books to her, I dedicate this one to my children and grandchildren.

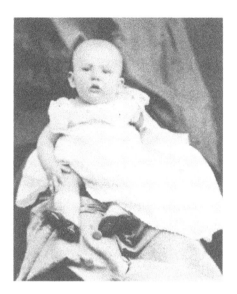

Ernest Drury as a baby

The young Ernest with a friend

Charles Drury, Ernest's father, and Ontario's first minister of agriculture

The Ontario Agricultural College, Guelph, as it was when Drury attended it, 1898–1900

The graduating class of 1900, Ontario Agricultural College. Drury is seated third from the left.

Ernest and Ella Drury, 11 January 1905

E.C. Drury shortly after becoming
premier

Ella Drury

The first cabinet of the United Farmers of Ontario government, 1919. From left to right: Manning Doherty, Henry Mills, Walter Rollo, Harry Nixon, F.C. Biggs, E.C. Drury, W.E. Raney, Peter Smith, Col. Carmichael, R.H. Grant, Beniah Bowman

Manning Doherty, the minister of agriculture, about to milk a cow on the steps of the legislature to promote the Pure Milk Campaign in Toronto, part of a public health program, June 1921

W.E. Raney, attorney general

Peter Smith, provincial treasurer

Frank Biggs, minister of public works

Beniah Bowman, minister of lands and forests

At home at Crown Hill: Drury in old age, surrounded by his grandchildren and family

E.C. DRURY: AGRARIAN IDEALIST

1

The Road from Kenilworth

Some one hundred miles northwest of London the town of Kenilworth lies in the pleasantly rolling Warwickshire countryside. Despite the heavy inroads made by the twentieth century on that part of England, the charming picture offered by a traveller's guide of the mid-nineteenth century can still be evoked: 'The fine, quiet, old English beauty of the scenery around, so softly undulating in its surface, so calm and hushed in its feeling, as though it had been charmed to sleep some thousand years ago ... '[1] The small community is still dominated by its castle. Built in the twelfth century, it has occasionally intruded on the centre stage of English history, finally being damaged in the Civil War and never restored.

Stories of English history, generated by the castle's imposing presence, were brought to Upper Canada by Joseph Drury when he emigrated to that part of the imperial frontier in 1819.[2] And clearly they were passed down to his great-grandson Ernest, the future premier of Ontario. Ernest took considerable pride in the knowledge that his ancestor was a yeoman farmer, from 'freedom-loving stock' to boot, a point assiduously stressed by his father, Charles Drury, and before him by his father Richard, who had accompanied Joseph to Upper Canada. Many years later Ernest Drury underscored the factor of permanence that these pioneers and their offspring had bestowed on the community: 'of the eleven farms [in the area] four are farmed by the descendants of the first settlers.'[3]

Why had Joseph Drury left the agreeable Warwickshire countryside? His farm of some one hundred acres was only slightly short of the average holding for that time. If he were as shy and insular as most Warwickshire farmers were reputed to be,[4] then it is unlikely that he was lured away to the new world by the spirit of adventure. Perhaps the general depression that stalked England in the aftermath of the Napoleonic War forced him to emigrate to supposedly greener fields. It is more likely that the effects of the parliamentary enclosure movement on the ancient open fields system may have taken their toll of Joseph and other small freeholders, who could not afford to cultivate the profitable new root crops that enclosure favoured and which were in demand in England's burgeoning industrial towns.[5] Add to these factors the growing promotional literature extolling Upper Canada's advantages, and some plausible picture can be formed of the motivations that spurred him to emigrate. He came with two of his grown sons, Richard and Thomas, leaving behind his wife, and his youngest son, Edmund, until he had established himself and could send for them. In the end his wife and daughter did not join him.

Joseph Drury was drawn to what became Oro Township, Simcoe County, by the possibilities afforded by the new road connecting Penetanguishene on Georgian Bay with York, Upper Canada's capital. Originally used by Indians and European entrepreneurs to tap the fur trade of the upper lakes, this access route had been improved by the British to retain their own dominion in that vast hinterland during the War of 1812. A part of their plan had been the establishment of a naval station at Penetanguishene and the building on the present site of Barrie of a storehouse for supplies and weapons in transit to the northwest. It was this modest rendez-vous, overlooking scenic Kempenfeldt Bay, that greeted Joseph Drury and other English arrivals in 1819. The area's link with the country beyond the lakes would never be severed and would serve to inspire the local tales spun to entertain and educate generations of Simcoe County youth, the young Ernest Drury included. Indeed, his family forged their own tentative ties to the interior. Richard and Thomas Drury briefly offered their services to the expedition organized in 1825 by Sir John Franklin to reach the Arctic Sea.

The area would lead a Janus-like existence, however, for the Penetang Road also brought it within the orbit of the lower lakes and would serve to consolidate York's hold over that part of Upper Canada. In due course the highway would also spawn the villages and hamlets that arose to cater to the immediate and varied needs of the Drurys and their neighbours. Thus Barrie progressed from storage depot to market town as more British immigrants moved in to join Joseph Drury and his sons in this strategic locale.

After filing the customary petition on 4 November 1819, indicating that he had the 'means to cultivate a new farm,'[6] the middle-aged Joseph was given a 'location ticket' for one hundred acres comprising Lot 30-1 in Oro Township. According to family lore he had some difficulty obtaining the necessary legal title, a problem that was not resolved until shortly before his untimely death in a raging snowstorm late in 1823.[7] From the beginning, Joseph relied heavily on his two energetic teenaged sons who, like able-bodied offspring elsewhere on the Upper Canadian frontier, were highly important economic assets. In 1820 the two men branched out on their own and were given title to an adjoining lot, with Richard occupying its northern half and Thomas the southern. Sometime after Joseph's death his other son, Edmund, came to Canada and settled on his father's property. While clearing and working their bush farms the older brothers also hired out their labour to neighbours and built a number of corduroy roads in the Barrie area, the remains of which were still in place over a century later.[8]

Thomas, who was to outlive his brother Richard by nearly twenty years, became actively involved with public affairs in the locality, as Oro Township councillor and reeve, and finally as sheriff of Simcoe County, an office that virtually became a family preserve. He appears to have had a reputation as a harsh dispenser of justice, particularly when he dealt with miscreants in Barrie's small black community.[9] Richard, on the other hand, when he served the public, refused to stoop to such questionable behaviour. Whatever their virtues or short-comings, the Drury brothers carved out a tradition of public service that first Richard's son Charles and later his grandson Ernest would find difficult to ignore. There is also a hint that Richard and Thomas Drury may have covertly supported the rebellion in Upper Canada in 1837. Their grandson once claimed in an interview that just after the turn of the century he had been shown a book containing the names of local settlers who had helped to underwrite William Lyon Mackenzie's uprising. 'I was astonished,' he recalled, 'to find the names of many people I knew ... including [those of] my grandfather and great-uncle.'[10]

In 1831 Richard Drury brought out to Upper Canada a Warwickshire girl, Elizabeth Bishop, to be his bride, and over the years she bore him twelve children, six boys and six girls. Richard's home reflected the taste for reading he had inherited from his father. In the homestead he built in 1836 were to be found books Joseph had brought with him to Canada: a Shakespeare, works by Milton and Thackeray, Pope's *Homer's Odyssey*, Bunyan's *Pilgrim's Progress*, Alison's *History of Europe*, and Bloomfield's *Poetical Works*, which dealt with English farm life. Tucked away in the collection, which Richard had augmented, was a copy of Macaulay's *History of England* and an edition of Adam Smith's *Wealth of Nations*, the classical treatise on political economy that would later become one of Ernest Drury's secular bibles. As well, there was a bound set of the English publication, *The Family Herald*, in which he first read of the stirring battles of the Crimean War and the complex vagaries of Victorian politics.[11]

Not surprisingly, education was a major priority in Richard Drury's household. He had been among the small band of trustees who in 1847 contracted to pay the teacher assigned to the community's original log schoolhouse where his son Charles would be tutored.[12] When the time came, Richard also saw to it that Charles went on to Dr Gore's District Grammar School, established in nearby Barrie in 1849. This was in keeping with his conviction that the emergent yeomanry of old Ontario should be properly schooled in the verities so that every farm would have, in his words, an 'educated man behind the plough handles.'[13]

To further this end Richard helped to launch the Oro Agricultural Society. Like its counterparts elsewhere in the colony, it sought to acquaint its members with agricultural innovations and the need to adapt to new challenges, brought on by the demand for more mixed farming and the large-scale production of root crops. During the Crimean War Britain was forced to import more heavily from her granary colonies, guaranteeing profitable returns for those local producers who could fill the bill for cereals and foodstuffs. Accompanying the profits of this wartime boom were the advantages promised by the 1854 Reciprocity Treaty with the United States. Deemed the last triumph of the agricultural order in British North America, it would remain for the Drurys an exemplar of the commercial policy the emergent Canadian nation should follow.

The home market was also showing signs of life. The colony's fledgling cities and towns were being galvanized into action by the first tentative steps toward industrialization and by the arrival of the railway, which brought new initiatives in commerce and manufacturing in its wake. Barrie was one of the first communities in the province to benefit from this technological marvel. In 1853, the very year the town became a separate municipality after its divorce from Vespra Township, the Ontario, Simcoe and Huron Railway (the future Northern Railway) was linked with nearby Allandale. 'Before this a journey to Toronto took two or even three days,' an early history of Barrie exulted, 'but by the opening of this railway ... the journey could be made in one day and a return the next.'[14]

Clearly Richard Drury was influenced by these changes, but he died before their full effect registered on the community. Even so, he had made his own enduring contribution to the beautification of his estate by planting trees: Lombardy poplars, beach locusts, mountain ash, and apple trees – Talman sweets, northern spy, a red astrachan, and a crabapple. But it would be his son Charles and his grandson Ernest who would benefit most from the transformation of Ontario's landscape after the mid-century. A new attitude to that landscape emerged with the arrival of second and third generation Ontarians who had not known of the forest or of the long struggle with the land.[15] This outlook was given architectural expression as well when Charles Drury built close by the old farm home a new red brick residence, appropriately named 'Kenilworth.' Clearly Richard's son was qualifying as a member of that substantial class of farmers which a government publication reported as having been long settled in Simcoe County and whose property was worth something of the order of $80 an acre.[16] Meanwhile, the farming community that the Drurys and other English immigrants had fashioned in that part of the township had taken the name of Crown Hill. According to a story told by Charles Drury, the name had been conferred by a visitor inspired by the 'decent church' that topped the 'neighbouring hill.'[17]

It was also a time for fresh approaches to those matters which touched the spirit and the moral health of Canada's late Victorian society. Charles Drury broke away from the Church of England over the liquor question and took refuge with the Methodists, the most voluble advocates of prohibition.[18] Anglicans in Canada soft-pedalled the need for such a measure, arguing that drinking was a private matter that ought not to be legislated against, a point of view that found no favour in the Drury household. So strongly did Charles Drury feel on the question that he and his brother William refused to sell their barley if there was the faintest hint that it might be corrupted into beer.[19] Charles's spiritual migration, his active membership in the Sons of Temperance, and his labours on behalf of the Crown Hill Methodist Church had a lasting effect on his son.

The family's draconian approach to the liquor question bemused the Anglicans in Barrie, who twitted the Drurys on their puritanical ways. It may be that the issue was a class one, with the 'humble Methodists' opposed to the professional and business elite who for the most part congregated in Anglican and Presbyterian pews and who, according to their squeamish critics, were prepared to wink at social excesses. Unquestionably Barrie, like a good many Ontario communities, was a town with a distinctly British flavour and well-defined class lines. Indeed, any exaltation of the high and mighty, together with a dismissal of the righteous but supposedly lower orders of society, seldom sat well with any Drury. Charles and his Crown Hill neighbours derisively turned their backs on the pretentious urban residents of Barrie, a posture that characterized other rural communities before the turn of the century. They looked upon their pristine community of Crown Hill as a shining example of the society so glowingly described by a president of the Ontario Agricultural College, in whose native village 'everybody worked. There was no idle or leisure class. There were none wealthy and none improverished. There was little snobbery. The hired man of today bade fair to become the farm owner of tomorrow. Petty attempts to establish social superiority were derided.'[20] These themes were reinforced by a government brochure which asserted that the

typical [Ontario] farmer ... is a temperate and moral man and a law-abiding citizen ... [who] may not always occupy so good a social position as the British farmer, nor so well as the dignity of his calling entitles him to. This may to some extent be attributed to the system arising out of the custom of earlier times, under which the farm hands he employs, become practically members of his family ... living in the same house and eating at the same table.[21]

For that matter, Crown Hill in the late nineteenth century was not yet totally dependent on the growing market and supply centre of Barrie. A wheelwright, a pump-maker, and a blacksmith provided essential services along with a three-storied steam mill built and owned by Charles Drury and his brothers, William and Thomas, in partnership with another local family. Self-sufficiency was not achieved, to be sure, but a large degree of material independence and cohesiveness was bestowed on Crown Hill by these simple but vital operations. Into this unpretentious and rustic setting, colonized by his great-grandfather some sixty years earlier, Ernest Charles Drury was born on 22 January 1878.

2

Growing up in Simcoe County

Ernest Drury's arrival was accompanied by tragedy. His mother, Marion Varley, daughter of a Yorkshire family settled in Barrie, did not survive the birth of her first child, a stark event all too common in those days. Deprived of a natural mother he never knew, he was taken over and affectionately raised by Aunt Bessie, his father's unmarried sister. Bessie Drury found time to provide not only the mothering he needed but inculcated in him the family taste for reading. She shared with him such classics as *Oliver Twist* and *Uncle Tom's Cabin*, in spite of the disapproval of a local Methodist preacher, who took less than kindly to novel-reading by women, even if it were done for the entertainment of children.

The time that Charles Drury could devote to the growing boy was limited by his farming tasks and his activities as a public servant. The farm was some four hundred acres, half of it ploughed land. Operated in partnership with his bachelor brother William, it was stocked with about fifty head of cattle and thirty sheep, a sizeable inventory for that day. Although the chores Charles assigned to his son were arduous and time-consuming, they brought him into daily contact with his father and uncle and furnished him a sound education in what then passed for enlightened farming. His responsibilities also provided insights into the pressures, challenges, and opportunities that made up a farmer's life. On one occasion, shortly before he graduated from elementary school, his father learned that wheat prices had begun to rise. 'We had more than a thousand bushels in the bins,' Ernest Drury recalled,

and I was given the job of selling and delivering it ... I sold my first load on the Saturday before Easter at something more than ninety cents a bushel, and followed the same program every day of the next week. It was fun, for every day the price was higher and the buyers more eager ... I sold my last loads on the following Saturday ... for $1.25 a bushel. When I brought in the second load [the buyer] asked me if we had any more left, and I told him we had a little, not quite a load. He advised me to bring it in that evening, for he had received a wire that afternoon telling him that the market was about to break. So I ... brought it in and unloaded it ... into a freight car on the siding. Next Monday our daily paper reported that the market had broken and wheat was back to its old price, about ninety cents a bushel.[1]

In those days there was also time for leisure on the farmstead. Lazy afternoon picnics and special holidays like Victoria Day were welcome distractions. In time they were to be rudely shortened, or abandoned altogether, when more intensive methods of farming were introduced. It was ironical that mechanization, while it took much of the drudgery out of farm work, also expanded the work to be done.

In the late 1880s Ernest had his first taste of the new order when his father bought a Massey self-binder, after he had taken his son to a demonstration of the contrivance at a nearby Kempenfeldt farm.[2] At about the same time horse power was being replaced on many farms by steam power. These innovations, though they would be dwarfed by the technological wonders that came later, nonetheless dramatically set off that turn-of-the-century generation from the pioneering times of young Richard and Thomas Drury. In the latter's heyday no implement-makers apart from blacksmiths and small foundries had even been listed in the census returns, yet by the time Ernest Drury reached adolescence there were over two hundred such firms of every conceivable size and description scattered across central Canada.[3]

All the same, in spite of these refinements the farming community still remained innocent of such future commonplaces as chemical fertilizers, herbicides, fungicides, and effective means of controlling insects and other pests. Animal husbandry was still plagued by a woeful ignorance of bovine tuberculosis, mastitis, and Bang's disease – or contagious abortion – which reached epidemic proportions every other decade. Yet for all this ignorance, the farmer of Charles Drury's generation could, with forgiveable pride, catalogue the improvements and the rising living standards that had transformed country life in the last half of the nineteenth century.

Farm work, no matter how agreeable Ernest may have found it, was forced to make way for education. Ernest was sent to the school on the Penetang Road, a successor to the one his father had attended; it was framed with clapboard rather than logs and set against a 'beautiful grove of second-growth pines.'[4] Although the neighbourhood industries commanded much respect as symbols of accomplishment, it was the schoolhouse that was the community's pride and joy. The local control of educational institutions, though weakened elsewhere in rural Ontario by the growing independence brought on by urbanization and improved transportation facilities, was still very much alive in Crown Hill while Ernest Drury was attending school. Not only this, he and his school chum neighbour, Charles B. Sissons, were fortunate in their teachers. One of them, Andrew Kerr (who received $550 annually for his efforts), was reputed to have provided a quality of schooling 'denied to pioneers and even the sons of pioneers in North Simcoe.'[5]

On the other hand, observations on Drury's appearance and deportment as a schoolboy were at times not so flattering. Although some teachers and fellow students remembered him as the 'dark eyed boy with the firm jaw,' others freely disclosed that 'when he first started to school he had an awful temper and he would kick ... and go into all kinds of antics ... [However] he was a good natured fellow as long as you didn't interfere with what he wanted to do.'[6] Another former classmate, Arthur Lower's sister, recalled gigglingly that young Drury, given his facial features, was widely known as 'Catfish.'[7] The boy with the unflattering sobriquet built up a reputation as a quick learner who usually stood at the head of the class.

In his own recollections Drury was less complimentary about the school than his contemporaries; among his complaints was that there was no school library (to match his father's, presumably). One cause of the primary school's meagre offerings may have been the inauguration in the 1870s of the high school entrance examinations. By reducing if not eradicating the overlapping nature of the high school and the elementary school, it led, so critics charged, to the decline of advanced work in the local public school.[8] Even so, Drury's interest in history was aroused, but not as a result of the formal instruction he received. 'In the schoolhouse in Crown Hill,' he recollected, 'a boy sat across from [me] whose family had lived in California ... [He] had an American History book about England. It was full of anti-British sentiment. Probably not a good book but it had life in it and interest ... I read it surreptitiously under my desk (the teacher would have licked me if she had caught me).' 'Because of it', he claimed, 'I became a reader of history, a student of history.'[9] And yet, for all the short-comings he recorded, he eventually conceded what his friend Sissons rejoiced in – that this particular country school did, on the whole, 'very good work':

By the time we reached the Fourth class we could read and read aloud, fluently and with expression. We could spell correctly and had a fairly broad vocabulary; we knew English grammar and the parts of speech and could parse and analyse. In the Third and Fourth readers we had been given a taste of the best of English literature, poetry and prose. We had in short been given an efficient key to further education, and sometimes the desire to use it, and perhaps this is all that education, higher or lower, can do.[10]

The slim reading materials at the Crown Hill school were thankfully supplemented by the books his father supplied at home, notably those of Daniel Defoe, Jules Verne, and Rider Haggard, though not the stirring imperial tales of G.A. Henty, which Charles Drury might have thought too chauvinistic. When the time came for Ernest to graduate, there was no question in the household that he should follow in his father's footsteps to Barrie Collegiate Institute. This was a step that comparatively few young people in Crown Hill could take at that time. A contemporary recalled that given Charles Drury's education and standing in the community, 'Ernest was perhaps just a little bit better than the rest of us.'[11]

For the country student in particular it meant financial sacrifices for the family, even Charles Drury's. Well aware of this, Drury and similarly situated collegiate classmates were for the most part serious minded, purposeful, and self-reliant. Although most of his school friends would expect to go on to solid professional and business positions, Drury was one of the exceptions. In keeping with family tradition, he submitted to education mainly for education's sake. 'Very early,' he recalled, 'I had made up my mind to be a farmer.'[12]

Unlike the socially oriented and more 'relevant' curricula that began to come in after the Great War, the tutoring he received at the BCI was totally academic, a more sophisticated version of the instruction his father had received at the old grammar school, whose building the collegiate occupied. Latin and mathematics, which embraced Euclid and trigonometry, would be the bane of his existence, though in later years he took up the reading of Virgil in order to improve his knowledge of English.[13] On the other hand, English literature and composition, history, ancient and modern, and science, particularly botany and zoology, would prove more attractive. The academic limits to which Drury and his classmates were pushed were outlined in the examination questions set for them by BCI teachers: 'What evidences, independent of recorded history, have we of a Roman occupation?' 'Account for the Latin elements in our language'; 'Give the cause of the Hundred Years' War'; and 'Explain the causes of the changes of the seasons.'[14] Drury was peppered with these and other queries during his five-year stint at the BCI.

Yet his time there was not taken up entirely with a mixture of classroom stimulation and drudgery. Although he had the physique and stamina for organized athletics – he stood some five foot eleven and weighed about one hundred and eighty-five pounds, which he distributed on a broad frame – he lacked the desire to play or compete.[15] When he wanted to test his considerable strength or find an outlet for his energy he usually did so not on the school's football field or baseball diamond but on the farm where he enjoyed the hard physical work of clearing bush and pitching hay. When he sought extracurricular diversions in high school he joined the literary society and the glee club. He also became a regular contributor to the high school paper, which was written in longhand and read aloud every week to the literary society. Public speaking opportunities and singing with the glee club in Barrie's Music Hall, for which he had been prepared by a travelling tutor from Barrie, gave him a confidence and presence that he would put to good use later in his career.

Meanwhile, when the chores were done at home, he ransacked his own family's library. Progressing beyond the adventure tales of his boyhood, he began to savour Walter Scott, Dickens, Kingsley, Bulwer Lytton, and Ralph Waldo Emerson. Poetry and verse were not neglected either. Shakespeare's sonnets and the Romantic poets, who had been enjoying their heyday while his grandfather had been transforming Joseph Drury's original bush farm into a viable homestead, were eagerly devoured. These apparently were read and re-read so that, as one admirer later noted, an 'apt quotation is ever at command of his ready pen or speech.'[16]

Once again, history, self-taught, came in for marked attention. Reading Carlyle's *French Revolution* and Macaulay's *Essays* and *Lays of Ancient Rome* was a happier experience than the memorization of facts and dates that was then the stock-in-trade of the high school classroom. His friend Charles Sissons, the future classicist and historian at Victoria College, suffered through the same experience when they were classmates together in Barrie. 'Was there ever a subject,' Sissons later asked Drury, 'which you liked less at school as taught than history? ... It has always been to me an amusing reflection that Ancient History, which I professed for forty years, was as dull as ditch water as taught in the old BCI. The first ray of light came with [J.R.] Green's Short History of the English People, and, as you will remember, we read that pretty much ourselves without any assistance from [the teacher].'[17]

John Richard Green can still stir the imagination, so small wonder that he caught the fancy of the impressionable Crown Hill schoolboys. Its publication, barely twenty years before they devoured it, was a breakthrough in historiography because it reputedly provided the English-speaking world with the 'first coherent and satisfying account of its own past.' Instead of high politics and the rise and fall of dynasties, the meat of conventional treatments, the *Short History* used the people of England as its hero. Drury's indebtedness to this popular account which, in his words, extolled the 'freedom brought from the German woods,' was acknowledged years later when he reflected warmly on his Warwickshire ancestry.[18]

His reading of history served to reinforce his belief in the historically leavening role of the Gospel. His father's strong faith and Aunt Bessie's religiosity entrenched his own deep personal commitment to a practising Christianity. His active membership in the Epworth League, the Methodist youth movement that aimed at identifying the church's social responsibilities, provided an outlet for his views on the need for Christians to ensure the same freedom and justice for the poor and the weak as was conferred on the rich and the strong.[19] Doubtless his friend Sissons shared the same enthusiasms, for he and his father were often seen in the pews of Barrie's Collier Street Methodist Church in the company of Charles and Ernest Drury.[20]

Yet Ernest's religious commitment did not stifle, indeed it might even have abetted, an instinctive desire to cut complex and erudite theological issues down

to size. Sometimes the young Drury's reaction to a preacher's message or deportment would border on the anti-clerical. This early, even while completing
his high school course, he may have questioned the credentials and motives of
some of those who professed to be qualified for the pulpit, a predilection he
often betrayed in later years. He suspected them of 'over-weening ambition' and
other secular lapses that did violence to the spiritual obligation they should have
been discharging. Thus when one preacher appeared at a social function at
Kenilworth, attended by guests from Toronto, and ostentatiously 'put his best
foot forward,' he jaundicedly concluded that the visitor was merely angling for
a call to an affluent church in that city.[21]

Meanwhile, back at high school, life as a budding member of the literati was
rudely jolted when Ernest failed his senior matriculation. The bugbears of his
academic life, mathematics and Latin, brought him roughly to earth. Happily,
the anticipated parental displeasure did not materialize, and when he sat the
examination again in mid-summer 1897 he passed it. He was now nineteen, but
the question of his immediate educational future had already been settled between
him and his father before he put pen to examination book. Sissons, who was
bound for university, thought that his friend should do the same, certain that
Drury had the skills to make a go of it and end up with a productive teaching
career, particularly in English studies.[22] But Drury was still committed to farming
and he resolved, in agreement with his father, to enroll at the Ontario Agricultural
College.

The store of information and insights gained through formal schooling had
been augmented by the discussions that habitually swirled about the family dinner
table. There the perceptive adolescent had been acquainted with Liberalism's
virtues and Conservatism's vices, particularly the iniquities of John A. Macdonald's National Policy which had clothed the country's nascent industry with
the tariff protection it supposedly needed to survive the cruel world of international competition. The frequency of bank failures and business collapses in
Barrie in the early 1890s belied for the Drury family the oft-cited equation
between prosperity and protection.[23] The lament of a businessman elsewhere in
the province – 'I went out to try to get in some money but without avail for the
people seem not to have any'[24] – summed up the situation in Simcoe County
during Drury's adolescence. The alleged evils of protectionism, which kept the
price of manufactures farmers needed at the artificially high levels that lined
industrialists' pockets and which served to depress the prices farmers sought for
their products in urban markets – these were the charges made and the lessons
learned during Drury's impressionable youth.

Drury also learnt at home of the work of the Dominion Grange and of the
activities of the Patrons of Industry. The Grange had been formed in 1874 – in
emulation of its American model – as the first important agrarian forum in post-
confederation Canada. Concerned almost exclusively with educational matters,

it had forsaken politics, content to serve as a vehicle for acquainting legislators and governments with the farmers' needs.[25] This comparatively polite approach to the conditions many farmers saw as threatening their livelihood by industrialism and urbanization was unceremoniously thrown overboard by the more militant Patrons of Industry, organized in 1889 as an offshoot of an American body. After achieving its own autonomy, it proceeded to invade the Ontario redoubt dominated by the party politics of Grit and Tory. As a third party it won some impressive electoral victories in Ontario before it withered under internal stress and external pressures at the turn of the century.[26] Obviously the Patrons' dramatic tactics had not inspired Charles Drury who continued to repose his faith in the Liberal party's capacity to preserve the farmer's place in society.

Nor were Ontario politics neglected. Charles Drury's involvement with Queen's Park began with his election to the legislature in 1882 as a Liberal representing East Simcoe. For two years, from 1888 to 90, he served in Oliver Mowat's administration as the province's first minister of agriculture. The new portfolio was in part the child of a marriage between the farmers and the newly established Ontario Agricultural College, opened by Queen's Park in 1874 in Guelph. The body that presided over the nuptials was the government-backed Farmers' Institute that was designed in part to make farmers aware of scientific developments in agriculture. The institute was the brain child of James Mills, the OAC's president, who wished to bring the college and its work, as he put it, 'into closer communication' with the farmers of the province 'so that the dignity of their occupation' would be underscored and a means provided 'to develop their talents and their energies.' Among the institute's larger objectives was the achievement of greater recognition at Queen's Park for the role that agriculture was playing in the community. Specifically it promoted the creation of a department of agriculture as a major step in that direction. The lobbying clearly had an effect, for provision was shortly made for the portfolio that Charles Drury was the first to fill in 1888.

In the meantime Charles Drury had remarried, and on several occasions he invited his son to visit him and his new stepmother, the former Isabella Brownlee, in Toronto where they resided when the legislature was in session. For the first time Ernest Drury got a glimpse of Ontario's capital and of parliamentarians at work. The legislature was still housed in the old red-brick quarters on Front Street, although some of the burgeoning government departments had been dispersed throughout that section of the city. Thus Charles Drury's new department was accommodated in a building at the corner of King and Yonge streets, appropriately over a grocery store. In spite of the impressive tours his father laid on, Ernest claimed later that the only immediate parliamentary ambition he entertained after his visits was to become a page boy.[27] His stays in the city were enlivened by pleasant visits to what he called his urban relations – the three young daughters of his father's second marriage. There was another revealing side to one such visit. He recalled, with an equal mixture of wonder and shame, having been a spectator at a 'theatre leg show.' He described the performance as simply scandalous, with the girls on the stage 'all painted and powdered, and their dresses ... cut low ... and their skirts ... almost up to their knees [showing] tight stockings, mostly black.'[28]

Such distractions had to be foregone, however, when he embarked on the next stage of his formal education. Anxious to complete the required work at the OAC as quickly as possible and return to the farm, he ended up taking most of the three-year course in two years, an exercise that left him less time than he would have liked for campus activities. When he first arrived at the college in the fall of 1898 the once-modest campus had grown to five buildings. These embraced quarters for animal husbandry, experimental work, and chemistry and physics, and included a gymnasium and a college residence. Thankfully absent when his son arrived was the 'sorry plight of the place' that had astonished Charles Drury when he had paid an official visit just ten years before.[29] Already, under the guidance of James Mills, the college had established a healthy reputation throughout Canada, parts of the empire, and in major farming regions of the United States for the thoroughness and inventiveness of its instruction. That instruction had been enhanced in 1888 by the introduction of a three-year program leading to the bachelor of science in agriculture (BSA), the program Drury was about to enter.

Although Charles Drury was on good terms with President Mills, a fellow native of Simcoe County, it would appear that his son made it through the college gates on the strength of his own credentials. 'I was just another boy from an up-country farm,' Ernest would reminisce, 'come to learn something about scientific farming.' Judging from the cultural and educational deprivation that scarred a good many of the registrants, he was not exactly just another boy. Some of his classmates had been out of school for years and woefully lacked the kind of home tutoring and formal schooling that he had enjoyed in Crown Hill and Barrie.[30]

While the intensity of his studies ruled out much off-campus activity he found some time to devote to his high school interests, notably singing and the campus literary society. Obviously these extracurricular contributions were well received, for in his second year he was elected to office in the literary society, and to editorship of the *OAC Review*. His concerns were boldly reflected in his own editorial submissions: for example, the impact of protection on the living standards of the Ontario farmer, and rural depopulation, one of the leading agrarian problems of the day.[31] The training received in the classroom and the inspiration derived from earlier literary excursions were clearly stamped on these reasonably lucid and well-argued editorials – though in later years he dismissed them as 'pretty poor stuff.'

His articles in the *OAC Review* brought him to the notice of W.L. Smith, the influential editor of the *Weekly Sun*, the mouthpiece of agrarian interests in Ontario. Out of this came a hearty friendship that strengthened his ties to the organized farm movement. It also led to an introduction to Goldwin Smith, the owner of the *Sun* and its leading columnist, writing under the name 'Observer.' The newspaper had begun its career as the *Canada Farmer's Sun*, the official organ of the Patrons of Industry. But when Patron fortunes dramatically declined its circulation fell away. Yet almost as dramatic as that reverse was the impact that Goldwin Smith, academic, publicist, and critic, had upon the paper's revival. Eager to shore up the rural community's image of itself, and its place in the community, Smith set about to turn what would be called the *Weekly Sun* into the voice of rural Ontario.[32] The Drury household appeared to be among the first eager subscribers to the paper in the Penetang area. There, Smith was assured by a friend, its influence 'has been very marked as [the farmers] have developed an open-eyed independence in political affairs which puts them on better terms with each other and contrasts pleasantly with the savage partisan animosity which makes it impossible for some farmers who wish to remain friends to discuss political matters at all, to their great loss.'[33] The passage came uncannily close to describing the future inclinations of Ernest Drury.

To be commended by a person of W.L. Smith's standing was an exhilarating experience and it emboldened the young Drury to prepare other articles for publication on the social and economic problems facing the Ontario farmer. Although he was familiar with the rough economics of free trade and rural depopulation, he had, he later confessed, 'never heard of the science of Political Economy till I was introduced to it at Guelph.' He had spotted Adam Smith's *Wealth of Nations* in his grandfather's library but he had never more than scanned its pages. The economics course he took at the OAC tempted him to take on Smith more rigorously and to read more widely than the course required. Thus was launched a life-long interest in economics that coloured his public addresses whether to comrades in farm organizations or to friends and foes in the political arena.

Drury's college years proved stimulating, prying out of him talents untapped by previous educational challenges or strengthening those already emerging. Not surprisingly, he regarded his stay at the OAC with gratitude and affection, not least for the circle of friends it created. One classmate with whom he struck up an especially close relationship was Manning Doherty who later became an associate professor in the biology department.

Drury's stint at the OAC was capped in 1900 by the acceptance of his thesis, which was prepared to meet the requirement in chemistry, reputedly one of the most demanding courses offered at the college. The work that had gone into the thesis and the gratification it generated moved him years later to outline the project in his published memoirs: 'It involved growing peas under controlled conditions in bare sand inoculated and uninoculated, some supplied with complete fertilizers and some not, some grown in soil rich in humus under the same conditions and with a quantitative analysis of plant and soil in each case.'[34] C.B. Sissons, who had gone on to the University of Toronto from the BCI, may have lamented his friend's failure to accompany him, but clearly Drury did not. He had freely elected to go to the OAC in order to enhance his life and chosen career, and he would have the BSA and the citation of second place in the class to prove it.

The day Drury received his degree at the University of Toronto convocation, 13 June 1900, was doubly gratifying. It also happened to be the nineteenth birthday of his fiancée, Ella Albena Partridge, the Crown Hill girl whom he had known since childhood and who had gone on to be a teacher. The daughter of James Wharton Partridge and Annie Sopher, she too was descended from English pioneers who had settled in the area the same year that Drury's great-grandfather had arrived.[35] As youngsters they had attended the same Crown Hill school, taken part in the same round of social activities, and worshipped in the neighbourhood Methodist church. But a sober thought intruded on the happy mental association Drury's graduation day fashioned: before he and Ella could contemplate marriage he would have to establish himself as an independent farmer in his own right, BSA or no BSA. Five years would pass before that landmark was reached.

3

Rural Activist

Following his graduation, Drury returned to the farm of his fathers, an example welcomed by successive presidents of the OAC. As one of them put it some years after Drury left its halls: 'the thread-bare tradition that one hears repeated and re-iterated that the agricultural colleges failed to return men to practical farming has no foundation in fact.'[1] Drury was one of these returnees. Apart from teaching what he himself had learned, he would have found it incomprehensible to do anything other than what he undertook at Crown Hill after the turn of the century.

But what were his prospects? All along he had worked for his father and uncle and had been paid like any other hired hand. Yet he was well aware that he would inherit his father's share of the farm partnership. And he was gratified when he was admitted as an equal to that partnership upon his return from Guelph. All the same, one-third of the profits, though symbolically reassuring, still amounted to nothing much more than glorified wages. But it was a beginning, and a promising one. The farm, moreover, under Charles and Will Drury's guidance, had become highly productive and profitable. Now, however, it was mainly up to Uncle Will and his nephew to make it thrive. Charles Drury, diagnosed as a diabetic, was obliged to curtail his farm labours. Besides, what time and energy he had left he wished to devote to his duties as sheriff of Simcoe County, an appointment he had received in 1896 following the close of his legislative career. Consequently his brother took over the farm's management and assigned considerable work to the newly admitted junior partner. Ernest's tasks were sweetened by the knowledge that he was free to make changes and improvements which he judged essential to capitalizing on the farm's resources. How Uncle Will took to the enthusiasms of this freshly graduated 'scientific farmer' has not been recorded. His nephew, on the other hand, recollected how an older neighbour, after listening patiently to his ambitious plans, commented laconically that 'most farmers know how to farm much better than they are able to.'[2]

Nevertheless, Ernest proved successful in one of his prime objectives, the conservation of soil fertility, which was to become a life-long preoccupation. A system of silage, crop rotation, the growing of root crops for fodder, the subsequent enlargement of the farm's cattle herd, and increased use of manures, all enriched the farm's soil and led to more abundant and higher quality crops. At the same time the farm's clay loam was well suited to alfalfa, which he introduced as a fodder crop in Ontario. Other farmers soon followed suit when it was shown that a 'farm in alfalfa will produce so much more that ... it will increase the revenue, and that [an eager farmer noted], is what we are after.'[3]

In the summer of 1903 Drury was joined on the farm by Charles Sissons, who had launched himself on a teaching career after graduating from university. Yearning for a diversion, he eagerly took up his friend's invitation to spend the summer at Crown Hill. These weeks together were exhilarating for both men as they punctuated exacting farm work with worldly discussion. 'The week I remember with most pleasure,' Sissons recalled,

was spent of all things in hoeing turnips. Ernest and I both took pride in the job – in the long clean rows levelled to a nicety with single drooping plants left fourteen to sixteen inches apart ... As we worked side by side we talked on poetry and politics, tariffs, and world trends with our horizon still unclouded by war. The discussion we shared fairly equally, except when Ernest discoursed on some new theory or invention in science.[4]

Quite likely, too, they chewed over a theme that Drury would constantly return to – the place and role of the farmer in society, and how farming, to use his words, was not a business but a 'science, a way of life, a sort of philosophy.'

The hard physical labour of the farm still left Drury with time to pursue his intellectual interests outside his own fence lines. One such activity was the Ontario Agricultural and Experimental Union, founded at the OAC by Professor C.A. Zavitz, the agronomist. Zavitz's aim was to assist graduates of the college who might be thrown onto their own resources when they returned to their farms. He also hoped to make use of these young men in his plan to test new varieties of crops and the methodologies he had concocted in his laboratory. Drury enlisted in Zavitz's agricultural army and ultimately served as vice-president and then president of the union.

Among his contributions was a report on barn ventilation. In his grandfather's day, when barn construction, as he wrote, left something to be desired, 'the wind came in and did all the ventilating that was needed, and the cattle could testify that the ventilation was very complete indeed.' Now, however, with better materials and construction methods, that natural ventilation had been shut off, with adverse effects on the cattle, not to mention on the barn's ambience. To correct the problem Drury urged what seemed most practical, the installation of flues.[5]

Having addressed such barnyard problems, Drury soon made it plain that he had larger concerns, one of which was the condition of Ontario's forest lands, particularly those in his native Simcoe County. The latter, as he recollected, contained

some of the best farming land in the province, and also some so poor that it never should have been farmed but ... left in forest. There were also several large areas that once had been covered with valuable stands of red and white pine. These areas had been cut over by lumbermen, the brush and waste timber being left on the ground to be burned over and over again till all the seed in the ground was destroyed and natural vegetation was impossible.[6]

Sometimes the conflagrations got out of hand. As an awestruck boy he had seen the Collingwood train come into the Barrie station 'with the paint on the cars blistered from running through [fires] on the Angus plains ... and the night sky red ... at Midhurst ... and Orr Lake.'[7]

As it turned out, Drury was on the ground floor of a movement that aimed at discrediting a view of the forest that had dominated the thinking of his grandfather's generation. For them the forest had been the enemy and the sooner it was subdued the better for civilization. Looking into the distant future, they reckoned that once the forests had been conquered by the lumberman and the farmer who followed in his tracks, they would never return. After the turn of the century, however, the argument was reversed to embrace the view that the forest, far from being static and impermanent, could be rendered eminently renewable through the application of sound scientific principles. The indiscriminate assaults of the past and what was now deemed to be the gross wastage of pioneer days came under attack from conservationists, professional foresters, and civil servants sensitive to the social and economic ramifications of proper forest management.

Drury reflected these concerns, and as early as 1902 he was sharing them with the forestry committee of the Experimental Union, established just the year before.[8] Like the committee, he realized that some misconceptions about reforestation would have to be cleared away. As he somewhat wordily claimed in a letter to W.C. Good, a friend and supporter of the farm movement in Brant County: 'I was one of the first to put forward the idea of reforestation, *not primarily as a means of producing timber* but, in the farming community of Old Ontario, as a means of controlling ... water supply and certain weather conditions, in order that the country might attain the most favourable conditions for a successful and permanent agriculture.'[9] Not far away C.A. Zavitz's cousin, Edmund John Zavitz, was completing his studies at McMaster University before embarking on his life work as a forester and conservationist. Years later he recalled the solid work of Drury and other members of the union's forestry committee.[10]

Another active member, with whom Drury would long keep in touch, was Nelson Monteith, a future Conservative minister of agriculture from the Stratford area who served on local councils and agricultural societies. At the annual meeting of the union late in 1902 the following resolution was moved by Monteith, seconded by Drury, and carried:

The Experimental Union, recognizing the urgent necessity for action, in the reforesting of the waste lands throughout Old Ontario, would recommend that the Department of Crown Lands be requested to provide material sufficient to re-forest areas sufficiently large to provide forest conditions in typical situations throughout Ontario, the Union undertaking to supervise the distribution.[11]

While the authorities were left to mull over this proposition Drury, as newly named chairman of the forestry committee, drew up plans for the next annual meeting. For its principal speaker he landed the formidable Bernhard Fernow, the German-born scholar who had figured prominently in the American conservation movement as the director of the Cornell College of Forestry. When that operation was closed down, Fernow accepted the deanship of the newly established faculty of forestry at the University of Toronto. Thanks to Drury's persistence, Fernow was able to address his remarks to John Dryden, the Liberal minister of agriculture, who had been prevailed upon to come up from Queen's Park to hear what the eminent conservationist had to say. The minister seemed to be impressed by Fernow's remarks. The visitor emphasized, among other things that Drury wanted to hear, the importance of forest cover 'as a furnisher of material most needful to civilization, next to food, because of its relationship to soil and water conditions.'[12] The enthusiastic meeting then passed a resolution calling for the establishment of a nursery and seedling program at the OAC.

In spite of his warm response to Fernow's speech, this was too much for the minister. He bluntly told the gathering that while he favoured such a project in principle he would not permit it on the campus, arguing that the college already had enough to do. He then urged that crown lands in the north be pressed into service for the purpose, a new departure that led Drury to believe that 'our motion [of 2 December 1902] had been misconstrued at Queen's Park as a call for 'reforesting ... New Ontario.' If that were the case Drury hastily tried to clarify the question. The waste lands they had in mind were in the south, of not much value agriculturally, which 'could be reforested with great advantage, and our motion was that the Government should allow us to experiment with one such area, in the hope of inducing the municipalities to take hold of the matter.'[13]

These remarks contained the germ of the legislation his future administration would implement.

It soon became apparent that the union's original motion had been greeted with studied indifference at Queen's Park. Undeterred, the union members decided to push even more vigorously for their proposal. Furthermore, they called for the appointment of nothing less than a fully qualified provincial forester, and they mobilized the *Weekly Sun* and other agrarian journals in a campaign to arouse public support. In this effort Drury doubtless played on the rapport he had already built up with the *Sun*'s editor, W.L. Smith. Whether or not this agitation was the decisive factor, Queen's Park appointed the sought-after forester. To the union's delight, E.J. Zavitz was the successful candidate. It did not escape Drury's notice that Zavitz was not only the best man available, but was also Dryden's prospective son-in-law.

Over the next few years Zavitz made a point of keeping in touch with Drury and other committed union members as he visited and appraised those waste lands in the province deemed ripe for reforestation.[14] He paid one such visit to Simcoe County in the fall of 1905 and stayed for several days in the Drury household. This afforded Drury his first opportunity to meet the forester, and he was favourably impressed. 'We discussed the problem of reforestation in Old Ontario very thoroughly,' he recollected, 'and with our horse and buggy drove over the pine plains at Angus and Midhurst [which] Zavitz ... seemed to favour [as a] forest nursery and demonstration area.'[15] Although one small plantation was authorized in Simcoe County, Zavitz in the end selected another site for his project at St Williams in Norfolk County near the Lake Erie shore.

Drury's elation over Zavitz's appointment was matched by his response to the news that Nelson Monteith had been named minister of agriculture in the new Conservative administration of James P. Whitney. In a limited sense Drury had helped to put him there. In the provincial election of 1905 he deserted the Liberal party of his fathers when it stood condemned of blatant electoral abuses and questionable patronage practices, sins ordinarily associated with its despised Tory opponent. He therefore rejected the discredited Liberals and cast his ballot for the presumably more worthy Tory candidate. This commitment to political purity, while it salved his conscience, mystified some of his friends and later gave his gleeful enemies the opportunity of labelling him a political chameleon who could not be ideologically trusted.

For the better part of three winters, from 1902 to 1904, he lent his speaking services to the farmers' institutes. High on the list of topics were reforestation and rural depopulation, lower down such technical matters as the care of sheep and the rotation of crops. Although he was obliged to hire help to take his place at Crown Hill while he discharged these duties (his out-of-pocket expenses came out of the public treasury), he looked forward to the task as a means of honing his speaking skills. Indeed, that may have been the only dividend if he shared the experiences of another unfortunate institute worker whose complaints the president of the OAC recorded in 1904: '[The] ... Institutes are about played out ... I have been through four counties, have done my very best to interest people ... and I have apparently roused no interest and have nearly worn myself out in attempting to help the farmers in these counties.'[16] On the other hand, Drury may have felt then the way he did some twenty years later when he openly criticized government-aided programs such as the institutes, which supposedly sought to do the farmers' thinking for them.[17]

The travel and the exertions that sharply reduced the time he could spend at Crown Hill were suspended early in 1905 when he and Ella Partridge decided to get married. The farm, through shrewd management and improvements, was prospering as it never had before. Besides, his father had elected in the fall of 1904 to move to more convenient quarters in Barrie, where his work was, and leave the brick farm house as a residence for his son and his prospective bride. These welcome developments and the knowledge that he had managed to put aside a modest but still substantial nest egg led the couple to set the wedding date for 11 January 1905. At this juncture his father's health began to fail. Although the couple dutifully offered to postpone the ceremony, Charles Drury urged them to go ahead with their plans. The day following the wedding he lapsed into a diabetic coma and died, but only after he had briefly entertained his son and new daughter-in-law in his Barrie home.

His father's death meant that Drury would come into his share of the jointly owned farm – the two hundred acres which he had painstakingly been improving since his graduation from the OAC. He would also inherit 'Kenilworth,' though the old homestead built by Richard Drury would be left to Will and Bessie. 'There was nothing new,' he would later have the protagonist say in his unpublished novel,

yet it was all new, different somehow. To feel that it was his, that he was responsible, that all the varied life on the place, [the] old ... colt, and the calves in the box-stalls, and the little lambs in the sheep-pen, and even the greening fields of wheat in ... back of the bush – that it all looked to him for care ..., for direction, that it would thrive or pine according as he was wise ... and provident – there was a new interest, even a sort of protective tenderness, that he had never felt before.[18]

Such reflections soon enough collided with some sombre realities. For one thing, he would be required to pay the estate some four thousand dollars for his step-mother and her three daughters, a transaction arranged by a mortgage, and to purchase from the estate and from Will Drury their share of the stock and implements, amounting to almost as much. Fortunately for Ernest and his new bride, the farm proved even more profitable than they had dared to imagine and within a year he was able to discharge his debt to his uncle.

In the spring of 1905, barely three months after his marriage, Drury received a totally unexpected offer of employment. His modest fame as an innovative farmer, not to mention the high recommendation written by James Mills, now a member of the Dominion Railway Board, doubtless combined to produce the offer. It came from Principal James W. Robertson, a former OAC faculty member, who was in the throes of setting up, as part of McGill University, Macdonald Agricultural College at Ste Anne de Bellevue, near Montreal. Drury's first assignment, should he accept the offer, would be to organize and manage the main farm at the college and then, if mutually acceptable, assume an academic appointment. This was far too tempting an offer to go uninvestigated and so he and Ella set out early in June for Ste Anne. The trip, which turned into a deferred honeymoon, ended in the couple's infatuation with the situation and its prospects: a managerial position with the apparent promise of a professorship, an annual salary of two thousand dollars, and a free house. Even so, there must have been considerable soul-searching about the venture because Drury put off accepting Robertson's offer until the early fall of 1905. After all, the farm at Crown Hill had just come into his hands and he was anxious to maintain and extend the stimulating contacts with the farm movement in Ontario. Ste Anne, however, promised an equally exhilarating challenge. It would involve an experiment in improving the rural education of the English-speaking community in Quebec, an object by which Robertson set great store.[19] Moreover, it provided an opportunity to test his agricultural skills in a new setting.

When the offer was finally accepted it meant that once again he would be obliged to engage a manager for his own farm. This was done by early February 1906, and Drury was free to move to Ste Anne. But he travelled there alone. Their first child, Charles (Carl), had arrived just before Christmas and he was obliged temporarily to leave his wife and infant behind. In all likelihood he would have had little time for family life anyway in the first few weeks, given the tasks laid out for him – the management of a three-hundred-acre farm and the care of a large prize herd of Ayrshire cattle. To render his appearance more plausible for this considerable undertaking he grew a beard, a 'nice little Van Dyke,' to mask his youthful appearance. Almost immediately he ran into trouble with some of the farm's employees, whose notions of how cattle and land should be ordered did not square with those of the self-assured, better-educated Ontario outsider. His main difficulty, however, was with the principal, who was more of an agrarian theorist and planner than Drury had bargained for. The Scottish-born Robertson, after abandoning plans for a medical career, had been successively professor of dairying at the OAC, dairy commissioner in Ottawa, and an agriculturist at the Central Experimental Farm before taking over the fledgling Macdonald College. What Drury may have been to the farm staff, Robertson in turn was to Drury. In his memoirs Drury, while conceding Robertson's brilliance as an organizer and thinker, deplored his innocence of practical training and experience.

An explosive parting of the ways came in September 1906, less than eight months after Drury's arrival at Ste Anne. He complained of Robertson's failure to give him a free hand with the main farm, which he claimed had been pledged in the original agreement. He also resented Robertson's countermanding orders he handed out to the staff. Those who had observed Drury's volatile temper on the Crown Hill school grounds would not have been surprised to read in *Farmer Premier* that he 'went down to [Robertson's] office in no good mood, and after a rather hot exchange ... handed [the principal] his resignation.'[20] A history of Macdonald College, on the other hand, contented itself with the laconic observation (in a footnote) that Drury 'had been offered the position of Farm Manager but, finding himself in disagreement with Dr. Robertson as to plans, declined the appointment.'[21] There was no reference in all this to the eventual professorial appointment of which Drury had made so much. Perhaps this had never been a firm commitment on Robertson's part, a factor that may have played some role in Drury's departure. It may have followed, too, that in spite of the comparatively handsome salary that went with the position, he saw little point in working someone else's slice of arcadia when he had his own in Crown Hill. Besides, he was cut off from those contacts in the farm movement and the political scene in Ontario that had already made life so adventuresome. At any rate, he and his family, which had eventually joined him in Ste Anne, wasted little time in packing up and returning to the welcoming embrace of Simcoe County.

Even before Drury entrained for Ste Anne he had been caught up in the agitation sparked by an announcement from Laurier's finance minister, William Fielding. Trapped uncomfortably between free traders and protectionists, the harried Fielding took a time-honoured way out and struck a commission to examine the problem of the tariff. Suspicious farmers were already well aware of Fielding's drift into the protectionist camp and the Liberal party's reluctance to tamper with the National Policy lest they offend their friends in the manufacturing sector. Understandably, farmers feared an upward revision of the tariff that would further erode their place in the economy, a point they vigorously put to the commission throughout its nation-wide hearings in the fall of 1905. Stung by their failure to state their case effectively before earlier tariff commissions, they more than made up for that shortcoming this time around. In the forefront of the action in Ontario was the newly formed Farmers' Association, a pressure group that activists, aided by the exhortations of a sympathetic *Weekly Sun*, had succeeded in organizing in the fall of 1902. It was designed in part to fill the place of the ill-fated Patrons of Industry and of the Dominion Grange, which for many aggrieved farmers had been functioning all too fitfully as the defender of agrarian views.[22]

For the *Sun* and other restless spokesmen of rural interests, the new organization was needed to push the farmers' case for recognition and redress. Playing a prominent part in this revival was the formidable James Morrison (better known as J.J.), a farmer from Wellington County who rapidly became the most influential farm spokesman in the province. At one stage of his career Morrison had temporarily left farming and worked in a Toronto warehousing firm where, it is claimed, he learned the mechanics of trade union organization and how they might be profitably applied to the farm movement.[23] His city experiences may have inspired his potent distrust of what he ominously called 'urban man', and starkly revealed to him how that creature and its habits were threatening the countryside's way of life. Seldom did he take kindly to those farmers who broke ranks and made their peace with the city. In any case, Morrison emerged as a voluble defender of Ontario's agrarian order, and prided himself on being perceived as the undisputed interpreter of its needs and aspirations. It followed that he made a profound impression on those who attended the founding meeting that named him secretary of the Farmers' Association.[24] Apparently Drury first encountered him when Morrison ventured into the Barrie area to organize local branches of the association.[25]

When the new body decided to confront the Fielding Commission, Drury was gratified to be called upon to serve in the front line. He responded like the proverbial fire horse to the bell. He was joined on the representational committee by James McEwing, the association's president, and by J. G. Lethbridge, a farm leader from Middlesex County. To Drury fell the welcome task of preparing much of the association's case, and as on most such occasions he called on his wife for counsel. The hearing was set for 14 November 1905, which gave him several weeks to put his arguments together. The date turned out to be highly inconvenient for all three men. McEwing and Lethbridge were obliged to spend a long weekend away from their demanding farms, while Drury had to contend with the dubious delights of the Cobalt Special, the only train out of Barrie that would deliver him to Toronto in time for the day's events.

'I think we did a good job,' Drury reflected later, '[and] it earned us a leading editorial in the "Globe",' which had already called for a levelling down of the tariff. The Toronto paper reported the kind of homework Drury had done – compiling statistics that revealed the burdens imposed on the farmer-consumer by the 30 to 50 per cent tariff on household goods and implements – and the carefully prepared message to the commission that 'We farmers are not used to asking you for something.' Ridiculing the favour-seeking protectionists, Drury remarked that 'if there comes a storm we duck our heads and take it like men. We don't run to the country for aid.'[26]

The gist of what Drury prepared for the occasion was embodied in an article he wrote for the *Canadian Magazine*. He declared that higher tariffs would be the death knell of the farmer, 'a condition [which] cannot fail to have disastrous effects upon the nation at large, not only on its material prosperity, but on its political, social and moral life, the backbone of which is, and must be, the farm home.'[27] This declaration of the 'Rural Ethic' was also addressed to the urbanized, if not urbane, Canadian Club of Toronto, in February 1906. Drury told them what some in the audience may have scoffed at if standards of politeness had not prevailed: 'The farm is the bulwark of the land – the ideal social conditions exist there. It is the simplest, truest, and sweetest social life of the nation and the mainstay of its political upbuilding.'[28] Other farm leaders at the time, like W.C. Good, his Brant County colleague, echoed his sentiments and applauded the 'moral discipline which comes to those engaged in the more fundamental work of production.'[29] At any rate, all those winter months that Drury had spent speaking to meetings of the Farmers' Institutes were beginning to pay oratorical dividends.

In the end, the cavalcade of rural delegations that appeared before the commission had some effect on Fielding's final decision in 1907. Although the farmers' demands were not totally met, the new tariff made some concessions to Ontario's cultivators so far as farm machinery rates were concerned. Essentially, the measure was a compromise that made no appeal to ardent supporters of either side of the issue.[30] Indeed, as Drury saw it, Fielding merely 'abandoned his scheme to raise the tariff – for a time – and the protected interests had to content themselves with what they had.'[31]

All in all, the episode had provided Drury with vital experiences that sharpened his organizational skills, bolstered his already considerable self-confidence, and enhanced his public presence. On the other hand, it may also have inflated the egotism and cocksuredness that some would later have cause to complain about. At any rate, his solid and reassuring frame, steady and powerful voice, and effective responses to challenges and criticism, soon made him a highly respected and sought-after organizer and speaker. In this connection, he recalled the advice offered by W.L. Smith. No lover of longwindedness, Smith always urged Drury, when he thought he had something worthwhile to say, to say it and sit down. On the few occasions Drury failed to heed this advice in Smith's presence, he was brusquely told afterwards that he had passed several 'perfectly good places to quit.'[32]

The promise that C.B. Sissons and others had seen in Drury was being fulfilled. From his activities on behalf of the Farmers' Association in 1905 he graduated to the secretaryship and, finally, to the presidency of the Dominion Grange. He then played an instrumental role in bringing those two organizations into a merger in September 1907. The fighting spirit aroused over the tariff commission helped to engineer this coalition, and in the process encouraged a more militant approach to the publicizing of the farmer's plight. This was a far cry from the time just four years earlier when Morrison had attempted to organize a branch of the Farmers' Association in Wellington County. On going to a meeting on one particular night, Morrison disclosed to a friend in the late winter of 1903, 'I drove through a drenching rain, and was rewarded by an attendance of two, so don't be surprised if my faith in my fellow farmer is somewhat weakened.'[33] Periodically Drury had faced the same disheartening scene.

Now, however, the picture had changed. Both Drury and Morrison, who served as the Grange's auditor, were pleased by the show of organized support. All the same, the task of establishing local branches in far-flung areas of southern Ontario consumed many hours and much energy, and, moreover, subjected the missionaries to the wretched road conditions of the day. Yet it gave Drury the opportunity to appraise sections of the province he had never seen before. He also established lasting friendships with local spokesmen for the cause and built a storehouse of information upon which he would profitably draw in later years. For example, he visited Prince Edward County early in 1908 with H.B. Cowan, the editor of Peterborough's *Farm and Dairy*:

We had our meetings at two places five or six miles apart. It was after eleven o'clock when the meeting was over, and we left for Picton some ten miles distant ... in a cutter ... The temperature was well below zero, for there was considerable wind ... We must have taken a wrong turn for we drove for miles without seeing a house ... After a while we came to a better road with good farmsteads ... In one of the houses there was a light in the downstairs window ... When ... the man who answered [our] knock ... knew who we were he insisted that we should spend the night ... I think I have never met kinder people ... We sat and talked ... [over] sandwiches and tea ... until nearly three o'clock.[34]

The zeal with which Drury carried out his mission prompted at least one impressed farmer to introduce him to his family as 'this remarkable young man.'[35]

Not all of Drury's time, it would appear, was spent unremittingly on behalf of rural evangelization. He recalled another time when he found himself in Ottawa to confer with two prairie leaders, Thomas A. Crerar of the Grain Growers Company and Roderick McKenzie of the Manitoba Grain Growers. Noticing that the tango – 'thought to be the ultimate in daring' – was featured in an act at his hotel, Drury decided to shake his companions, for fear they would disapprove of his intentions, and catch the performance. But when he took a strategic seat in the hotel dining room that evening he observed the sheepish arrival of both Crerar and McKenzie, bound on the same questionable mission. 'I knew then,' Drury chuckled, 'why they had been so easy to lose that afternoon.' This episode says much about the public reaction, at least on the part of rural citizens, to what was then considered risqué.[36]

The liaison with such western farm leaders began during Drury's service with the Grange and was strengthened after he had been elected master of the organization late in 1908. The bond between the northwest and Drury's part of the country was cemented after many of Simcoe County's farm families, including some of his wife's relations, had migrated to the prairies after the turn of the century.[37] Drury proceeded to build on the connection. In February 1909 he sent a letter to Crerar and his colleagues which resulted in the attendance of a prairie delegation at the next annual meeting of the Grange and Farmers' Association.

The success of the self-styled grain growers in organizing their forces and bringing their influence to bear on the political process, not to mention the enthusiasm that attended their efforts, made them logical candidates for Drury's invitation. The massive immigration which had speedily peopled the prairie west after the turn of the century had ushered in an explosive combination. Mingling with American Populists, whose cordial hatred of monopolies and vested interests was well known, were Ontarians of a solid Grit persuasion who enshrined the democratic ethic, and fire-eating trade unionists and labour spokesmen from the United Kingdom. These and other arrivals had made for considerable political ferment in the west, and ensured that the farm movement there would be more aggressive than its eastern counterpart. Moreover, its farmers had in G.F. Chipman's *Grain Growers' Guide* a powerful sounding board for the heady stock of ideas, concepts, and programs that propelled the western movement. Many of Ontario's rural spokesmen acknowledged the east's debt to the prairies. 'The Western men profited by our mistakes,' H.B. Cowan wrote W.C. Good during the Great War, 'and their success proved inspiring to our Ontario farmers.'[38]

For his part, Drury betrayed his pessimism over farming conditions in Ontario in a speech he gave at the Canadian National Exhibition in the fall of 1909: 'General farming ... is not prospering as it ought. The majority of Ontario farms are not making a dividend equal to 4 or 5 per cent on the capital invested.' The tariff, the *bête noire* of the farm movement, both east and west, was then roundly and, by this time, ritualistically denounced by the Master of the Grange. To make matters worse, Drury continued, 'the great papers are not in touch with the farmer and the urban population takes no interest.'[39] There seemed to be general agreement among Ontario's farmers that the time had arrived for them to throw in their lot with the westerners and from that union draw greater strength and wiser direction.

The upshot was a meeting arranged at Prince Albert, Saskatchewan, in February 1910 of the three major western bodies – the Alberta Farmers' Association and the Grain Growers Associations of Saskatchewan and Manitoba – and a delegation from Ontario headed by Drury, representing the Grange and Farmers' Association. Because his organization lacked the solvency of the western groups, which could summon up revenue from their profitable grain companies, Drury was forced to occupy uncomfortable tourist-class accommodations on the train he took west. This was his first trip to the country beyond the lakes, but he gave no hint in his memoirs of his impressions of it. Nor did he comment on the prairies' fondness for utopian politics. It is unlikely that a man whose family roots in Ontario went back nearly a century and who had been brought up in the sober faith of liberalism would have had that much in common with the more radical and unstable representatives of a society so recently put together. In any case, Drury contented himself with recalling the discomfiture of his first night in Prince Albert cooped up in an unventilated and steaming Pullman car that the local board of trade had laid on to house the overflow invasion of delegates.

Out of the convention came the first attempt to co-ordinate formally the hitherto separate farm movements in Ontario and the west. The Canadian Council of Agriculture (CCA) was set up with Roderick McKenzie of Brandon as its president and Drury as its secretary. Its avowed intention was to organize the 'farm population of the Dominion for the study of social and economic problems having a bearing on the happiness and prosperity of the people.'[40] The council was to operate essentially as a federation. Each constituency preserved its own autonomy in local matters but deferred to the central executive in all those affecting general policy. When Drury was told a few months after the founding meeting that the new body represented a mere handful of farmers, some fifty thousand, he retorted that, formal numbers aside, it reflected the views of rural Canada generally and enjoyed the support of the agricultural press and the tacit backing of thousands of unorganized farmers.[41] W.C. Good, who helped to write the council's constitution, hailed it as a means of 'doing a great work for the masses of the people.'[42]

The next few months were hectic ones for Drury as he helped to prepare the farmers' case for tariff reductions. There were encouraging signs that some relief might be afforded through the negotiation of a reciprocity treaty with the United States, ever since the demise of the first treaty a half-century earlier the goal of generations of Canadian farmers. One ray of hope came from northern states opposed to the recently imposed Payne-Aldrich tariff, which had sharply raised rates on basic raw materials which they wished to import from Canada. The tariff was in retaliation for Ottawa's discriminating against the United States through the conclusion of reciprocal agreements with other countries outside the empire. Yielding to domestic pressure, the Taft administration turned a blind eye to these Canadian infractions in the spring of 1910, some two months after the organization of the Canadian Council of Agriculture at Prince Albert. Then in the fall came the startling news that Washington was prepared to discuss nothing less than reciprocity itself.

Against this encouraging backdrop the CCA stepped up its own campaign to bring about a general reduction of the tariff. They pulled out all the stops when they confronted both Laurier and the Conservative leader, Robert Borden, on their pre-election swings through the prairies. Although many grain growers took Laurier's promises of tariff reductions at face value, eastern spokesmen such as Drury and Morrison reserved judgment.[43] To press the anti-protectionist point home, Drury and D.W. McCuaig, who had succeeded McKenzie as the CCA's president, committed the council to a mass demonstration in Ottawa of farmers from the prairies and Ontario. To Drury fell the responsibilty for much of the planning of the exercise, including such mundane chores as hiring the hall, in this case Ottawa's Grand Opera House, for the mass meeting arranged for 16 December 1910.

No one doubted that the west, with its vaunted enthusiasm for the cause, would deliver a sizeable and committed delegation. But some concern was expressed about the possible response from Ontario. The concern was soon laid to rest. By late November W.L. Smith, who showered the rural constituency with exhortations and appeals in the *Weekly Sun*, was already looking for great results from Ontario. 'The work of organizing the tariff deputation,' Smith wrote W.D. Gregory, 'is proceeding in a most satisfactory manner. It really looks as if we were going to reach the 300 mark from Ontario ... I really believe we are in a fair way of bringing about an arrangement which will be a vast benefit for [our] ... farmers.'[44] This was good news for Drury, who was anxious that the Ontario wing of the CCA register a creditable showing at Ottawa. Better news was to follow. A few days before the scheduled demonstration, the Grange and Farmers' Association held a well-attended annual convention in Toronto.

The some seven hundred delegates who gathered at Ottawa's Opera House were described by a cynical *Globe* reporter as a 'prosperous and self confident body of men' who, 'despite their protests at being ground down under the heel of the manufacturers, evidently possess bank accounts that would put most city dwellers to shame.'[45] Predictably, the meeting discussed commercial reciprocity with the United States. But the assembled farmers appeared to attach far more importance to a gradual transition to free trade. This would provide manufacturers with a breathing space of adjustment – a compromise finally hammered out at the meeting – by arranging a reduction of the British preference conceded by the Laurier government in 1897. In their mind, this would have the effect of ensuring the 'establishment of complete free trade between Canada and the Motherland within ten years.' This resolution, which passed unanimously, reflected the concerns of all delegates.

What particularly agitated Drury and the Ontario group were the massive urbanization and its concomitant, rural depopulation, which protectionism had helped to inflict on the country. These problems were spelled out in the following official statement that appeared over his and McCuaig's signatures:

[T]he greatest misfortune that can befall any country is to have its people huddled together in great centres of population and that the bearing of the present customs tariff has the tendency to encourage that condition and realizing also that in view of the constant movement of our people away from the farms, the greatest problem which presents itself to Canadian people today is the problem of retaining our people on the soil.[46]

The statement was vintage Drury, having been presented in much the same form to farmers' institutes, Grange meetings, and the sessions of the Experimental Union for the better part of a decade.

Together with the other statements and resolutions, it was formally presented to the government on 16 December 1910. 'Several of the Cabinet were present,' Drury recalled, 'and old Sir Richard Cartwright, with his white-bandaged foot and his crutch, nodded his head and smiled approvingly as we presented our case.' The rustic presentation took place in the Commons chamber which few of the delegates had ever laid eyes on before. The *Globe* remarked that what followed was the 'most significant four hours of straight talk which has been heard in Parliament for years,' and then commented on the vigorous address that Drury made on the tariff question.[47] But Laurier deflected the delegates with his usual charm, pointing out that he could not risk the fiscal structure by opening the doors, however gradually, to free trade with the motherland.[48] On the other hand, he assured them that the second-best undertaking in the minds of many at the Ottawa meeting – reciprocity with the United States – would be pursued. Though disappointed, Drury and McCuaig realized that that pledge was better than nothing and if handled adroitly could become the thin edge of the wedge for undermining the whole tariff structure.

Some were disposed to be more lyrical about the arrangement than Drury. In words that would have done honour to the mid-Victorian pronouncements of the so-called Manchester School, one observer commented that 'in a way the cause of Reciprocity is the cause of Peace for nothing is a more fruitful cause of dissension than tariffs and nothing makes for Peace so much as freer trade.'[49] At any rate, although it had failed to carry Laurier wholeheartedly into the agrarian camp, the CCA's submision was transformed into the so-called Farmers' Platform which would be presented to the voters at the next federal election.

Laurier had promised to put reciprocity high on his agenda and he followed through by dispatching Fielding and William Paterson to Washington early in the new year to negotiate a treaty. The news, however, did not generate waves of enthusiasm in Drury and other CCA spokesmen. Both emissaries were perceived to be 'arch protectionists,' totally wedded to the defence of a Liberalized National Policy. As a consequence, they might conceivably bring off free trade in natural products but would see to it that the rates on imported manufactures would remain more or less firmly in place. What Drury and the CCA still wanted, of course, was something like free trade across the board.

As it turned out, the final agreement with the United States, concluded in mid-January 1911, was to be implemented not by treaty but by concurrent legislation. The Americans, for their part, approved the agreement the following July. On the face of it there seemed nothing in this species of reciprocity to warrant any hostile reaction in Canada. Though it modestly went beyond what Drury had expected – duties were to be lowered on a specified group of man- ufactures and semi-finished products – it appeared to pose no serious threat to protected interests even while it pledged a vast American market for a wide range of Canadian agricultural exports. It was tantamount to an expression of economic motherhood and seemed, therefore, unassailable. A good many Conservatives, caught off guard, were reconciled to making the best of it. Some indeed, eager to rob the Liberals of the glory coming their way, went so far as to claim the agreement as their own. Drury ran into an instance of this in his own county. A few weeks after the agreement had been announced, 'I was on the same train as Houghton Lennox, the Conservative member for South Simcoe, and asked him what he thought about the ... treaty. "Splendid!" he said. "But you must remember that it's our policy not [the Liberals']. It's the very thing Sir John Macdonald tried to get".'[50]

Whatever the merits of this argument, there was to be a dramatic turnabout in the space of a few weeks. Just as ardent free traders like Drury had tolerated reciprocity as a means to achieve greater ends, so the protected interests feared that however innocent its terms might appear, the agreement would ultimately open the door to the removal of the trade barriers upon which, they were convinced, their whole industrial future depended. But when these economic fears were not considered sufficiently noble to enlist the electorate's opposition, reciprocity's 'inner meaning' was underscored by its critics. They warned of the very real possibility that any form of commercial rapport with Washington would lead inevitably to the demise of the imperial connection and to Canada's annexation to the United States. What had originally been viewed as a comparatively straightforward essay in international trade was now being denounced as a dangerous political exercise.

To compound the problem, Laurier's recent interpretations of Canada's place in the empire provided his Conservative opponents with the kind of ammunition they needed to shoot down what Liberals had first trumpeted as a sure-fire election issue. His compromise on the question of support for Great Britain during the German naval scare of 1909 and his supposedly half-hearted response during the South African War were branded as part of a concerted attempt to weaken Canada's ties with the imperial parent. Reciprocity, by threatening to draw Canada ever more firmly into the American orbit, was condemned as another step along this lamentable road.

Rural free traders, who appeared to share Laurier's real or imagined sentiments on the empire, were included in the condemnation that was thundered from Tory platforms and the Tory press.[51] And, to be sure, there was considerable grist for this kind of political mill. Good, a vocal anti-militarist, was probably close to the truth when he cautioned Laurier in 1909 that there was a 'strong feeling against the naval programme among the farmers and ... [the] question has never been brought before the electorate.' He then bitterly suggested that the Liberals were 'becoming identified with that party in England which looks to the Colonies to enable the British Empire to maintain its arrogant, immoral, and impossible "two power standard".'[52] Farmers sympathetic to Good's position would have been even more disturbed had they learned that during the Imperial Conference of 1907 arrangements had been made for Laurier and other colonial premiers to visit British manufacturers of the most advanced designs of artillery and warships.[53]

That Drury would have been as forceful as Good on the subject is doubtful. Nonetheless he did make it plain in later years that he had never been happy with the leading strings by which Canada had been tied to Great Britain. On the other hand, his fondness for the old country tended to take the sting out of his reflections on imperial relations. Furthermore, he had never ruled out the desirability of closer economic collaboration with Britain, an objective that he and other members of the CCA had stressed in their submission to Ottawa in 1910. In effect, both he and Good had plumped for a closer Anglo-Canadian partnership in trade. To some minds this promised to cement the very imperial relationship that the anti-reciprocity people were championing. This theme, however, was understandably downplayed by their protectionist opponents who feared the kind of industrial competition that freer trade with the United Kingdom would unleash on Canada.

It followed then that Drury personally was not very sanguine about the prospects of closer economic ties with the United States. Small wonder that he reacted all the more sharply to the charges of disloyalty ultimately levelled, after economic arguments had failed to carry the day, against those who espoused freer trade with the Americans. He deplored the excessive patriotism and abuse of the flag that disfigured the debate. 'Reason was cast aside,' he wrote later, 'and shrunk, shamefaced, out of sight.' He was also put off by the cavalier attitude of those who questioned the legitimacy of the farm movement's intervention in the campaign.

When the summer of 1911 approached, opponents of reciprocity were in full cry. What was worse for Laurier, some of his staunchest business backers came out against the agreement, and Liberal MPs representing industrial constituencies crossed the floor of the House to join the opposition. At the end of July 1911 Laurier decided to confront his critics and call a general election. The battle lines were clearly drawn and no one was more aware of this than Drury. Though profoundly interested in the outcome, Drury was not disposed to enter the fray as a candidate but only to take part in his official capacity as CCA secretary. This decision must have come as good news to his wife and Aunt Bessie, neither of whom welcomed the prospect of his devoting more hours than he already was to public affairs. According to a diary entry made by C.B. Sissons, Aunt Bessie 'hope[d] that Ernest will not get into politics and damp beds and the troubles they bring. Another reason, a man sees nothing of his children.'[54]

Even so, Drury spoke in a number of fiercely contested ridings, including, of course, those in Simcoe County. At a particularly hot and heavy session at Stroud, a Conservative Barrie paper, the *Northern Advance*, marvelled that he could so roundly denounce Fielding and Laurier for their perfidy when it came to the promotion of free trade and at the same time come out for reciprocity, their brainchild. 'No Tory in South Simcoe,' it gleefully reported, 'ever painted so black a picture of the [Liberal] party (with whom Mr. Drury is usually credited to be allied) as was portrayed by Mr. Drury ... at Stroud.' At subsequent speeches elsewhere, his critics claimed, he seemed to hew more to the traditional party line. This was too much for the editor in question. 'What side is Mr. D. on now?' he asked in feigned confusion. 'At Stroud he was independent; at Stayner he was a Liberal, and it is doubtful if he will not soon be found in the ranks of the Conservatives.' And apparently the Conservative Lennox, who had executed a *volte face* on reciprocity since his talk with Drury, remarked that up until now Drury 'ha[d] been sitting at the feet of these political Gamaliels [the Liberals] ... not one of them noted for political honesty.'[55]

Drury responded by arguing that he had spoken solely as a representative of the CCA, which had always regarded Laurier's economic policies as leaving much to be desired. He tried to show that the CCA was non-partisan and sought not to promote the fortunes of a particular party but to seek support for agrarian aims wherever they could find it. Conversely, they would criticize the failure to back the Farmers' Platform wherever it arose. Then, for the first time in public, Drury took a strong populist line when he attempted to show that the choice before the electorate in 1911 was not so much between Liberals and Conservatives as 'between the People and the Trusts.' Yet in spite of misgivings about Laurier's earlier behaviour and the second-best nature of the reciprocal trade agreement, the CCA would endorse it as a step along the way to the achievement of free trade in manufactured goods as well as natural products. But the *Northern Advance* was not prepared to let the matter rest there. When he scanned the issue which printed his retort, Drury noted that it had been dismissed as a political brochure in an accompanying editorial.

Impassioned presentations of the Farmers' Platform, however, were not enough. When the votes were counted on 21 September 1911 Laurier and his Liberals had been swept from office and reciprocity decisively rejected. The Liberal chieftain philosophically conceded that 'Reciprocity did not play the part which it should. The people did not rally to it as they would have done years ago, for the reason that the country is so prosperous, and ... reciprocity did not appeal to them.'[56] Nineteen-eleven was assuredly not 1854, when the first reciprocal agreement had been concluded with the United States. The clock hands, so Laurier and others were resigned to thinking, could not be turned back to eradicate the urban and industrial transformation that had overtaken the country since the mid-nineteenth century.

Right to the end, Drury and other farm activists thought the electorate would function rationally and do the right thing by voting for the principle of economic freedom. Yet the farming community had been divided on the question. Niagara fruit growers, for example, feared a tidal wave of imports from the southern states that would swamp their own lucrative domestic market, and they ended up being just as protectionist as manufacturers in nearby Hamilton. This harsh fact of life helped compound Drury's misery on election night. 'When I went to bed,' he recollected, 'I lay awake in the grip of a vast discouragement.'[57] He was not the only insomniac that fateful night. For most farmers, the election of 1911 was a cataclysm, a great divide that separated years of hope, however muted it might have been at times, from a future of despair. The campaign, after all, had not constituted a mere battle like other electoral battles, a simple confrontation with an enemy fortified behind what Arthur Meighen, of all people, denounced as 'ramparts of gold.'[58] To the farmers it had assumed all the proportions of a crusade to liberate the country from evils that endangered its life and soul.

When the crusade faltered and failed to deliver the goods the emotional shock for the losers was all the more devastating. Drury, Good, and other dispirited rural spokesmen had vainly tried to use the CCA as a battering ram to break down the protectionists' awesome defences and emancipate what Drury fulsomely called the 'finest yeomanry that civilization had yet produced.' At an unhappy post-mortem it was agreed that further exercises in organization had best be deferred until the farm movement had recovered from the débâcle. There was also self-recrimination. One who attended the post-mortem was supposed to have made the bitter remark that the 'farmers have been fools again. Let them fry in their own grease for a while.'[59] The general disenchantment was soon reflected in the decline of local Granges and the poor showing made by the thinly attended annual convention of the Grange and Farmers' Association in 1912. Nearly two years would pass before the demoralized organization called another.

By this time Queen's Park had entered the picture with its own farmers' clubs. It was no secret that this initiative had been seen as an opportunity to head off the newly formed alliance between the Grange and the Farmers' Association and to undermine its influence on the concession lines. The clubs were unquestionably fashioned not as potential political forums but primarily as social organizations, so many convivial meeting places where the discussion of questions that had been the lifeblood of association meetings would be eschewed. The farm movement appeared to have been put back thirty years.

But for Drury the dark cloud of defeat and disillusionment had one silver lining: it provided a respite from the intensive labour he had put in on behalf of the agrarian movement for the better part of four years. It meant too that he would absent himself for at least two years from the annual meetings of the CCA. The respite's timing was fortuitous because Crown Hill needed his attention, as did his wife and family. From the work of organizing conventions, drafting platforms, waging political battles, and stumping the province, he turned, with some relief, to the more mundane tasks of farming.

A Farmer in Wartime

Farm chores, long deferred by what he referred to as his mission work, occupied Drury for some months after his return from the political wars. They included the remodelling of a sheep pen to accommodate a larger flock, the repairing of a well, and the moving of an old barn and its transformation into a horse stable with stalls for work teams and the occasional 'old pensioner.' So much for the barnyard; the house would also be improved. The outdoor privy was unceremoniously relegated to the scrap heap when Drury added a bathroom to the house – one of the first in the township – complete with septic tank and water pumped from the refurbished well. W.C. Good's home was also embellished with a similar technological refinement. Indeed, the two friends may have conferred on the subject; they certainly did on the merits of other mechanical improvements. Years later Good's daughter echoed the delight of Drury's children when she looked back on the modern conveniences her father had introduced. She waxed enthusiastic on the 'coal furnace and stationary washtubs in the cellar, the bathroom upstairs, the hot and cold water in the kitchen, the laundry and bath.'[1] Urban comforts, however much their source might be questioned, were thus finding their way into the farmsteads of Ontario and transforming not only habits but domestic architecture as well.

In the midst of his improvement program at Crown Hill Drury became involved in an experiment in social justice. In 1912 he agreed to take on help in the form of a Scottish immigrant family, and house them in his ample home until they were able to find their own accommodation. At that point it came to light that the wife's sister had been detained at Quebec City, the port of entry, and threatened with deportation on the grounds that she was deemed feeble minded. Drury's reaction was immediate and characteristic. Dismissing the action as 'inhumanly cruel,' he cabled the minister of the interior and requested that she be admitted. He followed this up with a letter explaining the circumstances. His intervention, according to his recollections, paid off. The woman was admitted for one year on condition that Drury monitor the situation. He was specifically asked to report any plan to marry her to a Canadian citizen, an action that would bring instant deportation. When such an eventuality loomed the next spring Drury complied and duly reported it to Ottawa. Whereupon no less a bureaucrat than the deputy minister himself descended on Crown Hill to investigate the matter personally. The official, after surviving a hair-raising encounter with the swain in question, succeeded in keeping the woman in a state of unmarried innocence and the regulations intact.[2]

The upshot, however, was that those regulations were amended, requiring that medical examinations be made at the port of embarkation so that in future similar unhappy circumstances could be avoided.

While dealing with these and other matters at Crown Hill, and while the farm movement still seemed relegated to the fringes of his thinking, Drury found time to keep up with his reading, particularly of the classical political economists such as Smith, Ricardo, and Mill. He also delved into Henry George, the apostle of the single tax. After first dismissing George's ideas as unsound, he came around to a grudging acceptance of them. George had argued that the growing scarcity of land as population expanded, and its 'selfish monopolization' by a few, had denied access to its ownership by the many. With the enhancement of land values, powerful landowners had exacted constantly soaring rents that produced the paradox of progress and poverty, the phrase George used for the title of his highly popular work. To remedy the situation the reformer, after discarding confiscation and the socialization of land as alternatives, proposed instead to 'appropriate all rent by taxation,' in effect to abolish all taxation save upon land values. Hence, the single tax that would dispossess holders of unearned rent or increment, eradicate a social injustice, and emancipate those who had hitherto been denied the joys of landownership.[3] What may have helped to convince Drury of the merits of *Progress and Poverty*, even more than the arguments for the single tax, was the knowledge that its author was a convert to free trade as an instrument for reforming the international economic order.[4]

While thus engrossed in the fall of 1913, Drury received a letter from J.J. Morrison, still secretary and auditor of the chastened Grange and Farmers' Association. Two others long active on the agrarian front, W.C. Good and Colonel J.Z. Fraser of Burford, were also approached and invited to come to Toronto in late October to discuss the serious impasse facing Ontario's organized farmers. Clearly, Morrison wanted to discuss the feasibility of revitalizing the farm movement. Both Good and Drury, whom the former described as a 'man of some clearness of vision,' felt a sense of obligation and, in spite of previous disappointments, duty bound to seize a fresh opportunity to mobilize the rural troops.[5] What followed was touched upon in the participants' varied memoirs and in a published account that Drury prepared some years later for Melville H. Staples's history of the United Farmers of Ontario. Of the memoirs, only Morrison's offers more than a skeletal outline of what transpired.

Morrison was well aware that although some of the otherwise innocuous farmers' clubs set up by Queen's Park were beginning to thrive as centres of community interest, there was no effective central organization to co-ordinate their activities. 'There was no money to carry on a [publicity] campaign,' he lamented, 'no organizing machinery or office equipment,' or, for that matter, an office.[6] To address these and related problems the four men met at the Kirby House on Toronto's Queen Street West. This was a second-best rendez-vous; their original intention had been to meet in the office of the *Weekly Sun* but its doors were locked in deference to the 'city man's habit of taking Saturday afternoon off.'[7] They were therefore obliged to make do without editor Smith's counsel when they gathered in an alcove off the hotel's bar. Of the four only Fraser was not a committed tee-totaller, and he presumably polished off the mandatory liquid refreshment that came to their table.[8]

Morrison promptly submitted his plan to rejuvenate the farm movement in the province. Stated briefly, it was, to use his phrase, to steal from Queen's Park's control of the farmers' clubs that were still flourishing, form a central body to direct their operations in conjunction with the Grange and Farmers' Association, and thereby launch a new and more vigorous organization. In this way it was hoped to bring agrarian pressure once more to bear on politicians and bureaucrats and carry the rural message to the general public. With all in agreement, Morrison was designated the organizer of this program and the informal founding committee undertook to make good his out-of-pocket expenses.

Two months later the annual Grange meeting, which turned out to be its last official one, was urged by Good, its president, to support the Kirby House initiative. Anxious to yield to new schemes and fresh blood anyway, it needed little urging, and Good's eloquent call for action met with unanimous approval. He exhorted his listeners to join in the fight against the 'giant of special Privilege, who has enslaved and degraded this nation for so long [and who] is beginning to tremble in his castle.'[9] This statement was echoed in Morrison's fervent message to Thomas A. Crerar on the eve of the Toronto meeting: 'Our ... hope is to break the power of the vested interests that are destroying [what] ... our pioneer fathers wrested from the wilderness ... It is,' he concluded, 'the fight of my life.'[10]

Morrison, who throughout had made a point of keeping in touch with the leadership of the prairie farm movement, was overjoyed when they accepted his invitation to attend the Grange convention. Appropriately they pledged their services and financial support. In turn Morrison advised Crerar, whose Grain Growers' Company gave a welcome one thousand dollars to the neophyte Ontario organization, that it was going to be formed along western lines by keeping alive existing bodies but making them 'subsidiary to the new organization.'[11] What he had in mind was the array of co-operative societies which owed much to the example already set by Crerar's company and the evangelizing work of the CCA.

Drury, for his part, had personally backed the co-operative movement, described by OAC president George Creelman as the farmers' most crying need while waste and corruption in the market place and the profits of middlemen dominated the economy. In practical terms Drury had helped organize in Barrie a so-called beef ring – a co-operative butchering firm – which supplied its members with good-quality meat and staged annually a community supper.

In the meantime, Morrison was well aware that even while he was courting prairie support, Crerar and other westerners would have to be acquainted with certain Ontario facts of life. The farming scene in the east was fragmented into heterogeneous interest groups – fruit growers, truck farmers, livestock men, to name just a few – that set it off from the monolithic western community of graingrowers. Morrison was obviously trying to stress that in Ontario he had to deal with what he called a motley crowd. At a meeting in late November 1913, a month after the Kirby House deliberations, Morrison complained that the Niagara Apple-Growers Association, convinced that they had a captive western market anyway, saw little need for collaboration with the graingrowers and were 'blinded to the broader bearing of the movement.'[12] This sort of particularism and myopia had for Drury too long been the bugbear of all the varied species of farm organizations in Ontario. Morrison, who had a jaded view of human nature in any case, was under no illusions about the difficulties that lay in the path of the new venture and seldom did he permit high-flown oratory, least of all his own, to cloud his perception of reality.

Yet he shouldered aside his doubts and with the active support of Drury, Good, and Fraser, pressed ahead with plans to enlist the aid of existing organizations and to arrange a formal meeting for launching what would shortly be called the United Farmers of Ontario. Over their signatures a printed invitation was mailed out on 28 February 1914 to every farm group in the province urging them to send delegates to an organizational meeting, set for 19 and 20 March in Toronto's Labor Temple. In the interval Morrison undertook a barnstorming tour on behalf of the campaign, an exercise that earned the warm praise of George Keen, the founder of the Co-operative Union of Canada, who commended him for his 'great capacity for self sacrifice.'[13]

Two weeks before the founding convention opened, Drury and Good had an opportunity to ventilate the problems they saw facing the countryside, in no less a setting than the nation's capital. The Social Service Congress of Canada, hastily convened in Ottawa, was the first such national forum for identifying and discussing the country's social problems. By virtue of their standing in the farm movement, Drury and Good were invited to share the proceedings with representatives of other interest groups that had for some years been pinpointing the difficulties accompanying Canada's large-scale industrialization and urbanization. On hand were spokesmen for varying versions of the Social Gospel, which called upon the churches to take the lead in Christianizing the secular world and ushering in the Kingdom of God on Earth.[14]

At the time Drury, a former member of the conscientious Epworth League, appeared to write or say nothing explicit on this particular appeal. But the spirit that informed remarks he made years later may have shaped his responses on public issues in those late winter days of 1914. In unpublished writings of the 1930s he would stress the need for a new sort of church 'with a work to do in keeping with the times – the salvation of ... the whole, wide world – not just a few individuals here and there [but] the creation of the Kingdom of Heaven on Earth ... a Golden Age.'[15] His later brusque dismissal of personal salvation as a selfish goal he may not have expressed so blatantly in 1914, preferring instead to twin it in importance with the pursuit of social purification.

While Good addressed the problem of 'political impurity' at the Social Service Congress, Drury chaired the section dealing with the 'Problem of the Country.' He minced few words in his opening remarks, starting off with the bald assertion that the section he chaired was the most important of the congress. 'The other conferences deal only with the cleansing of the sewers of our civilization; we have to deal with a much more important and greater problem – the preservation of the springs of our civilization, of the fountain-head on which the whole depends.'[16] This was no new message. Drury and other farm activists had been preaching it to audiences for the better part of a decade. Yet there was seen to be an even greater need for the rural ethic to be forcefully stated in the years of dispiritedness that followed reciprocity's rejection at the polls. It was almost as if Drury was preparing the community at large for the debut of the United Farmers of Ontario just two weeks hence. That event, he and Good hoped, would help to bring closer to fruition the Golden Age they liked to talk about.

Drury's combative words in Ottawa ill matched the trepidation that seized Morrison in Toronto, when he pondered the problems that faced the new farm organization. The prospect that it might encounter rough weather, or worse, sink without a trace even before it was launched, brought on an attack of anxiety that hospitalized Morrison and sharply limited his attendance at the founding convention. Some who came to it would have added to his anguish, for they included the plainly curious who merely wished to take in a spectacle and harboured no great certainty that the new organization would fare any better than its hapless predecessors. They might have agreed with the caustic view of Humfrey Michell, a Queen's political economist, that 'farmers left to their own devices will surely make a mess of things.'[17]

None the less, some two hundred farmers responded to the invitation, and to Morrison's earlier swing through the province. The turnout at the Labor Temple was everything that Drury could have wished. Indeed, for some time he had been far more sanguine of success than Morrison. For one thing, he and many other farmers were once again spurred on by the exhortations of their prairie counterparts. Their cables of support Drury read out to the gathering and saved for his own account of the founding of the UFO. But the graingrowers' stimulus did not end with wordy messages of encouragement. Westerners of the calibre of Manitoba's Roderick McKenzie came and addressed the convention like so many rural crusaders and, in the end, wrote Drury, changed 'doubt to faith and hope.'[18]

The result was the formal endorsement of not one but two organizations – the UFO, of which Drury was named president, and the United Farmers Co-operative Company, an enterprise long championed by the small co-operatives that had sent representatives to the Labor Temple. Formally incorporated on 7 February 1914, the company was the brainchild of Good and farmer neighbours of Brant County. It predictably received the enthusiastic support of George Keen, the co-operativist, who had prepared the papers and secured the charter of the new company.[19] While the UFO sought to provide its constituency with the means for self-improvement, the United Farmers' Co-operative Company was set up to 'carry on the business of farming in all its branches on the co-operative plan for the mutual advantage, accommodation and convenience of ... the [Company's] members.'[20] Western influence was clearly stamped on the enterprise when it was announced that it would seek to do for the UFO what the lucrative graingrowers' co-operatives had done for the prairie organizations.

While Drury's interest in co-operativism was respectable enough, it never matched the zeal that Good lavished on the movement. Even so, Drury, as president of the UFO and a modest stockholder, was elected to the company's permanent board of directors.[21] Morrison, whom Drury with good reason called the real founder of the UFO, was unanimously named secretary-treasurer of both the UFO and the company. This was done to ensure that both organizations, though autonomous, would be handled from one office so that each would be kept informed of the other's activities. Given his command of the rural scene, Morrison seemed an eminently suitable choice for this appointment. But in spite of the company's brave beginnings and the attention paid it by Good, who was named its first president, it started life inauspiciously. 'I remember one emergency meeting of the directors,' Drury wrote in *Farmer Premier*, 'called by Good ... in late August [1914] at which all the directors subscribed for additional stock and paid for it on the spot, in order that the company might be able to carry on.'

The modest euphoria that greeted this latest adventure in the Ontario farm movement was countered by the outbreak of the First World War. The *Weekly Sun* had captured the mood of most of the concession lines when it editorialized against militarism overseas. Some months before Britain found herself at war the paper had repudiated the young Winston Churchill as a dangerous contributor to the makings of the conflict. The anti-militarism of Goldwin Smith, who eloquently articulated many farmers' reactions, dominated the weekly's columns in the summer months of 1914. The mid-Victorian liberalism that seasoned Smith's writing neatly combined with the farmers' aversion to war to provide another argument in the debate over free trade. Just as the defeat of protectionism would liberate humanity from its economic bondage, so the eradication of war, to which the emancipation of trade would make a signal contribution, would lead to the total fulfilment of man. In the minds of many rural leaders, Drury included, it would be up to an aroused farming community to promote these noble ends.[22] 'Agricultural peoples,' Drury would write with a blunt conceit and a fine disregard for historical realities, 'are almost invariably inclined to peace.'[23] His friend Good would have agreed. Before the war he had urged the country's political leadership to forsake armaments, arguing that 'if we are unarmed we cannot be dragged into quarrels not of our own making.' Moreover, sounding an isolationist note, he remarked that 'whatever the fancied necessities of the European powers, Canada's position is unique insofar as she has lived for 100 years in peaceful relations with the only country able to do her serious harm.'[24] The war was barely three months old when concerned and well-placed citizens in Toronto were showing their distress over such statements and deploring the 'great apathy ... throughout the Country Districts ... owing probably to a lack of appreciation of the serious aspects and vital importance of the great struggle in which we are engaged.'[25]

Drury's despair over the conflict almost matched that generated by the events of 1911. At UFO meetings he denigrated war as a destroyer of ideals. To Good he wrote that 'It is hard to see any real progress. The Germans, educated, Christianized, are as barbarous, as ruthless as their Roman prototypes, 2000 years ago. Our own people, in the face of the greatest calamaty [sic] of the ages, remain calloused, flippant, or worse, selfish ... I must confess I see little hope except in Divine interference.'[26]

When news of the war's outbreak had reached Simcoe County Drury had been 'greatly troubled as to where my duty lay.' In the end he reckoned that deafness in one ear, and the demands of his farm and his large and growing family of four children would rule out military service. Carl, the first-born, had been joined by Varley, Elizabeth, and Mabel in 1908, 1910, and 1912 respectively. He was also troubled by what he called a 'derangement of semi-circular canals on one side of my head,' which produced a condition like seasickness. 'I can now remain at home,' he wrote Good, 'and still get the full benefit of an ocean voyage.' In his published memoirs, he claims that he spurned a suggestion that he become a recruiting officer on the grounds that 'I could not see myself urging others to do something that I could not do myself.' On the other hand, after the war when he was running for office he made a point of telling an audience packed with veterans that he had helped a battalion stationed in the Barrie area with its recruiting drives.[27]

His decision to remain on the home front was reinforced by word that soon came from Ottawa, urging farmers to produce to the limit as a patriotic duty to meet the needs of the Allied Powers. In any event, Crown Hill's demands could not be ignored, war or no war. The months of activity devoted to floating the UFO, like his work earlier for the Canadian Council of Agriculture, had robbed the farm of vital direction and labour. To correct this he decided in 1915 not to let his name stand for re-election to the UFO presidency and instead to support the candidacy of R.H. Halbert. A matter of principle had also been involved – the belief that new blood should periodically be injected into the structure of the organization. Even so, he was gratified when he was elected perpetual honorary president in recognition of his contributions to the farm movement. Nor did he turn down the vice-presidency when it was offered him in 1917.

Back on the farm, there was a considerable backlog of work. Like others during the war, Drury had to put up with labour shortages, as more and more able-bodied men either joined the armed forces or moved to the city to take more lucrative employment in war-oriented industries. By the summer of 1916 Drury was complaining to Good, who had the same problem, that there was so much work that he couldn't concentrate at night to write. 'Not quite the same capacity for long hours of work – ... 5 am. to 8 pm. – that I had ... At one time I could work on the farm all day and read or write half the night.'[28] He reported also that the burdens of running the house were making his wife nervous and unwell. Those burdens, as he explained elsewhere, arose from the farm house's being 'not only a home, but a part of the business, and on the farm women devolve many duties not strictly domestic in their character. Under the best condition [and wartime assuredly was not] the farmer's wife is bound to work harder than her city sister.'[29] In spite of the claims on his time, Drury managed to find some hours to peruse his colleagues' writings, particularly Good's contributions to the *Farmer's Advocate*. He complimented him on giving 'economic truth in small, easily digested doses.' Characteristically combining bouquets with brickbats, he added that 'if they have a weakness it is that you are possibly a little too cocksure in the conclusions you draw from statistics.'

But even if Drury's literary pursuits suffered, his technological ones did not; he busily drew up plans to market an automatic regulating device that he had perfected for his water system and that Good had already used on his own farm. Though a firm expressed interest, wartime priorities must have intruded to shelve the scheme. In any case, nothing more was heard of it.

Although he wrote in *Farmer Premier* that he gave comparatively little to the farm movement during the war, he maintained a lively interest in the UFO and the co-operative company. At first, he was inclined to play down Good's qualms about the state of the company and its management. Unquestionably it had got off to a shaky start, caused in part by the unfriendly economic conditions that marred the early months of the war. Another problem stemmed from the importance that Good and Keen, the idealists of the co-operative movement, attached to the autonomy of local co-operative societies.[30] According to their critics, however, and these included J.J. Morrison, those societies lacked the leadership and drive to make the company the success that its founders had envisaged in the spring of 1914. Good was obviously disturbed by the criticism, so much so that Drury felt compelled in the spring of 1915 to assure him that he was being unduly pessimistic. Yet he did share some of Good's concern about the company's management and feared that through 'lack of business ability [it would] fail to give value to the [Farmer's] Clubs and so [would] fail to hold them.' Nevertheless, he urged Good to continue to put his faith in Morrison.[31]

A year later, however, Drury changed his tune and became almost as disturbed as Good about the kind of service and direction Morrison was providing both the UFO and the company. Although the documentation is fragmentary, it would appear that both men were anxious to block Morrison's plan to centralize the direction of local co-operatives and reduce their role.[32] In spite of his protests that the move would bring greater efficiency and enhanced returns to the company, Drury and Good suspected that the real reason was Morrison's desire to strengthen his own position at the centre of affairs. They both readily acknowledged Morrison's skill at dealing with the ordinary farmer but feared that what they saw as his ambition would eventually do more harm than good to the farm movement.[33] On the other hand, Drury had to face up to the reality that many of the UFO members were coming down on the side of Morrison's centralization strategy.

Meanwhile Drury had already been on the receiving end of an unpleasant letter from Morrison, who was presumably smarting from the charges of company mismanagement and complaints about the wide latitude he seemed to enjoy. To complicate matters further, Good accused Morrison of failing to promote what the UFO had ostensibly been formed to do – vital educational work among Ontario's farmers. Good held little back: 'So far as any activities emanating from the head office are concerned, the organization has been dead.' His distaste for centralization of any sort sharpened this criticism of 'head office,' a phrase that became a pejorative one in his literary armoury. Morrison fought back by asking how the UFO could play its propaganda role without any money. Moreover, he charged that if the UFO's educational work was not measuring up to Good's and Drury's expectations the fault lay as much with them, as directors, as it did with the secretary. At least Morrison, unlike his more self-assured colleagues, could include himself in the following indictment: 'We have been a blundering lot of men, remarkable only for our incapacity to do things.'[34] The misgivings which had haunted him at the outset were now breaking through the thin veneer of whatever optimism he still possessed.

What also emerged was Morrison's impatience with the apparent conceit of the formally educated leadership of the UFO. Although no real hint of academic arrogance intrudes on Drury's or Good's evaluation of Morrison, they may well have left the impression that their cultural and educational attainments somehow put them above one who, without benefit of their advanced tutoring, had long laboured in the trenches of the farm movement. Convinced of his superior ability to read the mood of the Ontario farmer, Morrison would tartly remind them that 'in addressing the rank and file ... you must speak to them on a level which they are accustomed to, otherwise your effort is a failure.' H.B. Cowan, the influential editor of *Farm and Dairy*, echoed this line. Drury was urged to speak and write in the simplest possible language because 'many farmers are ... ignorant ... of even the simplest principles ... [and] nearly everything will have to be handled in an almost ABC manner.'[35] The rift over co-operative policy was thus widened by the clash of backgrounds and personalities. Drury's own quick temper, when troubles for the UFO and the company multiplied during the war, seldom found much room for tolerating Morrison's shortcomings, real or fancied. For a time both he and Good pondered ways and means of getting a new secretary and ensuring that Morrison's appointment would never be made permanent.[36] But their plans never proceeded beyond mere contemplation. Morrison's hold over the membership, though challenged or questioned from time to time in the agrarian press and elsewhere, made him virtually impregnable.[37]

Although the secretary's career was not at risk, the company's general manager's was; Anson Groh, who did not get on well with Morrison, had held that office from the beginning. He came in for much criticism not only from Drury but from T.A. Crerar, whose intervention in the company's affairs had been invited. Groh was denounced as an absolutely hopeless general manager and Drury called for his dismissal. 'We can't allow personal considerations for any man,' he wrote Good, 'to wreck the movement.'[38] The upshot was that Groh resigned in July 1916 and was replaced by a reputedly more efficient and acceptable officer. And yet, though described by Drury later as honest and devoted, he lacked solid business experience. But the gulf between Morrison and the 'college farmers' was not entirely bridged, a state of affairs that boded ill for the future of the farm movement in Ontario.[39]

Meanwhile, Drury had been deflected by politics. The move chagrined Good who had wanted him to 'come in and give [local] co-operatives ... a boost.' Drury's decision in October 1916 to attend the Liberal nominating convention of North Simcoe riding at Stayner was shaped in part by the latest chapter in the unhappy chronicle of rural depopulation and farm labour shortages. In greater numbers than ever young people were being enticed to the cities to replace factory hands who had responded to the call of recruiting sergeants.[40] What had once been regarded as an irritant was now being described as a calamity. Just as urban spokesmen bemoaned the loss of the flower of Canadian youth in Flanders, so rural leaders were decrying the drain to the cities of the best blood of the farming community – for them another kind of Western Front. The lament came from many quarters: from the halls of the OAC where theses were being prepared on the subject, from editorials in the agrarian press, and from the writings and speeches of activists such as Drury and Good. Good probed to the heart of the problem when he wrote that the 'mere fact of decreasing numbers is not in itself of vital importance. *The vital question is that of the quality of those [remaining] in the country.*'[41] Drury would recall his own mood of the moment when he wrote comparable lines for his unpublished novel some twenty years later: 'The pioneer stock was leaving the land, or petering out in child-lessness, or deteriorating through a process of inverted selection, by which the cleverest and most ambitious were continually drained away to the cities.'[42] Resentment was also building over the way agrarian interests were overlooked when wartime prices were arbitrarily set for farm produce and, to quote Morrison, 'war conditions aggravated the inequalities [already] existing between the urban and the agricultural communities.'[43]

Drury expected to hear these and other issues aired at the North Simcoe federal nominating convention, and he was not disappointed. But much to his surprise, he was nominated as the Liberal standard-bearer even though he had warned the gathering that he would stand only as an independent Liberal, given his aversion to Laurier's economic policies. Although Drury and others hoped that an election would be deferred until after the war, he felt obliged to tell Good, who had wanted him to campaign in aid of the co-operative movement instead, that 'from now on I will have to give considerable time to the riding.'[44]

Drury's decision to venture into federal politics was taken in spite of the long-standing advice of Aunt Bessie and his wife's supposed dislike for the role of a politician's spouse. Ella feared that he would be away from home for even longer periods. In any case, Drury may have concluded by the fall of 1916 that he had made all the contributions of which he was capable to the UFO and the cause of co-operativism. At the same time he may have had enough of the infighting with Morrison. Then again, he may have thought that activities con-fined to the Ontario stage were marginal at best, a departure from the kind of national role he had sought to play, first with the Dominion Grange and then with the Canadian Council of Agriculture. After all, the issue that had com-manded the bulk of his attention for years was protectionism and the battle against the tariff could only be effectively fought at the federal level.

In spite of his dissatisfaction with party programs and leadership, Drury was still a firm believer in the party system itself. For this reason he looked unkindly upon the nostrums that Good and more radical elements in the farm movement were promoting. Morrison, already distrusted by Drury for his ambition, came under even greater suspicion when he espoused the initiative, the referendum, and the recall – all devices favoured by American Populists and those other backers of so-called direct democracy who wished to rein in their elected rep-resentatives. Morrison was also urging the substitution of what would later be called group or class government for the party system, which he roundly denounced as the tool of the very vested interests that were persecuting the farming community. Although Morrison may have imbibed some notions from American initiatives in these matters, it is altogether likely that some of his proposals for reforming the political system stemmed from his own practical experience with county and township councils.[45]

What pained Drury more than Morrison's flirtation with such panaceas was Good's defence of them. Disenchanted with a party system that seemed a mere plaything of vested interests, Good also called for sweeping electoral changes and the development of a keener sense of class consciousness among Ontario farmers. 'The parasitic classes,' he wrote early in 1917, 'have developed class consciousness ... and have thus [been enabled to] prey ... upon agriculture.'[46] Drury, with his strongly held view of a well-ordered and harmonious society, could not bring himself to support this kind of polarization or sanction schemes that would undo what was for him the only workable system in a parliamentary democracy. On one point, however, he was prepared to yield; he did come out in favour of the transferable vote. This formed part of Good's scheme of proportional representation which would ensure that parties or preferably groups would hold seats in a legislature in proportion to the support they received at the polls. The transferable vote would have the effect of guaranteeing that the victorious candidate had, in fact, obtained an honest majority of the votes cast.[47]

In the framework of wartime politics, however, prospects were bleak for achieving these or any other electoral reforms. This was made even more obvious in the summer of 1917 when the political crisis in Ottawa assumed explosive proportions. The military stalemate and the bloodletting on the Western Front prompted Prime Minister Robert Borden to call for the introduction of compulsory military service to meet Canada's manpower crisis. This was accompanied by a call to the Liberals for a coalition or union government. This would, it was hoped, put a gloss of national endorsement on a measure whose use had been solemnly foresworn at war's outbreak in deference largely to French-speaking Canada. Drury and other farm leaders learned soon enough that some leading Liberals had bought Borden's arguments and, over Laurier's protests, elected to join the projected coalition. These included none other than T.A. Crerar, the farm movement's principal western spokesman, and N.W. Rowell, Ontario's Liberal chieftain. In spite of this impressive show of commitment to the national purpose, Drury shared the view of many of his eastern colleagues that the coalition was 'merely the old Government with a bit of window dressing.'[48]

On the conscription question Drury had some agonizing moments. He realized that it could, by inflaming French Canadians, endanger the very national endeavour that Borden was seeking to mount, and threaten to entrench at home those 'Prussianizing' influences on Canadian life that the war had already condoned. In the end, however, he satisfied himself that conscription, though an evil, was a necessary one if the country were to continue to play its part in suppressing the heartland of Prussianism overseas. Although *Farmer Premier* makes no reference to the subject, he claimed in postwar statements that his grudging support for conscription had always been coupled with a call to conscript wealth through heavier taxation.[49] This approach assumed all the proportions of a battle cry when taken up by other rural spokesmen and by disgruntled labour leaders. At its convention in March 1916 the UFO had gone on record with the following statement:

Since human life is more valuable than gold, this convention most solemnly protests against any proposal looking to the conscription of men for battle while leaving ... plutocrats fattening on special privileges ... in undisturbed possession of their riches.[50]

Good appears to have been more vocal than his Simcoe County colleague on this theme and charged that compulsory military service was another means whereby the 'vocal Imperialist majority' who controlled the press were stampeding the country into bondage. Drury shrank from the vehemence of Good's assaults if only because of his fondness for the imperial connection and his belief that the empire could some day emerge as a 'galaxy of free, independent and equal nations.'[51]

Following the formation of the Union government and the political convulsions it created, Drury felt obliged to have his North Simcoe nomination reconsidered. When he protested that the changed political situation invalidated it, the executive disagreed and urged him to run in the riding as originally planned, as an independent Liberal. Then, in November 1917, about a month before the election called to endorse the Union government and conscription, he was thrown off stride by the news that most of the riding executive had switched to the coalition. 'No doubt they followed their consciences,' he consoled himself in his memoirs, but he probably thought he was being victimized by the very wartime hysteria that had already drawn his anger.[52] The defection of his erstwhile supporters punched a hole in his campaign, one that was enlarged by his subsequent reluctance to conduct a personal canvass in the riding that would have required him to pry into a voter's political preferences. It was an uphill battle from the start, made more so by the strength and following enjoyed by his tough Conservative opponent. Colonel John A. Currie had swept the riding in the reciprocity election of 1911, and in the interval had served overseas as commanding officer of the Simcoe Foresters, in the circumstances a virtually unbeatable combination.

The campaign turned ugly at one point when Drury was accused by a recently organized Ku Klux Klan of supporting 'slackers' and 'traitors' in Quebec who were refusing to aid the empire that had long safeguarded their rights. Drury suspected that it was mainly the Orange lodges at work stirring up the potent anti-Catholicism that was said to abound in certain parts of the county. He was not the only farm spokesman concerned about the way the war and its unrelenting appeals to patriotism had played into the hands of extremists in general and the Orange Order in particular. Ironically, Drury ended up being sniped at from both sides. In the strongly Catholic Phelpston district he was branded a member of the Klan, in the Orange-tinted Elmvale area his wife was unaccountably denounced as a Catholic. And in Barrie, the *Northern Advance* ridiculed his much-heralded independence and lampooned him, as it had in the past, as a chameleon who should not be trusted by the electorate.[53]

In spite of these frustrations, Drury campaigned vigorously. Volunteers, who recalled his services to the farm movement, particularly his work for the CCA, sent out promotional literature at their own expense and otherwise tried to smoke out a favourable vote. Lacking access to a party war chest, Drury had to foot his own election expenses, which amounted to the not inconsiderable sum of eight hundred dollars. His opponent's much more lavish expenditures he probably likened, as he did in his later writings, to a form of electoral bribery. 'Undoubtedly money spent in this way ... [on] political advertising,' he had a character in his unpublished novel say, 'is a far larger factor in elections ... than it has ever been.' Although Drury won in Oro, his home township, he went down to a convincing defeat, one perhaps assured by a shrewd cabinet decision taken in Ottawa two weeks before the election. It had provided what many farmers had long been requesting, exemptions for their sons from military service. Even so, Laurier Liberals fared better than Drury in other rural ridings, and where the Union government's candidate did carry the day he did so with a modest majority.

Drury's defeat was doubtless seen by him and his supporters as a microcosm of the setback suffered by the farming community in 1911. It was accompanied by the chilling realization that the war's end appeared to be more remote than ever. True, the Americans had entered it but they were not yet ready to fill the void created by Russia's dramatic withdrawal from the conflict. Some observers talked gloomily about the prospect of several more years of carnage on the Western Front. And yet, cynically motivated or not, the exemptions provided farmers' sons had resolved one festering problem on the home front. Not only this, farm prices had begun to climb well beyond the depressed levels set during the early stages of the war. Drury recalled that in the last wartime winter his wheat fetched over two dollars a bushel and he sold his lambs for the highest price ever paid on the Toronto market. Heartened by an improvement in his material fortunes, comforted by Ottawa's pledge on exemptions, and gratified by his well-received exertions on behalf of the UFO, Drury could live more comfortably with the chastisement he had received at the polls in late 1917.

5

With the UFO in Politics

The election of 1917 provided Canada, or so its backers claimed, with the physical means to carry the fight against Prussianism abroad. Yet, as conscription's critics were quick to point out, it threatened to impose Prussianism at home and, by breaking pledges made to French Canada at war's outbreak, destroy the unity of the country. The new year was barely four months old when the farming community received a dose of the same bitter medicine. Pleading the grave military situation overseas, Ottawa went back on its pre-election pledge and on 20 April 1918 decided to conscript farmers' sons after all. This latest betrayal was the final straw, clear proof that the wishes and aspirations of the rural community, particularly in Ontario, were to be buried by a political system that made a practice of minimizing their importance.

To be sure, not all farmers greeted the changed situation in this apocalyptic way, but the sense of grievance compounded by bewilderment was there. 'Many farmers,' wrote a Burlington farmer in late April 1918, 'accept the principle of conscripting single men with a fairly good grace – but most of them are indignant with the Gov' for breaking faith with them after having promised them exemption.' For this farmer the rude awakening had come when he realized that 'it was only an election ruse.'[1]

The same realization jolted Morrison, Good, and other activists into co-ordinating a demonstration against Ottawa's action. Drury, along with other UFO directors, received an invitation to attend a rally Morrison orchestrated for 13 May 1918 in Toronto's Labor Temple. According to the UFO secretary's recollections he had merely been the stage manager for a spontaneous production put on by outraged farmers aiming at nothing less than organizing another 'siege' of Ottawa.[2] Put in charge of logistics, Morrison asked a willing Crerar, by now minister of agriculture in the Union government, to reserve the Grand Opera House in the capital for the expected influx, and prevailed upon the railways to lay on extra coaches out of Toronto. In all, some three thousand angry farmers eventually descended on the Labor Temple, and after impassioned oratory resolved to protest the government's shift on the conscription question.

In all this, however, Drury kept his distance and took no active part in mobilizing the demonstrators and preparing their presentation. For this he took the full brunt of Morrison's displeasure. Years later Drury would admit that he should have publicly expressed the reasons for his aloofness in Toronto and not kept his feelings to himself.[3] He later claimed that he had opposed the planned confrontation on two grounds. In the first place, he thought it would be a futile gesture; secondly, and more importantly, he was becoming alarmed by the growing hostility of the urban press to agrarian remonstrances and by the public's resentment of rising food prices which were attributed solely to the farmers' wartime greed. These reactions would, in his view, only have been exacerbated by any further rural demonstrations while the fighting overseas was in such a crucial stage. Others were also alarmed. O.D. Skelton, the Queen's political scientist who frequently served as a consultant to the CCA, confessed to Good how 'astounded [he was] ... by the violence of the anti-farmer sentiment among even educated city people, resenting the alleged profiteering and the selfish slackening of farmers on the military issue.'[4]

Having made his decision to steer clear of the planned confrontation, Drury was obliged to read about it in the newspapers. As he had predicted, this renewed siege of the capital had quickly disintegrated under the ridicule of the press and the stony indifference of the government. Drury and other farm spokesmen had already had a taste of press hostility. At a meeting arranged by the *Sun's* W. L. Smith and W. Toole of the *Farmer's Advocate* with the editors of Toronto's dailies to discuss the farmers' case, Drury recalled how John ('Black Jack') Robinson of the *Telegram* had angrily scolded farmers for failing to do their duty in a national emergency. Whatever their differences over other matters, Drury doubtless agreed with Morrison's vilification of the *Telegram* as a yellow sheet which sought to poison its almost exclusively urban readership against the legitimate aspirations of the countryside.[5]

The fact remained, however, that Drury's virtual snub of the Ottawa deputation irked Morrison and a good many of the rank and file. Drury could have retorted, but did not, that neither Morrison nor Good, though they had helped to prepare the presentation, had gone to Ottawa. Their absence was explained away by the argument that the deputation, to be effective, should appear to be what it in fact claimed to be – a spontaneous reaction to a perceived injustice which had arisen independently of the farm leadership. In any event, the farmers' case at Ottawa was ultimately put by other UFO spokesmen – R.H. Halbert, Manning Doherty, and W.A. Amos.

Their rebuff at the hands of Borden and his colleagues, which had included a refusal of their request to address Parliament, was probably the decisive factor in turning the farm movement into a dynamic political force.[6] In the process it became the most politicized in the country after the ordinarily militant United Farmers of Alberta acquiesced in Ottawa's decision on conscription, a surrender that temporarily ruffled the relations between the UFO and their western brethren.[7] Indeed, the president of the Ontario organization went out of his way to stress the difference between the two wings of the farm movement by noting that the easterners' 'independence of political action rather than the graingrowers' economic doctrine had been the motive force behind the political movement in Ontario.'[8]

Meanwhile, as an antidote to the ill-disposed urban press, agitated farm spokesmen called for the establishment of what the UFO had long sought: an official paper of their own that would effectively champion the rural point of view, in effect an eastern equivalent of the *Grain Growers' Guide*. At the heavily attended convention held in Toronto's Massey Hall in June 1918 the principle was endorsed enthusiastically, and the following September the Farmers' Publishing Company was formed with an authorized capital of some half a million dollars. Although the company functioned autonomously, with its own president and board of directors elected by the shareholders, some of the directors also served on the UFO's board. After toying with the possibility of starting a paper from scratch, the UFO directors settled for the less expensive and more convenient step of acquiring the venerable *Weekly Sun,* which had just been put up for sale. After this decision was ratified at the annual UFO convention late in 1918, the Farmers' Publishing Company became the proprietor of the *Weekly Sun* (to be renamed the *Farmers' Sun*) the following April. Its first president was Colonel Fraser, a co-founder of the UFO, who appropriately provided a 'Word of Greeting' in the first issue of the transformed paper.[9]

Before the *Farmers' Sun* was launched, Drury and other rural spokesmen were treated to another stirring spectacle down on the farm. Local UFO clubs, their fury and frustration still very much intact, jettisoned their ancient Grit and Tory loyalties and boldly announced their intention to nominate and run Farmer candidates in two provincial by-elections. One was in the Manitoulin riding opened up by the death of the incumbent MLA in late 1917. There a committee representing all the island's clubs had put forward the name of Beniah Bowman, a former Mennonite missionary turned farmer, who was described by Morrison as a 'fairly good speaker, good-looking, robust and honest.'[10] At a later stage Morrison was called in to provide some organization and guidance. Throughout he was obviously impressed, as was Drury, by what he would wordily call the 'democratic tendencies' of these local farmers who, without benefit of a 'centrally controlled machinery of direction,' effectively brought out a 'concencus [*sic*] of opinion of their political desire.'[11]

In spite of the appearance of Sir William Hearst, the Conservative premier, in the riding, when the votes were cast on 24 October 1918 Bowman had won convincingly. The hapless Hearst, who made the error of publicly insisting that no election had been necessary and that the Conservative candidate ought to have been acclaimed, clearly contributed to the government's rude setback. At one stroke he had become the local focus of the boiling agrarian resentment against the Union government, which throughout Hearst had warmly supported.[12]

Bowman's triumph was matched by the success of a UFO comrade, John Widdifield, in North Ontario the following February. These electoral victories galvanized local organizers into action in other sections of the province and produced an unprecedented expansion of UFO clubs and memberships. By the end of the war, which came unexpectedly and mercifully in November 1918, the number of clubs had tripled from the modest 1916 figure to over six hundred. In the space of the following year alone, like a grass fire, they would almost double again to some 1,130 with a total membership of over 40,000, a ninefold increase since the midwar years.[13]

To this point Drury had been nothing more than a spectator on the provincial scene, albeit a keenly interested one. But in June 1919, with all the signs pointing to Hearst's need to call an election, he was thrust forward to centre stage. Along with Manning Doherty, a defecting Conservative and one-time classmate at the OAC, and his friend Good, he was asked by Morrison to help draft a platform for the burgeoning political movement triggered by Bowman's and Widdifield's victories. Whatever reservations Morrison might have had about Drury's luke-warm response to the demonstration of 1918, he obviously swallowed them when he sent out the invitation.

The resulting document (later published verbatim in Staples's *Challenge of Agriculture*) constituted a revealing though 'nebulous' blend – Drury's word – of the major preoccupations of its authors.[14] Thus Good's predilection for 'direct legislation,' which excited little enthusiasm in Drury, was reflected in the ninth plank calling for the initiative and the referendum. His fondness for electoral reform was clearly betrayed in the last one, which dealt with proportional representation. Drury's long-standing promotion of reforestation secured sixth place, while the reference in the fourth to the provision of 'equal educational opportunities for all the children of all the people' was unhesitatingly agreed upon by all three men. The rest of the program was a potpourri of the varied resolutions offered up over the years at UFO conventions. It embraced pledges to abolish party patronage, to support legislation expediting co-operatives, to foster regular road maintenance, to cut public expenditures, and to reduce the cost, though not the expansion, of the Hydro-Electric Power Commission, the popular public power enterprise initiated under Sir Adam Beck's leadership before the war. Armed with this statement of purpose, exhilarated UFO clubs and newly created constituency organizations forged ahead with plans to run their own candidates in the forthcoming provincial election. While the rural press understandably found much to applaud in the platform, Toronto's *Globe* predictably poured cold water on it. 'It is difficult to find in the Farmers' platform,' its editorial sniffed, 'sufficient cause for the decision to secure an increase of agricultural representation in the Legislature by the formation of a distinct party from the ranks and platforms of which Grits and Tories are to be driven with "bare knuckles" if necessary.'[15]

The date finally picked for the election – 20 October 1919 – had already been set aside by the premier for the referendum he had promised on the Ontario Temperance Act. This measure had been instituted in 1916 ostensibly to provide 'economy, thrift and efficiency' while the war lasted. The act closed down bars, clubs, and liquor stores for the war's duration, forbade the sale of intoxicating liquor 'unless authorized by the laws of Ontario,' and restricted its use to the privacy of a citizen's home. Although its legal sale for sacramental, medicinal, and other more or less respectable purposes provided potential loopholes, the legislation was vociferously supported by the Evangelical church press and the Dominion Alliance for the Total Suppression of the Liquor Traffic. No less enthusiastic were such committed agrarian drys as Drury and Good. Indeed, for many of that generation, who thought the issue could be taken out of politics through a referendum, it cut across party and class lines. For this reason the drafters of the UFO platform promised in the summer of 1919 that their group would support the enactment and enforcement of 'such prohibitory legislation against the liquor traffic as the people may sanction in the approaching referendum.' Paradoxically, while the war on booze made Hearst and his rural critics awkward bedfellows in one area, the farmers' angry campaign against the old-line parties and their supposedly undemocratic practices and anti-agrarian policies created a wide gulf between them in another.

In spite of their sense of outrage, the euphoric by-election successes, and the astounding growth of the farm movement, few UFO members contemplated the creation of anything so ambitious as a fully constituted farmers' party. What many would have preferred instead, and this was particularly true of Morrison, was the election of a sizeable bloc of agrarian candidates who could act as a pressure group forcing whatever government that was elected to pay heed to rural interests. By the time the battle lines were drawn sixty-four Farmer candidates had been nominated by local clubs and constituency organizations. And these preparations had been carried through without any financial help from the central office in Toronto. Typical was the action taken by the East Lambton club, which early on decided to underwrite the campaign of its duly nominated candidate, Leslie W. Oke. By September, with a month to go before the election, the unheard-of sum of five hundred dollars had been added to the club's coffers.[16] The same pretty well held true for a UFO club in Drury's area. The Edenvale group, besides providing their candidate with campaign funds, heartily applauded the speakers, Drury included, who came out to address them on the importance of the election.[17] In due course Morrison himself had been urged to join this political groundswell and run in his home riding. But he promptly declined, explaining that he was 'married to the job I am on now,' his duties as secretary-treasurer of the UFO and the co-operative company.[18]

Outrage and resentment, however, were not the monopoly of the concession lines. Organized labour had for some time been alienated by the wartime actions of Ottawa and Queen's Park. Some of their basic demands – a shorter work week, higher wages, and the relaxation of the liquor laws, which one vocal section was demanding – would not have been warmly endorsed on many farm-steads. But in other areas some farm and labour leaders recognized grounds for common action. Thus, when spokesmen for the Independent Labour Party, founded in the factory city of Hamilton in 1917, condemned waste, profiteering, inflation, extravagance, and political corruption and, moreover, urged the conscription of wealth as well as manpower, they were echoing the UFO's major concerns.[19] Again, when the ILP challenged the banking and credit system or called for loosening the ties with Britain they evoked a hearty response in Good and Morrison, though probably only a lukewarm one in Drury.

Morrison readily recognized a kindred spirit in a labour movement organized to do battle with the same implacable enemy in the industrial establishment. For a time he had actually flirted with the idea of encouraging trade unions to organize themselves into a 'co-operative purchasing concern' so that they might serve as marketing outlets for Ontario's rural co-operatives. On some occasions he had taken the trouble to have trade union representatives address UFO meetings, and also to serve as an intermediary between the CCA and the Trades and Labour Council of Toronto.[20] The upshot was that as election day approached no fewer than ten candidates ran on a combined Farmer-Labour ticket. One of them, J.B. Johnson, ran in Drury's own neighbourhood of East Simcoe; another, Frank Campbell Biggs, campaigned in North Wentworth. Biggs made a point of ad-dressing enthusiastic joint picnics of local UFO clubs and ILP branches.[21]

Such developments would have been dismissed as pure fantasy in prewar years. But now they were considered by many to be the natural though not necessarily welcome concomitant of a world turned upside down by the greatest war in its history and by the political disenchantment it had spawned. Many, like Drury, looked forward as hopefully as they could to a brave new world freed from the corrupt and manipulative parties that had grown up with Con-federation. With the emergence of politicized farmers and workingmen as threats to the old order, the press and journals of opinion talked freely about the 'complete change in the face of politics.'[22] The *Globe*, with an eye presumably on the leaderless rise of the UFO, exclaimed that the 'prestige ... [of leadership] counts less in determining the result than it had done in any other contest since Con-federation.' 'The Ontario election campaign,' the *Hamilton Herald* exulted, 'has been distinguished by a display of independence and a breaking away from party that can only be described as marvellous.'[23] E.D. Smith, the nearby Winona jam-maker and opponent of reciprocity, fully agreed but without exultation. He told Hearst on election eve that 'more people are independant [sic] in thought than ever before.' A complacent Hearst remained unruffled. His sizeable majority in the House seemed unassailable; out of 111 seats his Conservatives held 78.

But for some there was an uglier side to the picture that Smith had painted. 'People are not in a normal condition,' N.W. Rowell anxiously wrote his chief, Robert Borden, shortly before the armistice. 'There is less respect for law and authority than we probably ever had in the country.' He then predicted that there would be more turmoil in the postwar years than during the conflict itself.[24] The spectre of Bolshevism, recently triumphant in Russia and haunting many a board-room and political strategy meeting, also deepened the alarm that was frequently sensationalized in the press. Sometimes paranoia seemed to cloud good sense when predictions were made that, should Ontario's aggrieved farmers ever achieve power, a home-grown form of Bolshevism would be foisted on the province. But the fearful, as one magazine writer would sensibly point out, could take 'comfort from the fact that the farmer [who] ... does not deal lightly with property ... will be the uncompromising foe' of this foreign ideology and would not consider that the 'first duty of citizenship is to cause an upheaval.'[25] The writer was not whistling in the dark so far as Drury was concerned.

Meanwhile fear and despair were not in the organized farmer's vocabulary as he prepared to do battle with the old-line parties, denounced at one noisy UFO meeting as eggsuckers. Diehard Liberals and Conservatives alike were exco-riated, in part because Hartley Dewart, who had replaced Rowell as the new provincial Liberal leader, had not only taken the 'wrong position' on the Union government but was soft on prohibition. Most farmers would have readily agreed with the Ottawa official who announced that the 'time is now ripe ... for a movement [of protest] of this kind ... The influences at work are overwhelming ... and there will be an entirely new alignment of political forces.'[26] Erstwhile Liberals and Conservatives were joining the farmers' political movement, and the *Farmers' Sun* marvelled that in Peel County the UFO candidate Manning Doherty, a Catholic and Conservative, was being publicly supported by a Baptist minister of Liberal persuasion.[27] The times were indeed 'topsy turvy,' the only phrase the *Globe* could think of to characterize this remarkable turn of events.

Drury's involvement in the campaign was limited to speaking out on behalf of Farmer candidates over a two-week period in scattered sections of the province. He declined to run, even though he would in all likelihood have won a nomi-nation, probably because he had suffered through a costly election battle less than two years before. More to the point, the provincial stage was not the appropriate one for waging war on the tariff, still his principal preoccupation. None the less, he thoroughly enjoyed his speaking forays in the fall of 1919, particularly his invasion of Grenville County, the stronghold of Howard Fer-guson, Hearst's minister of lands, forests and mines. For many farmers Ferguson exquisitely personified the waste and corruption of which the Hearst government stood accused. Drury personally promised a Prescott audience that if the UFO were ever fortunate enough to form a government, Ferguson's department would immediately be investigated for all its alleged wrongdoing in the handling of timber leases in New Ontario.

Throughout his tour Drury made full use of his considerable speaking skills and his ability to handle audiences. He also had a cynical press to contend with. One paper in his riding mocked his supposed adventures in turncoating, deemed unfashionable and downright dishonest by those committed to blinkered political fealties. 'Drury must have had another change of heart,' its editor smirked, 'which, of course, is not hard for E.C. At the last Election [1917] he was the Laurier Liberal ... and shouted the virtues of Liberalism, French domination ... from the house tops. His cry now is for wisdom, justice and liberty. He has need of them all.'[28]

This election would mark the first time that Ontario women, by virtue of the wartime enfranchising legislation, would be able to cast ballots. Drury wistfully recalled that historic day nearly half a century later: 'On Monday morning, October 20 my wife and I walked together to the polling place in the old Temperance Hall some half mile down the [Crown Hill] road ... It was a bright fall morning and the roadside maples were dressed in autumn glory ... I found it a very pleasant experience, going with my wife beside me to cast our votes.'[29] Many were convinced that the votes of farm women such as Ella Drury ensured a dry Ontario when they voted on the Ontario Temperance Act referendum and helped to elect forty-five Farmer MLAs to the legislature. One Conservative worker was afraid that by scheduling the referendum and the election for the same day many farm women, while voting for prohibition – the issue that would genuinely lure them to the polling stations – would also vote for UFO candidates. His worst fears seemed to be confirmed by the results.[30]

That same day, after casting his own ballot, Drury briefly deferred to his first love, federal politics, and to a friendship, by hurrying off to speak at Beaverton on behalf of R.H. Halbert, who was running in a federal by-election. When he returned home late that night he learned that the Simcoe County ridings had been swept by Farmer candidates. Later the electrifying news came that the UFO would emerge, if not with a majority, at least with the largest number in the legislature, having won forty-five of the some seventy predominantly rural ridings, mainly at the expense of the Conservatives. The UFO were followed by the Liberals who, with twenty-nine elected, had more or less held their own, and a band of eleven ebullient Labourites. The shattered Conservatives were reduced from seventy-eight to a mere twenty-five. Only four of the ten Tory cabinet ministers had survived the débâcle, a rump that included Howard Ferguson and George Henry.[31] For the UFO, the frosting on the cake was provided by the ringing endorsement given the temperance act in the referendum.

The startling proportions of the Farmers' success dumbfounded many old-line partisans, political observers, and businessmen who kept in touch with the political scene. *Maclean's,* whose owner, Colonel J.B. Maclean, was kindly disposed toward the UFO, could not resist chortling at the expense of the supposedly more radical graingrowers (and, as well, those who feared the advent of rural Bolshevism). 'Down in old Conservative Ontario,' its editorial ran, 'regarded by the newer West as hopelessly slow and unprogressive ... this new rebirth has taken place, where the cows feed on the old homesteads and where the ... husbandmen watch their ancestral estates.'[32] The calmer sort of reaction from the business community was probably summed up by Joseph Flavelle's comment to an English friend that 'we have emerged from the war with a class consciousness which was emphasized in a somewhat spectacular manner in the recent elections in ... Ontario.'[33]

The outcome also surprised and unnerved some of the UFO candidates. This much electoral success, in their most rhapsodic moments, had never been anticipated. The reaction was echoed by their spouses and other farm women. Ella Drury was quoted as saying that 'I don't quite realize it yet and hardly know what I think or feel. You see it is all so unexpected.' The wife of Harry Nixon, the successful UFO standard-bearer in Brant, also made no secret of her surprise.[34] Drury shared this bittersweet experience, remarking in his memoirs that 'we were not ready to form a Government, if, as seemed very likely, [the Farmers] were called upon to do so.'[35]

For Morrison there was another danger. While he had looked forward to the election of a solid Farmer contingent, he recoiled from the prospect of the UFO's actually forming a government and assuming the direction of provincial affairs. He feared that the farm movement would be drawn into the same political traps and damaging compromises that had been the undoing of the old parties and the country. He now had to live with what his beloved rustic democracy had done. Without waiting for a lead from central office, the UFO had, to quote the *Globe,* 'taken the bit in their teeth and ... determined to discover at the polls to what extent the idea of agricultural solidarity in politics had taken hold.'[36] A related problem, as Morrison took pains to point out at a post-election meeting of the CCA, was that the 'political movement in Ontario had resulted in placing many men into prominence in a political way who had not been prominent before in the UFO.'[37] There was the very real danger that such people would be more interested in political power for its own sake than in the agrarian principles of the UFO.

Immediately after the election, by pre-arrangement elected Farmers and UFO directors met at central office in Toronto to chart the future and select a political leader. So far as the elected group was concerned, the meeting resolved to eschew any alliance with either of the old parties.[38] They were then instructed to 'assume the fullest share of responsibility and form a government in co-operation with such members of other parties as are in sympathy with their platform and principles.'[39] Lacking an overall majority, the Farmer contingent had no alternative.

Accordingly, a predictable overture was made to the leadership of the eleven-member Labour contingent that had been elected. A UFO committee of three was struck to sound out the views of a similar representation from the ILP at a meeting arranged in Hamilton, a Labour stronghold pardonably described by a local paper as the centre of Ontario's political stage. After several days' discussion, most of it amicable, the Labour members, anxious to exert their influence, indicated their willingness to join a coalition and accept whatever leader the UFO should choose. An ILP spokesman told reporters that his organization could 'more conscientiously co-operate with the UFO than any other party, because their platform, aims, fundamental principles and aspirations are similar.'[40] This brave statement was made in spite of the different backgrounds, vocations, and outlook of the two prospective collaborators, the one often employers of labour, the other almost exclusively wage-earners. There was also the rural aversion to those who seemed to spend so much time trying to shorten their work week when the farmer's own vital labour was all but interminable. On the other side of the coin there was the workingman's thirsty impatience with the agrarian righteous who would deny him his beer. All the same, many in both camps, excited by electoral success and the disarray of their foes, believed that in double harness they could do much to reform the political order, advance the cause of co-operativism, and otherwise usher in what Drury and others had called the Golden Age.

When the UFO finally tackled the long-deferred leadership question, several names were informally put forward, among them Manning Doherty's and Peter Smith's, representatives respectively of the UFO directorate and the MLAS-elect. Although a highly respected luminary of the Ontario farm movement, Doherty had two strikes against him. First of all, in spite of the support of the local Baptist parson, he had failed to win a seat in Peel; and secondly, as a Catholic in the Protestant citadel of Ontario, he was not exactly a prime political asset. The rising influence of the Orange Order in the province would be arrayed soon enough against seemingly aberrant and radical organizations such as the UFO, which threatened the sanctity of the traditional party system. To have installed Doherty in the Farmer leadership in these circumstances would have been to court sure disaster. As for Peter Smith, it was decided that in spite of his congeniality and popularity in his own Stratford riding, not to mention his having piled up an impressive majority of some 2,500 votes in the election, he was deficient in the qualities perceived to be needed in the premier's office. In the end neither he nor Doherty was formally presented to the gathering.

The name that soon caught the attention of all was that of Sir Adam Beck. At the end of the war the formidable chairman of the Hydro Commission was riding high politically and being acclaimed by Conservatives as a worthy successor to Sir William Hearst. At the same time he was well regarded by those

Liberals disenchanted with the leadership of Hartley Dewart. In the end Beck had tried for a seat in the legislature as an independent, explaining, to squelch reports that he was aspiring to Hearst's crown, that the 'Hearst government contains everything that is good, so we can endorse it, but only as an Independent can I look after the interests of Hydro for the people of the Province in the most efficient manner.'[41] Beck's visibility, his independent stand, and his easy rapport with dissidents in the old parties made him welcome to some UFO leaders. Carried away by his charisma and his accomplishments as the engineer of public power in Ontario, they were eager to sound him out.

Indeed, it was rumoured that feelers had been made even before the election. According to Morrison's memoirs, the UFO secretary had been urged by a Beck associate to have Farmer candidates stand aside in key ridings so as to ensure the election of certain others who could more effectively promote Beck's candidacy for the leadership of a victorious Farmers party. Morrison recorded that he and the UFO executive had promptly turned thumbs down on the scheme and advised Beck's friends to 'let him run as a UFO man and take his chances.'[42] When questioned many years later on this episode, Drury was incredulous. Even as a director of the organization he had obviously not been privy to all that must have transpired at central office. He ruefully told his interviewer that 'if Beck was scheming for the leadership, I for one did not know it and I don't think anyone else did except Morrison.'[43] For his part, C.B. Sissons, although not part of the meeting, clearly thought he was tuned into events and subsequently dismissed as bizarre the story that 'Beck saw himself or was seen by the farmers as their Moses.'[44]

It is clear, however, that active negotiations were begun with the Hydro chieftain shortly after the polls closed. Drury claims that he was named to a committee despatched to offer Beck the leadership if he wanted it, after Doherty had formally proposed that Beck be approached. Although one account claimed that the Hydro chairman was smuggled up the Church Street office's fire escape so as to thwart 'violently antagonistic' newspaper reporters, Drury recalled that he used a staircase and 'made no attempt to conceal the matter.'[45] After making what was called a nice little speech, Beck declined the offer of the leadership, fearing presumably that it was too risky. That appeared to be that.

But Morrison and others recalled it differently. If their versions are to be believed, Beck gave every indication of his willingness to assume the burden but his way was blocked by a disturbed Morrison who suspected that once ensconced in office, Beck would ride roughshod over his Farmer followers and arrange matters to suit his own political tastes. Morrison then apparently used his influence to scotch Beck's candidacy, a move that reopened the whole question.[46]

Not surprisingly, in view of his own past services, Morrison himself was mentioned for the leadership after Beck's name was dropped. The secretary speedily discouraged the move, arguing that a younger man – he was fifty-eight

– should assume that role. Besides, he pointed out plausibly enough, he could render greater service by continuing as secretary-treasurer of the UFO, the post he had filled from the beginning. Drury might have put Morrison's reluctance down to the secretary's apparent fondness not for the crown itself but for the role of king-breaker or maker. Nor could Drury and others at that meeting ignore the very real possibility that Morrison, perhaps as Beck might have, fully expected that the UFO's adventure on the political stage would degenerate into a misadventure. Would he want to skipper a supposedly sinking ship?

At that point most eyes in the room turned to Drury, who throughout had not been placed on anyone's short list as a possible front-runner for the leadership. He had, to be sure, contributed his own thoughts to the UFO platform and had added his supportive voice to those of candidates on the hustings. But he had not contested a riding as had Doherty, Smith, and Beck for that matter. Yet, as well-wishers and backers now assured him, Drury had much to commend his candidacy, even though it was being touted only after a process of elimination. He had, it was pointed out, presence, debating skills, speaking talents, and an enviable capacity for solid administrative and organizational work, reflected in his labours for both the CCA and the UFO.[47] The upshot was that he was formally invited to assume the leadership.

But for Drury such a challenge far eclipsed the responsibilities that had come his way in the farm movement, and there were many factors to ponder before he could come to a decision. He told the meeting that he would need time to think it over and they responded by giving him a week.

6

Pondering the Options

Drury was well aware that he was a last resort, that in effect he was being 'pitchforked' into the leadership.[1] Certainly he had good reason to turn down the offer. A demanding farm and a growing and equally demanding family – a fifth child, Harold, had been born in 1917 – not to mention his continuing work with the farm movement, were enough to tax any mortal. Moreover, the prospect of having an outsider manage the farm in his absence did not appeal to him. Besides, life in Toronto, even if intermittent, was not an attractive future for a farm parent who set much store by the advantages an arcadian environment could confer on growing children. There was also Aunt Bessie to consider. Now eighty-four, she had been a member of the household ever since William Drury had died in 1911. Could a suitable place ever be found for her in the hurly-burly of the provincial capital? The same question could be asked about his wife. Would Ella welcome a life away from the familiar surroundings of Crown Hill?

So much for personal concerns. The political dimension – the heart of the problem – now had to be assessed. Even if a coalition with Labour were brought off, the Farmers would still be saddled with a minority government and, more-over, one made up for the most part of neophytes, the word that a chortling Howard Ferguson would later use to brand Drury's legislative followers. None of this was appetizing. And even if these problems sorted themselves out, was the constitutionally limited provincial scene the most productive one for his purpose? Beyond this, his recent setback in a federal contest must have given him pause when he contemplated the fact that he would have to put his head on the block again in a by-election to gain a place in the legislature.

Then there was his relation with Morrison. He might have to depend on him now, much more than in the past, for help and counsel. Morrison's knowledge of the Ontario farmer and his ways could prove invaluable when it came time to fashion political strategy. Much would depend, however, upon how forth-coming the UFO secretary would be. He had already been gratuitously forthcom-ing in one area, if one is to believe his memoirs.[2] After drawing up a list of

Drury's perceived strengths and weaknesses, Morrison informed the prospective leader that while his oratorical talents and educational attainments would stand him in good stead, he should guard against his openness to flattery, his gullibility, his egotism, and his misjudgment of public opinion. Morrison's candid assessment, which was echoed by others over the years, must have added to Drury's disquiet about the political future and his ability to handle the challenge.

Again, Drury may have resented being shunted down the list of possible candidates. Whatever distress it caused him, that process of elimination had forcibly brought home to him and others at the Church Street meeting the leadership crisis that faced the Farmers. If he or someone like him did not step forward, the UFO might be condemned to forfeiting its right to govern and be reduced to playing the role of an overblown opposition in a fractured legislature. If that happened, the whole farm movement in Ontario, to which Drury had dedicated so much time and effort, might disintegrate with calamitous consequences not only for its supporters but for the whole political process. Drury feared for the future of representative government in Ontario if Farmers did not assume the responsibility the ballot box had thrust on them and shoulder the administration of the province's affairs.

As a prospective leader he was not entirely devoid of political blood. He recalled how he had thrilled to his father's stories of legislative combat and the accounts of a cabinet minister's awesome responsibilities. He had learned how in England a generation before his own birth decisions had been taken that launched her on the liberal course that abolished protection and afforded Drury's generation with the almost sacrosanct solution to Canada's economic ills. To his way of thinking, the remarkable events of 1919 constituted for Canada the kind of turning point that Britain's embarking on free trade had proved to be in the mid-nineteenth century. The Farmers' success in Ontario might well be duplicated elsewhere in the country to pave the way for what Progressives would hail as a new national policy that would free Canada from John A. Macdonald's tariff program. But the spur provided by the victory of 1919 might lose its driving edge if the UFO remained leaderless in the House. And in that sorry state it would be in no position to advance its cause and preserve, to quote Drury's comment at the Social Service Congress, the 'springs of our civilization.' Conceivably it could also grasp an opportunity to 'cleanse the sewers' of that civilization, and in the process improve the texture and quality of all forms of life, urban as well as rural, in Ontario.

Drury may have shared the sense of destiny that William Irvine, the agrarian radical, saw in the farm movement at the close of the war. In a reversal of Marx's ordering of the future, Irvine sought the 'universal class of the future' not in the industrial proletariat but in the farming community, the independent producers who in their avocation combined the antagonists Marx had seen as the moulders of the future – the farmers in effect were both 'capitalists and laborers.'[3] In his view labour, despite the drama of the recent Winnipeg General Strike, was a negligible factor in Canada compared to rural power, not only in numbers but in spirit and sense of purpose. That spirit for Irvine was fashioned by what he called the farmers' 'discovery of the higher law of co-operation,' which would eradicate conflict between competing groups in society.

Like Irvine, Drury perceived the significance of the agrarian upsurge and the vital role that the rejuvenated farm movement could play in bridging the gulf between warring parties and ushering in a society shorn of tensions and instability. The farm population, Drury would write, 'with its physical vigour, its mental poise and balance ... and in this country at least, *its unique combination of laborer and capitalist* in one person supplies a human factor of great importance in our national life.'[4] However, while Drury seemed to share Irvine's excitement about the role that a politicized farming community could play in shaping the future, he did not endorse the concept of group or class government that served as the underpinning of the radical's program.[5]

In fact, while making up his mind about assuming the leadership Drury fashioned the process that would be dubbed 'Broadening Out': the expansion of what had admittedly begun as a class movement into a wider one embracing citizens of all classes, occupations, and parties who shared the farmers' concerns about the direction society had been taking. Drury maintained that his only intention was to include people of like minds to form a new party and in the process adhere to the conventions of the parliamentary system and to spurn procedural nostrums like group government.[6] Years later he would have a character in his unpublished novel assert that the farm movement of his day had heralded the 'spontaneous up-rising of the people against the corruption of the old two-party system.'[7]

What probably swung Drury around to an acceptance of the leadership was his growing conviction that he could take full advantage of the current political mood of the province and forge ahead with plans for a genuine 'people's party.' As a young man Drury had been sensitive to the rise of American Populism. Characteristically, he was disposed to dress it up in biblical and simple terms when he wrote: ' 'Vox Populi, vox Dei' – the voice of the People is the voice of God. An ancient proverb, but a true one. You can always trust the Many, the People. You can never trust the Few.' In any case, the farmer by whatever measurement – demographic, moral, or political – had every right to speak out against evil and express the grievances of those who had not yet found their voice.

The farmer's claim to respect and attention in this campaign of enlightenment and purification was strengthened for Drury by the factor of permanence.[8] While recent demographic studies have shown how constant uprooting and migration destabilized some parts of old Ontario's rural community,[9] others clearly demonstrated their capacity to put down roots. It was from the latter that some of the more prominent farm spokesmen had emerged. Drury's own forebears had come to Simcoe County exactly a century before, almost to the month. This kind of residence and commitment to a locality, he reasoned, provided solid credentials for political recognition. There was also the matter of his English heritage, though for Drury the two formed part of a natural equation: 'We were brought up in a neighbourhood largely English, with the English farmer's idea of permanence, and that the land deserved the best.'[10]

In the end, his own interpretation of the historical process and its projection of the future, his political heritage, his commitment to the farm movement, and not least his conviction that he could make some personal contribution to the amelioration of society's ills overrode his doubts. But one other influence must be taken into account. Had Ella Drury not been willing to share the political burden and the privations of a premier's spouse – the long absences, the disruption of the household – her husband may well have rejected the leadership. Whatever qualms she might have had she squelched. Much must have passed between them during the week of soul-searching, and doubtless she offered the kind of counsel that he had come to expect over the years. His tributes to her understanding and advice were embodied in a number of places, notably in *Farmer Premier*. But he probably best caught the spirit of their relationship in the unpublished novel he wrote after her death in 1931. In her presence

he felt young ... adventurous – as he used to feel ... when they were children, and went beech-nutting together ... on a Saturday afternoon in the fall ... What [an] understanding comrade she was, this wife of mine! ... But something more was growing between them, a strange and wonderful intercommunion of mind that at first they had been slow to believe ... It had begun casually enough. Sitting by the fire, on an evening, after the children had been put to bed ... one of them would fall musingly into a train of thought. And presently, the other would speak only to reveal that their thoughts had been the same. At first they thought it chance, and had laughed together ... Then, as it was repeated time and again ... they came to believe that somehow ... their minds were turned to each other, their thoughts shared without words.[11]

Apart from his wife, only his boyhood chum, now turned academic, Charles Sissons, was approached for advice, and then only on the evening before he had to make his decision known. 'I appreciated his asking my opinion,' Sissons recalled, 'while fully aware that he would be likely to accept it only if it coincided with his own.' Apparently Drury still had Morrison on his mind and had to satisfy himself that the latter was not the fitter candidate. If in fact he wanted confirmation of his own view that the UFO secretary was not, Sissons certainly furnished it. When Drury left, his friend had 'no doubt that he would take the position, whatever attitude Morrison might assume.'[12]

His mind made up, Drury immediately arranged for a local man to take over the management of his farm. The next step, taken on 28 October 1919, was to advise the UFO caucus of his decision. He used the occasion to read out the text of the statement he had prepared on his projected people's party. As expected, the press was sufficiently interested to print it verbatim. 'May we not hope,' he told his followers,

that this political movement, which has begun as a class movement, representing farmers and labour, may expand and *broaden out* until it embraces citizens of all classes and occupations and becomes indeed a People's Party.[13]

On the whole the urban papers, seldom anxious to see a boat rocked, welcomed what appeared on the face of it to be an eminently accommodating and sensible clarion call of intent. *Maclean's,* whose owner, Colonel Maclean, commended Drury for his cleanness and sincerity, went so far as to echo the hopes of those who championed a more militant expression of the rural ethic. Its editor hailed Drury's 'broad minded regard for all classes. He has shown to the world that agricultural minds are bigger than farms or even production ... So that again the world has come back to the land to get its saner viewpoints and its resolute though unconventional impulses ... many see in the farmer movement a new birth to national ambitions and greatness.'[14] Parroting Drury, the magazine concluded that 'this is a people's movement and they demand that virile leadership be in its van.' Drury hoped that he qualified as he set out to rally the troops and to prepare for the formation of a government with the active co-operation of the Labour contingent. When asked by a Hamilton reporter if the ILP was satisfied with the choice of Drury as leader of the coalition, Walter Rollo responded diplomatically that he 'thought the best interests of the party could be assured if left to the guidance of the leader chosen.'[15]

Mutterings were heard, however, from scattered UFO clubs about the dangers of consorting with the ILP and, for that matter, of taking on the business of governing at all. Others were concerned about the implications of Broadening Out and would soon echo Morrison's distrust of a procedure that might dilute the farm movement's political aims and create yet another party of special interests at the expense of the general good.[16] Morrison served notice of his displeasure, pointing out that he promised to support Drury 'to the last ditch so long as you stand true to the organization; but not one inch further.'[17] On the other hand, Drury claimed in his recollection of events that on the morrow of his announcement no overt hostility greeted his scheme to work toward the organization of a people's party. Soon enough, however, he would be made painfully aware of it.

Taking Charge

The weekend of 31 October to 2 November, following his address to caucus, Drury retreated to Crown Hill, without benefit of advisers, and occupied himself behind a plough. He explained to a curious reporter that the exercise enabled him to think better about the cabinet appointments he had to make. Using the farm as a getaway soon became an established practice. 'I go home to Barrie for the week-end,' he wrote a friend a year later, 'leaving on the Friday afternoon train [or taking my car], as Saturday is really the only day I have the opportunity of spending with my family and getting a little rest.' His children recalled how they would anticipate his arrival, excitedly watching for his car when it came along the Crown Hill road as the Friday evening dusk settled.[1]

This first weekend did not, however, produce the sought-after cabinet list. His ruminations on the subject, continued after his return to Toronto, were interrupted by constitutional formalities. The first priority was an audience with Sir John Hendrie, the lieutenant-governor, who had to be formally advised that Drury had been named UFO leader and was prepared to form a government. On the automobile trip to Government House Drury was accompanied by Morrison who, in his caustic memoirs written years after the event, took credit for sprucing up an allegedly dishevelled premier-designate, who was not noted for fastidiousness of dress in any case. Morrison also claimed that he succeeded in keeping the voluble Drury out of reach of reporters eager to draw him out and, if possible, embarrass him.[2] Whatever Drury's flaws and weaknesses, Joseph Flavelle, the Toronto businessman, described him to a British colleague as the 'most representative man amongst the United Farmers and for that reason [he] was now being sent for by the Lieutenant-Governor.'[3]

After the visit to Government House a spruced-up Drury paid a visit to Hearst, the outgoing premier. Expediency as well as courtesy dictated the move. Drury needed time in which to complete his cabinet nominations, a more taxing challenge than he had imagined, and to that end urged a compliant Hearst to stay on for the time deemed necessary to complete his choices, that is, until 19 November. A major concern for the incoming premier was his ignorance of the cabinet material available to him. For the most part, the prospective appointees were virtually unknown to him and to one another and, moreover, had no experience in the legislature. Indeed, at least one of them, Harry Nixon, had never before set foot in the building at Queen's Park.[4]

So that he could concentrate on the problem, Drury took himself off to a dingy rented room on Adelaide Street, hired a typist, and recruited two men to brief him on the backgrounds and abilities of prospective ministers of the crown. One of them was F.M. Chapman, a rural journalist and personal friend who was now employed by *Maclean's;* the other was a newspaper reporter recommended by central office. Among those farm leaders who called on Drury in his retreat was Good, whose memories of one visit remained unpleasant. Two successful UFO candidates, whom Good had boosted on the hustings in spite of his reservations about them, showed up at Drury's quarters 'incredible as it may seem ... togged out in silk hats and frock coats!' 'Drury,' he added, 'was the last man in the world to be favourably impressed by such odd behaviour.'[5] Yet Good was to see both men selected for cabinet. He named no names but the pair were most likely Frank Biggs of West Flamborough and Peter Smith of Stratford, appointed respectively minister of public works, and provincial treasurer. According to Sissons's memoirs, Drury had earlier suspected them of conspiring to become, in the classicist's apt phrase, 'first and second in Rome.'[6]

On the other hand, Good may have been seeking too much perfection in the group that began assembling about Drury's standard or simply failed to detect virtues ultimately spotted by his friend and others. One factor that may have told against Biggs was that he would come to cabinet not from an active life in the farm movement but from years spent in local government. Although this was also a matter of concern to Morrison, it was a bonus for Drury because he was well aware that he would need as many politically experienced ministers as he could muster. Not only this, Biggs, an OAC graduate like himself, was from the Hamilton area, which combined symbiotically a flourishing agricultural domain and a powerful industrial base, a natural setting for an enduring Farmer-Labour alliance. To the distaste perhaps of more conservative farmers, Biggs seemed to be an early prototype of the agri-businessman; besides his successes as a herdsman, breeder, and dairyman, he was profitably involved in commercial and real estate operations in nearby Dundas and Hamilton. He seemed to be a striking example of what would later be called an assimilationist, the farmer who recognized current trends for what they were – in this case urban tastes, technology, and business techniques – adapted to them, and in the process made farming an economically attractive occupation.[7]

Biggs's record in local government, which was spread out for Drury's eye by

Chapman and his fellow scout, seemed compelling. He had started off as a township councillor and then had been elected to the Wentworth County Council. There he had served vigorously as chairman of the roads and bridges committee and of the crucial financial committee. His years of service at this level were capped by his being named warden of the county early in 1919, less than a year before his successful bid for the legislature as a UFO candidate. A long-time Liberal, like so many other Farmer hopefuls at the end of the war Biggs had become disillusioned with his party and switched his allegiance. Not surprisingly, Drury made a mental note to assign him, among other tasks, the maintenance and construction of roads.

At about the same time Drury reluctantly gave his approval to the other MLA-elect who had so dispirited Good – Peter Smith. The fact that Smith had been briefly touted as leader probably played some part in the decision, along with the knowledge that he had piled up the largest majority of all the prospective ministers. Sissons recalled that when he dropped in to see Drury one day, his host was being assured by one of his two advisers of Smith's solid record in local government and of his having received an 'excellent bill of health from his bank manager.'[8] The Stratford *Beacon-Herald* made even more of Smith's efficiency and well-ordered farm, not to mention his leadership in Perth County's affairs. What counted among both Liberals and Conservatives were Smith's reputation as a good neighbour and his standing as a local entrepreneur.[9] He appeared to be another Biggs in the making. Drury kept his fingers crossed.

Meanwhile other positions had to be filled, and quickly. At the same time the other party to the coalition had to be considered when portfolios were being handed out. From the beginning the Labour contingent had expected adequate cabinet representation, two positions at least. Harry Mills, a railway engineer elected in Cobalt, was named to the newly created Department of Mines. It was hived off from the Department of Lands and Forests out of respect for the mining industry and those northern affairs, other than mining, that supposedly needed closer attention. To charges that Mills had no practical knowledge of mining and its problems, Drury might have responded the way one friendly newspaper did: 'If Mr. Drury were to choose a mining expert, ... he would have to go outside the ranks of his supporters as well as outside the legislature ... If Mr. Mills is a man of intelligence and energy – and we have no doubt that he is – he will soon familiarize himself with the conditions and needs of the mining industry.'[10]

There was considerable competition for the new post of minister of labour. For a time Morrison MacBride, the vociferous ex-mayor of Brantford, was in the running, but his supposed lack of commitment to Labour and lukewarm response to the coalition told against him. The upshot was that the aggrieved MacBride bolted the coalition; fortunately for Drury and his minority phalanx, MacBride was the sole outright defector and for his pains was drummed out of the ILP. None the less the noisy and well-publicized episode did little for Drury's equanimity at this stage of the proceedings, particularly when it was prominently discussed by the hostile *Toronto Telegram*, reputedly friendly to MacBride.

With MacBride out of the way, Walter Rollo, a broom-maker by trade and a former Liberal, emerged as a creditable choice for the labour portfolio (to which health was subsequently attached). The need to give Hamilton proper representation combined with Rollo's credentials to make him acceptable to both parties to the coalition. Leader of the Ontario wing of the ILP, he had been a vigorous though unsuccessful campaigner in the volatile wartime election of 1917. Rollo had also gained considerable committee experience as a member of N.W. Rowell's War Resources Committee, struck to promote industrial and agricultural productivity on the home front.[11] Rollo's campaign tactics in Hamilton West, which had paid off handsomely in 1919, had featured full-page newspaper advertisements proclaiming that 'Your vote for Water Rollo is a nail in the coffin of the profiteers.' This so-called red rhetoric had to be balanced against Rollo's well-publicized moderation and reliance upon constitutional methods of obtaining reforms. Clearly there was to be no bomb-thrower in the ranks of the Farmer-Labour government. Rollo indeed appeared to be a Druryite in Labour's clothing. At the very least a new broom, Drury might have mused.

Another Labourite ostentatiously passed over was George Halcrow, who had carried Rollo's sister constituency of Hamilton East. Openly critical of Drury's stand on the liquor question – he was an unabashed wet – Halcrow had briefly sided with MacBride, and commented critically on the farmers' 'dilly-dallying' with 'irrelevant' issues such as the tariff. Relations between Halcrow and the premier were not improved when the former became involved in a 'drinking incident' on his return from a visit to Toronto.[12] Although he remained in the coalition, thanks to Rollo's efforts as conciliator, he was always a restive member of it.

With Labour's aspirations more or less fulfilled, Drury turned his attention to those in Farmer ranks who merited recognition. For example, something ought to be done for those who had served in the vanguard of the UFO's victory. Beniah Bowman, who had carried Manitoulin before the general election, had helped to establish a beachhead on which the UFO's main force had stormed ashore in the fall of 1919. Drury had some qualms about his abilities, as did those who reported to him, but this political pioneer, situated in a strategic northern riding, might perform acceptably enough in lands and forests, the department ultimately assigned him.

So much for obligations and regional interests. The agricultural portfolio was a crucial one and to fill it Drury had little hesitation in selecting Manning Doherty. Like Drury and Biggs, Doherty was a college farmer, having taught for four sessions at his alma mater, the OAC. His business skills had been honed in the Maritimes and Ontario, where he served as president of the milk and cream producers of his native Peel County and as a director of the United Farmers Co-operative Company. Some jaundiced Conservatives, who never forgave his defection from their ranks, complained that his OAC appointment had been a junior one only and political at that, having been conferred by Queen's Park over the objections of the college's president.[13] So far as Drury was concerned, this outburst was as good as an encomium, and besides, he knew for a fact that Doherty had been an associate professor, hardly a junior position. The additional charge that Doherty had been a 'profiteering contractor' while managing a dredging and construction company before the war,[14] Drury dismissed too after being assured of his business probity. What also commended Doherty was that he was from an old farming family like Drury's, the Dohertys having settled in Peel a year after Joseph Drury arrived on the Penetang Road. The premier sounded a nativistic note when he rejoiced, as he did before a receptive Woodstock audience, that his associates 'could trace their ancestry back to those fine pioneers who first settled in this country, and regarded it as significant that they should have risen to the top as they had.'[15] In any case, Doherty's intimate knowledge of farm problems, his business acumen, and his insights into the urban environment promised to make a productive combination in the agriculture portfolio.

Another working farmer who had a respectable pedigree in Brant County, and who came with Good's strong recommendation, was rewarded with the office of provincial secretary. Harry Nixon, an articulate native of St George and at twenty-eight, the youngest of the prospective ministers, was also an OAC graduate who enjoyed ready access to both rural and urban worlds. Regarded by Drury as an ideal choice for the position, Nixon would oversee penal institutions and asylums and, as well, administer the fish and game laws. According to a family story, his youthfulness had prompted his sceptical father to query: 'Who's going to vote for a kid like that?' As it turned out, a good many did, for Nixon emerged a handy winner in a sharp three-cornered contest in Brant North, on a day that he spent pulling turnips after casting his own ballot.[16]

The spectre of the war hung over the proceedings at one point when Drury reached out and named as minister without portfolio Lieutenant-Colonel Dougall Carmichael, a twice-wounded veteran who had led the 157th Regiment overseas. A popular farmer in the Meaford area, Carmichael had been the nominee of three hundred enthusiastic UFO members of Centre Grey. They had not been disappointed. He would be a reminder to the large veteran constituency that they would have a vigorous friend in court. Carmichael would also serve as government representative on the Hydro-Electric Commission.

For the education portfolio Drury finally settled on Robert Henry Grant. A native of the Ottawa area, Grant was described by Drury as a scholarly old chap with a good presence in spite of his want of a university degree. All the same, Grant was a graduate of the OAC and had briefly savoured higher education at the University of Toronto before being obliged to return home and assume family responsibilities. Certainly his selection met with the hearty approval of *The School,* the monthly journal of Toronto's Faculty of Education, which hoped that he would bring an empathic outsider's fresh approach to the problem.[17]

Even so, rumours circulated that others had been seriously considered for the post before Grant's name came up. These included Louis Aubrey Wood, a controversial instructor at Western University who would later write a history of the farmers' movement.[18] Another rumour touted C.B. Sissons, but it seems without any factual basis.[19] Apparently Drury made no overture to his old friend; perhaps he had no wish to enmesh him in what might prove to be an embarrassingly brief political venture.

The ultimate selection of Grant also had a bearing on the major portfolio Drury still had to fill – that of attorney general. And to fill it he would be forced, as he had not been hitherto, to go outside caucus simply because no one with legal training had been elected under the UFO or Labour banner. Although Drury sweepingly states in his memoirs that Morrison was reluctant to help in cabinet-making, there is little question that he offered suggestions, particularly when the attorney general's post came up for discussion. Morrison's first choice was Gordon Waldron, on the grounds of his active support of the UFO and his respectable standing in the legal profession.[20] Drury and others, however, demurred on Waldron because of his supposed 'strangeness' and the thinness of his prohibitionist credentials, a matter of no small importance to the premier. The rejection of Waldron could well have given Morrison a legitimate excuse to wash his hands of co-operation and to back off from making further recommendations. Understandably the decision sat no better with the victim. Over the years Waldron seldom concealed his dislike for the man whom he accused of having absorbed from the Methodist Church a 'ministerial hash of social justice.'[21] Others too would have cause to complain about Drury's holier-than-thou attitude.

At any rate, in his memoirs Drury made much of Morrison's refusal to help further in the task of cabinet-making. 'Whether he did not care to share the responsibility for something that might be a failure or whether he was already opposed to me on account of the policy of Broadening Out ... I do not know.'[22] And yet, as Drury admitted in a letter written in 1952, Morrison had in fact come up with still another nominee for attorney general – W.F. Nickle, a prominent Kingston lawyer and an active supporter of Queen's University. Drury gratefully acted on the suggestion, for Nickle, though an avowed Conservative, was on friendly terms with Drury and several of his prospective cabinet colleagues.[23] Nickle's acceptance would matter a good deal not only to the government generally but to Grant in particular. The latter was anxious that the cabinet secure as much representation as possible from eastern Ontario so as to avoid an unwelcome imbalance in favour of Toronto and its immediate hinterland. The point was well taken by Drury, who had already been warned that Nickle's part of the country wanted its fair share of representation in the government.[24] But after initially agreeing to accept the position, Nickle reversed himself at the last moment and elected to stay out, pleading a heavy case load and his commitment to Queen's. By this time Morrison had entrained for the west on farm movement business, ruling out, according to Drury, any chance of his offering further counsel. Yet Morrison claims in his recollections that he kept in touch with Drury and the situation in Toronto through his assistant at central office.[25]

With Nickle definitely out of the picture, Grant had to be mollified, no easy chore. It was only after considerable persuasion that he stayed in the cabinet, particularly when he learned whom Drury was next going to approach for attorney general. William E. Raney, whom the premier later claimed he had preferred to Nickle all along,[26] came warmly recommended by W.D. Gregory, a director of the *Farmers' Sun,* and by J.E. Atkinson of the Toronto *Star,* who was backing Drury's progressive and prohibitionist aims to the hilt. Morrison, for one, did not share their enthusiasm for Raney's candidacy. The UFO secretary complained that even if his legal credentials were impeccable, Raney's urbanite ways and innocence of the farm movement would make him a less than believable spokesman for rural interests and a farmers' government. Morrison even wondered aloud if Raney would bring all that much prestige to the government whose precarious position in the House should have told it to clothe itself with all the prestige it could mobilize.[27] Morrison may also have been put off by what one journal called Raney's 'natural pugnacity' and his constant 'moving in a hurricane.'[28] Drury ignored Morrison's complaints and stepped up the wooing of Raney. He was desperate, for his ministry had to be sworn in no later than 19 November. Raney was hesitant in the face of central office's criticism and did not accept Drury's invitation until the last minute, and then only after an urgent telephone call and a meeting. It had been a close shave. Even so, all the pieces had finally been fitted together into the cabinet jigsaw. The exercise came mercifully to an end when all the nominees were formally sworn into office.

So far, so good, but Drury was well aware that from pulpits, the press, and pundits much was being made of his followers as amateurs, neophytes. But if it was amateurism, at least it was, as Drury's son recalled, an inspiring species that generated a new kind of political freshness.[29] And oddly enough, the situation could be turned to Drury's advantage. 'We have a young government and everyone expects us to be green,' he conceded at the warden's dinner of the Wentworth County Council. But characteristically he went on with what he hoped would be a winning anecdote: 'When I went to Toronto [to take office] I was getting a shave, and the barber said to me: "What do you think of the farmer government?" I replied that I thought it would be all right. He answered that at least they would be honest. His was an unbiased opinion.'[30]

When all this has been said, however, one question is still begged. There was many a critic who clung to the notion that farmers, for all their virtues, lacked the 'intellectual resources which the old parties, even in their hour of decay, retain to a certain extent. [The Farmers] have yet to prove their capacity in the supply of adequate candidates and ... develop real views upon non-economic problems.'[31] Undoubtedly the elected Farmers were neophytes so far as Queen's Park was concerned, but how accurately does that word describe their political, administrative, and business experiences at other significant levels? Arguably a more plausible picture might emerge from a general profile of the UFO caucus. By and large it had been the most educated and articulate representatives of the farming community that had succeeded in making their presence felt on 20 October 1919. This was a point that Drury never tired of stressing on the lecture circuit in the early weeks of his administration. Justices of the peace, county wardens, reeves and deputy reeves, councillors, directors of co-operatives and mutual insurance companies – all these had ended up in the Farmer caucus which an exuberant Drury had addressed in late October 1919.[32]

Many of these veterans of local government, at times the most gruelling of political exercises because it served as the buffer between the citizen and Queen's Park, came to Toronto with a good grasp of parliamentary technique and a facility in debate. These assets would be in great demand in their new political quarters. So would their administrative efficiency and fiscal responsibility, as Morrison and the *Canadian Forum* were at pains to point out. 'The townships which are controlled by farmers,' the UFO secretary boasted in the summer of 1919, 'are practically free of debt while almost every urban centre is in debt up to its eyes.'[33]

At least seven of the victors were OAC graduates, a statistic that warmed the hearts of those in charge of the institution. President George Creelman made a point of telling audiences, including one at Brockville, Howard Ferguson's bailiwick, that the 'present agrarian movement had sprung from the College' which had built up a 'strong, useful and fearless class of men who [would] be able to take their part in the affairs of the farmers.' He stressed that farmers were now being recognized not only as farm workers but as capitalists and that they were being accepted by society at large as typical citizens.[34] And a leading Ontario academic echoed Creelman's sentiments and put his imprimatur on recent events. At a Canadian Club luncheon Principal Bruce Taylor of Queen's University remarked that a 'movement like the UFO does not sweep a level headed province of Ontario without some good reason for it ... I certainly hope they make good.'[35]

But were farmers being accepted as typical citizens? As Drury well knew from personal experience, the image of the farmer as a hayseed or hick had to be dispelled before the UFO legislator could become acceptable in the eyes of some urban voters. One of the more serious magazines of the day picked up on the point, observing that there was a certain urban class, more provincial, in the unpleasant sense of that word, than any other unto whom the farmer is an object of ridicule. The members of this 'league of darkness' are utterly ignorant of the conditions of life on the modern farm and of the mental equipment of the men who are officers of the UFO.[36]

Farm women too had cause to complain about ignorance and prejudice, particularly the social inferiority to which their daughters were often reduced when they went off to attend high school or visit relatives in the city. And like the men, they found a voice, in their case in the United Farm Women of Ontario, which was established as a section of the UFO, in spite of some male objections that it would harm the prestige of the farm movement.[37] Mrs. G.A. Brodie, first president of the UFWO, lamented, among other things, the all too familiar cartoon depicting the whisker-bedecked, mud-caked farmer and his drab, spiritless spouse. On one important public occasion – the presentation of Drury's ministry – she twitted the gathering: 'It did look nice to see the cabinet ministers on the platform last night, and the only bewhiskered one [W.E. Raney] was a Toronto man.'[38] Some newspapers, including the *Globe*, were convinced that the 'legend of the [yokel] ... survives only among the flippant, ignorant and vulgar ... Intelligent city people,' the editorial concluded firmly, 'have quite a different view of farm life, and are apt to idealize it rather than to despise it.'[39]

And the fact remained that certainly not all the forty-five Farmer MLAs had been elected by an exclusively rural constituency. The UFO's membership of some fifty thousand accounted for only a quarter of the ballots cast for rural candidates. Some urban voters, disheartened by the excesses of Grits and Tories, perhaps saw in the UFO a welcome expression of that arcadia many of them might have been longing for as a substitute for urban regimentation. The *Globe* predictably dwelt on this theme, pointing out that the 'majorities recorded for the Farmers ... are so extraordinarily large as to dispel the fears of a distinct cleavage between the people of the smaller towns and those of the rural sections.'[40]

Drury, for his part, did not wish to leave things to chance. Almost as soon as the swearing-in ceremonies ended and the last notable had held forth, he set out on a swing through the province to make his presence felt and his views more visible. Besides, having been sequestered in his downtown retreat for nearly a month he was eager to get some fresh political air and do what he had always enjoyed – public speaking. Eager to publicize his plan for a people's party in the non-farming sector, he made a point of speaking in Toronto and visiting, among other urban strongholds, Hamilton and London. Morrison, back at central office, doubtless wondered why this farmer premier should spend valuable time in places which in all probability had ignored Farmer candidates in the election. The secretary, so committed to the farm movement and so suspicious of Broadening Out, confessed to another rural leader that he was 'not particularly interested in ... [urban man] right now.'[41]

Out on his expedition Drury was gratified by the way the newspaper reporters followed on his heels and provided fodder for their editors' desks. In Simcoe County one paper brought its readers' attention to the kind words of the Toronto press and remarked that the *Globe's* estimate of the premier was 'complimentary enough to have been written by Mr. Drury's bosom friend, Mr. W.L. Smith.'[42] On some occasions Drury met newsmen more than halfway. In late November he accepted an invitation to address an editorial conference of the Canadian Press Association, and asked it for helpful advice and constructive criticism. Among those who showed the greatest enthusiasm for the new administration were understandably the so-called people's press. These papers – the *Hamilton Herald* was representative – had rebelled earlier against the conventional sort of journalism that paid scant heed to the interests of the lower classes of Ontario society.[43]

Drury clearly enjoyed himself on his travels, so much so that not even Morrison's acerbic criticisms troubled him. By the end of November, the premier recalled with a boast, 'it was quite apparent that urban public opinion was swinging in our favour and that we would at least have a chance to show what we could do.'[44] At any rate, a good many city people appeared to be disabused of the notion that their political fate was being delivered into the calloused hands of a dim-witted rustic. As one observer enthused, Drury had already cultivated an 'enormous amount of good will in the urban communities.'[45] One letter that came to Toronto, its spirit enhanced by illiteracy, announced that its writer 'Ham feeling quit Proud of you Fellows Down there. Eaven the Maill [the leading Conservative paper] aint Critising you so you Must be Pretty near all Right.'[46]

It was not all bouquets. Every once in a while the urban press squared off against the strong moral touches with which Drury always liked to clothe the issues of the day. In spite of efforts to reassure the non-farming community that his government was not wedded to a narrow class outlook, he sometimes gave his journalistic critics unnecessary ammunition. Thus when he smugly suggested that farmers were more sincere than other groups an otherwise friendly editor was outraged: 'The truth is, we fear, that Mr. Drury's head is just a little bit turned by his amazing and unexpected rise to power and place, and his arrogant, injudicious talk reflects his state of mind.'[47] There were indeed times when the premier was carried away by the ambience and the opportunity of the moment and doubtless sounded like the haughty agrarian who had addressed the Social Service Congress years before. Nor did his ordinarily well-received performances on the speaking circuit move some hardened politicians to change their minds about the long-term prospects of his administration. 'I doubt if he and his government,' wrote a sulphuric Clifford Sifton, 'has the slightest grasp of the problems that they are attacking.'[48] Given the acclaim that greeted his statements, Drury was able to absorb this kind of criticism.

One nagging problem remained to darken an otherwise serene political sky. Drury and two of his colleagues, Doherty and Raney, had no seats in the House. To meet it a three-man committee was struck, made up of Biggs, Dougall Carmichael, and Morrison as chairman. According to his own account, Morrison was a highly reluctant participant, fearing that the UFO secretary should not be so glaringly identified with the political process.[49] Drury did not see it that way. After all, having come this far along the road, he asked, should Morrison not go further and use his vaunted knowledge and expertise to find a haven for homeless candidates? Drury may well have played upon Morrison's conceit when he assured him that his contributions to the cause were vital. But the stratagem could backfire. When news of the secretary's role in the process reached the papers they were prepared to agree with Dewart, the Liberal leader, that Drury was 'Mr. Morrison's premier' and that the selection of constituencies was a matter not for the government to decide, but for the 'people,' as mobilized by Morrison.

Morrison did, at least in part, co-operate fully to meet Doherty's and Drury's needs. For Doherty he had astutely picked Kent because he had learned that the county was comparatively free of religious prejudice and Orange influence, a vital factor in the case of a Catholic candidate. In the end Doherty was acclaimed and, unlike his chief, was not obliged to fight a by-election. But the seat had come on the political market only after the sitting Farmer member had resigned and, for his self-sacrifice, been installed in a local public office just made vacant. Morrison later claimed that Drury had been unwilling at first to sanction this deal for fear it would smack of the old-fashioned patronage that the UFO had set its face against, and only gave way when Doherty threatened resignation if the move were not made.[50] In his own case, Drury ended up running not in his native county but in Halton where the incumbent, John F. Ford, made way for him, much to the premier's relief, without expectation of any reward.[51] Simcoe County had been barred to him even though all three elected Farmers had agreed to step down in his favour. When shrewdly contrived election protests were made by Conservatives the resignations, because of regulations governing this kind of situation, could not be tendered.

But trouble came over Raney. The matter of finding him a seat, complained Drury, dragged on for nearly two months. All along Morrison claimed it was a virtual impossibility to parachute Raney into a suitable riding. Drury and others suspected that the secretary was manufacturing problems in order to embarrass a candidate who had never enthused him and many a rank and file member of the UFO.[52] Finally, Morrison satisfied himself that the problem was insoluble and so advised Drury.

The time-consuming and frustrating task of finding the right ridings and the squabbling over Raney did much to widen the gulf already opening up between the premier and the UFO secretary. Drury recalled in his published memoirs how he had been 'cudgelled' by Morrison's bleak report and how he had felt obliged to offer the caucus his resignation should Raney, for want of a seat, be compelled to stand aside.[53] Although *Farmer Premier* makes no mention of Morrison's possible motives, Drury was much more explicit in a letter he sent to H.B. Cowan some fifteen years before that memoir was published. He disclosed that after making his announcement to caucus Morrison had replied: 'Well, in that case we'll have to get another Premier.' 'I have often wondered,' Drury went on, 'now that the [government] seemed likely to go ... whether [Morrison] did not deliberately plan to oust me and take the leadership himself.' Cowan seemed to agree, for he later interjected when he read the letter to an interviewer that Morrison 'had some hopes for himself.'[54]

Whatever the merits of this speculation, Drury did not resign, Morrison remained the UFO's secretary, and, in spite of the difficulties, a seat was found for the attorney general. Ironically, it would be none other than Morrison's brother-in-law, Albert Hellyer, the winner in East Wellington, who would make that riding available in return for other considerations. Apparently Hellyer himself had been briefly considered for a cabinet post but the proposal was discarded for fear his selection would smack of political cosiness. At any rate, East Wellington was surrendered to Raney, and in the end he was acclaimed after a much publicized opposition failed to materialize.

With Raney's immediate future secure, Drury could breathe a sigh of relief. But only a brief one because he himself had to seek election. The hope that he might share his colleagues' good fortune and be acclaimed was soon dashed when a self-styled Soldier-Labour candidate, E.W. Stevenson, presented himself to the voters. On the other hand, the Halton Reform Association, after a protracted discussion, decided to give the government a chance to see what it could do and, like the chastened Conservatives, declined to contest the seat. Drury was grateful for these favours but he still had to contend with Stevenson. The veteran's candidacy was said to appeal to a good many Halton voters if only because they were, as one paper put it, 'always fond of an election' anyway.[55] There was another factor. Drury was solemnly warned that the county seldom took kindly to outsiders being foisted on it. Consequently, during his swing through the riding the premier did his best to disarm local hostility.

In the process he ran headlong into another problem. Understandably Stevenson, like so many soldier candidates after the war, was bent on reminding the electorate of the battlefield sacrifices that merited political recognition in peacetime. In the course of the campaign Drury had to defend himself against thinly veiled charges that he had been a slacker, or had come out and condemned conscription. 'If any married man between the ages of 35 and 40, who hadn't gone to the war, had nothing to be ashamed of, I hadn't,' he told a large gathering in Milton late in the campaign. He went on: 'I had my wife and family, and a big farm. I thought it was my duty to work my farm and produce all I could. I am not ashamed of what I did. I was not an anti-conscriptionist. I stood for the conscription of men, coupled with the conscription of wealth.'[56] Even so, he was reduced to producing an affidavit affirming that he had not, as charged by his opponent, called the police to arrest two returned men for trespassing on his farm.

On the whole, the premier had little trouble fending off Stevenson and keeping election meetings good-naturedly on his side. His speech-making capacity had always been marked and though nervous before the event, he easily remained in control throughout his presentations. He obviously enjoyed the opportunity to present, defend, and rebut and did the task with 'great charm,'[57] and without going out of his way to take advantage of an opponent. He realized, of course, that by graciously deferring to even the most impolite foe he would win support and sympathy from most audiences. He also had a prodigious memory and a feeling for locality, both of which he effectively deployed to convince the voters of Halton that he was the man to represent them at Queen's Park.

At the same time, like other UFO candidates before him, Drury repeatedly promised clean government and the repudiation of the time-honoured use of patronage. The Milton paper, he was pleased to learn, commended his administration for appointing as Halton's returning officer an individual who had ably served previous ones. Ironically, Drury's position had not always pleased UFO clubs that had put forward farmers for local offices for no other reason than that they were farmers. The Strathroy club, for example, had roundly condemned his refusal to appoint such a candidate when a more qualified person lacking UFO credentials had been recommended.[58] But this kind of refreshing departure from past practice was applauded by the Haltonites who came out to hear what candidate Drury had to say.

For a good many of them the issue was not in doubt as polling day, 16 February, approached. And they were not surprised when Drury was handsomely elected, in a light vote, with a majority of 2,308.[59] For a time the victor had feared – he himself was snowbound in Barrie on election day – that bad weather would keep many farmers from the polling stations. Only in Milton and George-town did the premier lag behind his opponent. The rebuff in Milton was explained away by a local paper in terms that may have ruffled Drury, given his aim to maintain a profitable alliance with labour. 'This is a manufacturing centre,' the Canadian Champion explained, 'and many workmen were not ready to endorse the Farmers' Government. Milton was [also] the headquarters of a famous over-seas battalion, and a lot of returned men lived here. It was natural that they should rally round their comrade.'[60]

The euphoria of victory submerged any concern that the Milton setback may have caused. The work of government, already under way, could now be offi-cially tackled. And that task was made the smoother by the efficient staff Drury recruited to serve his office. His friend Sissons knowingly commented on Drury's want of system and told him that 'his most important cabinet minister would be his private secretary.'[61] So far the premier had no cause to regret his decision to retain Horace Wallis, who was thoroughly familiar with the work of the office, having served both Whitney and Hearst. Indeed, Drury made Wallis his deputy, a new post. A veteran, George Grant, was kept on at Hearst's request as private secretary. These appointments released Drury from a myriad details and helped to impose the system that Sissons, jokingly or not, had insisted was so vital in those first hectic months. He could also undertake his chores with some heady praise ringing in his ears. Typical was the one he passed on to his attorney general. A friend had written to say that 'Mr. Drury was the ablest Premier that this Province has ever had. So good clean government is expected, you have no one to satisfy but yourselves, no clique, corporation or financial interests have elected you to power.'[62] That admonition was a good spur for action.

Another was the formal opening of the legislature on 9 March 1920, less than four weeks after Drury's triumph in Halton. It was also a day to savour. Close observers of such ceremonies noted that there was a larger than usual attendance of families and friends, and commented on the festival air and the enthusiasm of the assembled. Some newspapers were pleased that in this agrarian gathering there was 'no display of extreme democracy' and that the wives and daughters of cabinet ministers and Farmer MLAs were well turned out and 'avoided fashion extremes.' Harry Nixon's wife recalled that the opening was indeed a 'lovely affair,' though a good many spectators acted as though they had expected rubes to show up and embarrass those who had organized the proceedings.[63] Anyway, basic traditions were upheld for the occasion and the ministers – Biggs and Smith must have been in their element – appeared resplendent in frock coats. But those rural activists who had long protested the military presence in the country were pleased by the absence on opening day of the customary artillery salute.

The speech from the throne was in keeping with the mood of the day and reflected the forces that had put the Farmer-Labour government into power. It also captured the spirit of the UFO platform and brought it to the very floor of the House. After referring to the anti-party sentiment that had recently gripped the country, it spoke about the need for a 'greater freedom on the part of [all] representatives of the people' when the government undertook its legislative business. And that business would embrace, among other priorities, education, veterans, reforestation, a new department of mines, and what was called special labour legislation. Then upon Drury's motion, seconded by Hartley Dewart, the suitably named Nelson Parliament, a Liberal, was elected Speaker of the House. Appropriate to a honeymoon period, the debate on the address lacked the cutting edge of usual Queen's Park confrontations, though Dewart, after he had excoriated the sins of the Hearst administration, did angrily dismiss the Farmer-Labour program as a mere carbon copy of the Liberals'. For his part, Ferguson, the temporary Tory leader, contented himself mainly with complaining about the well-known free trade proclivities of both Drury and Dewart. The address was passed at the end of the month without division or amendment.[64]

This kind of political reception was a relief for a government that was perched uncomfortably on a political razor's edge from which its fifty-five coalition members – forty-five Farmers and ten ILP – faced an almost equal combination of Liberals and Conservatives. There were other comforting developments early in the session. The opposition benches sometimes went out of their way to offer advice and suggestions to inexperienced Farmer MLAs and to do 'many kindly things' for them. Drury and his colleagues properly appreciated these courtesies, but they were shrewd enough to realize that the opposition knew that if the government were toppled early on a vote of confidence and another election called, there was every likelihood that an even more formidable UFO and labour group would be returned. Even allowing for sincerely offered hospitality and help from both Grits and Tories, at least some of their solicitude sprang from a desire to preserve the health of Drury's administration until such time as their own parties had recovered from the 1919 disaster and mended their misfortunes at the local level. Moreover, as one observer noted, if they acted otherwise, and in a churlish way, they would leave themselves open to charges of trickery, the last label that Liberal and Conservative leaders wished to be tagged with at that moment. Besides, as Drury also realized, there were some half a dozen Liberals in the House, the 'best of them,' according to one commentator, and at least two Tories who did not share their respective leaders' distaste for the government and could frequently be counted upon to vote for its measures.[65]

In this way, with the assurance of vital support from the other side of the House, the UFO minority government could get down to the serious business of addressing those questions that had loomed large in the throne speech. One of them was education and, although not the most pressing of the many issues lodged on the agenda, it had long been central to the concerns of Drury and other farm activists.

8

Tackling Education

In education, as in so many areas of public policy, the advent of the UFO coincided with major problems and difficulties. The concept of a brave new world that was supposed to undo the effects of wartime slaughter and prewar failures stirred the professional educator as well as the social reformer. Visionary farmers, including Drury, were not far behind in their campaign to improve the educational standing and cultural well-being of Ontario's countryside. With a committed government now installed at Queen's Park, the cry went up for the eradication of those shortcomings which a generation of rural critics had been calling to the public's attention. Such items as woefully cramped school grounds, poorly qualified teachers, shortages of supplies and equipment, not to mention demeaning salaries, headed this catalogue of grievances.[1] A clear index of the concern was the number of theses prepared at the OAC which pinpointed education as the principal engine by which the rural community might be propelled into a new and better era.[2] An improved educational system would in turn put a brake on rural depopulation. The *Globe* did its bit by suggesting that 'our school readers ... might be made to lay more emphasis on the dignity of agriculture and of all other useful work.'[3]

For some, like F.C. Biggs, the new minister of public works, reform meant higher salaries for rural teachers and amendments to curricula 'so that a farmer's son who passes his entrance [examination] need not take an office education, which is of practically no use to him.' 'Children who wish to complete their education,' Biggs told a Hamilton church meeting, 'must now come to the city, and they leave home when the home training is most needed.'[4] His approach, however, did not mesh with the premier's. Although Drury was as anxious as his cabinet minister to revivify rural education and the spirit of the countryside, he was reluctant to do so at the expense of the kind of general education he himself had received.

Early in 1920, some weeks after Biggs had stated his views in Hamilton, the premier appeared before Orillia's Canadian Club with a statement of his own.

After complaining about the general inadequacy of the public school system, he claimed that 93% of Ontario's pupils went no further than the passing of the high school entrance examination. For Drury this was hardly a suitable beginning of a life's career. He urged, moreover, that 'vocational training not be overdone to the point where it overshadowed the general education needed to stimulate independent thought and allow for the pursuit of knowledge for its own sake.'[5] This was a theme he was to repeat on numerous occasions. What he wanted was what his grandfather had sought – an 'educated gentleman behind the plough handles on every farm.' Some educators would have agreed with him, like the American who wrote the following to an OAC professor:

My objections to the county agricultural school ... is that it separates the agricultural students from all others and tends to make farmers a distinct and inferior class ... I would teach agriculture just like any other large subject as a part of ... education and not the whole of it because one's occupation is secondary to the man.[6]

Drury, of course, was calling upon his own experiences as a high-school student a generation earlier, when he had enjoyed such extra-curricular pursuits as writing, debating, and singing, which some of his teachers had actively encouraged.

Like so many in Farmer ranks, Drury paid particular attention to the teacher, described glowingly by the activist, Agnes Macphail, as the great country teacher, particularly the one responsible for those at the primary level. What Drury emphasized was that that teacher should be a fully qualified *male* teacher and be rewarded with a salary the 'same, at least as a country minister's.'[7] Not only this, but the traditional one-room village schoolhouse, revered by the nostalgic, should give way to a more commodious and well-appointed consolidated or graded school which could better serve a larger rural area. In all this can be seen the fruition of ideas exchanged between Drury and his schoolboy chum turned classicist, C.B. Sissons, who also favoured the appointment of more male teachers who knew 'something of country life, able to lead in sport, fit to discipline [the] mind and morals ... and able to instil a love of the soil' and to advance general learning as well. Sissons then urged a restructuring of the rural school so that it might 'become the centre and influence in the community which it once was and be regarded as offering a man's job to the teacher.'[8] Dissatisfaction with the presumably flighty and impermanent female teacher exploded in a variety of criticisms and often reflected something more than male chauvinism. Too often, the complaint ran, the lady in the classroom was urban-bred and conditioned, and merely serving a brief apprenticeship before she returned to greater opportunities in the city. Hence she was not only an alien influence but a less than dedicated bird of passage in the countryside.

Thus the school was seen not only as a place for instructing the young in the 'ultimate verities' of life in the complex modern world but as a cultural oasis to which the community could repair for social and educational enrichment. 'The farmer has the intelligence of other classes,' a student wrote in an OAC thesis, 'but due to his isolated position there is a great tendency for him to 'get into a rut' and not keep abreast with the times.[9] While Biggs might assure Drury that he could beat down this isolation with improved highways and the automobile, educators were advising an appreciative premier that there was another way: 'Intelligence,' a director of the Toronto Public Library boasted, could be taken to the farmer and others 'who dwell apart and have not the opportunities of educating themselves to the understanding of the problems of modern life.'[10] The fate of this proposed exercise in outreach was not recorded.

Others claimed that the problem of uplifting the farmer and his school-age son or daughter was complicated by the social and economic diversity that was supposed to abound on the concession lines. An OAC thesis in rural sociology echoed the point made earlier by Cowan and Morrison about the hierarchical nature of farming society, how dirt farmers at the lower end of the scale were set off sharply from the likes of Drury and Good, the well-placed yeomen at the upper end. The thesis went even further and suggested that certain kinds of farmers, especially those who raised livestock, ended up being more innovative and inventive and, accordingly, more effective leaders of their community.[11] It followed that such people would respond more imaginatively to educational refinements than their less progressive brethren, no matter what educators might do by way of bringing enlightenment to the countryside.

While digesting these varied arguments Drury tried to stay conversant with educational proposals in other parts of the rural constituency. The shadow of the Great War fell on some of the discussions. Thus the *Farmers' Sun* charged that the province's schools were being turned into a means of imperialistic propaganda. 'These schools should be Canadian schools for the development of the Canadian idea ... Canadianism means peace and the well-being of humanity.' The peroration ended with the hope that Drury's administration would put a stop to the 'turning [of] boys and girls into a lot of jingoes.'[12] Such talk alarmed parts of the urban press, which sneered that 'we may expect to see radical changes ... probably a new series of readers from which all favourable allusions to the British empire are carefully excluded and the institutions of the United States glorified.' And dedicated imperialists bitterly condemned as a 'thorn in the flesh ... the present Ontario Local Government headed by a Reciprocity advocate wedded to Free Trade.'[13] Had Drury's eyes come to rest on these passages he may well have smiled. Ordinarily he took an unfriendly view of the United States – rarely did he enjoy travelling there and did so only when he was forced to – and never did he equate the promotion of Canadianism, in school or out, with American ways and customs. On the other hand, he saw Canada playing a linchpin role between Britain and the republic, a theme popular with politicians, educators, and others who made a practice of keeping service club dinner speeches sentimentally enlivening.

Drury contributed his own homilies to this script, at the same time stressing what Canadians with a background similar to his owed their English heritage. Nevertheless, like so many of his generation, he exalted Canada's supposedly stimulating northern latitude.[14] 'Where is a child,' Drury asked in his unpublished novel,

who does not thrill when first he breathes the clean crisp air that sweeps across Ottawa from the untainted North ... And Ottawa, to the Canadian, fitly symbolizes his country – the City thrust boldly against the very borders of the northern wilderness, the Parliament buildings standing bravely on their noble hill, against the clear northern sky ... ah, hope is there, and courage, and faith, and the far-off vision of the pioneer.[15]

Though this outburst was written over a decade later, it probably expressed the image he had long held of Canada.

No one could deny Drury's right to speak of the pioneer's vision, and he doubtless sympathized with the United Farm Women of Ontario when they urged the Department of Education to prepare graded readers 'in which pioneer history of the province shall be given prominence,'[16] or at least equal time with recorded events in other sectors of Canadian history that too often had to do with the history of wars and bloodshed.

In the midst of his musing on educational matters Drury received a surprising offer from Vincent Massey, the Oxford-trained heir to the agricultural implement fortune. Massey was prepared to finance an educational commission to review the problems facing Ontario's school system. Drury's initial reaction was to welcome the initiative and offer Massey his support,[17] particularly when he learned that he would have two friends on the commission, Good and Sissons. Ordinarily the overture would have appealed to the economy-minded UFO, who were only too happy to have private organizations shoulder the financial burden government might otherwise have to assume. In this instance, however, some vocal farmers and labourites protested the 'impertinent' intervention of one of those corporate interests against which the UFO had long railed.[18] So did some of the press, including an angered *Farmers' Sun*. 'I suspect,' Sissons recollected, 'we looked like a high-brow aggregation (the current term is 'egg-head') supported by funds coming from the farmers through a rapacious implement company.'[19]

What was more important, the proposal was not well received by Robert Grant, Drury's minister of education, who grumbled that no one had consulted him on the matter, and came out unequivocally against the scheme. Drury may also have harkened to his department officials who wanted no outsider, least of all a Massey, muddying the waters of their preserve. In spite of this, Drury was still eager to accept the Massey offer as a way of easing the government's task. Grant, however, remained adamant and apparently threatened resignation if the premier did not give way.[20] Drury, already buffeted by other protests, eventually yielded and advised the public that unforeseen problems would force the government to leave the proposal in abeyance. His statement was followed by Grant's letter of explanation to Massey on 3 February. It covered an additional point that rebuked the practice, which Drury would soon follow, of striking commissions to investigate the province's problems:

... if the Department were thus to commit itself to an independent organization, however well meaning and public spirited, I know that some persons would feel that an attempt was being made to evade an obligation placed upon the Government and its officers ... we cannot afford to run any risk.[21]

Grant added that his department was already hard at work collecting the information that Massey's group would have accumulated. This effectively killed off the proposal and, as his biographer observed, Massey 'absorbed the lesson that, without political power, private resources and superior ideas must accept a limited role.'[22]

As it turned out, whatever information came Grant's way seemed to make no appreciable difference to the school system or its curriculum. From remarks Drury and Grant dropped, the situation may have resulted from the minister's being under the thumb of senior officials in his department who were disposed to drag their feet.[23] This inertia was a cause of concern to Sissons, who complained later in the *Canadian Forum* that while 'Mr. Drury in his earliest speeches ... had much to say of an educational awakening, it is equally significant that [since] ... he has been almost silent on the subject and that nothing striking has been done.'[24] Drury countered by insisting that productive action was being taken on a number of fronts. For one thing, financial support was increased for schools, particularly rural ones; for another, changes were made in the high school curriculum to improve not only academic but vocational, technical, and agricultural training.

As for the preparation of teachers, the Drury government took credit in 1920 for the establishment of the Ontario College of Education, a move that accompanied the closing down of the faculties of education at Queen's and Toronto. The new institution, long sought by the Department of Education which much preferred a provincially controlled facility, was dictated in part by the supposed inadequacies of the university programs. The reaction from Queen's was predictable. A faculty member accused the government of a breach of faith because it did not establish an independent college but only the Toronto faculty under another name. W.F. Nickle, the stalwart Queen's supporter who had turned down the attorney generalship, strongly criticized the action taken in Grant's name.[25] Whatever misunderstandings Grant may have sown, the fact remained that the new college was only nominally a division of the University of Toronto and was under the department's control, or so Drury and his minister of education would have the academic community believe. All the same, some members of that community were convinced that the arrangement would have a stultifying effect on the graduates of the new institution.

In spite of the controversy, Drury and his colleagues could take pride in the organization of the Ontario College of Education. On the other hand, they had to concede failure in their attempt to cope with a problem closer to the heart of Sissons and other educational reformers – the province's bilingual schools. Regulation 17, which since 1912 had sharply restricted instruction in French to the primary grades of the bilingual schools, had long been under attack from l'Association Canadienne française d'education d'Ontario (ACFEO).[26] The advent of the Drury government coincided with the appointment of Senator Napoleon-A. Belcourt to the association's presidency. A highly regarded Franco-Ontarian, Belcourt used quiet diplomacy, and through the aid of Sissons and other well-wishers, sought to build up in Ontario a public climate opposed to Regulation 17. Drury himself made a number of encouraging statements on the need for unity in the country and for respecting the rights of French Canadians generally and Franco-Ontarians in particular. Indeed, he hoped the province would play a key role in holding together the diverse ethnic, religious, and sectional interests of the country. Not surprisingly, hopes soared that the premier would shortly wield a new broom and, with the aid of his friend Sissons and the newly organized Unity League, an ACFEO ally, sweep out the problems spawned by Regulation 17.

Equally encouraging was a pamphlet put out by the UFO which solidly backed the association's position; it described the Franco-Ontarian claim that their children should be educated in French as well as in English as natural and just. The statement went on to stress that the 'teacher makes the school, and [that] the French-speaking people of Ontario should have as good teachers as their English-speaking neighbours.'[44] Morrison played a vital part in this campaign, making a point of providing a forum at Farmers' conventions for Franco-Ontarian members of the organization to express their views on the question.[27]

All in all, the time seemed propitious for change, and Sissons and Belcourt set about to make the most of it. One of Belcourt's chief concerns was the plight of the Ottawa Separate School Board which was denied crucial public aid because of Regulation 17. 'I do not think public opinion in Ontario,' Belcourt sanguinely wrote Sissons, 'would for one moment tolerate the idea that half the children of the Capital of Canada are to go without education because of some miserable regulation.'[28] At their first meeting with the ACFEO Drury and Grant lent an appreciative ear, but before long both men were backing away. Grant took refuge behind the purportedly serious differences of opinion between Ottawa's English- and French-speaking Catholics on the question, arising from the ancient antipathy between Irish and French communities. He pleaded that before he could make any move in the direction of discarding or modifying the 'miserable regulation' he would have to have unanimity in Ottawa.

This position only exasperated Sissons and Belcourt. They suspected that Grant's argument was a smoke screen for his real fear – the rising power of the thoroughly incensed Orange Order. As the premier and others knew, Grant was saddled with more than eighty Orange Lodges in his riding, which would not take kindly to any move that would aid a Catholic and francophone community. When Grant, in Sissons's presence, finally threatened resignation over an issue that was so explosive in his own constituency, Drury immediately retreated. However much he privately endorsed the ACFEO's campaign, he realized that he could ill afford to lose his minister of education and his only cabinet minister from eastern Ontario. The Farmer caucus was also entertaining second thoughts and opposing action for fear of the political consequences in Orange-hued sections of the countryside. Furthermore, Drury had good reason to dread how Howard Ferguson, now the acting leader of the Conservatives, might take advantage of the situation at a time when the government was precariously situated in the House.[29]

In defence of his inaction, Drury could legitimately claim that he had only so much time and energy to deal with what he identified as priorities. The bilingual schools question, a time bomb if ever there was one, was not to be upgraded as one of these. As expected, Belcourt challenged the government's agenda and dismissed Drury's excuses as so much political expediency, a vice he had not expected of an administration that had set out so hopefully to purify politics. The smarting premier needed no reminders of what political facts of life could do to good intentions. The upshot was that Drury made no move to revise or jettison Regulation 17, and the matter was still hanging fire on the eve of the next provincial general election.

Accompanying the premier's retreat on the Franco-Ontarian front – some would say an ignominious one – was an advance in another sector. The interests of northern or New Ontario, dismissed by Belcourt as a side issue, were met in part by the opening of a new high school at Monteith. The facility was designed to serve the educational needs of a wide area where advanced courses had previously been deemed unfeasible. The move gratified those residents of the New Liskeard district who had written Drury early in 1920 that the drift from the farms there could be arrested only if suitable education in more scientific farming and domestic sciences was quickly established.

Another move in the right direction, or so it was hailed, was the legislation of 1919 which raised the school-leaving age from fourteen to sixteen. Framed by the Reverend Henry Cody, Grant's predecessor, it was adopted by Drury's government as a means of raising the countryside's 'standard of citizenship' and creating a 'more enlightened agricultural class.' Indeed for some of its supporters the 'day when a farmer regarded his children as economic assets and hence [schooling and] play as wasted energy [was] largely past.'[30] Nevertheless, the legislation was condemned by a good many farmers who found a champion in the voluble W.H. Casselman, the UFO member for Dundas. He charged that the Adolescent School Attendance Act was the work of dreamers, idealists, and faddists who had no conception of the practical requirements of farming and who failed to realize that such an extension of formal education would ill prepare its recipients for the rural life. When Casselman threatened to bring in a countermeasure, Drury and Grant relented and provided for the exemption of farm youth should their 'services be required in the household or on a farm of [their] parents or guardians ...'[31] In the depressed agricultural circumstances of the early 1920s children would still be regarded on the marginal farm as important economic assets, in spite of what learned OAC theses might have to pronounce on the subject.

Resentment was also expressed over the allegedly heavy expenditures the government was lavishing on non-agricultural education, especially on the technical and vocational sides. 'Since the elections,' one farmer complained to Grant late in 1919, 'a new [financial] scheme more favourable to Technical Departments has been announced.' He went on to recommend that the funds awarded agricultural departments be made equal to those given their technical counterparts.[32] Others maintained that technical education should be a function not of the state but of its principal beneficiary, the industrial sector itself. True, technical instruction was furnishing the skilled personnel who might enable Canada 'to hold her own in the great industrial warfare now in progress among the nations,'[33] but it would also serve to strengthen the farming community's principal foe. To have that kind of education take precedence over the agricultural was particularly galling when it blatantly constituted another triumph of the corporate world whose growing power was causing so much apprehension in agrarian ranks. Nor, given its complexity, could training in industrial techniques be funded on the cheap, another sore point with the UFO. Morrison's brother-in-law put the issue bluntly in a letter to Raney early in 1921. 'At a time when farmers' incomes are cut in two,' Albert Hellyer wrote, 'it seems to us that some curb should be put on the amount of appropriations [to Education]. A good deal ... are along the lines of Fads and go largely to the cities. Why should such large grants be made to Technical Education, to Dental Inspection and Nurses ... It seems the interests of those who wish to see money spent has [sic] prevailed.'[34]

Some of the criticism that descended on Queen's Park was spiked when Drury and Grant subsequently made plans for special schools of agriculture at Ridgetown and Kemptville. Set up to provide courses in scientific farming for rural adolescents, a goal long demanded by some farm groups, they departed in spirit from the premier's insistence on the need for combining general education and 'intellectual uplift' with vocational training. Once again political considerations appear to have intruded on principle. In the meantime, at least one act of retrenchment commended Queen's Park to the Hellyers of the UFO. When the premier turned down Western University's request for an affiliated college of horticulture he not only pleaded economy but added 'that the best place for [such] a School ... is [not] in connection with the University.'[35] All the same he may have reached this conclusion after the generally cool response from the concession lines to Western's scheme.

The coupling of higher education and economizing betrayed one of Drury's preoccupations in policy-making. Indeed, the so-called University question consumed time, resources, and energy that he might have preferred to spend resolving problems at other levels of education. To a marked degree the question stemmed from the financial straits into which institutions of higher learning had been plunged after the war. As the 'Provincial University,' Toronto had always been on the receiving end of Queen's Park largesse. In order to stabilize the institution's financial structure the legislature, acting on a royal commission recommendation in 1906, had set aside a sum equal to 50 per cent of the receipts from succession duties, averaged over a stipulated period. Subsequently the limit on the university's annual share of the duties was placed at half a million dollars, on the understanding that additional grants would be forthcoming should an urgent need arise. Shortly before the war, the practice had begun of awarding modest subsidies to Queen's and Western universities as well, a form of support that by Drury's premiership was no longer seen to be all that modest. In spite of this funding, all three institutions were pointedly requesting additional aid in the postwar period.

Just as Drury and other rural activists were seeking a more generous treatment of school teachers, they were being reminded by Sir Robert Falconer, the forceful president of the University of Toronto, that professors' salaries also required attention. *Maclean's* had obliged Falconer and other university heads by publishing late in 1919 an essay entitled 'Can Canada Afford Cheap Teachers?' The information it embodied came in from all points of the higher education compass, and stressed the need for competing with the financial rewards of the business and industrial worlds.[36] Before long Drury and Grant were being visited by university deputations anxious to make themselves and their needs known to the administration.

Although the so-called outlying colleges posed special problems of their own, it was Toronto that constituted the major challenge, with its soaring postwar enrolment (up from a wartime three thousand to over five thousand) and the corresponding need for expanding its faculty and paying it more. The situation was put squarely before Drury and his colleagues in the spring of 1920 when the university's board of governors presented their annual estimates calling for an across-the-board salary increase for all faculty. Drury's composure was shaken not only by the request but by Falconer's letters to the newspapers bemoaning the university's financial woes.[37] Whatever his own views on the board's submission, Drury was soon made aware of the UFO's position. The farm body went on record with the following statement:

For the first time in the history of the University the farmers take an interest in the finances of University education ... The setting aside of an annual payment of 50% of the succession duties averaged over three years, *the gradual assumption of the cost of professional education* ... the conversion of endowment into buildings and the actual deficits which have been met by higher fees and by executive grants, and the sale of state guaranteed bonds, [all] have raised among the farmers a natural anxiety.[38]

Solemn reference was also made to the considerable assistance furnished the outlying colleges.

The UFO submission then hastened to say that the concern of the farm community was not restricted to finances: there was the semblance of a class issue too. 'Ontario's rural population of 900,000,' the statement noted, 'only sends 351 out of 1,833 students entering for study, and Toronto is favoured most of all.' The trend to centralization and the urbanization of higher education were both deplored. Then the major point was addressed: 'The question arises as to what extent a wise public policy will seek to decentralize education and bring it to the doors of those who pay for it.' This statement, advocating a kind of concession lines university, demanded a decentralization of the 'teaching of culture, that is of languages, literature, mental and moral science, economics, mathematics and history.'

The UFO statement went on to show how, at the very time such lavish sums were being demanded at the University of Toronto, farmers were 'in full view of an enormous depreciation of the value of their products and property.' Implicit in all this was that professional and business education, which after all benefited only those sectors of society that seemed insensitive to the farmers' needs, ought not to be generously funded by the hard-pressed rural ratepayer. Also given black marks were the university's 'bad situation in the business section of a great city' and its envelopment by a 'foreign population.' Might not the rural ethic, the statement seemed to ask in a fit of xenophobia, be subverted by urbanized instruction and by an alien society ignorant of the history and requirements of the farm community? The *Farmers' Sun* called for the abolition of the university's board of governors and the placing of the institution under the direct control of the Department of Education. [39]

When the universities' requests were made known, Peter Smith, whose appreciation of higher education fell lamentably short of Falconer's, put up the stiffest opposition in cabinet. But some colleagues were more tractable, including

Grant, the minister responsible, who was usually swayed by the tightly knit arguments and impeccable logic that graced Falconer's submissions. Other ministers stated no pronounced opinion of their own and coalesced loosely around the respective banners of Smith and Grant. That left the premier who, Falconer was convinced, held the key.[40]

Years later, the president's son would recall that his father had enjoyed good working relations with all the premiers of Ontario 'except for that farmer.'[41] Falconer's impatience was triggered by what he took to be Drury's reluctance to address the problems he had raised. At least twice during the summer of 1920 he sought an appointment with the premier only to be refused. For a person of Falconer's standing it must have come as a shock to be fended off by an untried farmer politician. He also complained that Drury had no first-hand knowledge of what a university was supposed to be, even though some hoped that a proper understanding would flow from the honorary Hart House membership conferred upon him for his term of office. But Falconer failed to realize that Drury was still trying to make his neophyte cabinet work and to cope with problems that went beyond the difficulties facing higher education. Besides, there was the urgent need to mollify the UFO membership and neutralize as best he could those anti-intellectual forces inside cabinet and out that could subject any serious discussion of university affairs to a cold shower. This work had to be accomplished before he could turn aside and do justice to Falconer and his preoccupations.

Anyone who knew Drury well – and Falconer, who had never met him was not one of these – would have scoffed at the charge that he was insensitive to a university's role in society. More knowledgeable about public issues than many politicians, well read, a competent stylist, and a vigorous and colourful debater, Drury entertained notions of education that would not have jarred Falconer's equanimity. Indeed, the president's assertion that 'character is the crown of our education and the safeguard of our educational efficiency' was a slightly more elaborate way of stating what Drury had long professed.[42] Nor would Falconer have been unsympathetic to the rustic remarks that Drury subsequently addressed to rural students at the university. 'If we can develop the reading habit,' he told them, calling on his own experiences at Crown Hill, 'and not only the reading habit, but the habit of rumination – the quiet chewing of the cud of reflection – then I think we have gone a long way toward acquiring for ourselves well-stored lives.'[43] Drury also ventured to Hart House and was accorded a 'tremendous ovation' by Toronto undergraduates when he skilfully explained the merits of third parties.[44]

However the premier sized up the university's place in society, he shared the UFO's view that no institution, regardless of its prestige or repute, should necessarily be immune from review. Like the parsimonious among organized farmers, Drury had pledged himself to reducing if not eliminating the fat of public expenditure. Retrenchment, the Liberal battle cry of the Victorian century, was boldly emblazoned on his own political banner, at least in these early months of his administration. Indeed, he entered into the spirit of things and set a dramatic example by announcing that he would not accept his full premier's salary.

In the meantime an anxious Falconer, distressed by Drury's standoffishness in the summer of 1920, sought help from the university's board of governors. Fearing, among other things, that the UFO might seek to reduce the faculty to the status of civil servants, he prevailed upon banker Edmund Walker and T.A. Russell, owner of a Toronto automotive firm, to intercede with the premier.[45] To their relief, Drury responded to the approaches and offered to see Falconer and work out some arrangement that would at one and the same time slake the university's financial thirst and pacify a suspicious UFO, no mean chore. Drury also had to satisfy himself that the president was not exaggerating the problem.

Even after the belated ice-breaking exercises had been carried out, Drury still needed convincing. He may have been anxious to placate his treasurer, Peter Smith, who was very much opposed to the university's request on the grounds that an increase had been granted two years before and this one was unwarranted. Happily for Falconer and the board of governors, the opposition jam began to break up early in September 1920. Walker reported to a relieved but still irritated Falconer that Drury was showing signs of coming around. All the same, the premier still worried because the university was asking for salaries higher than any university's except those at the very top in the United States. If that was the case, it would have been a great source of satisfaction to Falconer, who all along had hoped to ensure that American institutions, with their vastly greater resources, would no longer be able to entice away valuable Canadian talent needed at home. In the end, Drury pledged to recommend to cabinet that the university estimates be passed without amendment. What may have been a crucial factor in making up the premier's mind was the high regard he came to hold for T.A. Russell, who deftly handled the negotiations on behalf of the board of governors.[46]

When Drury took the matter to cabinet, however, strong doubts were still expressed by Smith and others. The discussion, if their meeting followed the usual format, must have been a freewheeling one, with everyone given the opportunity to offer his views before the final judgment was made. Although it is difficult to determine how vigorously Drury and Grant pressed the university's case, a compromise of sorts was hammered out in deference to the opposition. It fell to Grant to disclose to Falconer what had transpired: the government, while allowing a temporary increase to instructors only – staff and maintenance personnel were excluded – would not sanction an all-round salary boost. And in no case would an increment exceed five hundred dollars.

This news galvanized the board into a round of aggrieved discussion, the upshot of which was the despatch of another deputation to the premier's office. Drury was advised that the university was adamant in tying faculty salaries to those of qualified staff. Drury may have surmised, given his dependence on the ILP, that the board was indulging in blackmail when they predicted labour trouble on the campus should machinists and stationary engineers be ignored in the settlement.[47] In the end, a face-saving formula was worked out. Falconer recommended that the increase for both faculty and staff be classified as a bonus – a device that might be swallowed by the parsimonious in the cabinet – so that the ultimate salary arrangements could be held over for future discussion. Drury readily understood why Falconer wanted the issue resolved one way or the other: the academic session was already under way and he needed to set his house in order. Before September ended the bonus formula was, to everyone's relief, agreed upon by both parties and the budget was approved. The university gained a breathing space.

Clearly a long-term formula would have to be devised, however, and to that end a decision was reached in cabinet to appoint a royal commission to investigate the problem. It was to report upon the whole question of provincial aid to universities 'in order that a definite and comprehensive basis may be arrived at on which to rest the policy to be pursued.' Drury knew full well that the increases grudgingly made to Toronto would open the door to renewed financial requests from Western and Queen's; all the more reason, he comforted himself, to have a commission investigate university financing in general.

The Royal Commission on University Finances was to be, in fact, one of a series struck to review contentious issues. The practice, however, speedily brought down on the premier's head accusations that his government was shirking its parliamentary responsibilities by transferring them to others outside the system. But Drury reasoned that it was high time that a problem hitherto considered piecemeal and sporadically should be explored in depth by people with expertise. Of course, it was also a convenient way of delivering him from a dilemma that was consuming valuable time, making the UFO rank and file nervous, and shunting other major concerns undeservedly to the sidelines.

Whatever the circumstances, Falconer and the board welcomed the initiative, convinced that their university's case was irrefutable. Besides, those appointed to the commission were favourably disposed toward higher learning in general and the provincial university in particular. The chairman of the commission was Canon Cody, Grant's predecessor as minister of education, and adorning it were the influential Sir John Willison, a friend of Falconer's, and J. Alex Wallace, a well-regarded UFO member and graduate of McMaster University. They were joined by T.A. Russell, A.P. Deroche, who would speak for eastern Ontario, Queen's hinterland, and C.R. Somerville, who would act correspondingly for the western part of the province.[48] The three universities then receiving public assistance were visited in due course and much material prepared for the commission. On the other hand, denominational institutions such as McMaster fell outside its scope.

One potentially explosive issue that put the universities on edge arose when Wallace and other commissioners, out of respect for UFO feelings, proposed that the bulk of first-year university work be thrown upon the collegiate institutes. This would have had the effect of keeping farm students at home an extra year and available for chores when they were most needed. Whether or not Drury had a hand in the proposal is an open question. What was predictable was the universities' solid opposition to a scheme that threatened the very fabric of the province's institutions of higher learning. In the end the proposal was abandoned.

As the commission travelled, investigated, and met deputations, Drury did some homework of his own, buttonholing and interrogating journalists, university people, and others conversant with the academic scene. Nevertheless, when the Commission's report was submitted in February 1921, the premier was disturbed by the scope of its recommendations. For one thing, it urged the restoration of the support furnished by the Act of 1906 – a portion of the succession duties – and, moreover, a capital grant of $1.5 million for construction on campus. This was twinned with the recognition of the claims of Western and Queen's to 'such reasonable support ... as will be just to them and to the districts which they specially serve.'[49] What this meant in cold financial terms, the report went on, was an outlay of some one million dollars.

Drury's research had ill prepared him for this kind of thunderbolt and, according to one commissioner, he went into a financial panic. Drury countered that, should this costly transfusion be given the academic patient, the donor would be accused in his own constituency of the rankest extravagance. He was painfully aware, as Willison noted, that a 'certain UFO element is opposing such liberal treatment of the universities as the ... Commission recommended.'[50] Surely, the premier seemed to be asking, a less expensive solution could be prescribed? The result was that Drury announced his intention to hold up the report and defer a decision on its implementation. When Western and Queen's learned of this, they wasted little time despatching deputations to Queen's Park. They may have been asking themselves whether Drury's discomfiture was the result of personal qualms about extravagance or of fears of a backlash from his Farmer-Labourite caucus, or both. By this time – the spring of 1921 – he was fully engaged on other fronts, notably with Hydro and northern Ontario, and he could ill afford to alienate friends and supporters.

The following September a partial turn-around came. A hopeful Sherwood Fox of Western, in company with other university heads, learned that Grant, after long delays, intended to pledge the full amount the commission recommended for campus construction projects and to offer, as well, sizeable annual grants. The minister of education, impressed by Falconer's submissions and concerned about the needs of what had once promised to be his alma mater, supported the implementation of the report and urged MLAs to plump for it. For his part, a worried Drury had made an effort to see for himself what the universities needed and why their requirements were so essential. Thus, while he and his cabinet were on a tour of eastern Ontario, ostensibly to inspect Biggs's provincial highways, he paid a visit to a delighted Queen's campus. There he had a conversation with the voluble W.F. Nickle, who pressed the university's case for enlarged support. The forceful chancellor, Edward Beatty, may have relayed the message, similar to Belcourt's over bilingual schools, that 'such [public] economies as are necessary could ... have been effected without disturbing in any way the vote for educational facilities.'[51] Drury's response to the cordial treatment he received in Kingston was not recorded but he obviously came away with the conviction that the recommended support for higher education was by and large in order. In any event, Grant shortly announced the awarding of some $415,000 to Queen's, which was to be used for rebuilding the local general hospital, home of the university's medical school, and for other facilities and operating expenses. Although Fox had anticipated that Western, because of its rapid development, would be treated more handsomely than Queen's, the institution in London had to settle for comparable assistance. Even so, it was warmly welcomed.

In the meantime, the University of Toronto, the customary beneficiary of Queen's Park's generosity, seemed, in spite of Grant's support, to lag behind Queen's and Western when the time came to implement the commission's recommendations. The proposal that a portion of the succession duties again be made available did not see the light of day. In spite of frequent appeals from Falconer's office and the boardroom, the university was reduced to appealing every year to the legislature for the subsidies needed beyond the annual statutory grant of $500,000. In effect, the cabinet decreed that Toronto along with Queen's and Western would not be given a fixed income over a period of years, as had been requested by it and urged by the commission. Although Queen's dean, O.D. Skelton, allowed that his university was 'doing not too badly under the temporary system' of subsidies, one of his colleagues prayed that 'some government might come into being that would have ... regard for the things of the spirit and would not give to education only the fag-ends of their consideration.'[52]

Another irritant for Toronto, which all along had felt unjustly done by, was Drury's apparent disregard for the board of governors when he made new appointments to that body. Ordinarily, J.A. Wallace, the commissioner and UFO member, and W.C. Good, alumnus and Progressive, would have been perfectly acceptable, but what irked Walker was that both appointments were made without consulting the board. Drury contended that he was simply following past practice, which brought from Falconer the revealing comment that 'one was hoping that the new government would have changed that part of ... its predecessor's ... methods.'[53] The president need not have worried about Good, who had always taken considerable interest in his old university, particularly when academic freedom or student affairs had come under review.[54] As it turned out, disenchantment with the board's work and his political responsibilities in Ottawa soon combined to bring about his resignation.

For a time the university question, though not totally resolved to the satisfaction of Ontario's institutions of higher learning, was thought in many quarters to have been adequately addressed. Nevertheless, with the possible exception of Western, the universities still felt uneasy and unsure about their relationship with Queen's Park. And, as Willison had observed, there were vocal elements in the UFO still aggrieved by what they considered the government's unwarranted generosity to institutions that had all but fallen under the urban spell. There were others who grumbled that what had been awarded higher education far exceeded the support offered primary and secondary instruction. All this produced a tension that rarely left unruffled the minority government over which Drury presided.

9

Confronting Adam Beck

While Drury had been trying to pick his way through the labyrinth of education he had also been forced to deal with what turned out to be one of the major problems of his administration. Again, bigness was involved, but, financially speaking, Hydro was to dwarf all other concerns. While higher education made demands of Queen's Park in the hundreds of thousands of dollars, the Hydro-Electric Power Commission, under the dynamic leadership of its chairman, Sir Adam Beck, was seeking funding in the tens of millions. For a premier and a government pledged to economy, if not parsimony, Hydro came to constitute a kind of financial obscenity. At least it provided Drury with a handy excuse for turning down other supplicants. 'Owing to stringent financial conditions and the necessity of providing vast sums for Hydro Development,' he convincingly told the Canadian Deep Waterways Association, for example, 'we cannot possibly make a grant to your association.'[1]

Hydro had travelled a considerable distance since the time in 1906 when business leaders in western Ontario had banded together to promote a public power project that would confer on their municipalities the industrial and energy benefits that private companies were already bestowing on the favoured metropolis of Toronto. Ever since its victories gained at the expense of those private firms, Hydro had become an integral part of the economic and technological matrix of Ontario. The decisions it made, the policies it adopted, and the charges it set for its product, touched every man, woman, and child in the province.[2]

As the Drury government embarked on its self-appointed task to investigate, prune, and retrench, it was only a matter of time before Hydro and its chairman came under closer scrutiny at Queen's Park. Drury's approach was promptly interpreted by the press as an attack on the principle of public power itself. The *Toronto Telegram* led the way and saved up its most vituperative editorials for the 'upstarts' of the Farmer government who had the temerity to call to account the policies of the 'Hydro Knight.' On the other hand, the *Farmers' Sun* had been quick to criticize the arrogant tone of Beck's speeches on Hydro matters and what he expected in the way of support, financial and moral, from Queen's Park. In fact, UFO reactions to Beck's aggressive posture did not mean that the principle of public power was in jeopardy now that Drury was in the premier's office. Indeed, he moved to set the record straight, not only in the legislature but on the speaking circuit. Thus at a Toronto luncheon meeting early in 1920 he assured a party of fellow diners, which included Beck himself, that 'our government is not in any sense ... tied up by sentiment, or otherwise, to private enterprises.'[3] Typical, too, was the statement he made at Chippawa when a major Hydro project was officially opened late the following year:

I intend to take the opportunity ... to clear up ... some misrepresentations there have been, as to the attitude of the Government on various issues connected with the Hydro Electric Development. In the first place I want to tell you that there never has been a question of the Government of which I am the head, not supporting public ownership enterprises where these enterprises are sane and sound. It has been a plank of our platform from the beginning ... Those things which, by their nature, are a heritage of all the people should be treated, and are treated, and will be treated by the Government in the interests of all the people.[4]

'Sane and sound' were the words he stressed, another way perhaps of saying 'respect reasonable and realistic spending limits,' the watchword of his regime.

In this case, however, Drury was up against not a reserved university head like Falconer but a powerful public personality who was capable of making the following remarks at a dinner attended by the premier and his ministers: 'I take this to be an honest cabinet until I find otherwise. I have not been able to get hold of all the members yet – they are pretty oily for all the experience they have had.'[5] Nor was Drury permitted to forget that it was Beck who had been approached by UFO and particularly Labour MLAs and offered the leadership before Drury's candidacy was contemplated. Again, the premier needed no reminder that his name, unlike the illustrious Hydro chairman's, was not exactly a household word in the province. But Drury was not inclined to take a back seat to anyone when fundamental issues were under consideration. 'I think probably Beck has been accustomed to having his own way a good deal,' one of the premier's western friends observed understatedly, but 'Drury has a very square jaw.'[6]

At any rate, Drury pressed ahead with his own inquiry into the workings of the Hydro system and with plans to hold Beck in check on a reconstituted commission. Though it was virtually impossible to remove the popular Beck from the chairmanship, at least an effort could be made to neutralize some of his power by making appointments to the three-man body that would be sympathetic to the government's restraint program. Drury must have been aware

that previous governments had also sought to rein Beck in, with less than gratifying results. What made him think that he would be any more successful? Not
only this, he had already been informed that highly vocal UFO members wanted
to put their own kind on the commission. A.B. Hellyer, Morrison's brother-in-
law, assailed a scheme to have the municipalities under contract with Hydro
appoint a commissioner because it 'would simply mean Beck would be the
Commission.'[7] At the same time various regional interests and groups such as
labour sought special consideration. That kind of unwieldy balancing act was
out of the question. In the end, for all his talk of a rejuvenated Hydro Commission,
Drury settled for the immovable Beck as chairman, while to the other two
positions he appointed Dougall Carmichael, his minister without portfolio, and
I.B. Lucas, a holdover from the Hearst government.

One of the early concerns that came to Drury's attention was expressed by
the Ontario Hydro Power Uniform Rate Association (OHPURA). Formed two
months before the Farmer successes at the polls in 1919, it was made up of
representatives of the smaller municipalities of western Ontario which had long
complained of unfair treatment at Hydro's hands.[8] W.S. Bowden, an officer of
the association and a UFO member from the Goderich area, told the premier in
November 1919 that a

large number of municipalities have been very much dissatisfied with the present system
of fixing the charges for power delivered to the Municipalities, and believe that they are
very unfair to the smaller and rural Municipalities; and also that the low rates charged
to the places located in close proximity to the sources of power creates a deplorable
system of municipal competition, that is very harmful to the best interest of the Province
as a whole.[9]

Cheap power meant industrial growth and much sought after economic diver-
sification such as that already enjoyed by the urban heartland at the western end
of Lake Ontario. Goderich and its sister communities argued that so long as the
hinterland was denied that advantage it would suffer the fate of a colonial
dependency. Not surprisingly, the UFO annual convention, which met within
days of Drury's receipt of Bowden's letter, approved in principle what the
OHPURA was seeking – a uniform rate for Hydro power regardless of where it
was distributed.

The proposal was anathema to Beck. A uniform rate would benefit the rural
community at the expense of the urban one that had already mortgaged its
resources on behalf of public power. The new formula amounted to a breach of
faith and would do violence to the service-at-cost principle the commission had
set for itself from the very beginning. The price was based not only on the
generation of power but its transmission to the ultimate consumer, which involved

lines and other costly facilities. Although Beck appeared to sympathize with the smaller municipalities' problems he was convinced that any significant departure from established practice would imperil the fabric of public power by driving the larger municipalities in southern Ontario into the waiting arms of private power companies.

Meanwhile Drury agreed to meet with officers of the OHPURA and discuss the problem Bowden had raised. To their considerable relief he appeared to support their stand. Meanwhile, J.G. Lethbridge, UFO member for Middlesex West, introduced a resolution calling for the appointment of a House committee to devise, with Hydro's co-operation, a more equitable distribution of power and a more uniform price. Predictably, when the committee was struck Lethbridge was named its chairman; he was joined on it by representatives of all other parties and groups in the House. The potential conflict between city and countryside, seldom far below the surface, came out clearly when the committee's report was brought down on 30 November 1920. While it threw cold water on the uniform rate, dismissing it as neither practicable nor advisable, it did urge a lessening of the cost of providing service to the small urban and rural districts. To that end it called for a horsepower rental charge on all power generated, the money to be used to provide financial assistance for those agricultural districts unable to enjoy Hydro's benefits.[10] Since the tax would fall only on those municipalities which paid less than thirty dollars a horsepower – a figure that included most of those in the favoured metropolitan area of southern Ontario – the plan attempted to achieve some kind of equitable treatment for those not so fortunately sited in the province. Once again Beck voiced his displeasure, denouncing the tax, as he had the uniform rate, as discriminatory and an act of bad faith.

So much for Beck. What of Drury's response to the report of the Lethbridge committee? Throughout the summer and fall, while the committee had been engaged in its inquiries, Drury had been subjected to the arguments of both sides. If he was not on the receiving end of Bowden's entreaties, he was being forcibly acquainted with the point of view of the counter-lobbyists, the Association of Municipal Electrical Utilities of Ontario and the Ontario Municipal Electric Association. While the OHPURA and the *Farmers' Sun* lauded the proposal to tax the 'favoured power users' in order to help less fortunate consumers, their opponents claimed the rental would jeopardize the industrial life of the province.[11] As he had when confronted by Ontario's educational system, the premier was forced to submerge his natural sympathies in economic realities. While understandably disposed to support any reform that might reverse the rural depopulation he had so often deplored, he could not ignore the potent arguments of the province's metropolitan interests. Doubtless Drury was made aware by Rollo and other ILP members of how the rental scheme might adversely affect the livelihood of many of their constituents should it lead to an industrial recession in a city such as Hamilton. In the end he distanced himself from the committee's report and announced that personally he was opposed to the uniform rate and thought the rental tax excessive.

But he knew that if he rejected the tax outright he ran the risk of alienating articulate spokesmen of his own rural constituency. More than one UFO club had written to Carmichael endorsing the Lethbridge rental tax recommendation. In an effort to sort matters out, Drury, at Beck's request, summoned MLAS to a private meeting which the Hydro chairman promptly used to discredit the tax scheme. The upshot was that the rental plan was disavowed along with the uniform rate. But Drury realized that this wholly negative reaction would have to be eased by some concession to the interests represented by the OHPURA.[12] To salvage some advantage from the situation, the government introduced a bill on 30 April that set up the so-called Power Extension Fund. Fed by waterpower rentals and other monies that could be periodically spared, the fund was designed to meet what hitherto the smaller municipalities could not – the high costs of installing primary rural transmission lines. The measure was immediately dismissed by the Lethbridge committee as a paltry alternative. Its chairman was so disgusted that he broke with the UFO caucus, while the *Farmers' Sun* bemoaned the government's surrender to what it called the 'Power Boss of the Province.'[13]

Although the premier realized that his actions had lost him support on the concession lines, he was convinced that by finding subsidies for the transmission of power to areas in need he was not only putting an important capital asset in place but providing some solution to the problems publicized by the OHPURA. He satisfied himself that, criticisms notwithstanding, he had realistically struck an acceptable balance between the requirements of the metropolis and the needs of the hinterland. At least a program had been launched that would bring electrification for farm and household use to a large section of the countryside hitherto unable to afford it.

The controversy over the uniform rate brought Drury face to face with the formidable personality and entrenched power of Sir Adam Beck. But that had been a mere skirmish, an armed reconnaissance, compared to the confrontations that followed. For Drury these came to revolve around a fundamental question: who should have the ultimate responsibility in the province, a duly constituted government or an autonomous commission? The question arose when Beck virtually dictated to Queen's Park what sums should be appropriated for the construction of major projects, notably the radials and the Chippawa Development.

When Drury entered office in 1919, radials, or electrified railways, were emerging from pipedream to reality. Proposed initially by Beck as a convenient means of consuming Hydro's surplus power, radials had come to be perceived in some quarters as an ideal form of rapid transit, free from much of the noise and all of the pollution associated with the venerable steam locomotive. But as Hydro surpluses were whittled away by the demands of the Great War, Beck reckoned that an even more prodigious supply of power must be harnessed to meet the radials' demands as well as those of industry and the householder. When that equation was forged there was launched, with much fanfare, Beck's most spectacular undertaking – the Chippawa Development on the Niagara River. Sanctioned by the Hearst government and floated by municipal by-laws, it was commenced in the spring of 1917 in the confident expectation that some ten million dollars would meet the challenge, the funds to come from bonds issued by Hydro and guaranteed by the province. Two years later that original estimate had grown alarmingly to fifty-five million dollars as unforeseen construction and labour costs multiplied.

As the new man on the legislative block, Drury was soon made painfully aware of the varied ramifications of this power extravaganza. It involved nothing less than the excavation of a large canal from Chippawa Creek above Niagara Falls to transport water to a new power house at Queenston where the flow would plunge to the river far below, thus providing an additional 100,000 horsepower. Equally fascinating for a political leader wedded to economy was the financial dimension of this technological achievement. As it turned out, early estimates had erred in not taking into account the awesome hardness of the underlying rock, a costly impediment to the work of excavation. An unhappy augury of things to come was the premier's discovery, shortly after taking office, that nearly half that much again of the fifty-five million figure had already been spent on the development.[14] He may be pardoned for suspecting, as a future historian would, that in order to get Hearst's approval for the project Beck had deliberately minimized its costs.[15]

The situation only worsened for Drury when still more unanticipated costs continued to inflate the estimates. He began to fear for the health of the province's credit, not to mention the security of his own administration. Mounting rural discontent with Beck's dictatorial manner and the *Sun*'s call for action against what it called his Tammany Hall methods reinforced Drury's own decision to challenge Hydro's soaring demands. As early as March 1920 the premier decided to take the bull by the horns and seek clarification of the entire Hydro system. He sought help from the chairman's auditor, who he hoped would place on his desk information on the kind of funds Queen's Park would have to set aside over the next two years for the completion of all Hydro projects.[16] When that official finally obliged, after a delay of some three months, Drury was treated to the stark news of expanding estimates and cost over-runs on virtually every Hydro undertaking.

Ironically, if the premier's memory served him right, Beck himself confessed to being flabbergasted by the costs of the Chippawa Power Canal and suggested in the summer of 1920 that outside advice be sought while the work was in progress. Without delay Drury appointed a prominent American engineer and dam-builder, Hugh L. Cooper, to scrutinize the operation. Not only did Cooper shortly question Hydro's designs for the development but insisted on some costly alternatives which would have added to the bill. While Beck understandably bristled at the professional rebuke, Drury appeared to welcome the office visits of the expansive Cooper. Ever on the lookout for information and insights, the premier questioned the engineer on a number of matters related to Chippawa. In the course of these conversations Cooper claimed that he could make improvements that would ensure far more horsepower output than Beck's plan ever could. A concerned Drury wondered why such alternatives had not been contemplated by Beck and his engineers before the mammoth project was launched.

An even more serious question was raised as the work mercifully neared completion at Chippawa. When, the premier asked, were Hydro's 'unauthorized expenditures' on that and other projects to cease? In the fall of 1921 he learned that funds were being used for purposes other than those specified in the special warrants he was being called upon to sign 'at the rate of a million dollars a week.'[17] A memorandum prepared at Drury's request by the Ontario Municipal and Railway Board bore out what a worried *Sun* had already told its readers, that the 'acts under which the Hydro Commission operates are much too wide and loosely-drawn.' The paper urged that legislation 'be enacted, under which all sums advanced to [it] should first be passed by the Legislature.' Much to Drury's satisfaction, an outraged Colonel Maclean took up the cry in the *Financial Post* and charged that the 'license allowed Sir Adam Beck in the expenditure of moneys and in its method of administration flagrantly ignored many fundamental principles of sound business, and democratic government.'[18]

In the meantime, Drury did not hide his concern from the government's man on the commission. The alarming over-runs that appeared in Hydro's reports begged an immediate explanation, which he directed Carmichael to extract from a silent Beck. When Carmichael's intervention failed to get results, Drury entered the lists personally early in December. He reminded the Hydro chairman that his explanation was two months overdue and that the worth of his own 'personal promise' was at stake. About a week and a half later, after he had already carefully shepherded newspapermen to view the accomplishments at Chippawa, Beck finally responded. The usual excuses were paraded before the premier, including the unforeseen expenses brought on by an unforgiving geology. They did not appease an impatient premier. As a result, Beck's office finally agreed to itemize their requests, a simple enough procedure which hitherto the commission, long accustomed to having its requests go unchallenged, had not bothered to follow. It was a victory of sorts for Drury but a modest one.[19]

In the meantime, as though it had a life and momentum of its own, the first stage of the massive Chippawa Development preened itself for the ceremonial opening scheduled for 28 December. Drury, of course, was on hand to help officiate. When his turn came to hold forth he managed to get a slight dig in at Beck's expense and instruct the assembled dignitaries in the high finance of power development. At the appropriate moment, when he switched on an enormous illuminated sign proclaiming immodestly 'THE LARGEST HYDRO-ELECTRIC PLANT IN THE WORLD,' he remarked that the event marked the birth, 'as Sir Adam has told us,' of the greatest project of its kind 'on this continent and perhaps in the world.' Then he plunged into the matter of responsibilities and costs. With Beck's bemused gaze on his back, Drury reminded his audience that the Hydro-Electric Commission

became the trustee for the Municipalities, but responsible, of course, because every trustee must be responsible to someone, to the Legislature and to the Government. I do not care who you get, I do not care what the abilities or the character of the man or the organization may be; we know from the experience of the ages that it is dangerous, that it is impossible to entrust absolute power to any man or any organization. There must be responsibility. There must be some connecting link between those for whom the trust is undertaken and the trustee ... the Government and the Legislature of the Province.

Having discussed high principle, the premier turned to high finance. He noted that at the end of the past fiscal year a total of sixty-three million dollars had been lavished on Chippawa, a six-fold increase over the original estimate. And then to stifle talk that his government had impeded the work by withholding funds, Drury announced that it had done everything in its power to supply the wherewithal 'to forward the work most expeditiously ... This has been no small task, and it stands to our credit that through it all we have preserved the credit of the Province unimpaired.'[20]

Although his words had been carefully chosen to stake out Queen's Park's responsibilities and to show Beck where matters stood, Drury still harboured a grudging respect for Hydro's architect. This was reflected in his published memoirs a half-century later. They also disclosed something about himself:

Perhaps it is indicative of the rather strange relationship that existed between Sir Adam and me that he asked me to turn the wheel that would set the first generator in motion. In spite of our many differences, and some things that were hard to forgive, I liked Sir Adam and I think he liked me ... Sir Adam's only child ... was standing beside me [at the ceremony] ... When it came time for me to open the valve, on a sudden impulse I took her hand and placed it on the wheel beside my own, so that she had a part in the ceremony. And when the great generator began to turn, and the lights began to glow, dimly at first, then brightly, a great cheer went up from the crowd.[21]

There was, however, little for the premier to cheer about in the ceremony's aftermath. The battle over funding and responsibility was resumed after a brief armistice. In early February Beck, plainly unmoved by earlier criticisms, calmly asked for additional funding for the work awaiting completion at Chippawa. Still smarting from their previous confrontation, the premier again talked about an

exceedingly grave situation when he responded to Beck's requests. Drury scold-
ingly reminded him that 'having exhausted the whole of your estimates for the
[current] fiscal year ... you are required ... to submit a new estimate for the
amount now to be established to be required for that year.' Beck was also told
that if special warrants were to be issued they must be for specific amounts.
'Unless this is done,' Drury warned, 'the Government has no authority to take
any action.' The strategy seemed to work, for it elicited an uncharacteristically
swift response from the chairman – a detailed statement and more plausible
estimates for completing the remaining Chippawa units a year hence. Even so,
Drury was still appalled by their magnitude.[22] So was Carmichael, who was so
distressed that he tendered his resignation and apologized for having deceived
the legislature on the matter of Hydro's costs. Drury, however, brushed his
protestations aside and refused to let him resign, pointing out that it was Hydro's
fault, not Carmichael's, that expenditures had gone out of control. All the same,
some of Beck's UFO critics hailed the minister's threat to step down as a signal
that 'Hydro affairs were going to be brought to a head.'[23]

The scale of Hydro's spending and the wrangling that soured relations between
Beck and the government prompted Drury to appoint yet another commission
in the spring of 1922. Its broad mandate was to inquire and report upon all
Hydro 'power developments ... and generally all matters of expenditure and
administration of the ... Commission.' Over the new body Drury placed W.D.
Gregory, formerly of the *Weekly Sun* and a friend of the farmers' cause. The
establishment of the Gregory Commission was a shrewd move. Among other
things, it would serve for a time as a buffer between the government and the
Hydro Commission and, as well, generate welcome advice and favourable publicity for Queen's Park.

Meanwhile, by the time Beck finally accommodated the premier's wishes on
accountability he had already lost out on another crucial battlefield. The bitter
encounter over radials had, in fact, helped to cloud the festivities at Chippawa.
From the outset, radials had been linked in many minds, not least the premier's,
with the extravaganza emblazoned on the Niagara River. The fear that large-
scale radial expansion would pose a similar threat to the province's financial
health galvanized Drury into action some months before the showdown came
early in 1922. Within weeks of assuming office, in fact, he began to wonder in
public about the advisability of pursuing the much-published radial venture,
given the increased service recently provided by the publicly owned Canadian
National Railways. Wouldn't the radials, Drury asked, be dangerously expensive
exercises in duplication that would speedily make all forms of public transport
unprofitable? The independently minded *Hamilton Herald*, one of the few urban
papers that looked unkindly on radials, opposed them in part because the by-
law that would bring them into Hamilton placed their control not in city hall but
in Hydro's dictatorial hands. On the other hand, George Halcrow, the restive

ILP member for Hamilton East, seized another opportunity to ridicule Drury's understanding of the problem. The *Herald*'s rejoinder to Halcrow, which was well received in Drury's office, was that the premier's position 'is evidence that [he] ... has thought like a sensible man *and an economist and not like a partizan.*'[24] At about the same time the UFO convention in Toronto, with the verbose approval of the *Sun,* sided with Drury's position.[25]

Apart from railways and the possible duplication of effort and expense should radials be promoted, there was the motor vehicle to consider, a point already hammered home by the *Financial Post* and other observers. When Hydro had launched its impressive career in 1906 the automobile's impact on society and the economy had been all but negligible. But the demands of the war and the needs of the country's burgeoning economy had helped transform the internal combustion engine from a plaything into an essential tool for serving society. By 1919 there were no fewer than 135,000 registered motor vehicles in Ontario, and Drury had had his own personal experience with the phenomenon. 'Ford was selling "Tin Lizzies" for about four hundred dollars,' he wrote in his memoirs, 'which placed them within reach of common men. I myself frequently drove my Ford to Toronto, in preference to coming by rail, though [as premier] ... I had a pass on the railway.'[26] 'I remember driving ... from Brantford to Toronto,' he recalled elsewhere, 'and it took from ten in the morning until three in the afternoon because the roads were so bumpy.'[27] The improvement of those thoroughfares – there were then some four hundred miles of provincial roads – was a goal that private enthusiasts and vociferous organizations were now seeking to reach through assistance from Queen's Park.

As Drury well knew, one of those enthusiasts was a member of his own cabinet. F.C. Biggs, the minister of public works, had an unabashed love affair with the automobile (at any one time he was the proud owner of at least two) and he made the government's road-building one of its most dynamic programs. At the outset, to be sure, Biggs had hewed to the UFO line that public funds should not be earmarked for broad-paved highways that would supposedly favour urban interests only; after all, they already had an elaborate railway network at their disposal.[28] Rather, all roads, particularly those serving the countryside, should receive just enough surfacing to provide the farmer with effective access to his markets and sources of supply. Drury, for his part, had early on made his position plain enough. 'I do not favour one superior provincial road ... I do not believe in building a road for pleasure alone.' Again he sounded the populist note that had shaped the UFO platform: 'good transport for all the people.'[29]

As Biggs settled zestfully into his work at Queen's Park, however, he soon responded to the appeals of good roads promoters who wanted large-scale public assistance for an ambitious provincial network of widened and permanently paved highways. Before long the Central Provincial Highway Association, which clamoured for through roads from Sarnia to Toronto and from Hamilton to Windsor, and the Good Roads Association were mailing in their requests to his office. The force of these appeals combined with his own enthusiasm for a province-wide system to erode the restraints imposed by county government and UFO philosophy. In short order Biggs became almost as visible as Sir Adam Beck as he dashed from one end of Ontario to another, determining where and when old highways should be refurbished and new ones built. In the process, this agribusinessman set out to achieve what Beck sought for the radials: the provision of cheap transport for goods and services and the means to travel for those citizens and families whose budgets could be stretched to purchase a Tin Lizzie. A clear enough sign of the times was the expansive newspaper space already being purchased by automobile and truck manufacturers to advertise their products. Promises, among others, that food costs would be reduced and rail tie-ups circumvented (with the resultant 'allaying of social unrest') sprang from prominently displayed advertisements. 'Ship by Truck!' as an alternative to the use of the radial soon became a kind of battle cry.[30]

Then Biggs's and the premier's horizons broadened to embrace the benefits of tourism. Only dimly perceived in 1919, the tourist industry became a major pursuit part way through the administration's course. A Hotel and Tourist Investigation Committee was formed in the legislature, and soon it was receiving requests for the establishment of a provincial tourist bureau. Understandably, hotel owners and proprietors of real estate, particularly in the developing cottage country, aided and abetted the publicity campaign. A shrewd appeal was made to Drury's own pastoral background. 'A very great portion of [tourists] particularly from large cities,' one report glowed, 'prefer to stay at the comfortable roadside inn, it being cheaper, more homelike and inviting, if properly conducted, which breaks the monotony of noise, hustle, and bustle of city surroundings.'[31]

Equally shrewd was the letter sent by the persuasive president of a Hamilton advertising firm who doubled as secretary of the Provincial Highway Association. Addressing one of Drury's principal concerns – rural depopulation – Russell T. Kelley observed that 'Canada's greatest need today is to keep the people on the land and good roads are one of the main avenues whereby this will be accomplished.' Then he moved on to stress the importance of building up the tourist trade and attracting affluent American visitors.[32] Still another entreaty came to the premier's office from the Canadian Automobile Association, which must have known of his penchant for conservation and reforestation: 'Every effort [should be made by government] to preserve ... the natural scenic attractions of Ontario such as waterfalls and trees bordering Highways as from a purely utilitarian standpoint the value of these attractions, in bringing tourists to Canada will ... far exceed any immediate economic advantages which might be gained from their destruction.[33] Although Drury wrote little about the subject at the time, he certainly reflected on it, particularly on the need to attract American visitors, when he composed his *Forts of Folly* a decade later. His running battle with protectionism was also insinuated into the discussion:

> One of the objectives [of the road policy was] the development of the American tourist trade. If our friends across the line persisted in keeping our products out of their country by high tariffs, we would bring their citizens over the boundary using the natural beauties of our country as a magnet to attract them, and sell them our products here. Good motor roads were a means to this end.[34]

Although Drury made his own contributions to the government's roads program, Biggs was obviously in full charge and directed the operation with a gusto and expertise that sometimes dazzled the premier. 'I have often been astonished,' Drury recollected years later, 'when some question would be asked in the house, perhaps about some piece of road at the other end of the province, that Biggs could answer it without referring to his Department.' There were times, however, when Drury could be put off by the brusqueness and 'dictatorial manner' that characterized the frenetic activities of his highways minister.[35] But as head of a cabinet which boasted few such talented ministers Drury was reluctant to rein him in, particularly when Biggs appeared to be achieving notable successes and building up a constituency that augured well for the government. Indeed, if Broadening Out were to remain a viable political stratagem, then Biggs, a personification of a growing bridge between rural progressives and urbanites, would be a large asset. And yet the freedom that he and other forceful ministers enjoyed caused some grumbling in UFO circles about Drury's inability to direct and control his colleagues.[36]

Biggs soon came to be seen as the Adam Beck of the highways. Like his supposed Hydro counterpart, he began to talk grandly of expenditures of the order of tens of millions of dollars and thought it axiomatic that whenever he requested funds from the legislature they would be delivered. Biggs emphatically denied the need for a network of radials to serve southeastern Ontario out of Toronto, what with conventional railways and his own provincial highways already in place or projected. Biggs's son remembers overhearing an angry confrontation between his father and Beck over a plan to have radials complement the roads system already laid down in Wentworth County.[37] With Biggs's forcefulness to draw on, Drury was strengthened in his own resolve to block the radials and thereby avoid costly duplication of facilities. Besides, he was already committed to Biggs's wide-ranging road program and no more heavy strains on the provincial treasury could be tolerated.

Even so, a price had to be paid for Biggs's substantial support. Attacks from Beck and the Hydro interests were to be expected and could, it was hoped, be properly dealt with. But criticisms of Biggs's ambitious roads policy by the UFO and sections of the rural community, while not unexpected, seemed not so manageable. Economy-minded and suspicious farmers condemned Biggs's policy as a departure from the original UFO platform and an unwelcome sellout to urban interests. Drury was admonished by one critic early in 1920: 'So every person can have a reasonably good road not all the money [should be] spent on a few trunk lines that does [sic] no person any good a few miles back of them.' As for the argument that an expanded highway system would improve the quality of agrarian life, the same critic countered that too many marginal farmers, attracted by the wages paid for road work, were 'sacrificing the land' for this kind of dubious employment.[38]

The high cost of macadamizing roads was also harped on by concerned farmers. A study undertaken at the time disclosed that while a more or less serviceable dirt or gravel roadway could be built for about one thousand dollars a mile, a more permanent, wider, and graded surface could cost anywhere from five to eight times as much. Furthermore, there were loud complaints about the expensive practice of removing bends from old roads and widening them to accommodate a greater flow of heavy motor vehicles. The big guns of the UFO itself also sent salvoes into Biggs's department. Albert Hellyer, doubtless speaking for J.J. Morrison, told W.E. Raney that the 'chief source of apprehension is in regard to Mr. Biggs' Road Policy,' not, it would appear, radials, the uniform rate, or the other pressing concerns of that generation of farmer politicians.[39] To defuse charges that high costs were running away with the road policy, Drury and Biggs pointed to the government's legislation ensuring that the chief beneficiaries, the motorists and truckers themselves, would pay for a 'fair share of the building and maintenance' of the highway system.[40] It was expected that revenue capitalized from the issuance of automobile licences over a twenty-year period – an estimated $50 million – would help to bridge the financial gulf.

The assaults, however, continued and took a more abusive turn when Biggs's extravagance and tendering practices were singled out for special attention. The Toronto *Mail and Empire,* early in 1920, pounced on a story that Biggs had placed an order of $100,000 for motor trucks with a local firm in Dundas without tendering the transaction. The story was picked up by other papers, including the unfriendly *Northern Advance* in Barrie. It sneered that 'Frank's friend got the job and what else matters?' The *Hamilton Herald,* in Biggs's own constituency, added information of its own – his awarding of a paving contract to a Toronto firm, an inexcusable action in the eyes of any resident of the 'ambitious city.' The unperturbed Biggs told a reporter that 'it has not been the practice of my department to advertise for tenders. I have not been able to trace anything that would show tenders were advertised for.' The *Herald* was obviously disconcerted and called upon Biggs and the premier to rid themselves of the 'fossilized methods' they themselves had attacked when followed by old line governments.[41]

Eventually the worst of the criticism subsided when Drury intimated that appropriate provision would be made for the sought-after tendering. In this instance appearances and politics combined to make the premier tread on the toes of his ebullient minister. He agreed with Sissons's statement in the *Canadian Forum* that 'fine moral fibre is an essential in Farmer Government members' and the 'wife of Caesar must be above suspicion; also the lieutenant of Abe Lincoln.'[42] All in all, however, Drury was gratified by Biggs's performance and believed that his questionable actions left no visible scar on the government's reputation. Drury probably shared Sissons's assessment of the man, made after he left office, one that confirmed the wisdom of selecting him for cabinet in the first place. 'One evening ... I was strolling through [Queen's] ... Park,' Sissons recalled:

The Parliament Buildings were ablaze with lights and I wandered in. An attendant informed me that the [Public Accounts] Committee was in session, and I dropped in to see what was going on. I found Biggs being questioned on private as well as public business. I was compelled to stay to the end, being fascinated by the ease with which he stood the five perfectly good Conservative lawyers one after another on their heads.[43]

Assured of the backing of a colleague of Biggs's calibre, Drury formulated his counterattack against Beck's radials. As a first step, he settled for a stratagem he had already deployed to meet other problems – a royal commission, in this case to investigate the varied pitfalls of the Hydro scheme. Plans had to be laid carefully, however. For one thing, the cabinet and the caucus had to be taken into his confidence before he embarked on this course. 'I always considered the caucus a very useful instrument of government,' he recollected, when asked how he approached particularly contentious questions. 'Meeting in secret behind closed doors men will speak their minds. They don't always speak their minds in the House ... I used the caucus lavishly. I didn't use it to coerce them but ... to come to a decision that we all thought reasonable.'[44] On the radials question and the approach he adopted to it, this exercise in consensus rallied the Farmer MLAS to his side. The *Sun* and UFO officers such as Morrison had all along been voicing their concern about the radials, and prominent spokesmen of the farm movement, among them UFO co-founder J.Z. Fraser, had organized the vocal Hydro Information Association to combat pro-radial propaganda. On the other hand, some ILP members, notably the prickly George Halcrow, who had consistently supported Beck and his works, may have cast dissenting votes after Drury aired his strategy. For them radials had always meant a more economical and efficient means of transport and diversion for the workingman.

The outcome of the discussion, first in cabinet, then in caucus, was the endorsement of Drury's plan to strike a royal commission and the decision to refuse further guarantees of municipal radial bonds until that body had completed its task. All realized that this manoeuvre would lead to a toe-to-toe fight with the redoubtable Beck, a confrontation that would go beyond the mere querying of financial procedures and technological decisions. The Chippawa Development, in spite of the bombardment of criticism from Queen's Park, had always remained inviolate. But, as everyone seemed to sense, the war over the radials could possibly end up in nothing less than the dismantling of Beck's favourite project.

If Drury had not felt so secure about his position and his relationship with the UFO, would he have taken the circumspect way out and retreated from the radials battlefield? That seems unlikely. The political animals of the day, Howard Ferguson included, may have grasped this option but not Drury. Populists, even the sober variety grown in Ontario, did not appear to function that way. The 'common weal' was in danger and in response to some basic instinct Drury felt compelled to charge to the rescue. 'So strongly did I feel on this question,' he wrote in his memoirs, 'that I stood firm in spite of the battering I received.'[45] Even so, practical considerations, already weighed, had also helped to determine his course. Biggs's costly road plans and the expensive duplication of transportation in eastern Ontario combined to demonstrate the shakiness of the radials scheme. Not only this, there is always the possibility that Drury squared off against the radials in order to spike the suspicions of central office and to mend fences in that part of his political domain.

The battering to which he was subjected came from many quarters – Hydro, pro-radial forces on the opposition benches, and much of the urban press. Drury soon learned that Beck had not been sitting idly by while he had been formulating his own plans. Always highly visible anyway, Beck made well-publicized speeches in strategic parts of the province on the iniquities of delay and the urgent need for Queen's Park to proceed with the undertaking. Throughout he left few in doubt of what he thought of the premier's tactics and motives. A *Globe* report that arrived on Drury's desk early in July 1920 had Beck telling the Hydro Radial Association that the government had been influenced in its decision to investigate the radials by 'considerations other than the public interest.' Those considerations, according to the story, involved certain financial and railway interests that were attempting to stampede the government into delaying or halting the project.[46]

After being called to account for the *Globe* report, Beck calmly claimed that he had been misinterpreted. 'I did not wish it to be inferred,' he wrote Drury, 'that you were appointing a Royal Commission to investigate the ... Radial project to please the enemies of the Hydro, but that such an appointment would give pleasure to its enemies [who have] ... carried on ... a systematic campaign ... to undermine public confidence in [Hydro's] ... various undertakings.'[47] Understandably, the premier treated this as an exercise in hair-splitting. Furthermore, he realized that reporting the incident the way it did was just the *Globe*'s way of advertising its own pro-radial stance. Drury bitterly denounced what he called the 'howlings of the Toronto press.'

Probably the worst offender in Drury's eyes was the publisher of the *Toronto Telegram*. John ('Black Jack') Robinson, who had constantly ridiculed the Farmer government and its 'red' Labour allies, published an editorial on the radials that parodied the hymn: 'What matter to you, all ye who pass by, what matter to you if the children die?' 'I think I was as much concerned,' Drury wrote later, 'for the welfare of children as ... Robinson, but I couldn't see how radials would help the children in the slums of Toronto.'[48] The running battle with the press may account for the sarcastic passage that later appeared in his unpublished novel: 'as we all know ... the press, the palladium of the people's rights, is quite incorruptible.'[49]

This, then, was the uneasy background to the royal commission the premier appointed in mid-summer 1920. The chairman-designate of the commission was Mr Justice Robert F. Sutherland of the Ontario Supreme Court, a former Liberal MP and Speaker of the Commons. The other members of the commission were Brigadier Charles H. Mitchell, dean of engineering at the University of Toronto; Frederick Bancroft, a Toronto Labourite who, it was hoped, could also speak for urban interests; W.A. Amos, vice-president of the UFO; and A.F. McCallum, Ottawa's city engineer. Initially Drury had wanted T.A. Russell to serve, but Russell's close ties to the automobile industry probably accounted for his being replaced by Mitchell. Clearly some effort had been made to ensure a balanced membership.

While the battle continued to rage in the press and Beck carried out his self-promoting swings through the province, Drury took comfort from having the Sutherland Commission in place. Equally important, while that body was investigating radials, he could turn his attention to other matters piling up on his desk. In the summer of 1920 he snatched some spare moments to review the political situation and to muse over incidents that had occurred in the first six months of power. One had been the contretemps between the lieutenant-governor and himself some weeks earlier. It had to do with the government's announced intention, as an economy move and one in keeping with a democratic administration, to close down the official residence of His Majesty's representative in the province. The incumbent, Lionel H. Clarke, was reported to have made a Rotary Club speech condemning the decision as a 'Red victory,' an example of the sort of radicalism rampant in the UFO. The impression given was that Armageddon would follow the closing of Government House, deemed a 'stable institution' of which an unsettled postwar society was sorely in need. Most of the papers instantly repudiated Clarke's constitutional indiscretions and delightedly pointed out that he was flying in the face of his own ministers' advice.[50]

The premier himself was quick off the mark. The day after the alleged gaffe he sent a stiff letter to the lieutenant-governor. He must have relished composing it for it gave him an opportunity to lecture him on accepted parliamentary practice.

'I think it desirable to ascertain from you,' he told Clarke, 'if the [newspaper] reports are correct, and I do this because they admit of several interpretations, all of which tend to destroy that appearance of unity which, in the interest of stable government, should be maintained between the representative of His Majesty and his constitutional advisers.' Replying the next day, Clarke went out of his way to provide a disclaimer, lamenting that the newspapers had deliberately distorted his remarks. Along with his regrets he offered the assurance that it 'was most certainly not my intention to give expression to my personal views upon any matter in any active public controversy.'[51] He promised that henceforth he would carefully weigh whatever he had to say in public – in effect to tow the line. This response satisfied Drury and, if one may judge from the kind of remarks Drury reserved for Clarke in his memoirs, the premier bore him no ill will. As for Government House itself, it gained a lengthy reprieve. Closing it down proved more easily said than done because of the varied covenants that legally blocked its ready sale.

What was far more important, particularly in view of the problems facing him in the summer of 1920, was the political state of the legislature. After the ILP member Morrison MacBride defected to sit on the opposition benches, the strength of the Farmer-Labour coalition stood at fifty-five (forty-five Farmer, ten ILP). This was a virtual match for the twenty-nine Liberals led by the mercurial Hartley Dewart and the twenty-five-member Conservative rump under the temporary leadership of the far from chastened Howard Ferguson. Although this official tally put Drury on a razor's edge, there were mitigating circumstances. For one thing, as Drury readily appreciated, the other parties were not only at loggerheads but in disarray, particularly the Tories, and anxious to buy time in which to mend their misfortunes at the local level.[52] Moreover, there were some Liberals in the House who did not share Dewart's noisy distaste for the government and could frequently be counted upon to vote for its measures. What one student of the provincial scene had to say some six months later probably held good for the summer of 1920: '[Drury] seems to have no fears for the session – he can rely on about half a dozen anti-Dewart Liberals, the best of them, and also to my surprise two Tories, who will not help Howard Ferguson.'[53] The latter's abrasiveness and impatience with parliamentary niceties alienated not only Drury but clearly some of his own people as well.

Some in the provincial bureaucracy also harboured misgivings about the Conservatives' provisional leader but they may not have come directly to the premier's ears. 'In this vicinity,' wrote A.H.U. Colquhoun, the deputy minister of Education, to J.W. Dafoe, 'we have the Tory crowd whom John A. kept at a distance by cajolery and Whitney by kicking them. They are now in charge of the ship and if they bring her into port then it's time for me to retire from prophecy.'[54] In these circumstances Drury felt reasonably assured, even with the potential for disaster in the divisive Chippawa and radials controversies, that he could steer his government to some of the goals he had set for it. He would have been cheered by the *Canadian Annual Review*'s conclusion that the government was measuring up to its work better than even their own friends had expected; 'better in all cases than their opponents had thought possible.'[55]

Yet in spite of the comforting political and personal factors that aided the survival of his minority government, the opposition had not hesitated to put its foot down on Drury's plans to make certain procedural and electoral changes. In keeping with the anti-party mood that had politicized the UFO, he had urged the abandonment of certain parliamentary rules that he considered unreasonable and that denied backbenchers the opportunity to bring in private members' bills of their own. When opposition members refused to sanction changes to the traditional rules of the parliamentary game and accused him of ignoring his own responsibility as head of government, Drury speedily backed off and shelved his proposals. Nonetheless, those same backbenchers probably enjoyed greater freedom during his administration than at any other time in the province's history.[56] A further proposal, endorsed by Morrison and other UFO leaders, would have provided for fixed elections every four years as a means of guaranteeing that the House would spend the bulk of its time addressing issues of state rather than partisan electioneering. But the opposition again forced Drury to retreat. However much the UFO's success in 1919 had shaken the opposition, the strength of entrenched procedure defied these essays in reform. The discomfort this caused to the premier was allayed to an extent by the warm response his 'purifying' efforts had elicited in certain quarters at home as well as abroad. The reformist National Municipal League in the United States, an organization on the lookout for constitutional and parliamentary innovations, was quick to praise his initiatives.

Reflections on these and other recent events were terminated by reports that the Sutherland Commission was about to announce its findings. Already by the spring of 1921 it had gathered considerable testimony and information, in spite of what some called Hydro's stinginess in delivering data to the commission.[57] And when the necessary information was finally gathered it proved costly, and added considerably to the investigation's price tag. Expenses also caused concern in Sutherland's office. On one occasion he had to upbraid fellow commissioner Amos for untoward hotel expenses, ironic in view of the UFO's vaunted devotion to economy.[58] After that, Drury, on Sutherland's recommendation, brought all commission expenses under the direct control of his own office.

Finally, after months of touring, investigating, and deliberating, the commission submitted its report in August 1921.[59] A pleased Drury would have had a difficult time convincing anyone that he was surprised by its findings. In a nutshell, the commission strongly advised against a provincial pledge providing credit to the municipalities seeking radial construction, particularly the Toronto-Niagara line and the eastern Ontario extension. It did so after examining the fate of similar ventures in the United States which had never proved to be self-sustaining, the critical factor the commission had weighed throughout.

The report unleashed a storm of protest from much of the Toronto press and their urban counterparts elsewhere in the province. On 7 September the *Globe* showed its displeasure in a leader – 'Hydro Radials Must Come' – that announced that no matter what the commission decided, the 'project will be pushed to completion, and if Mr. Drury and his Government will not help they can at least get out of the way ... and cease [their] obstructive tactics.'[60] Such editorial fusillades were followed up by hastily organized meetings of the Hydro Radials Association which predictably scalded the commission and all its works. Pro-Hydro circles, represented by George Halcrow, were pleased to learn that Bancroft, the ILP man on the commission, had dissented and submitted his own minority report backing the radials. Into the premier's hands came as well an ornately produced counter-report from Beck whose contents can easily be imagined.[61]

To neutralize Beck's reaction and give reassurance to what the Sutherland Commission had done, Drury took several opportunities over the next few weeks to present the government's side of the case. Indeed, he had anticipated it in a wide-ranging address at Glencoe on 24 August. 'This Government is not to be stampeded into any position, rest assured of that. We ... are not going to be forced into action which would involve the Province in the guarantee of millions – $45 to $50,000,000 – that is only a beginning.' Then he told his audience how he had deferred action in June 1920 on a request from Hydro, on four days' notice, for a public guarantee of radial bonds. 'So we held it up,' he reminded his audience, 'and there was a row. There have been a lot of rows since we came into power but ... nothing comes of it.' Then, after reviewing the events that led up to the Sutherland Commission's appointment and summarizing its recommendations, he delivered a characteristically defiant message:

In view of the evidence, in view of the changed circumstances, in view of the Commission's findings, in view of the great obligations of the country to hydro electric development in a score of places, the government must stand firm and refuse to guarantee any bonds for further hydro radial enterprises. In doing so we may have to face popular clamor. That will make no difference. I have faced popular clamor and ... I am not so much in love with political life that in order to save my political life I would do that which might prove to be a very serious handicap to the province for years to come. My stock in the province of Ontario is greater than my stock in merely continuing the political life of a party. My stock in the province is the stock of a hundred years of descent in this province, and of children whom I hope will carry on in the same old place which I occupy and which my grandfather occupied. And I certainly am not going to mortgage the future of this province as the political parties in the past have mortgaged the future in order to gain applause or political advantage. So that is final and there is no good of any further discussion about it.[62]

He was wrong; it was, of course, neither final nor closed to debate. The critics saw to that. Drury was obliged to use September fair meetings – the timing was heaven-sent – to argue the case against the radials. At the end of the month he was telling a large crowd of attentive fairgoers at Caledonia that the Farmers' government was anxious to assign vital public funds to ventures worthier than the dubious radial. He ridiculed the *Globe* and likened its treatment of the radial question to the 'little boy who was asked by his teacher to give a description of a crawfish.'

The boy described it as a red fish which swims backwards. The teacher replied: 'That is a very fine description except for three things. In the first place it is not a fish, in the second place it is not red, and in the third place it does not swim backwards.[63]

Some of his speaking time was taken up with dismissing Beck's charge that by refusing to pledge the credit of the municipalities Drury was repudiating a public agreement made by the Hearst government. And on the subject of funding, Hydro and supporting newspapers were quick to complain about the half-million dollars (Drury's figure was $469,754) the Sutherland Commission had spent on its lengthy investigation. Drury's standard retort was that had Hydro been more forthcoming with information less time and expense would have had to be devoted to research and interviews. Besides, he argued, the inquiry, whatever its cost, had paid for itself a hundred-fold by choking off an inflated expenditure that would have jeopardized the province's credit.

This trump card the premier never wearied of slamming down on the radials' table, particularly when he could address a gathering such as the Canadian Club. This businessman's forum was shrewdly told in November 1921 that it would have been eminently bad business to have acted otherwise than he did. He also stressed the importance of his pausing to evaluate the radials program before permitting his government to be stampeded into sanctioning it. In words that may have disarmed his audience and provided some chuckles, he allowed that 'slow people from the countryside' needed time to consider major undertakings and reminded his audience that 'most of the cabinet members ... are also more or less bucolic.'[64]

Yet others who may have sympthized with the premier's radials policy deplored his sidestepping resort to a commission. While Dewart of the Liberals ridiculed Drury's 'eternal delegation of power to Commissions,' the newspapers took up the cry of irresponsible government.[65] But Drury thought that he had an answer for that one too:

Frankly, the Government didn't feel itself capable of skilled investigation. We don't hold our abilities to be nothing, but we do hold that a matter of this sort, a highly technical matter, was one that required consideration by good men capable of weighing evidence, capable of listening to the evidence and knowing what to believe and what not to believe.

He then chided his journalistic foes for their refusal at the turn of the century to question the 'wild railway schemes,' about which they were now belatedly complaining, just as they were currently refusing to challenge Hydro. The premier ridiculed 'cock eyed' optimism about the radials' future: 'I have no faith in the sort of optimism that was evidenced by the man who fell from the twelfth story of a building and on passing the fifth story on the way down ... called out to a man ... at [a] window, "John, I'm all right so far".'[66]

Of the major media, only the *Sun*, the *Star*, and the *Canadian Forum* backed the commission's recommendations with any show of conviction. All the same, the support received from the small town press – the *Stratford Beacon-Herald*, the *Manitoulin Expositor*, the *Collingwood News*, the *Orillia Packet*, and the *Pembroke Standard*, among others – was warmly welcomed in those dark hours. But one rural journal, Peterborough's *Farm and Dairy*, paid the price for this support. When it received no lucrative Hydro advertisement that fall, publisher H.B. Cowan wrote Carmichael that 'naturally, this led us to wonder if we have been overlooked by Hon. Mr. Beck ... because of our stand ... on the radials.'[67] The fight was getting rough.

Drury took the gloves off too following the passage of legislation that repealed the Hydro Radial Act of 1914. The new act, passed over Conservative opposition but with Liberal support, made no provision for bonds being issued by Hydro and offered no guarantee by the province of any bonds or debentures. One notable exception was made: the vital Niagara and Toronto radial was temporarily re-prieved because of the some four million dollars already ploughed into it. Even so, the municipalities which had long clamoured for the line would have to reaffirm their decision in the forthcoming municipal elections, set for December 1921.

To ensure that those elections went his way Beck was prepared to use Hydro funds. To combat this initiative Drury took the dramatic step of tinkering with the commission's membership. He had no intention or desire to oust Beck from the chairmanship in spite of those who thought it high time for the Hydro Knight to go. 'My own opinion is,' Drury kept repeating, 'that it would be a misfortune to place ... Beck in the position where he could claim a martyr's Crown.'[68] Apparently when Beck challenged the premier on the issue of dismissal, the latter reacted by saying: 'I do not intend to give you any reasonable excuse for quitting.'[69]

Although Drury would leave Beck in place, he decided to arrange the removal of the Hearst holdover, I.B. Lucas, and replace him with an ally, who in concert with Carmichael might be able to hold the chairman in check. Lucas had already worn out his welcome anyway, having publicly criticized the government's radials policy. But the Lucas replacement, Frederick Miller, a Toronto engineer and contractor, proved troublesome. Though close to Carmichael and warmly recommended by Doherty, Miller turned out to be on friendly terms with the *Telegram*'s John Robinson. Before long a worried Carmichael advised Drury that Miller was wavering on the question, and the new appointment was promptly summoned to the premier's office. 'I ... reminded him of his promise [to back the government],' Drury recalled in *Farmer Premier*,

and told him that the time had come when I expected him to fulfil it. He did not reply for some time, and simply sat in that big leather chair with his head bowed. At last ... as he looked up his face was like death. 'Mr. Premier,' he said, 'I'm ashamed to say it, but I can't do it. You don't know this man.' Then he told me. In his student days he had been guilty of some indiscretion, a matter long ago forgotten, and he was now a happily married man. But the thing had been dug up and was being held over his head as a threat. I told him that under these circumstances I would not ask him to keep his promise, I would deal with the matter myself.[70]

The upshot was that Drury tackled Beck directly and warned him about the impropriety of spending Hydro money on the radials campaign, though whether or not the chairman was confronted with the Miller story is not revealed. The fight was getting rougher. Beck purportedly gave the press a different account of their conversation but, even so, the premier satisfied himself that no more Hydro funds would be deployed in this way.

Yet notwithstanding the Sutherland Commission's arguments and the government's exertions, the municipal elections of 1921 went solidly against the campaign to stop the radials. Worse was to follow, or so it seemed. It involved what Drury and others referred to as the 'waterfront grab' whereby a six-track right of way along the Toronto waterfront would be awarded by the city to Beck as part of his radial package. The plan also provided for a Hydro-operated subway on Bay Street, an alternative to a Sutherland recommendation that a municipally controlled radial system be set up in Toronto independent of any Hydro arrangement. The latter scheme, as Beck and Drury were well aware, would deprive Hydro municipalities of any kind of control over Toronto's radial entrances by placing them under the Toronto Transit Commission, a body opposed to Beck's encroachment on its own turf. The Hydro chairman charged that if the TTC was allowed to have its way violence would be done to previous government undertakings.

Whatever the merits of Beck's arguments, the plain and disagreeable fact for Drury was that the chairman enjoyed much support in Toronto's city council, where the issue would have to be decided. Much to Drury's chagrin, Beck seemed to enjoy a considerable edge over his adversaries from the TTC and the other organizations that had a stake in the 'grab' – the Toronto Harbour Board and the Canadian National Exhibition. Nevertheless, in spite of the support he received from the *Globe*, the *Telegram*, and Mayor C.A. Maguire, a Hydro addict, Beck did not win easily. The debate in council lasted a week and was not wound up until 6 September 1922. In the course of it, a more modest package endorsed in 1916 by civic ratepayers and calling for a four-track system under the joint control of Hydro, the TTC, and the Harbour Board, was resurrected only to be reinterred by an unsympathetic Beck. Alderman W.R. Plewman, who a quarter-century later would write *Adam Beck and the Ontario Hydro,* was there that day and tried to act as a conciliator. He told Beck that it would do nothing for Hydro's prestige to 'impose on Toronto a war to the death between public bodies and leading citizens, all of whom are equally loyal to the community.'[71] The Hydro chairman disregarded Plewman's advice and by refusing to accept the compromise plan forced a vote in council. Though not even close, at least five of the assembled twenty-two councillors put thumbs down on Beck's proposal.

If Beck had hoped that a council decision would be final he was in for a shock. In an office conversation followed up by a letter, Drury spelled out the next move to the Hydro chairman. The opposition of 'three public service corporations' and a substantial minority of city council together with the 'very important differences between the [new] Radial Entrance Scheme ... and that [of] 1916' convinced the premier that before his government could validate the agreement it would have to be approved by Toronto's ratepayers. The next day, 12 September, Drury added the afterthought that if there was opposition in Toronto to the entrance proposal, that fact should be made public along with the government's critical attitude.[72] In his reply, composed about a week later, Beck denied that he had made any request for Queen's Park validation when he had visited Drury. Moreover, he bluntly told the premier that since the city, not Hydro, should seek such an object he was forwarding the letter to the mayor.

Drury soon discovered how the mayor grasped what he had in mind. 'Your refusal,' Maguire wrote the premier, 'to give legislation validating this radial ... entrance agreement because of ... differences of opinion ... and opposition of certain public bodies, may have the effect of ... destroying the whole main radial scheme.'[73] Drury must have chuckled over that passage because that was the whole object of the exercise. If the entrance plan was thwarted, the rest of the radials program would collapse like a house of cards. In the end Drury had his way. After some hesitation Beck and Maguire agreed to have the proposal submitted to the ratepayers on the day scheduled for the municipal elections, 1 January 1923.

Although Drury claimed that no member of the government took part in the election campaign, there was considerable action behind the scenes. So that

Maguire would not go unchallenged in his bid for re-election Drury worked out a stratagem whereby a former mayor, R.J. Fleming, who had acted for the Harbour Board, would run against the incumbent.[74] In spite of his reluctance to play the sacrificial lamb, Fleming agreed and, though beaten by Maguire, his candidacy helped to illuminate the radial issue for those voters kept in the dark by Beck and Maguire. If Drury had stopped to think about it, his sense of the ironic would have been tickled. Here he was dickering with one set of urban and professional interests, with whom he was supposed to have little rapport, at the expense of another. The farmer as big city broker, he may have mused, particularly if he recalled a letter he had received in the summer of 1922. 'For some time,' a member of the Toronto community wrote, 'I have felt there was not sufficient courtesy paid by the City to yourself ... and it seemed to me ... a good thing if we met oftener at public functions.'[75]

When the electors of Toronto finally went to the polls, they delivered up a verdict that warmed the hearts of Drury and Sutherland. Plewman's 'war to the death' culminated in a decisive rejection of Beck's proposal, by 28,325 votes to 23,129. Just three days after the vote a memorandum came to Drury's office from the public works department. It was probably prepared by Biggs, one of the clear beneficiaries of the balloting. After commenting on the 'great relief [afforded] Ontario financing,' the memo expressed the hope that the ground would be swept entirely 'from the feet of Sir Adam Beck' and that he would be kept 'on the outside, so far as the operation of radials is concerned.'[76] According to one observer, there was another potential beneficiary of Beck's setback. The Canadian Pacific interests, already concerned about the expansion of the Canadian National Railways across Canada, had allegedly been lining up newspapers and aldermen for years to combat the radials.[77] Drury's announcement after the municipal elections, however, gave the Canadian Pacific little comfort. The government's intention was to have Hydro supply the power when and if it was required 'for the electrification of such National lines as it would seem to be for the general advantage to be electrified.'[78] The promotion of the public system was clearly going to take precedence in the premier's office.

In the aftermath of victory Drury weighed the varied factors that helped to produce the anti-radial turnout in Toronto. He clearly thought his own activities behind the scenes and the work of the Sutherland Commission carried great weight. All the same, Beck's cocksureness may have alienated some Toronto voters already put off by the way certain unique civic institutions – the CNE and the TTC in particular – were being sidetracked by the Hydro juggernaut. Again, in the chilling economic climate of the early 1920s there were citizens who felt that Beck's projected expenditures on radials were simply too much to swallow. However, if he had not kept the issue squarely before the public, Drury concluded, Beck might have carried the day. At any rate, the financial consequences of defeat, nearly every observer now concedes, would have been hazardous to the province's financial health. W.R. Plewman, whose admiration for Beck can hardly be questioned, had this to say some twenty-five years after the event:

The only chance of making a veto effective and other than politically disastrous to those who imposed it, was to place before the public all the information about the tragic experiences of radial railways in the United States and the effect on radial revenues of good roads, motor buses and motor trucks. Whatever errors may have been committed by Premier Drury in dealing with the radial question, his course required the exercise of more courage and sagacity than are usually found in public men. The average businessman today [1947] might give his verdict that the vast sum spent upon the radial inquiry yielded a handsome dividend.[79]

Yet all that Drury could recall, as he told Mackenzie King some years later, was that he earned only abuse for having undertaken to save Ontario from economic disaster and the CN from expensive competition.[80]

Nonetheless, Drury's solicitude for the provincial treasury had been acclaimed in certain quarters. The *Hamilton Herald,* which had consistently tried to give the Drury government a chance, anticipated Plewman's later assessment. It hailed the premier as the 'first responsible man in public life in this province who has dared to set his will against that of the popular and autocratic Sir Adam Beck and let him know where he gets off at.'[81] Drury soon got wind of Beck's reaction to what had happened. C.B. Sissons, who had kept track of the protracted radials debate, recounted the following story, which doubtless was passed on to the premier:

I talked to Sir Adam only once. That was when Dean DeLury and I called at his office to ask him to speak at [our] Open Forum. He did not answer us at once, but without the slightest pretext embarked on a regular tirade against Drury. Only at length when he had calmed down did he vouchsafe a negative answer ... We could hardly believe our ears, and concluded that his imperious mind had been pretty well shattered along with his vaulting ambitions.[82]

Even if Beck's mind had not been shattered, certainly his physical health had. Throughout much of the controversy he had been ailing and showing all of his sixty-six years. He was, after all, a veritable greybeard compared to the hale and hearty premier of forty-four years, a fact seldom alluded to in the literature of the day. For his part, Drury did allow, from the safe distance of memoir-writing, that while he had had his battles with Beck, he had always admired his enormous energy and less arrogant side when he had chosen to display it.[83]

In the weeks that followed Toronto's electoral decision Drury and his cabinet conducted mopping-up operations. These involved the passage of legislation terminating the earlier agreements between Hydro and the municipalities regarding the now doomed Toronto and Niagara line. Henceforth any undertakings entered into were subject to the understanding that no provincial aid would fund them. The only radial line that the government was prepared to underwrite was the short Toronto and Oakville venture which, like intercity systems in heavily populated sections of the United States, showed the ability to sustain itself, the condition on which the Sutherland Commission had put special stress.

By this time Drury was receiving interim reports from the Gregory Commission, struck on the eve of the radials showdown and following the completion of the first phase of the costly Chippawa Development. The launching of that investigation – its final report was issued after Drury was voted out of office – and the resolution of the radials question served notice that the government, for all the battering it had taken, intended to govern. And when the financial well-being of the province was threatened, that government would do so, to quote Drury's parting shot at Glencoe, 'in the best interests of the people of ... Ontario who want no showy clap trap policies ... that would have left it to our successors to bear any burden that might accrue.'[84]

Drury's determination and fiscal conservatism, as reflected in the radials battle, and his plea for a return to responsible government during the course of the Chippawa Development, commended him in a number of political and business circles that had hitherto kept their distance. Among the other matters Drury turned to after the confrontation with Beck was the cultivation of ties with Ottawa and the entertainment of ambitions that ranged beyond the political stage of Queen's Park.

10

Political Hopes and Fears

Drury's joust with the Hydro Knight made him something of a national political figure. The admittedly friendly *Canadian Forum* under C.B. Sisson's influence was even prepared to assess Drury as a possible federal leader.[1] It reminded its readers that Drury's work for the Canadian Council of Agriculture and the UFO had clearly established his solid standing with the Farmers. What was even more important from the *Forum*'s point of view was that the premier's 'resolute position on Hydro-radials has given him the confidence that he has administrative ability to match his unusual powers in public debate.'[2] Indeed, some members of the business community were impressed by how Drury's persistent homework had deflated Beck's long-standing boast that Hydro, a public project, was the quintessence of private enterprise. The revelations of waste, faulty estimates, and costly over-runs would never have been permitted in conventional business operations, or so these defenders of the gospel of free enterprise would have liked to think.[3] Drury's growing acceptance in such circles was brought to the attention of the self-important J.W. Dafoe. Ever anxious to be informed of political trends, the western pundit was told that Drury had 'pleased greatly a Board of Trade audience [in Ottawa] ... most of [whom] would not naturally be sympathetic to him.'[4]

The *Forum* editorial went on to observe that Drury had some standing in Quebec because of his reputation for racial and religious tolerance, even if it had not been translated into scrapping the notorious Regulation 17. The journal then envisaged the role that Drury might play as the country's prime minister. 'His type of mind,' it observed, 'is essentially antithetic to that of Mr. Meighen [the Conservative incumbent], and the Parliament of Canada would regain some of its prestige lost during recent years were two such able exponents of opposing schools of thought to shape Canadian policy as first minister and chief critic.'[5] The Toronto *Star*, an unflagging Drury booster, also commended his talents, claiming that he possessed 'to a rare degree the combination of qualities requisite to success in the realm of politics. [His] mind goes unerringly and with almost uncanny quickness to the heart of a problem.'

If Mackenzie King, the recently named Liberal leader, had happened to peruse these dazzling kudos he would not have welcomed the prospect that voters might elevate someone other than himself to Meighen's high office. Yet he would not take lightly Drury's qualifications for a federal role. Among other things, King was impressed by the confidence that business and financial interests were now reposing in the UFO leader.[6] Drury's relationship with King had begun months before the critical general election that enlivened the year's end. Early in 1921, while the premier was on a business trip to Ottawa, he received a call from King and a meeting was arranged for that night. In the absence of his own account of what happened, King's must be recruited. 'We talked over the position of parties,' King wrote in his diary for 13 January. 'He was very frank and open, asked me what my view was & I told him I would like to see open coalition before an election of farmers and Liberals, that I believed we would sweep the country, wipe out [Meighen's] ... reactionary government and get Liberal measures assured.' The specific group that King had in mind was the recently organized Progressive Party. Like the UFO, the new party, which drew its strength mainly from the prairie west, had sprung in 1920 from the anti-partyism and wartime discontent that had produced the Farmers' platform. Transformed into the New National Policy, the platform sought to re-order the country's priorities and undo the legacy of Macdonald's tariff program. Under the leadership of T.A. Crerar, who had long since washed his hands of the Union government, it laid plans to challenge Meighen in the forthcoming general election.

Drury appeared to favour King's plan but made it plain that such an alignment should not be engineered at the expense of the Progressives. 'The farmer knew what he wanted,' King was told, 'the movement had fervour and conviction back of it, and it would not do to destroy its idealism.'[7] Drury had good reason to underscore the aims and the spirit of the movement. More than once over the past year he had been forcibly reminded that his views on Broadening Out had not been palatable to many in the Ontario wing of the farm movement. However much he wanted to rally other progressive forces to his 'people's party,' he knew that his standing hinged on the rural support that alone gave him credibility in the eyes of the Mackenzie Kings. Furthermore, that rural backing and its idealism might be jeopardized by any move that threatened to align the farm movement with one of the flawed old-line parties. Drury soberly reminded himself that just a month before, at the annual UFO convention, a proposal to create a People's Progressive Party out of the UFO's political arm had been summarily shelved.[8] Not only this, Morrison had even hoped to keep the premier from attending the gathering, though talked out of it by a disturbed Crerar who feared the political consequences of such a rebuff.[9]

In the end Drury was invited not only to the plenary session but also to a private conference beforehand where he was allowed to present his case for Broadening Out to the assembled UFO directors. At the same time he took pains to urge that all complaints about his political stewardship be brought to his personal attention. While his views on a people's party gained no ground at this meeting and were left in abeyance at the convention, his conciliatory approach was applauded as an act of good faith. Clearly the premier's presence and candour went down well with most of the directors, if one can judge from H.B. Cowan's assessment. He advised G.F. Chipman of the *Grain Growers' Guide* that Drury made a good impression, which he trusted would undo some of the harm done by a Broadening Out speech the premier had made at Chatham some weeks earlier.[10] But the points that Drury scored at the pre-convention meeting and the standing ovation given him at the plenary session were dampened by the realization that his major political objective was still as far off as ever.[11] Moreover, it was equally obvious that Morrison, whose influence at central office was often decisive, was still implacably opposed to anything more than a 'class' or 'occupational' group in the legislature.

Indeed, Morrison's campaign against Broadening Out had heated up considerably after Drury sounded its clarion call in his Halton nomination speech early in 1920. At the secretary's urging, a secret meeting was called by UFO county directors with Farmer MLAS and the whole cabinet. The directors demanded that henceforth their advice be courted, even on such procedural matters as the appointment of a parliamentary whip. They also insisted that retrenchment take precedence when legislation was drafted, and that the government generally harken to what their organized rural constituency perceived the function of that government to be. In addition, they unanimously and pointedly endorsed the device of the recall for the benefit of the assembled parliamentarians.[12] Few in attendance were left in any doubt that the extra-legislative group wished not merely to monitor but to regulate the government. They looked upon the Farmer legislators not as representatives in the traditional parliamentary sense but as delegates of their constituents, in this case the UFO clubs and organizations.

All of this posed a problem for Drury and his fellow MLAS. To what degree must they defer to a body outside the legislature that insisted that government's function was not to govern as it saw fit, in the light of its own principles and the circumstances of the moment, but to serve primarily as a conduit between that body and the legislative process?[13] Drury, a creature of parliamentary orthodoxy, saw in this arrangement a potentially dangerous concentration of influence in the hands of one social and economic group. Though democratic in one sense – making government responsive to grass roots aspirations – was it any better morally than the means by which the supposedly protected interests had previously manipulated the old-line party politician? The author of Broadening Out, as eager as ever to form a liaison with progressive elements in other quarters, not to mention being his own man, did not look kindly on the prospect of his serving as a mere mouthpiece of the organized farm movement. As Drury repeatedly pointed out, the 'political organization born of the UFO,' while it must never ignore its agrarian roots, must also seek to 'live its own life distinct from that of the parent.'[14]

In the summer of 1920, goaded by the *Globe*, which looked askance at what the UFO government was promoting, Morrison took off the gloves and berated not only Drury but the ridiculing press.[15] They and the Liberals were accused of trying to hatch a takeover of the Farmers' contingent in the legislature. Morrison's outbursts were fuelled as well by the government's hotly contested superannuation bill, designed for the first time to provide adequate provision for those retiring from the provincial public service. Some one hundred government employees, many of them holdovers from the era of Confederation, could not, it was claimed, afford the luxury of retirement.[16] To combat what he called a general feeling of insecurity in the public service, Drury brought forward a morale-bracing palliative. Apart from a humanitarian concern, Drury doubtless felt that a more contented civil service, freed from the spectre of want in old age, would provide better service to his fledgling government, which needed all the bureaucratic guidance it could get.

He discovered soon enough that considerations of this sort cut little ice in Morrison's office. In the spring of 1920 the secretary sent an indignant letter to all UFO clubs and constituency organizations, condemning the legislation, a move the *Globe* called an unwarranted interference with the duties of the legislature. An undeterred Morrison, after reminding his correspondents that 'Our motto says: "Equal Rights for all, special privileges to none",' explained how the superannuation measure violated the principle. Superannuation and retirement allowances he described as class privileges. 'Is it wisdom,' he asked rhetorically, 'for a permanent class distinction to be created in this country, especially by a UFO Government claiming to be the embodiment [*sic*] of democracy ... ? Would farmers enjoying ... salaries [of the order of $1,800 to $2,300] until they are 65 ... living as they do, require public support by the people?' Having considered principle, Morrison then denounced the legislation as much too expensive for the taxpayer.[17]

Several farmers' clubs responded. One agreed that the bill would unfairly tax one class to 'provide for the old age of another.' But at least it had the good sense to add – in this case price was less of an object – that if the 'civil servants do not get enough salary to provide for old age the remedy is to pay them enough.' Another club passed a resolution heartily opposing the bill and giving the local MLA 'authority to move a 6-months hoist for [it].'[18] When Drury subsequently submitted the proposal to caucus that MLA, Leslie Oke, was one of the seven Farmers who stood out against it. Although the measure survived the effort to 'delay' it – it came into force in mid-June 1920 – Morrison and other disaffected executive members and vocal members of the rank and file continued to grumble audibly in the months ahead.

The legislation led to a bitter confrontation between the premier and the UFO president, R.W.E. Burnaby, who took Drury on publicly at a farm picnic where they shared the platform. Then, according to Morrison, during their automobile ride back to Toronto Burnaby kept up the heated argument.[19] It was left to Gordon Waldron, who seldom missed an opportunity to ridicule the man who had denied him a cabinet appointment, to put the situation in some perspective. He maintained that it went far beyond the superannuation issue. 'Drury, you will remember,' Waldron wrote Crerar, 'took the stand at once after his selection [as leader], that he was appointed, I might say, without irreverence, by God to do what he thought was right without any regard to anybody or to consequence. He took no counsel of the farmers as to his Cabinet – wanted to be leader of a new party.' Then he concluded on a bloodthirsty note that probably put off the western farm leader: 'Drury should be destroyed if he wishes to battle farmer friends.'[20] The defeat suffered by Morrison and the UFO executive on the su-perannuation question convinced them of the need to put greater pressure on the government and force it to honour the mandate the farm movement had assigned it. Obviously the reactions of individual clubs lacked the kind of punch to overawe the cabinet.

By the end of the year, after the UFO convention had put Broadening Out in its place, some observers had made up their minds that Drury's main trouble was not so much with foes in the legislature as with Morrison and the clique in the UFO office. Drury may even have got wind of the story that the Canadian Manufacturers' Association was subsidizing a defector in Morrison's group to 'spread discord in agrarian ranks.'[21] Plainly, the premier's task amounted to convincing the UFO membership that an enlightened program of reaching out to sympathetic and like-minded groups would provide the farmer with reliable allies in the struggle against those forces that had long sacrificed the common good to selfish interests. The reverse of the coin was equally important: to convince people outside rural ranks that a progressive movement in Ontario was the answer to their problem in an age of rapid change and much confusion.

For Drury, this approach was infinitely preferable to Morrison's alternative – group government. Early on Drury freely admitted that that formula had left him bewildered. But thanks to a public debate arranged by Sissons at Victoria College, he tackled Morrison on the subject and in the process learned about it the hard way.[22] Drury's perception of it was recorded bluntly in his memoirs:

It was based on the theory that the citizen's chief interest was his occupation, and that class consciousness was the citizen's highest virtue. The seats in Parliament were to be apportioned to the various occupations according to their numbers, and occupational constituencies rather than geographical ones were to be created. The Executive (the Cabinet) were to be elected individually by Parliament and were to be individually responsible to Parliament. There would be no such thing as Cabinet solidarity. Caucuses would be abolished, and there would be no government policy and no opposition.[23]

As one committed to a laundered party system and the principle of cabinet government, Drury had little patience with the scheme backed by Morrison and W.C. Good. The premier later recollected that 'we would have been laughed out of court ... if we had tried to introduce [it].' Mackenzie King heartily agreed. So did Drury's opposite number in Saskatchewan. 'The more I see of the development of this class consciousness and group government idea,' Charles Dunning wrote, 'the more I am convinced that, – despite the faults inherent in the old two-party system, – it still promises the best results so far as sound and stable government is concerned.'[24]

But Drury realized that the concept may not have originated with Morrison or Good at all; it had probably been borrowed from Henry Wise Wood, the one-time Missouri populist who had taken Alberta by storm and organized what contemporaries called a radical and revolutionary movement – group government or the 'Alberta scheme.' It aimed at nothing less than depriving the 'plutocratic interests' of the control they allegedly enjoyed over supine political parties.[25] What the UFO secretary had picked up on was Wood's insistence that 'class organization was the only way the farmers could ensure democratic control of their own movement [but if] they widened their base to include other groups they would weaken its democratic character.'[26] Armed with this kind of ammunition, Morrison had stepped up his campaign against Broadening Out, which Drury with equal fervour gave no sign of abandoning. Indeed, the premier urged King in his January conversation to back farmers in some by-elections. '[Drury] hopes,' King wrote in his diary, 'to make a Progressive Party [out of] ... those who would leave old parties ... and go to the Province on that.'

The Liberal leader then added a sentence that speaks volumes for Drury's concern about the state of his Ontario following and Morrison's influence: 'He spoke of not plucking the plums before they are ripe.' This was in response to King's talk of a possible pre-election coalition between Progressives and Liberals on the federal stage, an arrangement that Drury feared might have an adverse effect on the farm movement's momentum. The premier then unburdened some home truths on King, pointing out that Liberalism 'had been hurt by the Tories in the Liberal ranks [notably Lomer Gouin]' who had set their faces against social reform and tariff reduction. The January interview appeared to come to an end with Drury suggesting nothing much more in the way of federal collaboration than an avoidance of three-cornered fights at election time. In the meantime, he advised King to 'let matters shape themselves.'[27] And one that did proved gratifying to the premier. Within a week of his cautious interview with

King he received from the Farmer caucus a unanimous endorsement of his leadership and the stand that he had taken on group government, if not on Broadening Out. The endorsement came soothingly on the heels of Morrison's denunciation of that stratagem in a speech in Wilton Grove, one that had the full backing of the UFO executive.[28]

Drury's comparatively low-keyed response to King betrayed his understandable preoccupation with the provincial scene and his ongoing confrontation with Sir Adam Beck, not to mention the other concerns of his administration. Again, he may have felt that in spite of the publicity that had attended King's assumption of the Liberal leadership two years before, he was still a totally untried federal leader. True, King had heralded his advent with a testament of sorts – his book *Industry and Humanity* – which purported to offer a blueprint for resolving the pressing social and economic problems of that generation, but there is nothing to indicate that Drury ever examined the work. Perhaps at this stage the premier merely regarded King as one of many hopeful politicians seeking support on the national stage and saw little point in attaching all that much importance to what he had to say. Certainly the *Canadian Forum* (and Sissons) had seen it that way. In these quarters King's chances were not rated highly on the eve of the election of 1921. Yet to be singled out and discreetly courted by the leader, however newly installed, of a national party and one, moreover, who appeared to be on the side of the Progressive angels, must have been a mildly heady experience for the premier. And one burning question probably remained with him for the rest of the year. Should King ever succeed in translating his federal hopes into reality, might he call upon Drury's services?

Certainly, the premier's progress was carefully monitored in Ottawa. King told his diary four days after their meeting that he had read a *Globe* article on the growing fight between Drury and Morrison, one that he hoped would 'help his party and ours coming together.'[29] The very next day Drury was at it again, calling in a speech for the withdrawal of the UFO from the political arena and the nurturing of its legislative child into a broadened party. The *Farmers' Sun*, which had solidly backed Drury during the radials battle, nonetheless dutifully aired the views of the UFO executive. Like them, the paper resented the premier's 'flattening out' policy and alleged spurning of the farm movement, though from time to time it did allow him space to present his opinions.[30]

Years later, Drury made a revealing remark to Good when the latter's memoirs were published. 'It appeared to me,' Drury told his friend, 'that you did not know all the circumstances with which I had to deal in the period 1919–1924, *as I did not know much of what went on in the UFO in the same period.*[31] It was almost as if Drury had wanted to distance himself from the organization that had spawned his political following and to draw a sharp dividing line between the UFO – principally its personification, the inflexible Morrison – and its political expression. It was at about this time that M.H. Staples, the UFO's educational secretary, had called on the premier for help with a book he was preparing on the history of the organization. For one reason or another, Drury seemed less than enthusiastic. At that moment the challenge of government might have been seen as more pressing than the 'challenge of agriculture,' the title Staples subsequently gave his work. On the other hand, Drury's slowness to co-operate may have stemmed from his growing impatience with Morrison and others in the UFO executive. Why take time out, he may have asked himself, to reconstruct the origins of an organization which was then causing him grief? But Staples would have the last word. 'Finally, one day, I became so insistent in his office,' he recalled for Good's benefit, 'that [Drury] summoned his stenographer and as he paced up and down dictated the chapter just as you find it in the book.'[32]

At this juncture, Drury probably did not wish to arouse the hostility of any more leading members of the UFO, least of all its respected educational secretary. Even so, as Sissons pointed out in his *Forum* review of Staples's history, Drury seized the chance to show off the 'sprightliness of his wit' and to shove some literary barbs into Morrison. For example, on the secretary's alleged stealing of farmers' clubs the premier remarked parenthetically that 'this was Brother Morrison's first venture in Bolshevism.'[33]

The demarcation line that Drury sought to draw between the UFO and his government was, ironically, also welcomed by officials of the organization. Thus President Burnaby told readers of the *Canadian Baptist* early in 1920 that

the U.F.O. and its aims and objects are not understood. In the opinion of some, the U.F.O. is looked upon as a political organization. To these I wish to say most emphatically it is not. Any political activity on the part of U.F.O. members is the result or effect of our organization rather than one of its aims. Its whole object is to further the interests of farmers in all branches of agriculture.[34]

In any case, by the early weeks of 1921 it was clear that Morrison was determined to apply a brake to a government that seemed to be losing touch with its principal constituents. This reaction committed Drury even more vociferously to his own cause, as King was in the process of discovering. Not even the time-consuming battle over the radials could crowd out Drury's emphasis on the need for a broadened party. As the spring approached he could sustain this commitment in the comforting knowledge that, however much central office and its friends might threaten to rock the boat, he had little to fear so far as the legislature was concerned. The *Globe* agreed. 'Supporters of the government,' it editorialized in March, 'are reported to be so confident of its popularity that they are disposed to meet criticism with defiance and to welcome any test of strength in the House or the country.' Drury's personal popularity also seemed to be at an all-time high. The *Globe* then went on to underscore another asset for the government: the factiousness of its critics in the legislature.

One of them, Howard Ferguson, had not yet come into his own as the most biting critic of the government front benches. But Drury knew that he was gearing up for that kind of political assault and battery. And it would be undertaken in part to help federal Conservatives undermine Progressive strength in the province before the impending general election came along. Soon committed Ontario Progressives such as W.C. Good were receiving as much critical attention as Crerar and his prairie colleagues. Although some of the Progressives' less thoughtful critics feared their supposed social radicalism, Drury would have agreed with a later historian's judgment that they were radicals in tactics only. They wanted a sweeping adjustment of national policies 'for a conservative purpose' – in other words, a lower tariff, reciprocity, and measures to safeguard the grain growers' interests.[35] A relieved John W. Dafoe, the pundit who ran the *Manitoba Free Press*, welcomed Drury's Broadening Out program as proof that the Progressive movement need not be a class or even sectional one, against which he always pontificated. Dafoe kept close tabs on Drury's activities for the edification of his prairie readership.

So did Morrison. Convinced, as Wood was, that the Progressives should preserve their class consciousness, he was disturbed by news that reached him in the early summer of 1921. A.G. Farrow, the local UFO director in Halton and a member of the central executive, had been instrumental in organizing the so-called Halton People's Party in an obvious attempt to apply the premier's formula to his own riding. The move, which an aggrieved Morrison was forced to accept as a fait accompli, was made primarily to furnish a launching pad for the local Progressive candidate in the forthcoming federal general election.

The date of the election – 6 December – was announced in early September. Using the recent provincial voting as a guide, observers prophesied the election of a minority government on whose complexion, however, few of them were prepared to wager. Shortly before the news was made public Drury sent a cable to Crerar requesting a meeting with the prairie Progressive leader. Whether Drury wished to discuss overall strategy or to seek advice on his own populist endeavours cannot be determined. At any rate, Crerar wrote back: 'I do not know what change the announcement [of the election date] will make in your plans' and went on to 'welcome most heartily your appearance with me at public meetings.'[36]

That same week Drury was treated to a contretemps between his minister of education and Arthur Meighen, one that foreshadowed the kind of bitter rhetoric that would punctuate the campaign. The Toronto *Star* of 5 September carried the story of an interview in which R.H. Grant was supposed to have said that Meighen's 'previous reference to farmers being Reds and Bolshevists strengthened our party a lot.'[37] Ever on the alert for the ill-advised generalization, the prime minister was quick to challenge Grant's statement. Grant was equal to the occasion. A few days later he assured Meighen that the reporter had misrepresented an overheard conversation, and that it had in fact been Sir George Foster who had uttered the unfortunate words, or something like them, about a year before. All the same, Grant warned the Conservative leader not to be 'too caustic in your remarks' because Foster was, after all, a member of his cabinet. However, the minister ended his letter by saying that he was pleased that Meighen resented having 'any such meaning attributed to words of yours as that the "farmers of this country are Reds or Bolshevists".' Grant added: 'As one who, I understand, has sprung from farm surroundings you know how foreign such sentiments are to that class.'

But Meighen would not let the matter rest. He proceeded to state explicitly what he had actually said on the subject. 'I asserted,' he told Grant, 'that though no people in the country were further from being Bolshevists than the farmers, still their party had gathered ... men of extreme views and seditious principles.' 'The words since,' he added ominously, 'have been vindicated by events in Alberta,' a reference to the recent electoral win of the United Farmers of that province.[38] Drury and Grant probably chuckled over this indirect allusion to Morrison as a person of 'seditious principles.' Anyway, for the premier and his colleague the exchange said much for Meighen's political paranoia and helped to get the Ontario section of the campaign off to a colourful start. Drury used more than one opportunity to condemn what he called the prime minister's Bolshevik slur, pointing out that while his government had grown out of a class movement, it had overturned nothing but rottenness and corruption.

At the outset of the campaign Drury was reluctant to wade too far into debates on national questions. A provincial premier seen to be too intimately involved with the federal scene might needlessly alienate those Ontario voters who customarily made sharp distinctions between Queen's Park and the world of Caesar that was Ottawa. Crerar understood this feeling, but he bluntly warned Drury that 'Meighen and the Government ... will centre their attack on the Farmers and you may possibly be driven to the position where you will have to take part in the issue.' Crerar returned to this point a few weeks later when he exhorted the premier to take actively to the stump and join him on his Ontario odyssey. Drury was advised that his province 'will be the real battleground in the election.'[39]

There was another consideration, however. If Drury invested heavily in the Progressive campaign and it ended in anything less than a convincing demonstration of strength, his own political stock in Ontario might be sharply devalued. Yet he also had to bear in mind that Morrison had been picked by Crerar to head the provincial campaign organization, a chore added to the secretary's political workload in the Maritimes and Quebec. In these circumstances Drury could ill afford to stand aside and risk being accused of shirking his duty while his nemesis in the UFO was discharging his for the good of the movement.

Morrison, too, had some qualms. These Crerar addressed with some brotherly advice: 'Don't go at it too strongly, I am sure you can render the best service by keeping yourself in a sufficiently detached position that you can think over problems and advise the course of action that should be taken.'[40] Morrison's intimate knowledge of ridings and personalities, the envy of Drury and his colleagues, was a reservoir of insights and information that Crerar was anxious to tap as he prepared to do battle. All the same, the Progressive leader was nagged by the same problem that disturbed Drury. He gloomily described it to Good: 'Morrison hopes to see [Progressivism] ... as a movement that will not be called upon to assume the responsibilities of office but ... will be always occupying a cross-bench position, seeking to force its programme upon governments.'[41] In spite of this reservation, Crerar still deemed Morrison a first-class political asset. The secretary's entry into the fray may have forced Drury's hand, for by the end of September 1921 the premier was reported to be ready to do battle if the record of his government was attacked. Voters were subsequently treated to the spectacle of Drury and Morrison appearing on the same platform in unaccustomed double harness, a state of affairs that even the *Globe* marvelled at.

Drury had made his move, however reluctantly, but what of the caucus? Morrison enlightened Crerar on this point. Apparently the decision was reached that each Farmer MLA was to act as he saw fit. Not content with that, Morrison stressed the government's growing unpopularity with the rank and file of the province's farmers. He warned that the MLAS' appearance on the hustings in support of Progressive candidates could trigger hostile criticism and defeat the purpose of the campaign. Moreover, their campaigning might even 'turn the trend of the argument towards Provincial matters rather than the real issue of the Dominion.' Morrison then betrayed his anger with the Drury government by summarily dismissing the provincial scene as inconsequential. After all, he remarked condescendingly, 'Provincial Politics are only a local matter, more of detail than policy.'[42] The venom was ill concealed. Had he known of the letter's contents Drury would have fumed, but on reflection he might have grudgingly agreed that the presence of some cabinet ministers or Farmer MLAS in certain sensitive ridings – Biggs's name came to mind – would do the campaign little good. Even so, he was not prepared to swallow the notion that there were as many liabilities as Morrison claimed. Indeed, he reckoned that at least some of his ministers would add lustre to the Progressive campaign.

Here he was probably thinking of the minister of agriculture, Manning Doherty, whose contributions had made him welcome in some rural ridings. For one thing, he was striving to end Britain's wartime embargo on Ontario cattle exports brought on by unsubstantiated reports that they were infected with pleuropneumonia. Doherty resented the slur all the more when he learned that the embargo was mainly aimed at protecting cattlemen in the United Kingdom. His lobbying junkets to Britain combined with the efforts of a friendly Beaverbrook press to discredit the government's action and help reverse it.[43] Although others claimed that Arthur Meighen played a more critical role in the proceedings than the 'embarrassing activities of a ... Canadian Provincial Minister,' Doherty emerged with the praises of Ontario's cattlemen ringing in his ears and a congratulatory telegram from Beaverbrook himself.[44]

Another Doherty initiative which had elicited a warm response from farmers, though a less than cordial greeting from bankers, was the establishment of a system of rural credits to improve agriculture's financial standing and help check the population erosion in the countryside. This matter had periodically been discussed, with Drury's backing and George Keen's approval, at annual meetings of the UFO.[45] The Agricultural Development Finance Act set up a provincial savings institution which generated funding for farm loans and an inexpensive program of life insurance. The loans were to be regulated by an Agricultural Development Board and administered by a Farm Loan Association. To bankers' charges that these moves amounted to class favouritism, Doherty responded by warning them that their institutions 'derived their authority from the people for the purpose of rendering service to the people, not for the purpose of creating arrogant millionaires.'[46] Ontario populism had ventured into the banking business.

Drury's decision to play an active role on the Progressives' behalf was shaped in part by stirring events in his own riding. There the UFO organization had given way to Farrow's Halton People's Party though not without a price. For his heresy Farrow was promptly challenged and explanations demanded. In any case, a few months later he resigned from his UFO executive position and was named manager of Doherty's newly formed Farm Loan Association.[47] Meanwhile the party he had founded nominated J.F. Ford, the victor of 1919 who had made way for Drury, as the Progressive candidate. Drury, the unabashed populist, rhapsodized over the prospect when he visited the riding. 'I like the name ''People's party'' – body and soul to the people,' he crowed in Milton, where the crowd had applauded him for nearly five minutes before he spoke. He congratulated the riding's farmers on their enthusiasm and on their having invited 'townsmen' to join their organization.[48] Many hoped that this would be the thin end of the Broadening Out wedge.

Curiously, in view of his resolve not to engage in debate about national issues unless his own government were assailed, he offered some gratuitous comments on the tariff. Even more curiously, he reportedly told his Milton audience that the big issue in the election was not the National Policy. He insisted that Meighen was trying to force the tariff question 'so that farmers could be stigmatized' as free traders, as if to imply that the phrase was indeed a pejorative one. Later in the campaign he even allowed that a tariff 'divested of abuses would be acceptable to him.' All of this seems strange coming from such a committed anti-protectionist, and begs some questions. Was he concerned about the townsman's vote which just might be wedded to protection, and about his own Labour allies who were expressing strong doubts about the wisdom of freer trade? He was well aware that the Canadian Labour Party had decided to throw in its lot with the Progressives and that Good had been named by the UFO to serve on the executive of that party's Ontario section. Perhaps strong talk about the tariff would chill that relationship. Drury realized, in any case, that he would have to tread warily so far as labour was concerned because his ILP colleagues were 'asking for things that we cannot give' – unemployment insurance and the repudiation of debt, among others.[49] He may have felt that in these circumstances the discussion of other divisive matters favouring the farmer, such as the liberation of trade, had best be left in abeyance. Again, the consideration of harsh political realities, as it had in the case of education and Hydro, encroached on the populistic idealism that had coloured the UFO's platform in 1919.

What Drury thought he could discuss without fear of reaction was Ottawa's railway policy. He attacked, for example, the extravagance of the varied railway ventures the federal government had promoted and the surpluses piled up by the newly formed Canadian National Railways, particularly on the eve of elections. As in the radials' case, he was denounced for being an enemy of public enterprise and for wrongfully accusing Ottawa of political skulduggery. His retort was the same: extravagance, waste, and inefficiency were his enemy, not the principle of public ownership or control.

The reception Drury received in Halton and Ford's apparent popularity in the riding seemed to clinch it for the Progressive cause. Certainly the government candidate did not minimize his difficulties. 'The contest will be no "cinch" for any party,' he told Meighen. 'The United Farmer is strong and aggressive and their candidate is popular ... ' But he reckoned that the UFO could be undercut if facts were broadcast about their extravagance and the failure to deliver on their varied pledges. He then took a swipe at the premier: 'Only for Drury's record,' he asserted, 'we could not make a "dint" in the Farmers' Party.' Meighen wrote back his approval of the scheme to expose the provincial government.[50]

One possible attempt involved the United Farmers' Co-operative Company. Drury learned some two weeks before the election that a petition was filed in the courts alleging that certain financial interests had unearthed damaging information on the company's operations and called for its winding up. According to an affidavit subsequently submitted by a company director, the petitioner agreed to keep the matter out of the press if Burnaby, the UFO candidate, withdrew in North York (where King was running) and Morrison resigned as the UFO secretary. This essay in political blackmail fizzled at the end of November, however, when the petition was judged fraudulent and thrown out.[51]

Meanwhile, Drury's correspondents were fully alive to the Conservative strategy of fighting the issues on the record of his government. They made no bones about the need for Drury and his cabinet to come out swinging in support of Progressive candidates. As Tory attacks continued to mount, the premier needed no further bidding. Brampton, Sarnia, Oshawa, Kingston, Simcoe, Toronto,

Ottawa, and finally his own stamping grounds in Barrie – these were among the communities Drury visited, usually with Crerar and sometimes with Morrison in tow. By November, two weeks before polling day, he was properly warming to the task. It was 1919 all over again, or so it appeared. So enthusiastic did his canvassing become that he turned the tables on Crerar and urged him, as he had once been urged, to have more meetings than originally scheduled. Before long the premier was echoing the Progressive leader's conviction that Ontario 'is the real fighting ground' now that the west appeared firmly lodged in the win column. By this time Drury was convinced that a broad tide was moving in favour of the Progressives all across the social spectrum.[52]

In Toronto he linked city and country and his fondness for summoning up the British past with an apparent modification of his Milton stand on the tariff. He remarked that in the Canadian campaign for free trade history would be reversed. 'In England many years ago,' he lectured, 'the townspeople had gone to the farmers to convince them that *high protection* was not good. In Canada the farmer was coming to the city.'[53] As he had already intimated, there were lower and medium levels of protection that were tolerable, if not to the purist, as he had appeared to be, at least to the pragmatist. At any rate, he could argue that when he had appeared before the Tariff Commission late in 1920 he had urged the retention of a revenue tariff only.

At Barrie, where Crerar wound up his eighteen-day swing in Ontario, he was excited by the two large audiences that greeted him in spite of bad weather and equally bad roads. Perfectly at home as host, Drury rattled off figures on the enormity of rural depopulation and how it had been spawned by the National Policy. He had probably not enjoyed himself so much since his Halton campaign, a year and a half earlier. He even took in stride reports that W.A. Boys, the local Tory candidate, in the august company of Arthur Meighen himself, had laughingly dismissed him as 'the chance and a fluke' premier.

Toward the end of the campaign Drury took himself off to Ottawa to do battle in Meighen's own backyard and savour some revenge. If the Conservative leader insisted on provincializing national issues, then he could return the favour. One way of doing this, dear to the premier's heart, was to brand Meighen as the Canadian archpriest of protectionism. This was not difficult to do, for Meighen made no effort to hide his keen solicitude for this supposed guarantor of Canada's economic and political well-being. In keeping with the stand he had already taken, Drury would stress 'high protection' rather than other less crippling species of the affliction. He chose to do this by mocking Meighen's earlier position on the question when he had come out against the Liberals' taking refuge behind 'ramparts of gold':

We looked over that young man [Meighen] with hope, and thought he might be the Moses that would lead us out. That young man came with Israel to the Red Sea, but the waters were cold, the east wind of public opinion had not yet risen, and to cross the sea meant separation from his old party. He looked across the sea, and saw the wilderness and years of wandering. The promised land was out of sight, and he turned and looked back to Egypt and saw the steaming fleshpots of office warm and inviting, and got in his nostrils the smell of onions and garlic, luring him back to the mess of the slave of those 'who helped him to power', to use his own words, and who now maintain him there 'behind ramparts of gold'.[54]

Then, with a passing reference to the advertising techniques of the day and some popular consumer items, he remarked that thanks to the billboard, Meighen 'was now almost as well known as the two old gentlemen who smoke Old Chum tobacco, the little girl with Dutch Cleanser, or the Sunny Jim of the good old days.'[55]

Eventually the travelling and the haranguing had to give way to the event for which all this had been hectic preparation – the election of 6 December. To Drury's unalloyed satisfaction, Meighen and the frayed Union government were handed a crushing setback and reduced to a mere fifty seats in the Commons. But the Conservatives' defeat in North York was engineered not by Burnaby, the UFO standard-bearer, but by the Liberal candidate, no less a person than Mackenzie King himself.[56] Before the election some observers, even outside Farmer ranks, had hoped that Progressive wins in Ontario would roughly match the UFO's victories two years before. 'The Farmers may drop down to 35 and they may go up to 45,' speculated Clifford Sifton. 'I shall be very well satisfied if they get 40.'[57] He, and all in the UFO who shared his optimism, were in for a rude shock. The chastened Progressives would have to be content with a mere twenty-four from Ontario. Had he been invited to do so, Sifton would have offered Drury and other UFO supporters the succinct advice he spelled out for Dafoe: 'The farmers' organization in Ontario will want jacking up if it is to be permanently successful.'[58]

As best he could Drury tried to shrug off the election results, pointing out that the federal vote had no appreciable provincial significance. He downplayed the results as well in his memoirs published nearly half a century later, off-handedly referring to the small part he had played in the election.[59] But that does not square with his considerable exertions on behalf of Progressive hopefuls, particularly when Crerar had been in the province. If he had hesitated to plunge into the fray for fear that it might boomerang on his own political standing, then he had some cause to be rueful after 6 December. What was genuinely disturbing, though he gave no outward sign, was that save for Harry Nixon, every cabinet minister, including himself, saw the Progressive candidate defeated in his home riding. In Nixon's case, Good made the grade and went off to Ottawa as part of the sixty-five-member Progressive contingent, one bright spot in the gloom. The outcome in Halton must have been particularly upsetting. The reputedly popular Ford, the 'people's choice,' was beaten in a three-cornered contest narrowly won by the Conservative candidate. In Wentworth, Biggs's 1919 majority was annihilated, while the Conservative won easily in Grant's Carleton riding. Labour had little to crow about either; Walter Rollo's majority, like Biggs's, was virtually wiped out.[60]

The press did not share Drury's view that federal voting was no reflection of provincial opinion, and rushed in with many and varied explanations as to why Farmer candidates had failed to carry as many ridings as they had in 1919. Excessive expenditures, particularly on Biggs's roads network, disenchantment with real or imagined group government, and a desire on the part of rural voters who now wished in the calmer political climate of 1921 to return to the comfort of traditional allegiances – these and other factors were authoritatively put to newspaper readers. The *Globe* added another when it suggested that Drury's opposition to the radials, the paper's pet project, had worked against Progressive candidates in urban or semi-urban ridings.[61] The conclusion drawn was that the UFO had been no asset at all but rather a crippling liability to Crerar's cause in Ontario. As for the Conservative opposition at Queen's Park, it was understandably jubilant, in spite of the disaster met by their federal counterparts. 'Taken as a whole,' Howard Ferguson wrote a successful Conservative candidate, 'the result in Ontario points with no uncertainty to the collapse of the class movement. Ontario refuses to accept the doctrine that we can be better governed by groups founded upon occupational distinction.'[62] Another critic was more vitriolic. 'It is quite time,' he wrote, 'that this UFO bugaboo was wiped out of existence ... the sooner people are getting to realize ... that class government will not do, the better it will be for all concerned.'[63] Drury would have been the first to agree with the substance of these critiques, given his own predilection for parliamentary government on a broadened political base.

At this point Morrison, the advocate of group government, entered the discussion with a predictable commentary on what had happened on 6 December. 'To the UFO an election is not a struggle for position,' he told a *Globe* reporter, 'but rather is it a means to secure the promotion of ideals for the betterment of our country.' His preoccupation with the special hazards in Ontario came out in his next observation: 'Now, whatever action is taken by our group [in Ottawa] will be dictated by a desire to project our ideals free from the fear of the fall of the Government.'[64] This cross-bench position, which Crerar had lamented early in the campaign, was vital to Morrison's scheme of things. That Progressive candidates had carried only twenty-four ridings was immaterial to the UFO secretary.

Throughout the gloomy post-mortems on the showing of UFO candidates Drury continued as plausibly as he could to gloss over the results. He soon had cause to rejoice when a provincial by-election in North Oxford resulted in a commanding UFO victory in, moreover, a tough three-party battle. The Liberals, who had held the riding, the Conservatives, and the government threw in all their available strength and the results, as the *Canadian Forum* noted, were 'striking.' The Liberal majority of 1919 was translated into a government one and Ferguson's candidate trailed badly in the polls. For some the Tory débâcle was welcome because it was also a slap in the face for the Orange Order, whose growing influence Crerar and Drury had grown to fear in the charged political climate of the postwar years. Resentful of Drury's alleged pandering to Roman Catholic interests and suspicious of his 'aberrant' administration, Orangemen had openly campaigned for the Tory standard-bearer.[65] The latter's poor showing was put down to the thinness of racial and religious prejudices in parts of the riding as well as to the bad odour of the Union government. But how was one to account for the Liberal rout? Drury and others preferred to think that it was his government's strong stand on the radials that turned the trick, and John Castell Hopkins of the *Canadian Annual Review* was inclined to agree with them.[66] Whatever conspired to produce the refreshing outcome in North Oxford, Drury wasted little time capitalizing on it. Even so, a cautious Sissons warned him that he still faced problems in parts of the riding, including the town of Woodstock where the Farmer candidate had actually trailed his two opponents. The implication was clear enough that difficulties in North Oxford might well be duplicated in key urban ridings elsewhere.

Meanwhile, as a result of the federal election, portentous developments soon loomed on Drury's political horizon. The strong national showing of the assorted Progressives had cut heavily into traditional political strongholds. The result was that King emerged with only 117 seats in a 235-seat chamber and had to settle for a minority government, as some had predicted. The west went almost solidly Progressive and Ontario was sharply divided between the latter's allies and the old parties, while the rest of the east, generally speaking, spoke with a Liberal voice. When King set about to construct his cabinet he would have to take these realities into account and try to entice Progressive leaders into his ministerial fold so that he might gain some standing on the prairies. If many Progressives were what they had been described, Liberals in a hurry, then he could quicken his own pace perhaps – in a dignified fashion so as not to alienate too many of the party's right-wingers – to catch up with the Progressives' demands for change.[67] In the process he might be able to pick up desperately needed support for his minority government.

This set the stage for the political wooing of Drury, Crerar, and other Progressives. Within forty-eight hours of the election King and Andrew Haydon, secretary of the national Liberal organization, were poring over a list of cabinet prospects which bore the names of these farmer politicians. Drury would learn later that King had stressed to Haydon that the 'alliance with the rural elements [was to be] the solid foundation of the Liberal party through the years to come.'

Drury himself was to be considered for the railways portfolio, not surprising perhaps in view of his assaults on railway mismanagement and his highly visible stand on the radials.[68]

In the meantime, Drury had not been idle. Shortly after the election dust settled the premier sought out P.C. Larkin, the so-called Tea King of Canada and treasurer of the Ontario Liberal Association. He wanted Larkin to tell King that 'if [he] had any trouble with the protectionist Montreal group [he] could count on [Drury's] support,' and that of other Progressives. Larkin came away convinced that the premier was really acting on Crerar's behalf. King in turn was convinced that if he played his cards right he might bring off a merger of Progressives and Liberals under his leadership. In any event, King wanted something more than a coalition, if there was any such possibility. A coalition, an alliance of virtual equals with each still clinging to their respective platforms and ideologies, might dilute his own authority. What King aimed at was a 'coalescence' of the two parties to produce a 'new, strong, vigorous, united, solid Liberal Party representative of the will and the wish of the great body of the people.'[69] For Drury this could have been represented as a national version of the Broadening Out program he still sought to install in Ontario, that is, if he decided to stay at the helm there.

The premier soon had occasion to think seriously of uprooting himself from Queen's Park and joining King in Ottawa. The process began when the prime minister arranged a meeting with him at Larkin's home. In the interval, Drury correctly surmised that King canvassed his closest advisers on the desirability of recruiting him and other farmer politicians for the cabinet. One of those advisers, W.C. Kennedy, a utilities executive who had been an anti-conscriptionist Liberal in 1917, did not take kindly to Drury's nomination, arguing that 'our men who had fought him wouldn't like it.' But King dismissed the criticism, at least in his diary, and complained that its author had 'no vision of national unity.'[70] Surprisingly, Lomer Gouin, the high protectionist former premier of Quebec, was one of Drury's strongest backers. Perhaps their common opposition to the railways' ambitions was a factor. Or Gouin may have hoped that Drury's selection would pose fewer problems for the conservative wing than Crerar's, if such a choice had to be made. Had the premier got wind of this he would not have been flattered; Gouin, after all, was a leading member of that very Montreal group that Drury had volunteered to help King keep in their place.

While the premier was pondering events in Ottawa, Morrison was being called upon by certain parties for advice and guidance. According to Clifford Sifton, Morrison agreed with both him and Dafoe that coalition was feasible but only if Crerar could work out an arrangement on a 'fifty-fifty basis.' Otherwise the Progressive leader should steer clear of King and his plans; in other words, it should be a genuine coalition, not the prime minister's sought-after coalescence under the Liberal party's umbrella. Morrison, it would appear, felt strongly enough about the matter to send that kind of message directly to Crerar. Sifton, anxious to hurt reactionary elements in the Liberal party, urged the Progressives 'to have the brains *and the grit* to hold together, doing nothing except through their accredited leader.' Any other course, he warned, 'is bound to result in disruption.' Morrison needed no urging from anybody. What Sifton had expressed adequately summed up the role he thought the Progressives should play in the House. Finally, Sifton gave Dafoe his own unflattering assessment of Drury, this hard upon the heels of his high praise for the UFO secretary. 'I should not depend anything on Drury,' he wrote. 'It is unlikely that he has [been?] approached [by King?] but I understand that he made a practice of consulting the wrong people and is getting very much weaker.'[71] The criticism could just as easily have come from Morrison.

The object of Sifton's scorn duly had his audience with King on 14 December. 'Perhaps it was characteristic of his extreme caution,' Drury recalled, 'that he said, "Don't bring a driver, drive yourself." So I went, parked my Ford car at the curb, walked up the pathway [to Larkin's home] and rang the doorbell.'[72] From that point in his memoirs Drury seems to confuse the meeting with the one he had with King earlier in the year, for he talks extensively of protectionism and free trade, the subjects which had monopolized the first conversation. In any case, King made no allusions to them in his diary entries for that day but concentrated instead on such problems as cabinet-making and the role that Drury and Crerar could play. Significantly, Drury 'agreed wholeheartedly' with the prime minister's argument that in the event of a merger Crerar should not make the mistake of pinning King down beforehand on such contentious issues as the tariff.[73] Given the way he had seemed to blow hot and cold on the question during the election, it comes as no surprise that Drury should fall in with King on this tactical point. All the same, King's version of the conversation contrasts sharply with Drury's memories. This was the scenario that appeared in *Farmer Premier*:

[King] proposed to form a union with the free trade Progressives and let the high tariff Liberals go where they would ...
  I said, 'Mr. King, you know where I stand on the tariff. How far are you willing to go?'
  'Just as far as you are,' he said.
  'That will be all the way,' I said. He answered, 'Yes.'[74]

Drury insisted in the 1960s, when writing Good and others, that his memory of the conversation '[was] as clear as if it happened yesterday.'[75] Perhaps not.

The impression conveyed by King's rendition of events is that Drury was hungering after an Ottawa appointment, a prospect he 'had cherished ... for years.' King also noted that Drury would have said yes at once had there been anyone in the provincial wings to succeed him. On the face of it, this was hardly the response of one totally committed to Queen's Park. At any rate, the premier indicated the obvious, that before he could come to a decision, he would have to discuss the matter with his cabinet and caucus. In his memoirs Drury states that he stressed the merits of a full coalition and that 'anything less would have been meaningless.' He may have said as much, but according to King the Liberal chief had the last word. 'I was emphatic in saying,' he recorded, 'it must be a straight Liberal government.'[76] This unequivocal position Drury must have accepted. Again, not a whisper of King's rejoinder appears in *Farmer Premier*. Drury's promotion of coalition at this stage of the proceedings may have been prompted by a concern for the feelings of those in UFO ranks who were supporting Morrison's stand on the question. His ultimate acquiescence in King's plan, however, reflects his own interest in the concept of Broadening Out, this time at the federal level. Furthermore, the plan would enable him, should he join King's cabinet, to battle for those national goals, notably the lowering of the tariff, which were denied him in the provincial field.

At this time King solicited the newspaper world for assessments of Drury. Atkinson of the Toronto *Star*, long a friendly figure in the premier's corner, rated him highly for the railways portfolio, though he had been told that he fancied finance. Stewart Lyon of the *Globe*, who had differed with Drury on the radials question, was much less enthusiastic and told King that among his other faults the premier 'doesn't finish things,' a complaint that others had expressed.

The alacrity with which Drury responded to King's overtures and his apparent readiness to leave Queen's Park deserve some comment. The conversation of 14 December took place while the by-election fight in North Oxford still hung in the balance. If it went against his administration, as seemed likely, than all the gloom generated by the general election's outcome would be justified. Sifton, for one, saw this clearly enough the very day of the meeting at Larkin's home. 'My information is,' he wrote Dafoe, 'that [King] will not find Drury very hard to handle ... Just now Drury is engaged in a very hot fight in North Oxford. If he wins that he will be considerably strengthened, but his Government is very much in need of strength in some particulars.' A few days later, with a welcome victory in North Oxford safely tucked away, the premier seemed less enthusiastic about accepting King's proposition, at least at that juncture. Moreover, even before the by-election results were known he did a turnabout on the coalition question. On 17 December he wired Crerar and urged him to hold out against anything smacking of a merger with the Liberals. Rather, he strongly advised the Progressives to insist on a genuine partnership that would honour their identity and exclude the 'Gouin bloc.'[77] It would appear that Drury was beginning to question the sincerity of King's overtures, as Sifton certainly was, or trying to head off complications in his own political camp at Queen's Park.

What is certain is that on 20 December the contents of Drury's cable to Crerar were disclosed to an annoyed prime minister who just a few days earlier had heard Drury accept his plan for an'alliance under his sole management. Drury 'phoned that very day' and conceded that, so far as his own role was concerned, the outcome in North Oxford on 19 December was 'not helping matters.' All the same, he agreed to come to Ottawa and talk further. The next morning Drury called on King and gave him some additional news that must have been anticipated. Other considerations aside, the entire caucus had insisted that Drury stay on in Toronto and continue to pilot the government through its varied responsibilities. They had been all agreed that no one else appeared ready, able, or willing to fill his shoes. Drury accepted their judgment and announced his intention to stay on at Queen's Park. Yet he did not abandon all thoughts of Ottawa. He pleaded with King to reserve a federal place for him should he be released at a later date from his provincial obligations. To this King apparently agreed.[78]

Whatever his views on the arrangements King wanted with the Progressives, Drury reaffirmed his own plans for 'coalescence' in Ontario. He had already received some welcome news from the Liberal benches in the legislature. Apparently Wellington Hay, the successor to the acerbic Dewart who had resigned, would look with favour on some kind of fusion with the Farmer-Labour group. Hay, who was on good terms with the premier anyway, thought the latter should stay at Queen's Park and not forsake it for Ottawa's dubious advantages. Obviously much would depend on how Drury fared politically over the remainder of his tenure. The unpleasant prospect that he might be denied a renewal of it had to be faced, but should some kind of Liberal-Progressive party – King's phrase – be forged in Ontario, then perhaps the spectre of defeat would dissolve. Into the bargain, King would be assured of a bastion to protect his own fortunes in that key province should he manage to bring off a merger with the Progressives in Ottawa.

That happy ending, however, was denied the prime minister at meetings arranged with the Progressive leadership in Winnipeg and later with the rank and file in Saskatoon and Toronto. Although the Saskatoon meeting furnished a glimmer of hope by authorizing Crerar's entry into the cabinet should the government's policy be acceptable to the Progressives, they insisted on King's recognition of their group as a distinctive force in the House of Commons. But King's proposals encountered much rougher sledding in Toronto, where the Ontario group met with Crerar on the evening of 23 December. Conspicuously absent was the premier of the province.

I did not know until I read ... Good's ... *Farmer Citizen* [Drury stated in his recollections], that two meetings of the newly elected Progressive members had been called ...; that the Progressive leader ... Crerar attended both and strongly urged that ... King's proposal

... be accepted; and that they should turn it down ... As head of the Farmer-Labour Government of Ontario and as one who had taken some part in the election campaign, I might reasonably have been expected to be invited to the Toronto meeting.[79]

Quite possibly Drury's memory may have been playing tricks for, according to Sifton, Crerar paid the premier a visit before he met with the Progressive MPs-elect. If that were the case, would not the western leader have told him of the gathering? But far more important than a possible memory lapse was Drury's renewed acceptance of King's political strategy. 'If I had been [at the meeting],' he asserted in *Farmer Premier*, 'I would have joined Crerar in urging acceptance of the proposal.' Again, he had reversed his position, now urging the endorsement of what he had warned the Progressive leadership against in his wire of 17 December. King's vaunted persuasiveness, combined perhaps with Drury's distrust of any kind of group politics, made him waver and, as the prime minister's biographer put it, 'prove fickle' on the coalition question.[80]

Drury's exclusion from the Toronto meeting should have come as no surprise, given his support of Broadening Out. The premier's suspicion that Morrison was at the back of the discourtesy was well founded. The man who helped to orchestrate the repudiation of King's merger plans at the Toronto meeting was hardly likely to afford its principal Ontario champion an opportunity to promote it. As it turned out, the UFO secretary was not reduced to twisting many arms on 23 December. Most, if not all, the Ontario Progressives had already flatly rejected a merger on King's terms. Good's stand was certainly typical. He recalled that the proposal was turned down with very little discussion:

The main objection we registered was that on occasion we would have to repudiate our principles or our representatives in the Cabinet ... Mr. Crerar [who] honestly believed that the two-party ... system was the best ... probably thought that in 1921 the Progressives should go into the Liberal party, drive out the reactionary Liberals, and create a new Liberal Party ... I did not share such views and hopes.[81]

Obviously Drury now did. Like King, who expressed surprise at the Toronto attitude until he learned that Drury was absent from the meeting, he mourned the lost opportunity. Forty years later, almost to the day, Drury told Good that when the Progressives had rejected the proposal they had made a big mistake.[82]

In any event, the federal opportunity presented Drury in late 1921 broke on the provincial obligations that were spelled out to him by his caucus. Had there been other considerations, however, that made up his mind? Years later he confided to a friend that King had left him uncertain about his prospective cabinet responsibilities, a hedging that may have weighed heavily in his calculations.[83] There was also his family to consider. Throughout his career his wife had been a close confidante. She took a keen interest in public affairs, and 'in all his reading and thinking had kept pace with him, step by step.' But as the wife of an MP, and a cabinet minister at that, Ella Drury would have had to involve herself in social activities the like of which had not seriously encroached on her life. Indeed, according to one account, much official entertaining which might ordinarily have fallen on her shoulders as the wife of a provincial premier was undertaken by the expansive Biggs household in Wentworth County which, after all, was geographically closer to the main political stage than Crown Hill.[84]

Ottawa, however, might well prove much more demanding. Her going there at this time, even more than her venturing to live in Toronto, was out of the question. A growing family of five and the duties of a rural chatelaine kept her fully occupied at Crown Hill. Even in the comfortable setting of her home could she ever find the time to perform those special duties that the community might well expect of the wife of an 'Ottawa man'? Inevitably there would be the 'speaking, the canvassing, the organizing' which some political spouses were now undertaking and which apparently some of Drury's colleagues thought she should. In the unpublished novel Drury wrote in the 1930s, Alice Brooks responds:

I wonder if they know how much I'm doing now? Of course, I want to help you [my husband] – all I can – But I've got to do it my way. I'm not a public person ... I'm a homebody, and I'm afraid I can't be changed. Besides some-one must look after things at home. There are the children. It's a pretty trying time for them ... and they need some-one ... You have no time for them, so I must give them all the more. One public person in the family is quite enough.[85]

And what about Drury's own circumstances? A life spent commuting between Barrie and Toronto was at times hectic enough. The longer trek to Ottawa, which would probably have to be undertaken by train, would be even more trying. Such problems would have to be faced before he made a decision to uproot himself and his family from the more manageable provincial setting.

Although these and other considerations shaped his decision to stay with Queen's Park, the courtship with King did not expire. On several occasions, when business took him to Ottawa the following year, Drury heard more tantalizing talk. For example, he learned that if King did succeed in assembling a Liberal-Progressive administration he would again be invited to serve. In such an eventuality his place in Toronto, according to the information that came to him, would be taken by Newton W. Rowell, a leading Liberal Unionist and, like Drury, a Methodist and prohibitionist.[86] Both Rowell and the premier were then high on the list of one political observer who held out little hope for the future of King's brand of Liberalism. 'The best of the Liberals,' he wrote Dafoe, 'will come to the [Progressives] once the Liberal party splits up ... King can be dumped and forgotten and a fresh start made in opposition with some *decent leader* like Rowell or Drury.[87] It so happened that Rowell had formed an equally favourable opinion of his prospective predecessor. Alluding to the Broadening Out controversy, Rowell concluded that 'as between himself and Mr. Morrison, Mr. Drury is undoubtedly in the right.[88] Rowell's reference to the running battle showed that it was not about to abate, and gave some hint that the worst of the squabble in the farm family lay ahead. All the same, the knowledge that Drury's political stock was intact in Ontario and still commanded respect in Ottawa took some of the sting out of Morrison's barbs. It also provided considerable comfort to the premier as he put aside, for the time being, any possible federal aspirations and returned to the full-time management of provincial affairs.

11

Entrenching Virtue

When Drury later recalled that he had been pitchforked into power, he might have added that similar circumstances played a part in keeping him at the helm in 1921. As in 1919, no one seemed a plausible substitute in the eyes of the Farmer-Labour caucus. The energetic Frank Biggs, who had certainly demonstrated administrative capacity, betrayed no ambition to occupy the premier's office. Besides, he was unacceptable in some quarters because he had not graduated from the ranks of the UFO; in others he was disliked for his opportunism and his 'wasteful spending' on the province's highways. Another possible contender, who like Biggs gave no sign that he coveted Drury's post, was Manning Doherty, the capable minister of agriculture. But in a community where the King Billy parade was still a commanding ritual, a Roman Catholic premier would have been unthinkable.

What about W.E. Raney? Many were agreed, Drury included, that after Doherty he enjoyed the edge as the ablest member of cabinet. Indeed, in some circles Raney was considered to be at least a match for Drury and better able than the premier to help inexperienced colleagues out of parliamentary and political difficulties.[1] The question asked was why could not the attorney general have taken over at Queen's Park so that Drury could sit at King's side in Ottawa? The answers were not hard to come by. For all his ability, energy, and capacity for hard work, Raney had not yet, and perhaps never would, overcome the hostility that had greeted his appointment in 1919. Morrison, when he was not battering Drury for trying to 'broaden out,' could be heard complaining still of the premier's unwise selection for the attorney generalship.[2] How a city man, whose legal credentials seemed to be less than heart-stirring, could successfully serve rural interests was a question that continued to agitate UFO meetings. Not even Raney's dedication to the cause of prohibition could erode his unfavourable image. Moreover, it was well known that some Farmer MLAs actually applauded the sallies that came from the irreverent opposition benches after Raney's humourless single-mindedness had worn out the House's patience. For some of his cabinet colleagues, described by Drury as a few wets,[3] the badge of rectitude the attorney general wore so proudly was often galling.[4]

Yet Drury never appeared to waver in his support of the man and his firmly held views. The premier, of course, would have added to his political vulnerability had he only lukewarmly supported the one person he had gone out of his way to lionize as the best possible choice for the attorney generalship. All the same, nothing had happened to make Drury change his mind about Raney or about his ability to spearhead a campaign of moral reform. And on one of the principal components of that campaign – prohibition – Drury saw eye to eye with him. Indeed, the premier had come to commune more with Raney on matters touching public morality than with any other member of cabinet. As the only lawyer on the government side Raney was asked for his counsel on every conceivable matter that came up for discussion and resolution, a task that went far beyond the already broad limits of what an attorney general was expected to do. Another factor must be given some weight: Raney could always find time for backing Drury in other schemes designed to rejuvenate and reform society.

In the beginning Drury saw the 'war on booze' as only a part, albeit a major part, of a larger cause. Although the UFO platform gave few solid hints of what a farmer group would do once it assumed office, there is little doubt that the premier had some decided views on what ought to be done to meet certain social needs. Much has been made of the derivative features of Drury's ventures into reform. In the case of mothers' allowances, for example, he was supposed to have merely presided over the enactment of legislation for which the Hearst government had set the stage.[5] Ranged against this is Drury's claim in *Farmer Premier* that his administration enacted 'such a program of social legislation as Ontario and indeed all of Canada and North America had never seen, or perhaps thought possible.'[6] This statement, written in old age, was an overblown version of the self-assessment he had made some thirty years earlier when he wrote that he had initiated and carried through 'as much good work ... as any government in a similar time in the history of the Province.'[7]

Although some of Drury's hyperbole has to be discounted, the fact remains that only after repeated remonstrances from the Local Council of Women, which had been backing a mothers' allowance plan since 1912, did the Hearst government give serious consideration to helping needy widows with dependent children.[8] The demands of the First World War, which had shown the urgent need for fostering the physically as well as the morally fit in society, had underscored the urgency of the program. The upshot had been a sympathetic report prepared by W.A. Riddell, a career civil servant who had investigated conditions in the cities and interviewed an assortment of civic leaders and urban reformers. Had Hearst survived the election of 1919 he may well have translated Riddell's report into legislation.

Even so, this possibility should not diminish the part that Drury played. His government's legislation, which went into effect on 1 October 1920 and was subsequently amended to provide more extensive benefits, created a Mothers' Allowance Commission and set up local boards. Appointed to it were the Reverend Peter Bryce, a Methodist minister active in Toronto's social work circles, who served as its first chairman; Elizabeth Shortt, a medical doctor and a vigorous activist, as vice chairman; and Mrs William Singer, a labour representative.

Administration by commission was settled upon so that Queen's Park's influence could be effectively shut out. 'The Government or any member of it,' explained Drury to someone who had plainly inferred otherwise, 'has not the power to say who shall or shall not receive Allowances under the ... Act ... To give to any Government [such] power would be so dangerous that it should not for one moment be considered ... It would become inevitably a means for the exercise of patronage and favouritism.' It then followed that appointments to the local boards would be strictly non-political, 'the one consideration being to have a representative Board of citizens of good standing in the community, and sympathetic with the Act.'[9]

Mothers' allowances broke with the Victorian notion that public home relief should be discouraged in favour of the institutional services of orphanages and industrial schools. The rebuilding of the family as the best possible environment for the child and the pursuit of the ideal of family unity and stability had long been the aim of Mrs Shortt and her associates. To a considerable extent Drury shared their enthusiasms. The premier had little patience with stark institutional settings that lacked the warmth and security that only a stable family could provide. His views on the subject, which recur frequently in his writings, were reinforced by personal experiences. The loss of his own mother, and the kindly attentions of Aunt Bessie, had brought home to him the poignancy of the situations that advocates of mothers' pensions had portrayed. But for the premier, who believed that women, urban and rural alike, ought to be politically mobilized as their spouses' equals, it went beyond this. He would obviously side with those who saw in the program a recognition of the state's duty to give full scope to the 'maternal potential for preserving community and race.'[10] He went even further and struck a nativist note: implying that the melting pot had somehow mongrelized the United States, he urged the need for more Canadian born and raised children so that his country would not suffer a similar fate.

At the same time, Mrs Shortt and her colleagues recognized the need for trained social workers who could seek out and identify the problems facing not only the widowed woman with a growing family but others victimized by deteriorating social and economic circumstances. Instead of the haphazardness that supposedly characterized the efforts of the untrained moral reformer, there would now be an efficient professionalism for resolving the difficulties besieging society. Drury, however, never wished to see such professional servants turned into mere government employees; there was still need for the more sophisticated voluntary worker, and the fewer 'intruders into the nursery' the better.[11]

In the UFO government Biggs was also a vocal champion of mothers' pensions, as was his Labour colleague Walter Rollo, who had been responsible for inviting Elizabeth Shortt to join the commission in the first place.[12] Rollo's advocacy, certainly explicable in the light of his riding's problems, strengthened the link between the Farmer and ILP contingents in the coalition. Furthermore, an effort was made within the year to extend the act's provisions to deserted wives (for a limited term), to wives whose husbands were totally disabled, and to foster mothers with dependent children. Permission was also granted the recipient of aid to take on part-time work to supplement income, preferably in the home. Special care was taken – a safeguard stressed by Drury who had to keep his eye cocked on the parsimonious in the UFO – to ensure that ineligible people were kept off the rolls.

One significant feature of the program was the assignment of investigators to so-called remote areas to determine eligibility and the extent of need. This meant that for the first time an agent of Queen's Park was figuratively parachuted into the fringes of the province to inquire into basic social problems, an expansion of governmental influence that went relatively unnoticed at the time. Before long the commission was receiving responses from its beneficiaries, which in several cases were passed on to an interested premier. The quasi-literacy of some added to their poignancy: 'If you were only like me amongst all the poor widows and hear there talks you would be pleased of the splendid work your doing ... for its certainly the best law ... that never was before.' Still another correspondent wrote: 'Before I received my Allowance I could not keep my children properly fed and clothed and was just on the point of giving them over to some of my friends.'[13]

Although Drury stuck to his arm's length policy for the government, he took a personal interest in some cases where no proof of marriage could be established, an omission that could deny benefits to an otherwise deserving candidate. In such cases Drury was prepared to bend the law so that a statement professing proof of marriage would be acceptable in lieu of a marriage certificate. 'The letter of the law,' he told one correspondent, 'may be varied in the interest of humanity to meet the needs of [particular and, as it turned out, isolated] cases.'[14] This, however, was the limit of the premier's 'interference' and on no occasion did he challenge what a local board offered or the commission approved once the law was 'varied.' As for funding the program, mercifully for Drury and UFO watchdogs, it proved much less costly than other government obligations. The expense was shared equally with Queen's Park by the province's municipalities, thus entitling them to places on local boards. In the first year of operation three-quarters of a million dollars were spent to provide allowances and services, including the work of eighteen inspectors. The sense of commitment that sprang from their sometimes harrowing reports dovetailed with the premier's concern for this social program.[15]

The whole process was given a boost when the press, irrespective of political affiliation, uniformly bestowed their praises on the legislation. The *Star* hailed it as a vindication of Joseph Atkinson's early campaign on behalf of mothers' allowances. The *Globe* rejoiced that the program 'springs from the social sympathies of the people of Ontario,' and was gladdened by the thought that 'many sad domestic tragedies were uncovered and ... healed.'[16] So was Drury, who revelled in the opportunity to legislate social improvements in areas where in his pre-office days he had seen such a need. The Social Service Council, a body organized before the war, praised his 'social convictions' and welcomed his intervention.[17] Drury was particularly proud of his so-called Adoption Act. In his memoirs he wrote:

Its need was suggested to me ... in 1917 when [a companion] and I were driving together from a Liberal ... meeting in Collingwood [on the eve of the wartime election] ... As we passed a farm he told me that ... it had belonged to a [middle aged] couple who ... had taken an orphaned boy whom they had regarded as their son. The [parents] ... died, both intestate. Distant relatives claimed the estate, and the boy who had every moral right to inherit, got nothing. Adoptions could then only be made by a private bill passed by the Legislature – a cumbersome and costly procedure ... The incident stuck in my mind, and so, when I unexpectedly found myself in the business of making laws, I had an Act prepared by which adoptions could be [cheaply] made by application to a county judge.[18]

This solicitude for children was reflected in other pieces of legislation that Drury, with the full support of women's groups such as the UFWO, backed in his first two parliamentary sessions.[19] In the Children's Protection Act, for example, it was laid down that foster homes for neglected children lodged in county institutions be located in the district where the children normally resided. Another act, inspired by the Social Service Council which, at Drury's request, had submitted a draft bill, sought to protect and maintain illegitimate children by compelling the father to assume all financial responsibilities for such offspring. A related measure, which plainly aimed at erasing the stigma of bastardy, ensured that children born out of wedlock would be legitimized by the subsequent marriage of the parents. The administration also put some teeth into existing legislation against wife desertion by making it an offence for a father to desert his children. On the side of medical care, provision was made for the appointment of public health nurses and for free children's clinics across the province.

In a move that delighted Elizabeth Shortt and other feminists, a law was enacted preventing a father from appointing a stranger to be a child's guardian, to the exclusion of the mother, and providing for equal rights of guardianship in both parents. Nor were the interests of parents to be neglected in this surge of family legislation. The responsibilities of offspring were spelled out in another act, the Parents' Maintenance Act, which required children to provide for indigent mothers and fathers. The burden of such care, traditionally and for the most part uncomplainingly shouldered by Victorian families, was not about to be thrust on the general rates at the expense of the taxpayer. What had once been more or less taken for granted would now in a more complex and perhaps less responsible age have to be insisted upon by the state. A recent study has sneered at the UFO's social legislation as 'conventional as yesterday,'[20] but that was the whole point of the exercise. It was the perceived values and standards of a Victorian yesterday that Drury and his colleagues sought to entrench through the actions of their government.

Whether it was the mothers' allowance or the Parents' Maintenance Act, a common thread binds together the fabric of these varied measures: the preservation of the family unit and its built-in obligations as a sure route to the salvation of society. And the premier placed these actions not in the context of collectivism but in a broader one of Christian humanitarianism. That force, as he never wearied of reminding listeners, had in the nineteenth century banished slavery, softened the effects of the Industrial Revolution, and sought to apply on earth the principles of the brotherhood of man and the fatherhood of God. In Drury's pantheon of heroes, Abraham Lincoln, William Wilberforce, and John Stuart Mill occupied prominent niches. The liberation movements with which they and other reformers were identified he lumped together with his own government's efforts in the twentieth century, all of which he characterized as the 'indirect results of the Great Christian Revival that began with John Wesley.'[21] This kind of continuum, with its 'deep-seated sense of justice and right' – not perhaps the comparatively recent arrival of the Social Gospel – served to forge in Drury's mind the link between Christianity and the reform impulse.

For the premier and others such as W.E. Raney, an equally important building block in the structure of reform was prohibition, the movement that would root out the physical and moral evil threatening the vitality of the community. 'Any physician ought to know by this time,' a typical letter advised Drury, 'that alcohol lessens the powers of the system to fight disease, when great medical associations, boards of health, government commissions, *and even the British War Office*, have decided it to be so.'[22] On the even more compelling moral argument, a denominational magazine rejoiced in the wake of the 1919 referendum that 'Never again will ... John Barleycorn ... be allowed to establish himself in the "lurking places of the villages" or "to murder the innocent".'[23]

For Raney, the war on liquor constituted the keystone in the arch of social rejuvenation. He bent every effort to bring it to a successful conclusion through an effective enforcement of the Ontario Temperance Act and by aiding the work of the Board of Licence Commissioners, the body that administered the legislation. If the war were ever going to be won, the *Star* and other sympathetic papers argued, bold action would have to be taken when the circumstances were so favourable. Yet, as Drury readily appreciated, probably more than the zealous attorney general, prohibition could excite more passions and trigger more debate than any other subject. A major problem was that it could be construed as a threat, direct or implied, to personal liberty and freedom of choice. Drury realized that this kind of issue, like frenzied theological controversies over fundamentalism and evolution, for which the 1920s would also be notorious, would be eagerly picked up by a press hungry for the sensational.

There was another major consideration. The premier knew that any fanatical approach to the liquor question would alienate those Labour supporters vital to the life of his government. Some of them were already restive under the obligation to support an avowedly 'dry' administration. The disgruntled George Halcrow, who had tangled with Drury earlier on the question, occupied an admittedly extreme position; all the same, his voluble opposition might prove catching should Drury and Raney make any unwise moves. Among these would be to put a ban on the relatively inoffensive 'near beer' (two and one-half proof spirit) that was permissible under the temperance act. At the very least they could anticipate an outcry from bartenders and organized brewery workers. As it was, Drury came in for heavy criticism when he granted municipalities the power to award exclusive rights to 'Standard Hotels' to sell beer in their jurisdictions. Small shopkeepers instantly complained. Unlike hotel-owners, they were required to buy a licence to sell their wares and to close up at a prescribed hour, while hotels could remain open for business much longer and retail non-alcoholic items that were the small stores' stock-in-trade.[24]

In the early weeks of his administration, indeed even before he had finished the trying chore of cabinet-making, Drury received more than one letter like the following:

You may think other matters will overshadow the question of prohibition, that the talk about it will die out, if you have that idea, dismiss it. The people are discontented at so many prohibition laws, possibly in the country around which you farm ideas may be different, but get the ideas of the workers in the Cities, in the Towns, get the ideas of the great majority and you will ascertain that prohibition of the People's liberty is not favoured.[25]

And the premier would probably have agreed with Clifford Sifton's judgment that if Raney, as rumoured, went 'searching ... cellars for Liquor,' there would be 'war declared on the Government of a different character altogether from what it has [had] to contend with heretofore.'[26] Drury swiftly quashed such rumours by announcing that the government had no intention of amending the Ontario Temperance Act so as to permit the 'transgression ... of private rights that ... every British subject holds dear.'[27]

The complaints from urban citizens, and particularly working people, doubtless played their role in shaping Drury's labour policy. Arguably the Minimum Wage Act of 1920 formed just as much a part of his family legislation as mothers' allowances, for it would cover every female wage earner in Ontario. But the act should also be assessed in the context of Drury's relations with the Labour MLAS and his need to mollify them. Not surprisingly, they had wanted a more comprehensive measure involving male workers as well. Even if Drury had wanted to meet their wishes, the UFO would have opposed such a move as class legislation, on a par with the mollycoddling of superannuated civil servants. The same rural reaction would have greeted the demand for an eight-hour day, dismissed as laughable on the farm where even Labour Day went unobserved.[28] For his part, Drury clung to a common belief that shorter hours might imperil productivity and the workingman's moral fibre.[29] Indeed, when he learned that the International Labour Conference had gone on record in favour of a reduced working week he immediately registered his concern with the Department of Labour in Ottawa.

Yet if newspaper reports had it right, not all of his ministers felt the same way. Biggs was supposed to have remarked at a church supper that he favoured nothing less than a 'six-hour day for all the workers of Canada.'[30] While Drury shrugged off this ill-advised outburst, he could not take so lightly the entreaties of his Labour colleagues. But fortunately for him, neither Rollo nor Mills pushed what Drury and others denigrated as class programs, like the ones consistently proposed by Halcrow. Among these was unemployment insurance, which UFO officials denounced as a 'premium on laziness' that would make urban life even more attractive at the expense of the countryside.[31] Years later the premier gratefully recalled that most members of the Labour contingent had not been 'at all narrow or selfish ... [and] did not use their position to demand unreasonable ... legislation.'[32]

Even so, prodded by Rollo and his own humanitarian instincts, Drury periodically took steps to cope with the unemployment crisis. Spawned by a severe postwar slump, it was one that beleaguered municipalities with strained treasuries claimed they could no longer handle on their own. In the closing days of 1920 Drury chaired a conference attended by representatives of veterans' groups, labour unions, and the business community. Out of it came a major recommendation that the province supplement municipal grants for what was called 'urgent and immediate relief,' and that a similar request be directed to Ottawa.[33] These deliberations and Drury's overtures to the Meighen government produced a plan whereby Queen's Park would defray one-third of a municipality's unemployment expenses and Ottawa would contribute a matching amount, but only as long as the so-called crisis persisted. The proviso demonstrated that this was viewed as a relief operation aimed at dealing with the immediate situation only.

In spite of the bad times, Drury still embraced the belief that much of the problem would dissolve if only the urban unemployed would help to relieve the labour shortage stalking the concession lines. Although realistic observers such as Good had long questioned the value of untried city labour, Drury continued to press the point. He minced few words when he addressed the problems posed by Toronto's joblessness. He told the city's treasurer that 'unless it could be shown that the people seeking relief in a city ... this size were willing to take employment outside of the city [he] would not be willing to consider favorably any request for assistance by the Provincial Government.'[34]

The Minimum Wage Act turned out to be the only significant piece of labour legislation that Drury put on the books, though he did not consider it his only achievement in this field. In a statement drawn up at the end of its term the government pointed to increased payments and allowances to injured workers and to widows under the Workmen's Compensation Act, and to improvements to the Mechanics' Lien Act which required the employment of journeymen electricians on the construction of rural Hydro lines. These admittedly brought complaints from Hydro about added labour costs and unpleasant letters from rural handymen who had used such work to supplement their income.[35] Yet the political risk of meeting some of Labour's marginal demands had to be taken, particularly if ILP men were to be reconciled to the indefinite deferment of their more ambitious programs.

It followed that Labour's backing for prohibition, so vital to Drury's plans, would be tepid at best. One recurring complaint was that the workingman's source of beer was now shut down by 'class legislation' while no such hardship was suffered by the wealthy. They could summon up all the so-called cellar supplies they could consume by simply resorting to purchases outside the province now that the federal wartime ban on importation had been lifted.[36] But the criticisms of deprived urban workers went beyond this. They accused some of their ostensibly dry country cousins of hypocrisy, of brewing or distilling in the privacy of the barn for their own use, while voting against alcohol for city folk. The charge may have had some substance if conditions described at the turn of the century still prevailed in the townships. A former president of the OAC recalled how his father had brewed a hearty beer for his farm workers and how he, his son, had sometimes drunk this home brew before handing on the pail to the next thirsty hand.[37] Beer plainly survived for some years to come, though there is no way of determining the extent of illicit rural moonshining at this time.

Yet the temperance act did condone the domestic manufacture for sale of one intoxicating beverage – wine. The promotion of this Canadian product was in deference to the grape growers of the Niagara peninsula, no mean pressure group, and quite possibly an expedient concession to the thirsty urbanite who might settle for wine if denied the hard stuff. At the very least the arrangement was a kind of safety valve for the government, particularly when it learned that under the temperance act no limit was specified on the strength of native wines, which sometimes soared to a staggering 28% proof. Left to his own devices Raney might have taken action against such a powerful libation, but in the light of certain political realities Drury persuaded him to change his mind. The influential Dominion Alliance and its formidable spokesman, the Reverend Ben Spence, were treated to the same kind of persuasion when they appeared at the legislature early in 1920. The previous day their open letter had arrived for Drury, complaining about the authorities' failure to consign to the sewer recently confiscated 'vile concoctions, poisonous swill [and] swine wash [that] were taken from dives and dens, from the unclean foreigner, from the offscouring of the Province.'[38] Most of the cabinet assembled to hear the impressive Spence on the main staircase of the legislature. After he held forth it was Drury's turn. After promising that he would spare no effort to enforce the Ontario Temperance Act, he warned the Alliance that he was opposed to the kind of enforcement that would provoke a hostile reaction and 'jeopardize the permanent cause of temperance.'

Drury was determined that the act should be amended, or even scrapped, not by the government of the day or by legislative action but only by the electorate. 'Let us enforce the law,' he sternly advised, quoting the text of populism, 'as the people have suggested.' Otherwise, if the question were thrown into the House or the cabinet it would be turned into a plaything of party politics 'where the financial strength of the liquor interest would make itself felt through campaign funds.'[39] The periodical submission of vital policies to the people – that is, government by referendum – was frowned upon, however, in those same circles that criticized Drury's penchant for government by commission. It was deemed, in short, unparliamentary and irresponsible.

The premier was subjected to the same charge when he sought through private members to plug a breach in prohibition's defences that threatened to make the act unenforceable. This was caused by so-called short-circuiting, which involved the purchase of liquor stocked in the province through an agent located outside it. In this case, with the government's hearty approval, a UFO legislator, F.G. Sandy, introduced the sought-after remedial measure and saw it carried by Farmer and Liberal votes. The same tactic was used and the same result achieved when advantage was taken of Ottawa's Bill 26 which provided for a referendum on the importing of liquor into a dry province should one be requested. If the referendum carried in favour of an import ban, then the federal government, which had sole jurisdiction in the matter, would oblige by proclaiming the necessary order-in-council. However, when the resolution seeking an Ontario referendum had been moved, again by a private member, the Drury government was immediately condemned for dodging its responsibilities.[40] As convincingly as he could, the premier shot back that this indirect procedure had the advantage of guaranteeing a full and uninhibited discussion of the question in the House. In fact, he and Raney knew that Labour men, with the possible exception of Rollo, were opposed to any further ventures down the prohibition road. Thus, by the stratagem of avoiding a formal government initiative, Drury was spared a hostile reaction from the ILP that could well have embarrassed his administration. Once again the politics of expediency had to be blended uncomfortably with the politics of principle.

The date of the referendum was set well in advance. It would be 18 April 1921, and in the weeks leading up to the voting, Raney, the Dominion Alliance, the evangelical denominations, and much of the press eagerly entered the fray. It was perceived to be crucial to determining whether or not Ontario would be rendered 'bone dry.' In his memoirs Drury described his part in the campaign as a small one, and, significantly, undertaken 'against the advice of some of my friends who thought it was poor politics.' Biggs might have been one of them. His ardour for the prohibitionist cause, never overwhelming, cooled considerably when he sensed a growing opposition to organized temperance.[41] Characteristically, Drury shunned the advice and spoke in a number of major centres, including Toronto and London. For the most part, however, immersed as he was in other matters – notably Hydro politics – he left much of the campaigning to the tireless Raney.

But when the premier did speak out he boldly defended the referendum. In meetings in Toronto, attended by citizens in their thousands who came out of either conviction or a desire for live theatre, Drury hammered away at what he called the 'clarification of the question.' Still wary of the fanatical approach, he stressed that logic and reason, combined with righteousness, could effectively destroy an evil that had inflicted so much damage on society. 'Speaking of the revival of crime in Ontario,' the *Globe* reported from an overflow meeting in Toronto's Mutual Street arena, 'the Premier declared that it was due to the influences let loose by the opening of the floodgates of liquor in the removal of wartime restriction.' Drury insisted that the question was not merely one of traffic regulation but of law-observing. 'Every cellar,' he warned, 'will be a potential centre of the illicit boot-legging trade' if the referendum did not carry.[42] Sharing the platform with Drury that tumultuous evening was N.W. Rowell, another staunch prohibitionist. Carried away by the enthusiasm of the cause, Rowell declared that 'this magnificent gathering typified the uprising of the people of Ontario, not against individuals, not against their fellow-citizens, but against the organized, legalized liquor traffic.'[43] He echoed Drury's assertions that when the referendum carried the observance of the law would triumph over its bending and breaking.

Others were not so sure. Aware of how the Americans' controversial Volstead Act threatened respect for the law by breeding lawlessness, these critics claimed that otherwise law-abiding citizens invariably reacted against enforced moral uplift and connived with the bootlegger. Remove the restrictions, they pleaded, and the unlawful, anti-social element would be shorn of their dubious livelihood. To such arguments Drury and his attorney general turned a deaf ear. 'If the referendum fails,' Drury warned early in 1921,

we would be confronted for a time with this unenforceable law. In the end public feeling would swing against us. We would have first a period of chaos, lack of respect for the law, and then a period of retrogression ... With the passing of the referendum you will have the liquor trade where it will be definitely possible to control it. You will have a generation of young people growing up who know not the taste of alcoholic liquor.[44]

Both men reacted similarly to an alternative put forward by the anti-prohibitionist Citizens' Liberty League that had long counselled respect for the democratic freedom of choice. Among other things, it called for government control and sale of liquor in the province as a substitute for the temperance act's arrangements. Predictably, the league was smeared as a front for those liquor interests who would stand to benefit from any erosion of the regulations, including government control however effectively it was handled.[45] Drury made the point that that kind of control in neighbouring Quebec, the principal source of Ontario's liquor supplies, had not checked its manufacture and sales in that province.

Then the evangelical church press took up the cry. 'As [Mr. Raney] has pointed out', the *Canadian Baptist* warned its flock in an editorial entitled 'The Duty of the Hour', 'Government control, with the door wide open to permit liquor in unlimited quantities to come into the Province, means no control at all.' To Drury's satisfaction the paper urged what he had throughout the referendum campaign, that 'Christian womanhood' rally to the occasion as they had so effectively in 1919.[46]

The results of the voting on 18 April 1921 were everything, or nearly everything, that Drury, Raney, and the Dominion Alliance could have wanted. The referendum was passed by a substantial majority of some 167,000 votes and the door was opened to making more effective the ban on importation and the defusing of short-circuiting. By the following July both had taken effect.

Even while the victors were rejoicing, they might have taken time out to ponder certain realities lost sight of in the euphoric moment of triumph. For one thing, considerable though it was, the margin of victory in 1921 fell short of the one two years earlier when the Ontario Temperance Act had been put to the test. For another, well-directed criticism had assailed Drury's program in the newspapers, in the pronouncements of labour organizations, and in the admittedly suspect advertisements of the Citizens' Liberty League. What could not be lightly disregarded were the reservations expressed by the Trades and Labour Congress and by the Anglican community, which were beginning to lean in favour of government control.[47] And while the *Farmers' Sun* hailed the verdict as a triumph for rural Ontario and its 'splendid men and women,' other voices in the countryside were not so certain that prohibitive legislation was the answer. These echoed the city-based Liberty Leaguers and called for 'education and moral leadership' as a means of solving the problem rather than recourse to the temperance act, which was held up as a confession of moral defeat.[48] There was also the prospect that such a visible commitment to prohibition would provoke ridicule among the articulate 'professional classes.' For the premier, however, these were the very sort who had long proved so repellent to him and his family. They were the 'smart set' who presumed to have the status and prestige to dictate community standards and to question the values of their 'inferiors.' Whenever he could, Drury took pains to excuse himself from those professional and financial gatherings that entertained with liquor.

The drys also had to reckon with the mocking humorist. The irrepressible Stephen Leacock, who had hailed mothers' allowances as the saviour of 'frail womankind,' could condemn in the next breath the 'un-British' attempt of the prohibitionist to stifle liberty.[49] In other writings he waxed more witty at the expense of such reformers as Drury and Raney. 'Landing in England after spending the summer in Ontario,' Leacock wrote, 'it seemed a terrible thing to see people openly drinking on an English train. On an Ontario train, as everybody knows, there is no way of taking a drink except by climbing up on the roof, lying flat on one's stomach, and taking a suck out of a flask.' And on prohibition's supposed powers to foster efficiency and dedication among workingmen, a favourite topic with farmers and the middle class, he remarked: 'In the old days they used to drop their work the moment the hour struck. Now they simply refuse to do so. I noticed yesterday a foreman in charge of a building operation vainly trying to call the bricklayers down ... [T]hey just went on laying bricks faster than ever.'[50]

Nor was Drury personally immune from this sort of treatment. Once, at a banquet in Barrie, a good-natured prohibitionist skit was performed that called for one of the participants to sing out at the appropriate moment: 'Ernie, Ernie, I've been thinking, what would you and Raney do, if all the citizens of this county drank ... home brew?'[51] From all accounts 'Ernie' took it in good part and laughed along with the audience. On the other hand, judging by what was said about Raney's stubborn resistance to cultivating a sense of humour, the attorney general may not have responded the same way.[52]

However they might have reacted to the scoffers, neither man took kindly to abuses in the system. One was opened up when physicians were authorized under the temperance act to issue prescriptions of alcohol for so-called medicinal purposes. The bulk of the liquor drawn off from the government dispensaries established by the Hearst administration went into the filling of such prescriptions.[53] In a good many cases they appeared to have been prescribed lavishly, particularly at Christmas time. Drury complained that medical men were betraying a trust and using their profession as a 'thin cloak for bootlegging.'[54] Furthermore, outraged prohibitionists queried the impressive inventories of the dispensaries which boasted spirits that an aficianado would have been happy to see reposing in his own cellar. 'Imagine, Mr. Premier,' fumed one critic, 'an honest, busy doctor specifically prescribing Kilmarnock's Scotch, or Thompson's Grand Highland, strictly for medicinal purposes. Or the ... Editor of the Christian Guardian asking for Usher's Green Stripe label for sacramental purposes?'[55]

To curb the practice, one that plainly mocked the law, Raney ordered doctors, on pain of prosecution, to limit their alcohol prescriptions to forty a month. Soon enough there were heated reactions in the legislature and in physicians' offices when prosecutions were carried out. Charges of partisan spite were laid when Dr Forbes Godfrey, MLA, one of the more rollicking Conservative members, lost his right to issue prescriptions because of his allegedly flagrant abuse of the service. The pejorative phrases dear to that generation, 'Bolshevik' and 'soviet,' were freely bandied about in the House and in the press to describe such punitive actions. The unlucky attorney general was caught uncomfortably between the arch-prohibitionists who thundered that, thanks to the dispensaries, the administration itself was the province's leading bootlegger, and the so-called moderates who accused him of high-handed tactics dangerous to peace, order, and good government. In an attempt to reassure the champions of uplift that his convictions were in the right place, Raney ran the risk of alienating law-abiding citizens who resented their government acting in a dictatorial manner. Even if Raney were not the unpleasant creature that the Godfreys and the *Telegram* tried to make him out to be, he gave the appearance of being one, and that was probably all that mattered.

A controversy swirled around Raney's scheme to restrict appeals in temperance cases on the grounds that they enabled bootleggers to 'frame up anything at all.'[56] A special committee of the House advised otherwise, and in the end Raney had to give way. In early March 1921 he brought in a bill that, while it ruled out retrials except on evidence taken before a magistrate, did concede the right of appeal to county court judges, a procedure which Labour MLAs had strongly supported. According to the newspapers, Drury was prepared to back his attorney general to the hilt, and told his caucus that should Raney's bill be defeated he would resign and go to the country. But the *Globe* suggested that if the story were true it amounted to bluster for there was 'but a small probability of a House majority standing out for admission of new evidence.'[57] Anyway, neither Dewart nor Ferguson was prepared to force a division that might precipitate an election for which the opposition was still woefully unprepared. Drury, as the papers rightly concluded, must have been fully aware of this fact of life.

Yet he was also made aware of another fact – that even if the MLAs opposite always stopped short of actually felling his government, they skilfully used the debates to paint Raney as a dangerous autocrat. Drury was always sensitive to this issue, and he betrayed his concern when the opposition, in a spasm of bitter name-calling, charged that Raney was transgressing the citizen's liberties and subverting the traditional appeals procedure. The attorney general was also accused of setting himself up as a 'bully of the law,' a charge repeated when he reorganized the provincial police to make them a more effective enforcer of the temperance act. Such a 'semi-military body' would not likely find favour with some vocal UFO members either. But what raised the legislature's temperature was the fear that Raney, under cover of enforcing the law, was becoming a kind of puritan theocrat out of control.[58] This reaction also greeted Raney's attempts to lay down the law to local magistrates in the determination of temperance cases brought before them. His actions were denounced as an unhealthy interference with the judicial system and destructive of the magistrate's discretionary power. Even some papers that had hitherto backed his crusade repudiated his removal of a magistrate who had allegedly been guilty of aiding the liquor interests and bringing the law into disrepute.

Another storm blew up over Raney's attempt to combat race-track gambling through the imposition of a 5 per cent tax on pari-mutuel betting. This particular battle in the war on evil turned out to be as lively as the prohibition campaign. Drury was buffeted by accusations that Raney was either trying to force such betting out of business or being a party to it by feeding off its profits. But he could take some comfort from the knowledge that his attorney general was in good company. At the federal level the premier's friend, W.C. Good, had also moved to have gambling taxed, an initiative that was instantly linked with Raney's at Queen's Park.

Raney was also accused of playing favourites, a charge which he quaintly dismissed in these terms: 'I am in favour of enforcing the law whether the party be a silk hatted gentleman or a poor Chinaman playing fantan in his back room.'[59] One charge brought against him Drury had to handle in his official capacity as premier. A Cuban official angrily wrote Arthur Meighen about Raney's reported comments that 'owing to gambling at the Race Tracks in Ontario, Canada was being placed on the level with the Governments of Cuba and Mexico.'[60] A bemused Meighen gratefully turned the matter over to Drury, who presumably succeeded in mollifying the ruffled diplomat.

A more serious question arose over the way Raney dealt with an injunction aimed at restraining the gambling tax. Even Drury might have been taken aback by the attorney general's blunt reaction to the court decision: he brought in a bill that amounted to nothing less than an assertion of the doctrine of legislative supremacy for it declared that 'no action could be [taken] against a Minister ... in connection with his official duties,' and, with regard to the tax measure itself, that any injunction is 'hereby forever stayed.'[61] The opposition promptly assailed Raney's actions as an insult to the bench and a violation of Magna Carta.

This episode did little to improve Raney's image as an even-handed minister of the crown. Sometimes, as Drury recalled, the abusive criticism of the attorney general's policies and methods could turn nasty, as when anonymous ill-wishers 'used to call his wife up on the telephone and threaten [his] life ... [She] was a very neurotic woman ... poor Raney had a life of it.'[62]

That may be one reason why Drury usually let his high-principled minister have his head and did comparatively little to restrain him. Another reason was Raney's apparent indispensability. And yet Drury might well have asked himself at what point this kind of indispensability priced itself out of the market and endangered the whole political economy. Certainly some of his critics in the UFO looked unkindly on his reluctance to control those of his colleagues who were commanding less and less respect on the concession lines. Instead of exploring the question, Drury sweepingly exonerated his attorney general of any fanaticism, vindictiveness, or insensitivity when he set about his tasks.

Indeed, Drury, once anxious to proceed with care in such a sensitive field as prohibition, was now being accused of a change of heart and of openly condoning Raney's harsh actions. The premier had initially set his face against the invasion of the citizen's home and castle in search of illicit booze; but by 1921 no liquor could be kept on the premises for a year if the occupant had been charged with an offence under the temperance act. And automobiles and yachts, highly mobile extensions of the household, could now be tracked down and searched for illegal liquor, as could ships in general whose owners or captains were to be held responsible for on-board infractions of the law. On the face of it, this seemed a far cry from the stand originally taken, and with so much fanfare, by the premier. Moreover, the employment of special officers (or 'stool pigeons') to uncover infractions soon came under fire when it was learned that undesirables with drinking problems of their own or even with criminal records were being used to trap the unwary drinker. However many special officers may have been properly sober and law-abiding, there was a visible minority who were not, and it was this questionable group that gave Drury and Raney recurring headaches.

Understandably, both men took steps to stop the recruitment of what one opponent called thugs and criminals. 'If you mean to enforce an act,' Drury repeated the obvious, 'you have to get popular sympathy, and you cannot do it by methods of this sort.'[63] His critics at the UFO central office would have been quick to agree. Probably welcoming another chance to put the premier and his attorney general in their place, Morrison stated publicly that those who 'leave the OTA to the mercies of enforcement officers are poorly serving the cause of true Temperance ... Supporting public opinion will not be developed with a club, and the sooner we realize that the better.'[64]

Soon enough Drury learned another lesson of government. Strong-willed and over-zealous agents who had the political and moral backing of their districts could frequently frustrate Queen's Park's intentions by embarking on unrestrained crusades of their own against bootleggers and law-breakers. But in spite of the notorious Spracklin Case,'[65] in which a militant parson shot and killed a suspected rum-runner, Drury constantly consoled himself with the thought that what was being done in the name of the law was, generally speaking, achieving its aim of reducing lawlessness and crime. He doubtless made as much of it then as he did so categorically in his published memoirs. 'Under Raney's enforcement crime reached its lowest [stage] in the history of the province,' a point he made before a Senate committee in the United States when he advised it on the workings of the Ontario Temperance Act.[66]

All this self-congratulation was sharply reminiscent of the praise he lavished on his family legislation whose objects he always twinned with the campaign to eradicate liquor. More dispassionate observers, however, took exception to his prohibition claims. 'The figures of the period,' wrote one historian, 'could be made to say almost anything a person wanted them to say. Drinking and boot-legging, violations and prosecutions, illegal importation, and rum-running continued. Speak-easies, blind-pigs, and illicit stills grew in number throughout the period – some apparently within walking distance of Queen's Park.'[67]

On the other hand, in spite of Drury's warm advocacy of a 'bone dry' province, he and his government had not exactly invented prohibition, the Board of Licence Commissioners, or the dispensaries. Instead they had inherited a system which they felt morally and politically obligated to make work. Moreover, they claimed to have done so, in spite of what the opposition might have said, without unduly imperilling individual rights and freedoms. Drury was convinced that, by and large, he had succeeded in treading a difficult middle path between the realities of this world and the puritanical otherworldliness of the Dominion Alliance. At the same time he had strengthened his resolve to use his government as a means of entrenching those virtues that had supposedly made Ontario the envy of the rest of the country as a 'stable and restrained society.'[68] He also liked to tell himself, as he proudly reviewed mothers' allowances, prohibition, and the other expressions of his social legislation, that those qualities had been shaped by what he called the permanence which the rural community had infused into provincial society.

12

Cleaning up the North

Shortly after taking office Drury received letters whose enthusiasm for prohibition was, to say the least, muted. Several came from northern or New Ontario, predictably in the main from outraged members of the Citizens' Liberty League. Among other things, they took unkindly to the premier's charge that their organization was a mere front for the liquor interests. One letter raised the spectre of the north's secession from the province. 'In this country,' Drury was told by a mining engineer, 'there are very few pleasures, few diversions, and we cannot see eye to eye with the Uplifters of the South, who have everything.' 'It was King George the third,' the writer warned, 'who lost the American Colonies. It is possible that you will be the man who will go down to posterity as the man who lost Northern Ontario to Southern Ontario.'[1]

Disgruntled libertarians and people ill equipped to deal in a manly way with social deprivation were one thing and could easily be dismissed by Drury and his colleagues. But certain species of critics were another. Thus the premier was advised that there were more solid reasons for the north's disenchantment with the southern metropole. 'I beg to say,' the operator of a silver mine wrote, 'that [separatist] discontent had its origin in the maladministration of a ring of Ontario Government officials and not with the laws of the province as a whole.' 'It appears to me,' he added ominously, 'that, although Ontario has a UFO-Labour Coalition government, the people of the North are still governed by the officials of the late and disreputable Ontario Government.' Others took up the ancient cry of Victorian colonial reformers that 'absentee government is not as good as local government,' and added that the province was after all merely a county writ large, and 'when a County becomes unwieldy a new [one] is formed out of it.'[2]

Some months later, Drury felt constrained to offer some remarks on the subject to a gathering of North Bay teachers. After characterizing the separatist movement as serious, he declared that 'Old Ontario could get along better without

New Ontario' than the latter could shorn of the former. A month later in Cochrane he softened an earlier suggestion that the north should resign itself to being a ward of the southern heartland. He noted that 'New Ontario is a treasured daughter in her mother's house. She can go out, I suppose, if she wants to, but if she goes, she goes, not as a grown woman but as a more or less helpless girl.' It could have been a Kipling speaking in the old family idiom of empire that had so appealed to Canadian imperialists of Drury's youth, and the kind of stuff upon which he himself had been raised. To a person who thought the integrated family a prerequisite for growth, harmony, and stability, the use of the family metaphor in this case seemed extraordinarily apt. Drury would not happily countenance a movement that would destroy the integrity of Ontario and prematurely thrust into the world a community not yet ready to face it. He firmly told his northern audiences that there 'are not two Provinces, not two sections but one,' and denied charges that New Ontario was being exploited 'like some milch cow for the gratification of southern appetites.'[3] He then promised his listeners that he would proceed more circumspectly than those who had earlier tried to develop the timber, mineral, and agricultural resources of the north. He also went out of his way to upbraid Howard Ferguson's handling of the Department of Lands, Forests and Mines, which he claimed had saddled the north with ill-advised schemes of development and given away a hapless colony's advantages to plunderers. Drury's first target was Kapuskasing and its precarious Soldiers' Settlement Farm Colony; the second was the alleged corruption that had disfigured the lease of timber limits to private concerns.

The once popular Kapuskasing scheme had been conceived during the war as Ontario's answer to Ottawa's back-to-the-land movement. It had provided an opportunity for veterans to try their hand at agriculture, and was also intended to check the farmers' drift to the prairies and reverse rural depopulation. For years favourable reports had been circulated about the potential of the so-called Great Clay Belt of which the Kapuskasing area formed a part. Promoters and boosters had once found a ready audience for their highly flavoured accounts of the potential of this 'true North.' The appeal was enhanced by the stress they laid on the benefits that would flow from the National Transcontinental and the Toronto and Northern Ontario Railway which had already been completed to Cochrane. Howard Ferguson had subsequently taken firm control of the colonization program at Lands and Forests, organized the Soldiers' Settlement early in 1917, and within a year established a hundred families at Kapuskasing, near the site of a former prisoner-of-war camp.[4] Unfortunately lack of planning, misplaced optimism, the faulty selection of candidates, not to mention the glaring shortcomings of the environment, combined to frustrate an otherwise praiseworthy experiment.

It was this unhappy situation that was brought to Drury's attention shortly after he took office. A delegation from the settlement showed up at the legislature and made no pretence at hiding their feelings about life at Kapuskasing. Although much of the Clay Belt was supposed to be moderately fertile, the task of clearing the land and coping with a cramped growing season and savage winters had taken much of the starch out of the enterprise. One correspondent had already spoken for many of the disaffected when he wrote of how he had been misled by the program's sponsors, while another wryly wondered if 'we will be compelled to sit back and wait until the arctic warms.'[5] Other criticisms poured from the delegation: supplies of seed and food were erratically arranged and, to complicate matters, a promised paper mill had failed to materialize. Consequently the settlers' pulpwood, their only source of revenue apart from farming, had no local market. In keeping with the 'manufacturing condition,' which decreed that raw materials must not be exported but rather processed on the provincial premises to provide cheaper products and gainful employment, the settlers ordinarily would not have been allowed to sell their pulpwood to exporting companies in the north. But the poverty facing these last frontiersmen was so heartbreaking, an historian has written, 'that not even the most determined administrator could dismiss their appeals without feeling some sympathy for their plight.'[6] It was obviously heartbreaking enough for Drury. As Hearst had before him, he relaxed the manufacturing condition enough to permit the kind of transaction the stricken at Kapuskasing wanted.[7]

This move was well received in the settlement. 'We realize,' one colonist wrote the premier, 'that your Government intends to be fair to the Soldier, and in our dealings ... since [your] coming into power we have every reason to be pleased with the treatment we have received.' Then he added a comment that must have been welcome in an office so eager to put Howard Ferguson in his place: 'I have in my possession a large number of letters that would certainly not make good publicity for the late Government, whose affair this Settlement really was.'[8] Among other welcome initiatives, Queen's Park decided to assist a local clergyman in the distribution to destitute mothers of needed children's supplies and clothing, to the value of fifty dollars. 'In extraordinary cases,' Drury wired him, 'you may increase the amount,' but always, he insisted, only with the 'concurrence of the husband.'[9]

Most of the information that subsequently came to Drury was collected by a three-man investigating team that he despatched to the scene in February 1920. He made much of its non-partisan character: it comprised a Liberal, Colonel J.I. MacLaren of Hamilton, W.F. Nickle, the Kingston Conservative, and Professor John Sharp of Haileybury. Nickle's appointment begs some comment. According to Morrison's memoirs, he was supposed to have parted company with Drury on unfriendly terms but here he was again, prominently placed on the premier's list. Obviously Nickle's selection (and his desire to serve) showed that Drury could expect considerable support for his clean-up operation at Kapuskasing.

The report that Nickle and his colleagues submitted on 16 March 1920 was all that the premier could have asked for; it found little to praise in the organization and planning that had gone into the settlement.

But if Drury hoped that the Conservatives would be properly chastened and Ferguson undone he was in for a setback. The former minister let go instead with a barrage of recrimination in a compelling speech in the House. On few other occasions apparently did he show to such effect the dramatic street-fighting tactics he had brought to Ontario politics. In the course of his assault he accused the commission of acting unprofessionally and inconclusively by failing to gather sworn evidence and by neglecting to seek out those in the settlement who may have been satisfied with their lot. In his memoirs Drury allowed that there was only one such person who elected to persevere. Ferguson told it otherwise, however, and he turned out to be right: there were at least eight other intrepid survivors. The Conservative spokesman also claimed that a number of settlers had written him to express their satisfaction with what had been done for their community.

Then Nickle and MacLaren came under the gun. 'These Commissioners,' Ferguson told an amused House, 'were accustomed to living lives of comfort or of luxury. Take them out of Kingston or Hamilton, put them in the north where the snow is deep and there is no carpet on the floor – do this, and then ask them if they like it, and they shake themselves, shimmy-like, and say "No".'[10] He polished off his presentation by charging the government with smear tactics which only discredited the north and the productive work already accomplished there in mining and agriculture. Drury never seemed quite capable of adjusting to Ferguson's jugular debating style or of understanding those otherwise friendly newspapers who thought that his opponent got the better of his commission in the free-for-all he staged in the House. Yet if the government failed to extract as much satisfaction from its Kapuskasing exposé as it believed it deserved, at least it could take pride in the successful rejuvenation of the settlement.

The fruit of the commission's report was the appointment by order-in-council of an arbitration board, on which one settler was allowed to serve, whose task would be to determine the financial compensation for those who wished to leave the colony. Drury urged the board to err on the side of generosity, and to treat more generously those who elected to persevere with the colony. As for the ones who left, Drury wrote, 'if [they] recognize that the Government wishes to provide every man ... with at least $500.00 to start him in his new life, it will be seen that it is hardly right to speak of any settlement as being unfair.'[11]

Meanwhile, the logistics of removal were prepared: a special train was laid on for the convenience of the evacuees, lumber was freely supplied for packing crates, and food prepared for the scheduled trip to Toronto, some five hundred miles away. At the same time concerned relatives were alerted by night letters to prepare for the arrival of the decamped settlers, a characteristic Druryesque touch. But it was made quite clear that these arrangements would 'afford the last opportunity [for people] to leave the settlement under [the plan] provided by the Government.'[12] In any case, Drury, once denigrated as an 'Uplifter of the South,' showed that however much moral issues might engage his attention, the material and emotional wants of the north were also going to be vigorously addressed while he was in control at Queen's Park.

Not long after the departure of the last group of settlers in early May 1920, the premier paid the first of several visits to the site. Not surprisingly, he took a special interest in the Dominion Experimental Farm established there in 1912,[13] and paid particular attention to the problems facing the soldier-survivors. Drury saw to it that they received what had already been pledged – sufficient seed and supplies – and that the educational needs of their children would be met. But one major condition for survival was an industrial base for revitalizing the community. To that end negotiations were opened with the recently formed Spruce Falls Company, a Kimberly-Clark venture that wanted to operate a paper mill in the district. The area's highly marketable spruce, the presence of hydro power, and solid river and rail transportation combined to make it an attractive proposition to the company and a boon for Queen's Park.[14]

An agreement was reached in October 1920 whereby the company undertook to supply at cost all the timber, lumber, and other building materials for their employees' housing and for others who would commit themselves to the model town planned for the Kapuskasing site. In addition, the company was bound to furnish electrical power, again at cost, for houses and street illumination and other municipal purposes, until such time as the new community established its own power plant. The firm was permitted under the agreement to house their work force in the shelter already in place in the settlement, but was required to apply to Queen's Park should they wish to build additional accommodation. Clearly construction was not to be haphazard or unseemly. For its part, the Drury government guaranteed municipal bonds issued to fund house-building for other would-be citizens, and endorsed further civic improvements to the value of some half a million dollars. In the event of a municipal bond default, assurances were given that half of any amount Queen's Park might recover would be shared with the company. A housing commission, a planned intermediary between government and consumer, was authorized to sell lots at a price not to exceed one hundred dollars.[15]

Less than a month after the agreement was signed Drury paid another visit to the area. On this occasion he determined that the eastern rather than the western and much swampier side of the Kapuskasing River was the better location for the town. His thinking was reinforced by the expertise of others – J.A. Ellis of the Bureau of Municipal Affairs and L.V. Rorke, director of surveys – who accompanied the premier on his tours of inspection. The eastern choice, though it meant a reduction of the site originally contemplated, had one enormous advantage over the alternative, indeed, to quote Ellis's memo to Drury, 'over any other north country town.' Fire, the dreaded scourge of New Ontario, would be held at bay if the eastern location were chosen because for about 'three-quarters of its boundaries it will be protected ... by a considerable body of water.'[16] As if to prove the point, fire eventually consumed much of the ramshackle community that had survived west of the river, including the prisoner-of-war barracks. In this case the disaster had a silver lining, for it swept away an alleged Sodom and Gommorah of prostitution, gambling, and other assorted vices that had battened on this frontier construction project. Apparently the temporary mayor of the town, who owned considerable property in the devastated section, had been urging newcomers to shun the eastern side and throw in their lot with his domain.

The town was formally incorporated on 8 April 1921. Its main features were in place, including the celebrated 'Circle,' a hub from which five streets would radiate to the periphery of the town. Goderich, the Lake Huron municipality, plainly served as a model for this arrangement, which aimed at providing the new community with a focus for concentrating business activities at its very heart.[17] When the time came to name the 'Town out of the Forest' (its motto), the original identification seemed the most appropriate though Drury claimed that he rejected a suggestion that his name be honoured. In the end his graced one of the main streets instead, and the town was duly christened Kapuskasing.

In the meantime, the local UFO organization, to whom Drury lent an attentive ear, was requesting consideration of their special concerns. Some of them were heeded. It would appear, however, that one was not, a request that 'one or two French-Canadian members of our club' be allowed to take part in the deliberations of the first municipal council.[18] But the following year this was rectified, much to the disgust of Orange Lodge spokesmen, when three of the six council members were elected from the francophone community and grounds were set aside for a Roman Catholic church and a separate school. On the economic front, the Spruce Company's mills were beginning to function, ambitious and optimistic newcomers were settling in, and the groundwork was being laid for a precedent-setting urban experiment in New Ontario. Drury was entitled to the satisfaction he derived from these circumstances.

The premier now turned to his next northern objective, the offensive against Howard Ferguson's handling of the Lands and Forests portfolio. 'At his nomination [before the election of] 1919,' Drury gleefully recalled, 'I went down [to his riding] on purpose and told him that if there was a change of government, there would be a clean up in the Department. And I made good on my promise.'[19] This involved striking a royal commission to review Ferguson's record and placing it in charge of two former Liberals, W.R. Riddell and F.R. Latchford of the Ontario Supreme Court. In March 1920 they were assigned the task of determining the 'accuracy or otherwise of all returns made pursuant to the Crown

Timber Act ... by a holder of a timber license.' The so-called Timber Commission, which gathered testimony and sifted evidence for the better part of two years on this and other northern matters, became a major theatrical attraction. Its every move and decision were avidly followed by the newspapers, particularly when prominent lumber barons appeared before it and admitted that they had knowingly ignored crown land regulations in their quest for profits. The premier's joy swelled when the commissioners began receiving allegations of Ferguson's own culpability. It was discovered, for example, that he had breezily abused his powers and defied timber regulations and in the process surrendered sizable tracts without tender or public competition for only a fraction of the normal dues.[20] The key indictment was reserved for Ferguson's dealings with the Shevlin-Clarke Lumber Company, a name that became a despised household word in UFO circles. For many a Farmer and, of course, the premier, those dealings constituted the most damning examples of the corruption so vociferously condemned in the weeks leading up to the 1919 election. In the Shevlin-Clarke case, Ferguson had entered into a transaction with a company whose president happened to be a fellow Tory MLA and which had amounted to the sale of a timber limit for dues below the ordinary rate. If there was to be a new era in Ontario politics, Drury announced, then obviously antics such as these would have to be condemned and their perpetrators brought to justice.

Drury's excitement over the disclosures put a cutting edge on the speeches he delivered that summer in various parts of the province. Typical was a performance at Strathroy, where he complained that thanks to Ferguson's 'pilfering,' the treasury received no more timber revenue than New Brunswick, which had only one tenth of Ontario's resources. During his speech-making junket Drury was bolstered by the realization that others in high places shared his loathing for Ferguson and the political vices he was supposed to personify. 'There has never been,' Clifford Sifton sweepingly wrote in the fall of 1920, 'such an exposure of systematic long continued corruption ... and violation of the law as there was in the case of the investigation into the Crown Timber Department ... Ferguson broke the law ... deliberately and frequently ... His attitude is that of a thief who is caught with the goods and starts to make charges against the character of the [arresting] ... officer.'[21]

That conclusion flowed from the strategy that Ferguson used before the commission. The self-assuredness that he displayed at the hearings must have appalled the premier, particularly after he had been told by a *Globe* reporter that Ferguson was in a state of despair over the question. Drury later claimed that the newsman 'thought it would be a nice gesture on my part if I would say, which was perfectly true, that nothing [to date] had come out which would implicate Mr. Ferguson. Well, I was fool enough to do it and of course ... [the reporter] blew the whole thing up.'[22] The premier would have been even more shocked to learn that the imposing Canon Cody had at this time given the grieving minister the 'heart and courage' that enabled him to 'strengthen his faith in God and man.'[23]

Meanwhile Ferguson predictably insisted at the commission hearings that what he had done, or failed to do, had been in the best interests of the province as he had been in a position to define them. Anyway, he stated that he was prepared to leave the matter not to a judicial commission which could well have failings of its own, but to what he liked to call the 'jury of the public'.[24] Ferguson then joyously turned to the counter-offensive, thus promptly laying to rest the rumours of his unaccustomed passivity. Having been grilled himself, he proceeded to grill his inquisitors. After underscoring his own personal integrity by demonstrating that he had not gained one nickle from the various transactions, he impugned the political honesty of the commissioners. He charged that they were interested not so much in arriving at the truth as in mounting a personal vendetta. He shrewdly pointed out that Latchford, who had held Lands and Forests in George Ross's Liberal administration, was limiting the inquiry to the Conservative years. In other words, Drury's judicial investigation might not be so judicial after all but only a thinly disguised exercise in political assassination. Besides, Ferguson added in the spring of 1921, 'the timber probe is befuddled [and] ...is inspecting the little, trivial office sweepings that are picked up by the Crown Counsel with a broom and dustpan, and it has been unable to find anything in the sweepings that even discolours ... my administration.'[25]

Perhaps only the politically imaginative Ferguson could have brought it off. But his tactics in this case – the best defence is uninhibited assault and battery – designed to blunt the serious charges brought against him, served an even more important strategy. This was the pursuit of the formal and permanent leadership of his party, an exercise that would be judged at a Conservative convention in Toronto at the close of the year. In spite of widespread newspaper criticism, including even the *Telegram*'s hostile editorials, and the rebukes ladled out by the Timber Commission, a happy Ferguson was duly acclaimed the Conservative leader. If Drury had hoped that the investigation would dishonour his enemy's credentials and hound him out of political life he was rudely disappointed. That Ferguson could emerge from the fire of criticism, charred admittedly but still very much intact, helped to season the pejorative terms the premier used to describe the man who exemplified for him all the evils of Ontario politics. It was bad enough that Ferguson had done something illegal; it was even worse when those illegalities could be shrugged off as the pardonable excesses of a colourful politician. Often Drury behaved as though he were performing in some kind of modern morality play where right and goodness, when properly demonstrated, would automatically command the community's support, and 'naked wickedness' be summarily punished. But the kind of political theatre that reality produced, particularly when it was enlivened by a performer of Ferguson's talents, provided poor shelter for Drury's brand of idealism.

All the same, the premier could take some comfort from the final report of the Timber Commission in the summer of 1922. As anticipated, it vilified Ferguson's tactics and, while it could not tag him with personal corruption, challenged the power he had exercised 'over large areas of the public domain ... without regard to Regulation[s].'[26] Yet Ferguson's well-publicized questioning of the commission's integrity and impartiality probably sapped some of its credibility. Furthermore, the noisy resignation of the commission's Conservative counsel over disagreements with Latchford, and charges that his government counterpart had received a private retainer to gather evidence against one of the companies under investigation, may have further eroded its image. On the other hand, Attorney General Raney convinced himself at one stage of the proceedings that sinister (though unnamed) forces had been at work impeding the investigation and trying to bring it into disrepute. As might have been expected, the *Canadian Forum*, which under Sissons's political direction had usually smiled on the Drury government, rejoiced in the commission's report and echoed the premier's denunciation of Ferguson. The journal approved the recommendations that Lands and Forests' 'slipshod' bookkeeping and timber-grading methods be cleaned up, and finished its account by claiming that whatever the probe's critics might say, the 'labours of the Commission have thoroughly aroused public opinion.'[27]

While Drury was turning to the task of remedying administrative deficiencies in the department, he must have been encouraged by a commission report that appealed directly to his own concerns. It cited the need for the more conservative use of timber, and for 'recuperative measures' not only in the north but 'in the older parts of the Province.'[28] These objects Drury had long sought himself, and he spelled them out again for the Canadian Forestry Association early in 1922. 'To administer our forest wealth wisely,' he told them, 'is not to hold large areas untouched, but to replace wastage with new growth ... Ontario's virgin pine forests are unpleasantly nearing their end to-day.'[29] But he knew that actions would speak louder than words. The premier recalled one of the visits that E.J. Zavitz, the provincial forester, paid him, when he 'drove over the barren lands of [Simcoe] county.'[30] The two men took off the shelf and revivified the Counties Reforestation Act, originally passed by the Whitney government in 1911. This led in 1922 to the establishment of the so-called Agreement Forests, planted on lands counties were allowed to purchase on the understanding they would be committed to reforestation. In return, Queen's Park would undertake to plant and administer the lands for thirty (later extended to fifty) years.[31] After that, the county could reimburse the province for the cost of planting and care and take the forest over, or share ownership with it.

Although Simcoe County speedily took advantage of the program by acquiring a thousand-acre tract, the future Hendrie Forest, the premier grumbled about the slow response of other municipalities. Just as farmers had been suspicious of such efforts at the turn of the century so now their descendants seemed indifferent to the virtues of reforestation and the benefits it brought in its wake – the combating of erosion, the conservation of moisture, the regulation of stream flow, and the moderating of climate. In the case of the apathetic urban dweller,

Drury probably blamed his all-too-ready acceptance of the new technology that improved his life, and his failure to see how it was greedily consuming the province's natural resources. The premier shared his concerns with Manning Doherty, who had long complained that the twentieth-century world was 'insanely drunk' with the desire for industrial development and who had urged that it sober up by promoting more agricultural growth.[32] That Ontario's cornucopia might already have been seriously drained of its treasures, most of which were not renewable, was a possibility not readily grasped by most people of Drury's generation.

Yet if the premier had cause to complain about the counties' foot-dragging, then Sissons in turn queried what Drury had done. 'For twenty years,' his column in the *Canadian Forum* complained, 'Mr. Drury has been a public advocate of forest conservation and ... extension. Yet his ministry has so far achieved little of a constructive character.' Sissons paid a muted compliment to the county scheme but added that a broad constructive policy still awaited a minister of vision and energy. This was an ill-disguised rebuke of Beniah Bowman whose lack of imagination had been noted by others besides Sissons.[33] On the other hand, Charles Stewart, a fellow native of Simcoe Country who served as Mackenzie King's Minister of the Interior, applauded Drury's endeavours and their contributions to international trade.[34]

In the meantime, the Timber Commission report touched on a major aspect of the 'Ferguson case' when it announced that action was being taken in the courts to recover all or part of the money that Ferguson's generosity to timber companies had allegedly cost the province. As a happy premier noted, a royal commission was not the only weapon that could be deployed in the war against wrong-doing. The courts could also be enlisted, in this case to redeem his pledge to make the companies pay for their transgressions of timber regulations and to draw even more attention to Ferguson's role in arranging the illegalities. In the action against Shevlin-Clarke, the most notorious offender, Drury appropriately called upon the legal services of N.W. Rowell, who had already fought shoulder to shoulder with him for prohibition.[35] Rowell had the satisfaction of winning the case and hearing the presiding judge roundly condemn the practices that had spawned the fraudulent grants. As a result of this and other judgments, something of the order of one and a half million dollars was recovered for the provincial treasury.[36] At a time when he was being assailed for frittering away taxpayers' money on commissions and investigations Drury extracted as much publicity value as he could from this bonanza.[37]

The taste of victory and vindication turned bittersweet, however, when Ferguson shrewdly exploited an arrangement entered into by the government with one of the major timber interests in northwestern Ontario. The story had begun in 1914 when one Edward Wellington Backus, a powerful Minnesota lumberman, purchased the Lake of the Woods pulp limit. Subsequently a number of factors

– the war, recurring financial problems, and concerns about water power problems – appeared to put the venture at risk. But Ferguson, the minister then responsible, had discounted these factors. Suspecting Backus of delaying tactics, he served notice that unless he complied with the original terms of the agreement his limits would be forfeited. Before Ferguson could take the appropriate action, however, the Hearst ministry was swept away. The Drury government that took its place also demanded results, and pledged itself to cancel the undertaking with Backus if they failed to materialize. Much to the premier's annoyance, Ferguson later claimed in the press most of the credit for this move.[38]

Like other freewheeling dynamos of his generation, Backus was not intimidated by threats that would have dismayed lesser mortals, and he responded to Drury's warning by boldly requesting a renewal and restructuring of the original contract. The proposal amounted to having Queen's Park sanction not only that arrangement but a lease of the White Dog Rapids site and a large pulp limit of some three thousand square miles on the English River. Backus grandly promised that if the Drury government approved, a truly productive pulp and power project would result that would dwarf the original. He doubtless used to good advantage his considerable charm and imaginativeness when he enlarged on his scheme in the presence of the premier and Raney.[39] Although they were plainly impressed by Backus's take-charge air, other factors merited as much attention. The two men were not so naive that they could not recognize big talk for what it was and cut through the smoke of the lumberman's glowing presentation to see that other interests would also benefit from an expanded enterprise in northwestern Ontario.

One of these was quite obviously the town of Kenora, the aspiring metropolis of the region. Indeed, when Backus appeared at the legislature in August 1920 he was backed by an awesome five-hundred-man delegation from the town led by its ebullient mayor, George A. Toole, who for years had been promoting industrial growth in his district.[40] His message was that if Backus were granted what he wanted Kenora would acquire those pulp and paper mills long regarded as the sine qua non of its future on the Laurentian fringe. An agreement to this effect, conditional upon Queen's Park's favourable response, had already been overwhelmingly ratified by the town's voters with Backus's Keewatin Pulp and Power Companies. In other words, Drury and Raney were told that if they rejected the proposal Kenora would go the way of the original settlement at Kapuskasing and the northland would suffer a major reverse. It was at this very juncture, of course, the summer of 1920, that the government was trying to sort out Kapuskasing's affairs and launch it as a model town. To have ignored the entreaties of a sister municipality, Backus's overtures aside, would have been inconsistent, not to mention impolitic. Drury doubtless reasoned that a kind of informal imperialism or empire by proxy could be arranged for Kenora whereby, for attractive profits and at little public expense, a private enterprise would shoulder an important public responsibility. Raney constantly underscored the point that 'so far as the water power [arrangement] is concerned the province [would] get all the benefits of public ownership without the investment of one dollar of public money.'[41]

At any rate, when Backus formally applied in writing for the new pulp limit on 20 August 1920, the government's response took the following form: that the English River limits be put up for sale provided that steps were taken to eliminate 'spurious bidders'; that Kenora's claims be reasonably protected; that assurances be offered that any development that did unfold be within the 're-quirements of the province'; and finally, that the area be properly defined.[42] At the end of August, when Backus showed up at Queen's Park to discuss the matter, he was advised what had long been promised, that his former properties were declared forfeited. However, at the same time he was assured that he would be given the White Dog Rapids concession and that the English River limits, on which the Kenora proposals hinged, would be put up for competition in a manner prescribed by the Crown Timber Act, the legislation that Ferguson had recently been accused of ignoring. With respect to the White Dog Rapids lease, Raney made it plain to Backus that it had been made 'subject to conditions which gave the Government absolute control of the development.' 'Under these con-ditions,' he continued, 'the government will require [Backus] to develop the full capacity of water power ... and to sell the surplus above his own requirements at such a price as the Government may see fit to dictate.'[43]

As he had at the beginning, the attorney general stressed what was obviously a crucial factor: Kenora's economic plight should the project founder. The town's indignation over the long delay in having its wishes met could no longer be ignored. Raney put it even more bluntly when dismissing an alternative scheme that would have located the projected mills not at Kenora but elsewhere in the English River limits:

I make no hesitation in saying that the interest of the people of ... Kenora ... was greater than the interest of the people of Toronto, and greater even than the interest of the whole of the rest of the province, and even if the location of the mills there [Kenora] had meant a little less revenue for the Government, which I believe is not the case, the Government would not have hesitated for a moment.[44]

As with prohibition or any other emotionally charged issue that came his way, Raney rarely did things by halves. And the premier, though he took no direct part in the actual negotiations, fully concurred in what his lieutenant proposed.

The agreement concluded with Backus on 30 September 1920, which settled the question of the power site and paved the way for the sale by tender of the English River limits, was fully reported in the press. Predictably, a Kenora paper greeted it as the best information in twenty years.[45] At the metropolitan level, both the *Globe* and the *Mail and Empire* dissected its major provisions, and the *Sun*, ever on the alert for the shenanigans of sharp businessmen, mildly rejoiced that Backus was forced to tender and that the Kenora situation was settled. 'The government,' it added more glowingly, 'made a very satisfactory bargain for the people of Kenora and the ... Province.'[46]

The paper's compliments contrasted sharply, however, with reports that the local UFO riding association had openly questioned the wisdom of doing business with the likes of Backus. One complaint was that his principal supporter, Mayor Toole, was an ardent Conservative and president of the party's local association. Not only this, Backus's American origins and flamboyant style did not endear him to some vocal UFO people.[47] Toole tried to minimize his Tory ties and to dismiss Backus's unflattering image in a letter sent off to the district's MLA, Peter Heenan. Heenan, an Irish-born locomotive engineer who had resided in the area for twenty years, responded by coming out solidly in favour of the undertaking.[48] A local form of Broadening Out that was welcomed in Drury's camp counted for more in some patriotic quarters in Kenora than a scrupulous adherence to UFO-Labour solidarity. Ideology was obviously going to take a back seat to pressing civic concerns in Kenora.

The September agreement contained the following protective features: the expenditure of some two and a half million dollars by Backus companies in the town of Kenora; the erection of pulp and paper mills having a daily capacity of at least two hundred tons of newsprint; the employment of a thousand people; and the observance of.the manufacturing condition whereby the timber or pulp-wood would be processed or manufactured in Kenora.[49] The hope was also expressed that railways would shortly be built to break down the English River's inaccessibility and open up the country generally. To expedite the proposed sale, the appropriate advertisement was prepared even before the agreement was con-cluded. Inexplicably, however, some weeks passed before it was placed in the province's major newspapers and trade journals. This omission was understand-ably clothed with sinister implications by Ferguson and others who were anxious to discredit a government whose Timber Commission had just discredited them. As it turned out, once the formal advertisement was placed on 11 November 1920 it ran in seventeen newspapers and through several editions. Drury and Raney satisfied themselves (with a smugness that enraged Ferguson) that the law had been observed, the appropriate advertising properly planted, and the required steps taken to put the limits up for competition.

On the whole, Drury and his attorney general were pleased by the reception accorded their initiative in the closing weeks of the year. Although some of the Toronto dailies were highly critical, the two men delighted in quoting a favourable editorial in the *Hamilton Spectator*, a paper that seldom approved of what the administration did.[50] Yet behind the scenes of editorial commendation there lurked suspicion and doubt. Some publishers were not as friendly as the *Spec-*

tator's and protested that the sale of the limits might actually endanger their paper supplies. For others, such as the jaded J. Castell Hopkins of the *Canadian Annual Review*, the Backus deal was not so much an exercise to condemn as an 'old story of monied interests seeing a chance to make some money, a Government seeing an opening for the important development of water-powers and timber, and increase in revenue, and critics seeing nothing but grants of water-powers and timber with little immediate return to the people.'[51]

By mid-December the Backus advertisement had run its course and the tenders were received. As well, E.J. Zavitz, who had been assigned to report on the English River limit, concluded that there was sufficient information upon which to base a sale. (His findings also revealed that of the limit's three thousand square miles, only about half bore serviceable timber, roughly a million acres.) A few days after his report was submitted the tenders were opened. 'Three of [the four received],' Drury disclosed on 23 December, 'are from the United States and one from British Columbia. No tender was received from any of the pulp or paper interests in ... Ontario or in Eastern Canada.' It turned out that Backus's tender, formally accepted by Beniah Bowman, the minister responsible, was the highest and that his firm pledged the largest bonus. But, as a gratified Drury emphasized in his December remarks, not only had the advertising and tendering regulations been scrupulously followed but – '*the really important thing*' – Kenora had been industrialized and presumably saved from extinction. He added some frosting to the cake of self-congratulation by claiming that the arrangement would also generate annually some two hundred thousand dollars in revenue, and 'eventually from the timber now standing an aggregate amount of from $8 million to $10 million dollars.' 'There can be no doubt,' he concluded, 'that the [undertaking] will help materially at once in relieving ... unemployment ... and contribute to the prosperity of the whole Province.'[52]

The joy in Kenora (that is, outside UFO headquarters) and the pleasure in the premier's office were soon punctured by Howard Ferguson's swift reaction. Mired in the Timber Commission's accusations, Ferguson grasped at the lifeline of the Backus deal to pull himself to political advantage. In a widely quoted speech at Uxbridge he charged that the opposing tenders had actually come from Backus's partner and paper broker – 'hardly fierce competitors,' as one historian has readily agreed.[53] Although two more plausible tenders had been submitted, the oft-repeated charge of spuriousness promptly stuck in the public mind. Then Ferguson set out to convince the electorate that what the premier had done far exceeded his own exercises in timber limit grants. He spoke repeatedly of secret deals with a questionable and, to boot, an alien entrepreneur beyond the scrutiny of responsible officials. It was vintage Ferguson. His attempt to demonstrate that the Drury government could well end up compromising their own high mindedness found a strong echo in those quarters not kindly disposed to Backus and his way of doing things. The *Globe*, for example, editorialized that the lumberman, the 'full fed gentleman from Minnesota,' had plainly got the better of the province and stood to profit handsomely.[54] Ferguson's shrewdly orchestrated counter-attack also confirmed the doubts of those who questioned Drury's tactics and staying power. Sifton was clearly one such sceptic, in spite of his now grudging respect for the Farmers' party. His commentary on recent events, ritualistically passed on to J.W. Dafoe, is worth presenting if only to show how certain basic points could be overlooked in a search for shortcomings. 'The haste with which the transaction has been carried through is one of its worst features,' Sifton's statement began.

But the unpardonable feature ... is the granting of such a huge limit of the public domain to anybody whatever ... the Government has plunged ahead giving over an enormous ... domain for practically no consideration whatever to a man who is not a citizen of Canada and who has shown himself defiant and impudent where ... Canadian rights [and] Canadian laws are concerned.[55]

Much of Sifton's statement merely amounted to a more civilized version of the kind of assault that Ferguson was organizing. With sincere friends like Sifton, the premier might have wondered, who needed foes?

On the other hand, Drury had to admit that some parties, like the aggrieved UFO constituency chairman in Kenora, had strongly advised caution in any dealings with Backus. He must also have realized that the award to the controversial lumberman would not only produce knowing winks and political leers but provide highly combustible fuel for Ferguson's counter-campaign. But perhaps the premier was becoming more accustomed to all this. He had survived similar taunts over the radials and prohibition and doubtless he expected to survive these latest.

Throughout the ordeal that was to come, Drury and most of his colleagues rose to the occasion in the rousing debates in the House and the speechifying on the road. Raney was the principal combatant for the government side and he left little out in his frequently ponderous recitations of the ancient history and recent affairs of the English River limit. At times it was an uphill battle. In spite of the cabinet's efforts, the Backus deal would continue in many circles to be regarded as a flawed and dubious transaction. For this, ironically, the government was to blame in a very real sense. Their highly publicized stand on probity and virtue in public life made it difficult for many a citizen to tolerate any perceived fall from grace. Another administration not so visibly committed to political righteousness might have had less trouble minimizing the charges that coloured Ferguson's counter-attack, a point not lost on that wily Conservative.

But Drury could spend little time agonizing over the implications of his recent actions. Other equally pressing problems had crowded into his agenda, including a crisis that arose within the very fold of the farm movement. He was brutally reminded of the festering dispute over Broadening Out which threatened to poison the government's relations with its principal constituency and in the process its political health.

13

Dissension and Defeat

One strong inkling of the dissension in Farmer ranks was the row over the control of the *Farmers' Sun*. It blew up in the spring of 1922 following reports that the UFO office – meaning Morrison and the president, R.W.E. Burnaby – were dissatisfied with the services of editor J.C. Ross. The complaint was that Ross, who had succeeded the aging W.L. Smith, refused to criticize the goverment for its various shortcomings. The upshot was that Ross vacated the editor's chair and took to managing the paper's business affairs. Still later, reports circulated that he was threatening to leave the *Sun* altogether and start a government-backed daily.

Upset by what he calld the hoop-la, Morrison tried to defuse the situation by claiming that every member of the board thought the reports about Ross were nonsense, and that Drury 'will not be so easily fooled as that.' Morrison went on to say that the new editor, John Hamm, had satisfactorily explained the situation to the premier and that M.H. Staples had moved in to calm down those Farmer MLAS who had been 'hot about it.' What Drury in fact thought about the situation was not disclosed either at the time or later in his varied memoirs. In any event Good, who shared Morrison's jaded opinion of the *Sun*'s editorial efforts, tried to pour oil on the troubled waters. He claimed that the premier was 'quite favourable to the idea of a change [of editors], so there is nothing in the idea that the Board has taken action because it wishes a critical paper. At least in the sense in which this word is generally used.'[1]

If that was the case, it may explain why Drury stayed above the strife that erupted between the executive and those caucus members infuriated by the circumstances surrounding Ross's departure as editor. Their resolve to confront central office would have been fortified had they learned that Morrison had asked Ross not to support a bill introduced by Manning Doherty. Although Doherty had earned high marks for his stand on the cattle embargo and for his rural credits program, his attempt to lay the basis of a provincially owned dairy company met with the determined resistance of independent milk producers and the United Dairymen Co-operative, a strong backer of the UFO. Whatever the merits of Drury's bill, Ross had not obliged Morrison and the dairymen. He had instead written a supportive front page story and an editorial, which were denounced by an angry secretary as a 'dirty slap on us.'[2] In the end Doherty's measure, introduced in part to improve cheese-marketing procedures, died still-born when threatened dairy interests, who resented any kind of interference from Queen's Park, successfully petitioned to have it withdrawn. In this and in other matters Ross had unmistakably sided with the government and ultimately he made good his threat and left the *Sun*.

What happened next was a secret meeting Ross arranged with angered caucus members for the purpose of challenging the incumbent directors' control of the paper. But secrecy was hard to protect because Morrison had a direct pipeline to caucus through his MLA friends. Soon enough he learned, as the *Sun* promptly disclosed, that a committee had been formed 'pledged to go on a hunt for proxies [in the ridings] in [an] attempt to outvote the present directorate.'[3] The paper also insinuated that Drury was not only privy to the scheme but aiding and abetting it while all along pretending that it had originated not with him but with an outraged caucus. While Drury was slapping down the insinuation, a bitter mud-slinging battle ensued between the *Sun*'s directors and the caucus committee. The latter again charged that Ross had been demoted for attempting to be fair to the government; the paper hotly denied it. Ultimately the committee lost the proxy battle and the impugned directorate was handsomely re-elected. So bitter had the fight been, however, that both sides threatened libel action, and only cooler heads in the UFO talked them out of it.[4]

In this unhappy atmosphere Ross's successor had great difficulty bridging the opposing camps in the farm organization. The one was prepared to sanction government schemes for large-scale public benefits and Broadening Out, the other was just as determined to block any program deemed an affront to the true purposes of the UFO. In spite of Hamm's ability as an editor and a writer, support for the *Sun* faltered as the conflict picked up steam, and its circulation began to plummet in the closing months of 1922. As for Drury, he may indeed have welcomed fresh editorial blood at the paper but he was never happy with Hamm's personal views and political approach. He 'has shown [no] inclination,' Drury later complained to Good, 'to give me fair treatment. I am sure I do not know why. Perhaps it is Tory prejudice, born in him.'[5] T.A. Crerar shared Drury's political opinion of Hamm, remarking that 'sometimes when I read [the *Sun*] 'I think that it is clever propaganda by Tory agents.'[6] There could, however, have been another side to the coin. That Hamm may have conceived that Drury was at the back of all the machinations that made his life an editorial nightmare never seemed to occur to the premier.

The *Sun's* misfortunes sadly reflected those that befell the principal adversaries on the question of Broadening Out. The battle already joined only intensified when rumours circulated in the fall of 1922 that Drury was planning that Liberal-Progressive compact in Ontario that he had once discussed with Mackenzie King. 'Quite a buzz in Queen's Park has been audible for some time,' the *Globe* crowed in a front page story. 'In private there has been frank and free discussion of "fusion", "alliance", and all the other near synonyms of co-operation ... surprising if something really tangible does not come out of all this talk.'[7] For obvious reasons Drury denied such talk lest it alienate those in UFO ranks who had once been of the Conservative persuasion and who wanted no truck with any form of Liberalism. This was the very danger that Good had stressed in 1921 when he sealed his own case against Crerar's campaign to lead the Progressives into King's fold.[8] While he may not have taken concrete steps to put together such an alliance, none the less Drury would have welcomed one. He was particularly pleased when the irascible Hartley Dewart was succeeded by the more accommodating Wellington Hay as leader of Ontario's Liberals in March 1922. Although a formal coalition may have been out of the question, there is evidence that Drury discussed electoral co-operation with Hay before the North Oxford and Russell by-elections. Moreover, he had scouted the possibility of bringing some Liberals into his cabinet before the next general election.[9] If this was not an exercise in coalition, an observer might have legitimately asked, what was it?

Yet if coalition or fusion with the Liberal contingent was not feasible, Drury still clung to the hope of organizing a people's or progressive party. At mid-summer 1922 the *Sun* learned that a confidential letter had gone out over the premier's signature to all Farmer MLAS urging their support for such an initiative. Morrison instantly complained that the views of farmers generally were being cavalierly disregarded, and even Drury's friends had reservations. C.B. Sissons entertained grave doubts about Drury's chances of forming a viable progressive party or of convincing a majority of the UFO membership to spurn Morrison and back him.[10] The opinions offered by Crerar and Doherty were equally gloomy. Crerar reported that the 'impression out [West] seems to be that Morrison has scored against the Government.' Doherty's demoralization was also beginning to show in the wake of recent setbacks in the legislature.[11] The agriculture minister, who may well have been going too far, too fast for rural opinion, told Crerar in the fall of 1922: 'I have been strongly tempted to resign ... many and many a night during the last twelve months ... When one finds his path strewn with obstacles placed there by your own supporters, you discourage of making progress.'[12] Yet in spite of all this Drury remained unperturbed, and doggedly persevered with his political plan.

Then in October 1922 he suffered a reverse. In the Russell by-election, in which he had hoped for local Liberal co-operation, the tables were turned by Howard Ferguson. In late September Ferguson had spelled out the issue for

Arthur Meighen: 'I much prefer to help the Liberals win that seat and my advice to all our friends who believe in the party system will be to vote for the Liberal candidate.' To this end he prevailed upon Charles Murphy, a King cabinet minister ill disposed to a Farmer-Liberal coalition, to use his considerable influence in the riding to have a 'straight Liberal' run against the UFO candidate and, further, to have him campaign not as a Druryite but as a 'Morrison farmer.' Murphy happily obliged and the formula worked: the Liberal was elected and the UFO standard-bearer suffered a stinging defeat. For the *Globe*, which rejoiced over the outcome, it was a clear rebuke to group government and 'class feeling.' Another complication, caused by Senator Belcourt's denunciation of the government's failure to act on the 'odious' Regulation 17, cost the UFO votes among Franco-Ontarians in the riding. These and other unsettling developments forced a chastened Drury to suspend plans for a populist party convention.

In the meantime the varied rumours, public statements, and charges and counter-charges generated by the row at the *Sun* set an unhappy stage for the UFO convention scheduled for mid-December 1922. While fully engaged in the task of governing and meeting a wide range of speaking commitments,[13] Drury found some time to cover the points he felt he should make at that annual meeting. These included, of course, the explosive one of Broadening Out, a subject sure to be on the agenda. Morrison shared that certainty and made his own preparations for the event, including an interview with a *Globe* reporter in mid-November. He allowed that any local riding association could 'broaden out' as wide as it liked, providing this did not affect the central organization or the farm movement as a whole. If the locals cared to call in 'urban people' and give them equal representation with farmers, as the Halton interests had done, then he would accept that too. 'But to throw wide the doors of the whole movement', he ominously warned, 'would be a different matter.' It would lead directly to what he despised – the creation of yet another political party burdened with the 'old political vices.'[14]

When the UFO convention assembled on 13 December, the discussion of Broadening Out was deferred a day because comparatively few members showed up for the opening session. Drury was rescheduled to speak on the evening of the next day but before he did so he took some precautions. These he described in *Farmer Premier*:

I asked Manning Doherty and Harry Nixon to attend the afternoon meeting to make sure that the question did not arise before my presentation. They stayed till ... the convention ... thinned out with only a few members left on the floor, and then came back and reported to me that the coast was clear.[15]

Reassured by their report, Drury confidently defended his Broadening Out program that evening in a speech that was warmly greeted by the 'capacity house.'

The next day when he scanned the newspapers he learned to his astonishment that 'in the last minutes of the afternoon session [after Doherty and Nixon had departed] a resolution had been passed unequivocally condemning me and my policy.' 'In my speech,' he recalled dolefully, 'I had simply been beating the air.'

At first glance the incongruity between the 'tumultuous' evening reception and the calm torpedoing of his plans in the afternoon is curious. But the reasons for this are not hard to determine. The evening session had hailed the most famous farmer in the province and one who also happened to be the premier of Ontario. Plainly many in attendance thought Drury's appearance the high point of the proceedings and were not disposed to let ideological considerations rain on them, even if Morrison had gone out of his way to have Broadening Out dealt with as the 'great question' of the convention. Moreover, probably few who assembled to hear the premier in that euphoric hour had been present at the sparsely attended afternoon meeting that had scuppered his program. And some of those who had attended may not have grasped the significance of what they had done. Crerar, who ought to have known what he was talking about, intimated that the resolution against Broadening Out had been passed almost perfunctorily. He also disclosed that after the departure of the premier's colleagues a small group led by Agnes Macphail, and presumably backed by Morrison, had railroaded through the controversial resolution. It had categorically called for 'no change ... in the form of the [UFO] ... for political purposes,' a reaffirmation of the policy of constituency autonomy, and opposition to the transformation of the farmers' movement into a new political party.[16]

Looking back on the event, Drury erred when he said that he had been personally rebuked, but even so his favourite policy had been dealt a crippling blow, and for this he predictably blamed Morrison's manoeuvrings. And Agnes Macphail's contemptuous words on Broadening Out were often quoted by its enemies. 'You see the broader one gets the flatter one gets,' she remarked, as if describing some kind of political peneplain, 'until finally there is nothing left but a large expanse of polished surface.'[17] H.B. Cowan, who had worked for reconciliation at the conference, held back few emotions when he recalled the episode a half-century later. 'Morrison was [Drury's] deadly enemy,' he told the interviewer, 'working against him all the time – every way he could – and he had lots of ways of doing it.' When asked to explain Morrison's behaviour, Cowan replied: 'It was himself. He wanted to get up, and he was pulling wires in all directions, utterly regardless of truth or anything like that.'[18] Others were also disturbed and, like the *Ontario Reformer*, were so bold as to suggest that the 'better type farmers were wearying of ... Morrison' and that his 'narrowness was being rejected.'[19] In scattered sections of the province there were some signs indeed of a swing to Broadening Out. Drury's supporters in Halton, where the first local people's party had been launched, urged him to 'make a personal canvass to ... get most of the principal people to commit themselves in your favour.'[20]

Once again, the notion was bruited about that class and other distinctions might be fragmenting the supposedly monolithic farming society of Ontario. What Morrison, Cowan, and OAC theses had asserted over the years could well have been emerging to sharpen the fundamental debate that Broadening Out had sparked. Some questions pose themselves. Was it possible that Drury shared the *Ontario Reformer*'s hope that the better type farmer, with material and cultural attainments comparable to his own, were seeing through Morrison's alleged posturing and manipulative wooing of the UFO rank and file? And what about Drury's relations with that rank and file, made up of so many of what Cowan described as average farmers? Echoing Morrison's wartime complaint, Cowan recalled that the premier's 'great difficulty was that he was way above [that] average farmer. He was a good farmer and could talk to good farmers fine. [But] he didn't know how to talk to dirt farmers – ones that were down near the ground – ones that were having a hard time getting by.'[21] As for Morrison, was he as convinced as ever that far more effectively than patrician farmers like Drury and Good, he could speak for the dirt farmer who stood in greater need of the UFO's services than their better-placed brethren? Would not Broadening Out, Morrison might have asked himself, destroy the last chance to save the marginal farmer from the rapacious 'urban man'? The next question was, might not Broadening Out serve only to advance the interests of those at the upper level of the farming community who had already accommodated themselves to city ways? That the UFO secretary entertained such queries can be safely inferred from a reading of his troubled memoirs.

If all this had been packaged as a formal debate Drury could have responded in kind. He had long been suspicious of Morrison's motives and doubtless he came to believe that the assaults on Broadening Out owed as much to the secretary's fear of how that strategy might dilute his own authority as to its possible impact on a pristine farm movement. And on the subject of his perceived advantages, Drury might have agreed that his background sometimes made it difficult for him to commune with less articulate and less affluent farmers. Even given this, he would have been justified in bristling at the insinuation that he looked down his nose at dirt farmers. His major objects in the farm movement had been to lift up the marginal or average farmer through education, guidance, and morale-building to the level enjoyed by the more fortunate members of agrarian society. If there was such a thing as a rural upper middle class and he belonged to it, then Drury was anxious that opportunities be created for opening its doors to those further down the scale. Yet in spite of Drury's protestations and reports that Morrison's tactics were alienating the 'better type farmer,' there was strong evidence that the farm bloc idea still commanded widespread support.[22] Halton, it became plain, could not speak for the entire rural community when it urged the premier to make a stronger case for his pet political formula before the next election rolled around.

Any kind of election talk in the face of recent flare-ups forced Drury into a contemplation of electoral procedures and tactics. With Morrison's opposition hanging over him like a sword of Damocles, he looked to the transferable vote as a possible deliverance from his predicament. Much would depend, of course, on how well he could foster the growing relationship with Wellington Hay's Liberal following. 'A ray of hope appeared', he wrote in *Farmer Premier*. 'If I could pass an Act providing for the transferable vote it seemed reasonable to suppose that Liberals ... would vote for the Government candidate as their second choice.'[23] And he was grateful for one small mercy from the UFO: they had endorsed the procedure in the 1919 platform and reaffirmed that endorsement at the recent convention. Yet in spite of this, a good many UFO members were left with the feeling that the transferable vote might boomerang and favour urban interests and the old-line parties. The *Sun* reported that some Labour men shared the concern that Liberal and Conservative voters in the cities might be disposed to 'leave farmers out in marking their second choices.' In any case the paper and other interested parties besieged Drury's office with requests to have what they considered a far better electoral guarantee introduced as well – proportional representation.

Unlike Good, Drury did not fancy this device. Yet out of respect for his friend's views, Drury compromised on the question and announced that he would experiment with it on a trial basis in certain urban ridings. This was coupled with a statement that he would also seek the widespread introduction of the transferable vote in all single-member constituencies. Good was happy enough to see proportional representation endorsed in principle but he was unhappy with Drury's piecemeal approach. 'The Conservatives will make capital of such a policy,' he explained to a receptive Morrison, 'because it will undoubtedly be presented as an effort to take unfair advantage of [their] ... party,' one that was based on the domination of Toronto, which happened to be one of the cities Drury singled out for the experiment. Good dismissed the whole plan as a 'policy of truckling expediency' which would give Ferguson a 'fine chance ... to strike a body blow.'[24] Then the *Globe* chipped in with a warning that limiting proportional representation to a few cities would be a farce unless it were accompanied by a general redistribution of seats recognizing the principle of representation by population, the battle cry of the paper's founder, George Brown. The *Canadian Forum* also wagged a finger at Drury and talked about the need to rectify the maldistribution that favoured rural ridings. Reminding the government of its moral mandate, Sissons urged the premier to 'make good his promise that he wishes not power but an honest and efficient administration.'[25]

In this particular case the *Sun* accurately reflected Drury's views on the subject and quickly responded to the *Globe* editorial. Fully expecting the government to oppose the principle of equalizing rural and urban votes, it reminded the metropolitan press that that kind of equality 'has ... never been accepted in this country ... not because there has been a denial of the spirit of Rep by Pop but because it has been recognized that the strict application of a population unit would not give equality in representation.' The reason, the *Sun* explained, was that cities had a 'superior community organization of industry and commerce,' and therefore were better able to bring pressure to bear on governments. This image of a hapless countryside intimidated by organized city slickers the *Globe* immediately held up to scorn and pointed to the 'pressure politics' of Ontario's well co-ordinated farming community.[26] When Drury, in response to the demand, settled down to drafting a redistribution bill he plainly embodied in it the principle underscored by the *Sun*. While it sought to correct some of the more glaring inequalities, it ensured that overall the farm vote would continue to count for more than the urban one.

If the premier expected any kind of genuine help from Morrison in promoting these modest electoral reforms he was in for the usual disappointment. Ferguson's opposition to proportional representation and the transferable vote could be taken for granted simply because they were tailored to the very multi-party system that he abhorred. But Morrison could have been another matter. Admittedly, he favoured proportional representation and actually urged the *Sun* to back the government's measures in spite of some UFO members' qualms. Yet his own personal effort on their behalf was half-hearted. In the expectation that Good would sooner or later pass it on to the premier, he relayed to him the following home truth in February 1923: 'I would take a much stronger stand ... if my actions in the past had not been challenged even by Drury himself and I was described as a dictator ... Therefore the very help that he needed now in putting through what I feel he conscientiously believes is in the best interests of the people is weakened.'[27] His critics, Drury included, accused Morrison of playing a 'Tory card.' It was generally well known anyway that if the secretary could seldom brook Grits, he tended to respect Conservatives for the sincerity of their beliefs, however mistaken they might have been.

While this contretemps was building, dramatic developments were gripping the legislature and making a mockery of sanguine forecasts that the newly opened session would be neither contentious nor controversial. Indeed, at the close of the 1922 session Drury had put more than the usual emphasis on the admonition to his ministers to so arrange their affairs for the new one as to ensure an 'orderly and uncomplicated presentation of government business.'[28] But serenity was the first casualty when a battle broke out in the Farmer caucus over the premier's apparent dickering with the Liberals at Queen's Park. No less a person than Andrew Hicks, the UFO whip, rose in the House on 11 April 1923 and condemned Drury's suspected flirtation with Wellington Hay. The press could not have asked for a juicier story,[29] with the possible exception of a toe-to-toe fight between fundamentalists and modernists on the theological front, an equally gripping item that seasoned front pages in the twenties. In a real sense the political squabble triggered by Hicks resembled the theological one, as Morrisonian defenders of rural fundamentals squared off against the modernist supporters of Broadening Out.

After the aggrieved Hicks read out a questionnaire purportedly asking Liberals to back a Farmer-Liberal amalgamation, other Farmer MLAS noisily voiced their disapproval. These included L.W. Oke, the member for East Lambton who had not forgiven the government for its controversial superannuation bill, and W.H. Casselman, the member for Dundas who had tripped Drury up on the Adolescent School Bill. Casselman brought in a resolution attacking Drury's extravagant spending and his failure to restore agriculture to its proper place in the province. Taken aback by what amounted to a want of confidence motion, an irate premier hotly scolded the dissenters, telling them that the Farmers' dirty linen ought not to be laundered in the House but in the sanctity of caucus. He added the promise that he would answer the charge in the legislature that evening.

At the appointed hour, newsmen and citizens eagerly converged on Queen's Park for what promised to be first-rate political theatre. They were not disappointed. In the few hours at his disposal that afternoon Drury had made good use of his speech-writing ability and honed those points that he instinctively reckoned would go down well with the caucus and the press. When he came to address the House he first stressed that a crisis had been fabricated where none really existed. He then set out, to 'loud applause,' to demolish the charge of dickering with the Liberals: 'It would be beneath me to ... bargain with the hon. gentleman [Hay] who sits across the aisle ... And I can assure the House that there has been no such bargaining, that there will be no bargaining.' But he did go on to say that the

Government will accept in the future, as it has in the past, support from those who have not yet, and maybe never will, call themselves by the name of the Progressive Party ... If the course that the Government has taken has appealed to the gentlemen across the aisle, and if it appeals to them when we go to the country, their support will be accepted, but for us our policy is definite and clear, and there can be no dickering when a policy and a record are at stake.[30]

Then a bombshell was thrown into Drury's camp by Colonel J.A. Currie, the Conservative member for West Toronto who had defeated him in the wartime federal election. Currie's repeated attacks on his old adversary had led some of the premier's more waggish friends to give him a gas mask for warding off the fumes.[31] In this instance he needed all the protection he could get when Currie read out a letter, mistakenly delivered to him, from Liberal Senator A.C. Hardy to J. Walter Curry, the Liberal member for South East Toronto. The letter promoted a scheme whereby, after an election which Hardy was sure the government would lose, Farmers and Liberals would come together and recreate the 'old time Liberal party.' The gloating Currie, who had forewarned the senator that he would divulge the letter's contents, sneered at a 'political morality that runs to hidden compacts, secret conspiracies, plots and tricks intended to deceive the straight Liberal and Conservative voters.'[32] What made Currie's disclosures all the more distasteful to Drury was his well-know fondness for watering down prohibition through amendments to the Ontario Temperance Act.

Following Currie's revelations, and continued angry bickering in the House until well past midnight, a vote was finally taken on the Casselman resolution. The government, to its great relief, emerged victorious; only the disaffected Hicks and Casselman failed to go along with the Farmer-Labour vote. Although Ferguson and the Tories backed an apostate's resolution to a man, most Liberals, to Drury's gratification, did not. All the same, the Liberal rally to the government side and the contents of Hardy's purloined letter disturbed those caucus and cabinet members 'brought up in the Conservative faith.' 'After this demonstration of [concern]', Drury recollected in *Farmer Premier*, 'I knew coalition was impossible.' He suspected something else as well, that Morrison was back of the recent protests and recriminations, though for a time he was prudent not to say as much in public.

The next day, April 12, following further heated exchanges, Drury lost his notoriously short temper and lashed out at his persecutors. Then, without pausing to consult either cabinet or caucus, the premier bluntly announced that 'we'll get to the people as quickly as we can.' May 4 was announced as the date of dissolution and a general election was set for late June. He may have ruefully realized then, as he certainly would later, that 'heads of government cannot afford to lose their tempers.' Had he been able to survive a full term, until, say, the following September, his political position may have been made more secure.

Some four days after the vote on the Casselman resolution, Drury addressed the Halton People's Party Association and his remarks were duly reported in the local paper. According to its account, Drury claimed that in the event he received no majority in the next election he would seek a government of 'shared convictions.' The *Sun* was more explicit and reported him as saying that 'if I find ... that we are a minority group and have men in the House who, *without bribes of position*, but through honesty of conviction, *Liberal or Conservative* ... if there are enough such men to support us, I shall advise His Honour that we can form a Government, *but I shall not sacrifice the principles of the Progressive movement.*[33]

What all accounts agreed upon was Drury's statement that in no circumstances would he consort with Ferguson's cronies in the legislature, whom he dismissed as the 'dregs of the leavings of the Conservative party,' a remark he would live to regret and for which he belatedly apologized. Good shared the premier's distaste for this group. He painted a grim picture of what life might be like under a Ferguson regime: 'Personally, I think it would be a catastrophe of the worst kind if a certain group of men should come into power in Ontario, not because they are called by a certain party name, but because so far as I can see they are personally disreputable and unreliable, and are allied with some of the worst faces in the country.'[34]

In the meantime the much maligned 'political dregs' decided to filibuster the electoral reform bills the goverment had introduced the day Drury announced dissolution. This came as a disagreeable surprise to the government benches. Drury had expected heavy criticism from all sides but not the stalemating that Ferguson and his followers orchestrated. But plainly that group had been angered more than usual by the premier's unflattering statements in Milton and elsewhere. A more basic factor was cited by a farm journal sympathetic to Drury when it reminded him that the Tories understandably 'mistrusted a measure to alter the election machinery ... introduced by one of the contestants just before the heralds had announced that the issue would be joined.'[35] Since every House member could speak to the question on second reading and no closure was in place for throttling the long-winded, they could talk until they dropped in their tracks. 'One night during the filibuster,' Drury recalled with a twinge of the frustration he had suffered at the time, 'Charlie McCrae [a prospective Tory cabinet minister] read from *David Copperfield* for several hours ... The only way to dispose of him was to let him talk himself out. This usually took all night [and] ... the House seldom adjourned till the April morning was breaking.'[36] The resulting frayed nerves and shortened tempers produced some bitter verbal clashes, high-lighted by a stormy confontation between Dougall Carmichael and Colonel Currie, whose revelations had launched the strife a few days before.

In the end, on 19 April, a beaten Drury, with the concurrence of the House, withdrew the controversial electoral bills. 'Barren, bitter and acrimonious' was how one disgusted newspaper editor aptly summed up the proceedings in the dying hours of the session.[37] Virtually the only thing all parties could agree upon was the voting of supply before the House wound up its sittings on 4 May.

All Drury could now do was to put as brave a face as possible on his government's chances of winning the election and the sought-after majority. Bravery was certainly in order given the gloomy forecasts already made, even by the well disposed. The previous summer, Sissons had written in the *Canadian Forum* that the government's 'success has not been so marked or so uniform as to assure a favourable verdict when an appeal is made to the country in a year's time.'[38] *Maclean's*, which now liked to describe Drury as the 'greatest talking premier in Ontario history,' reported that 'already the wise ones are saying, "Goodbye, Ernie, take keer of yourself".'[39] The only hope some observers held out for his survival was his getting together with Hay and the Liberals. As it turned out, the Liberals rejected all plans for collaboration with the Farmer-

Labour group and determined to enter as many three-cornered contests as possible in the hope of regaining their place in Ontario's political sun. Yet hope died hard in the farm press. Even after the Liberals declared official war on government candidates, the *Sun* stayed convinced that Hay would consider an alliance if the UFO ever gave the word. But predictably the word was never given.

On the very mid-April day the premier gave his fighting speech in Milton, he had received some strongly worded advice from Good. He was urged to waste no time in mollifying his UFO critics by assuring them that he would follow the 'same course as in 1919.' That is, Drury should decide only after consultation with Farmer MLAs and with the UFO directorate what approaches or alliances ought to be made if the Farmers were returned as a minority government. Drury took some convincing because Good remained unhappy with the ambiguity of his declarations after dissolution was announced. Once again Drury was subjected to the argument, so dear to Good's democratic heart, that the issue should be left to the rank and file to decide. The premier was also told to state categorically that the 'idea to which currency has been given that you ... would act in an autocratic way in linking up with the Liberal Party in a Coalition Government is absurd.'[40] At this point Manning Doherty, who shared Good's concerns, decided to enter the picture. In spite of his own difficulties with the UFO executive, he set out to patch up the differences between them and the premier. Confronted by his own awesome political problems, Drury finally saw the wisdom of this strategy.

Indeed, within a day of Good's latest admonition – 26 April 1923 – he and Doherty presented themselves at central office and conferred with Morrison and the executive on the political situation. Two items were placed on the agenda: the kind of support the farm organization would pledge in the campaign, and what the premier should do in the event his government was returned. The resolution offered by the executive was guarded. While it conceded that some of the government's accomplishments had been good, it reminded Drury that the UFO's platform and principles had not been adhered to at all times. On the other hand, it expressed the need to preserve a strong Farmer representation in the legislature, and promised that the executive would lend support to those UFO candidates committed to upholding the platform and the principles of the organization. In turn Drury, obviously anxious to mend as many rifts as he could, made the pledge urged on him by Good, that should his government be returned he would be guided by decisions reached by elected and defeated candidates and by the UFO executive. Faced with the toughest political battle of his career, Drury knew that he needed all the help he could enlist even if it meant cultivating the frayed ties with his original constituency.

Along with swallowing his resentment at Morrison's past obstructionism, he had to eat some humble pie when he spoke to the press after the meeting. First of all, he denied what assuredly he and others had long thought Morrison was up to – attempting to dictate the government's policy. He followed this with the assertion that, while he and the UFO secretary had differed on some questions, the latter had 'never sought to do more than express his own views and those of other members of the organization, in a proper and fitting manner, as he had a perfect right to do.'[41]

With Broadening Out now a forlorn hope and coalition more or less a dead issue, Drury was obliged to fall back on his last rampart – whatever support he could elicit from the UFO, the *Sun*, and friendly representatives of the urban press. There were pitifully few of the last. While some papers talked about the arrangement of an 'expedient truce,' the *Globe* lampooned the way the premier had 'trotted like a lamb into J.J.'s fold.' The *Hamilton Herald*, which had initially welcomed the Drury administration, sadly reflected that if the compact meant anything at all it meant that the 'Morrisonian idea of having the farmers carrying their class consciousness into the political contest would prevail.' In the editor's judgment, this left Drury little chance but as 'leader of the opposition farmer group in the next legislature,' for the *Herald* not an alluring prospect.[42] As for the *Sun*, it did not exactly trumpet the government's virtues, an act of negligence condemned by some rural voices, who contrasted its diffidence with the attacks of the 'party press arrayed against us.'[43] The loss of the *Sun*'s artillery support was keenly felt, as was the decline in the UFO's reserves, an unhappy augury on the eve of a critical election battle. The number of UFO clubs, as a disappointed J.C. Ross pointed out, had dropped alarmingly in recent months in the wake of dissension and disenchantment with the political process. The imposing membership of 1919 had three years later dwindled by a half, to some 22,000, and a good many clubs still on the books had become dormant.[44]

Besieged by so many unhappy tidings, Drury reacted characteristically by looking at the brighter side of the political ledger – the positive achievements of his administration. Although Sissons had constantly mixed criticism with praise when assessing the government's stewardship, he probably conveyed to the premier the following sentiment he later captured in his memoirs:

For my part, I am prepared to assert, as one who has studied the records of Ontario with some attention, that it will be difficult to find four years in the history of the Province marked by greater achievement than the years 1919–23 during which the Drury government held office ... I freely admit there were sins of omission and commission; but the sins actually committed were blown out of all proportion to the seriousness of their effect on the public interest.[45]

Yet when Sissons wrote this in the early 1960s he may have been judging the Drury goverment partly against what had been unknown and unanticipated forty years earlier. In the 1930s there had been the less than stirring administration of Tory George Henry and the less than reputable regime of Liberal Mitchell Hepburn, himself a young and ambitious UFO member in Drury's day. Set against these, Drury's tenure appeared eminently praiseworthy.

In any event, when the premier dipped into his bag of accomplishments he came up with some items he thought would be negotiable in the campaign, the kind that enthused one 'independent in politics' who congratulated him on his leading the 'fairest and squarest Government ... we have [ever] had.'[46] In each instance Drury hoped that his achievements would offset the minuses that critics were calling to the electorate's attention. Thus when he was charged with extravagance, he countered that he had saved the province millions of dollars by stopping Beck's radials in their tracks. Accused of sanctioning F.C. Biggs's costly roads program, he retorted that the internal combustion engine was here to stay and had to be catered to in a rapidly modernizing world that was putting a premium on mobility. Again, condemned for giving away northern resources to an unprincipled timber pirate, Drury responded that the Backus transaction was neither corrupt nor double-dealing, and that it promised, besides, to save the whole Kenora district from extinction. The news, moreover, that its sitting member, Labourite Peter Heenan, had been renominated by a joint ILP and UFO convention was hailed as an 'indication of the esteem in which ... the Drury Administration is held by area residents.'[47] Equally musical to the premier's ears were the expressions of 'deep appreciation [for] what the Government ... [did] for us' that came from fire-stricken victims in the Cochrane and Haileybury regions. Drury readily recalled the days he had spent at Haileybury in the fall of 1920 helping to direct relief operations and seeing to the reconstruction of that community.[48]

In his careful cataloguing of achievements Drury did not neglect his family legislation. Others had cause to rejoice over these. Typically, a Toronto dentist with a social conscience praised Drury as a 'man really very much interested in our social and economic problems,' and he looked forward to the premier's triumphant return to office.[49] Still others commended his government for having supported the medical research of Charles Best and Frederick Banting (another Simcoe County native) which had earlier led to the discovery of insulin for the treatment of the dreaded diabetes. Even in the heat of the election campaign Drury paused over the heart-wrenching letter he received from a diabetic's distraught father. After asking the premier to 'put Banting on easy street for life,' he pleaded, 'for God's sake, put [insulin] in reach of the poor as well as the rich ... My little girlie has a right to a chance as well as a rich man's child.'[50] Drury dashed off a letter to the appropriate authorities imploring them to make special provision for this sufferer. Although the government's plan for honouring insulin's creators did not put them on easy street, it did provide for what Drury called an 'adequate and honourable recognition of [their] services.'

One government accomplishment seemed to eclipse all others, however, as

Drury cast about for ammunition with which to fight the election. And that was the apparently successful promotion of the Ontario Temperance Act and the 'drying up' of Ontario. Why not, he asked himself, make prohibition the key issue? Some of his colleagues, however, did not welcome the rhetorical question and the strategy it signalled, and were convinced, as future historians would be, that it should not have been an issue. Though Biggs, for one, commended his chief for other virtues – manliness, decency, and straightforwardness – he was irritated by the time and publicity Drury subsequently lavished on the defence of the Temperance Act.[51] Biggs urged instead a liquor plebiscite for determining the wishes, be they wet or dry, of the municipalities in the province. This approach, already endorsed by many anti-prohibitionists, was not welcome in the premier's office and certainly not in Raney's, where determined efforts would be made to keep the temperance issue before the public. Apparently Biggs was not the only member of cabinet alienated by Drury's moral approach on the prohibition question. Harry Nixon also found it difficult to stomach Drury's righteousness, in spite of his strongly held religious views.[52]

For other more voluble critics of prohibition, many of whom appeared to speak from the ranks of Ferguson's supporters, the act had become a piece of 'Prussian legislation' (the worst epithet after 'Bolshevik' that that generation could bestow on what it disliked). Perhaps Drury seized upon the issue of prohibition as a sure means of distancing his administration from the Conservative 'dregs' who followed his arch foe. As for the Tory leader himself, he indulged in considerable fence-sitting on the question. Ferguson was well aware that his predecessor, Hearst, had been victimized in part by his prohibitionist stand in 1919. He also realized that when he made pronouncements that as premier he would soften the temperance act he aroused an instant reaction from the arrayed guardians of a dry Ontario. In any event, he, unlike Drury, sized up prohibition not so much as a moral issue as a political one, and therefore he elected to tread warily.[53]

In any case, as long as Ferguson tried to stay ambivalent on the question, which really meant a show of support for the wets, it seemed to Drury to make solid sense for his government to embrace prohibition as though it was their own special preserve. Besides, Drury could mix politics and morality in a crusade that was bound to appeal to many in the rural community, the bedrock of his support. Some newspapers, however, rudely suggested another political motive for Drury's draping himself in the prohibition banner: it would conveniently mask the government's shortcomings in other departments. Was prohibition, they asked in so many words, merely the last refuge of the incompetent? Although Drury obviously weighed the politics of prohibition, they really played second fiddle to its moral and social dimension.

Drury's personal commitment had, if anything, become even fiercer since the 1921 referendum. He had periodically conferred with Ben Spence of the Dominion Alliance on the best mode of publicizing the advantages of a 'bone dry' province and to that end had prepared late in 1922 a special foreword to Spence's prohibitionist tract, *Six Years Dry*.[54] During the election campaign Drury brought out his own appropriately entitled *Temperance, the Vital Issue*. For the premier, its vitality had much to do with the whole corpus of his family legislation, for by now he was making it plain that the eradication of liquor, the notorious crippler of family stability, was in fact the keystone of his arch of social reform. If prohibition were placed in jeopardy through the election of those who advocated a 'good glass of grog' then, he argued cataclysmically, the foundations of society itself would be undermined.

To battle that grim prospect Drury and Raney rode out to discredit the foes of the Ontario Temperance Act. What lent a special urgency to their expedition was the confidence with which certain anti-prohibitionist groups were anticipating public approval for the liberalization of the act, if not its repeal entirely, should Drury's government go down to defeat.[55] All of this produced the distinct feeling on both sides of the barricades that a showdown was looming even more portentous than the one that had marked the electoral endorsement of the act. Raney was so worked up by the challenge that he actually shelved resignation plans over Drury's truce with Morrison, with whom he was still at loggerheads.[56] Beseeched by a beleaguered premier to return to the fight, he did so with great enthusiasm on 19 May 1923. Raney immediately underscored the primacy of prohibition's cause by assuring voters that the 'issue ... today is not any subsidiary question. It is prohibition itself.' Ferguson, he charged, 'was to all intents and purposes the commander-in-chief of the liquor forces, and their war chest would be at his services.'[57]

Within the month, however, Ferguson seemed to be shedding all ambivalence, and was assuring temperance advocates in Tory ranks that if elected he would authorize no substantive changes in the temperance act unless they were voted on by the people of Ontario. On the face of it, he was calling for the full enforcement of the act but not in the 'spirit of fanaticism.' The announcement understandably knocked a good deal of wind out of Drury's prohibition sails. The press pounced on his discomfiture at once, asking 'if [Prohibition] is not the main issue then what is the rationale for returning the Farmer Government?'[58] On the other hand, Drury's friends at the *Canadian Forum* thought Ferguson's strategy would boomerang: 'So Mr.F. has at last declared himself a friend ... of the OTA. This declaration has been the most striking feature of the election campaign ... We confess that we should have liked Mr.F. better had he persisted in being bold and bad ... '[59] Drury may not have shared the monthly's certainty, particularly after an experience he recounted in *Farmer Premier*. To counter Ferguson's tour de force,

the young reporter in charge of our central office on his own initiative ... sent out a ... circular letter to every clergyman in the province, telling them that the OTA was [still] at stake and asking them to give their support to the Government candidates ... In reply he received a score of angry epistles from preachers who protested his attempt to 'bring the clergy into politics'.[60]

Ferguson and other Conservative candidates added to Drury's unhappiness by shrewdly turning the tables and tagging his government with charges of hypocrisy and immorality. One acute embarrassment arose over what an unforgiving Morrison referred to as the 'last awful night' of the 1921 legislative session. According to Drury's recollections it was R.H. Grant who told him the distressing tale. Peter Smith, 'like the good natured fool that he was,' had permitted some fellow MLAS, including members from the government side, to use his private apartment at Queen's Park for an end-of-session party. It apparently came complete with whisky and the appearance of 'scantily clad girls' from the secretarial pool. A disturbed Drury, after being assured that no minister was involved, angrily scolded the participants and urged their fellow legislators not to blow the incident out of proportion. He immediately took the practical step of instituting a nightly patrol of the Parliament Buildings to prevent the repetition of such a 'terrible event.' All too soon Morrison got wind of it through his caucus pipeline and passed the news on to an outraged *Sun*.[61]

The opposition, which had been quick to exploit the incident at the time, were understandably all the more eager to recall it for the voter on election eve as a reminder that Farmer MLAS too were morally flawed. 'That night' came back to haunt Drury and Raney, particularly in the former's own riding of Halton when he was renominated. When his Conservative opponent brought up the episode, to the predictable roars of disapproval from Drury's backers, the premier retorted rather ponderously: 'I greatly regret that one of the candidates has seen fit to descend to personalities and to make ... a statement that no decent man would make.'

Early in the year Drury had confessed that he would have preferred to run in his 'native constituency ... which my father represented for so many years.' But he had been prepared, if his Halton friends preferred it, to stand in that riding again.[62] The friends, in question, A.G. Farrow's People's Party Association, clearly did. At a convention in Milton on 9 May Drury was unanimously chosen as their candidate after pledging, among other things, that he would not send the temperance act back to the people. He was obviously touched by the show of affection in the place where he had scored his first-ever electoral triumph. Equally gratifying was the news that Andrew Hicks, the former whip who had made the government's life so unpleasant in April, failed to secure nomination in the South Huron riding.

Nevertheless, Drury was painfully aware of the organizational and financial problems besetting his campaign. For one thing, the UFO executive, in spite of the apparent reconciliation with the premier, was even less disposed than it had been in 1919 to direct the operation. For another, there was no war chest worthy of the name; Drury reckoned that he personally contributed the bulk of the pitiful fifteen hundred dollars that was eventually raised for the campaign. Few funds were collected by the UFO clubs, their memberships decimated anyway, and Farmer MLAS were reduced to foraging wherever they could for the meagre financing that did materialize. As for a campaign office, it was located not in the Parliament Buildings as was Ferguson's but in modest quarters on King Street, and manned by a lonely volunteer who had managed the Progressive organization in Ottawa.[63] The stark simplicity of the arrangements ought to have appealed to Morrison but if they did he gave no sign. In effect, Drury was venturing into battle with slim resources, a barebones organization, and no formal party structure.

Meanwhile, the imperfectly patched rift with the UFO executive had not succeeded in banishing lingering doubts and confusion in the minds of many rural voters. In more quarters than he cared to think about the premier was seen as having been remiss in his obligations to the UFO. According to a statement released by the organization's election committee, the government had failed to honour an agreement to appoint members to the committee so as to ensure that the principles of the UFO and the administration's record would go out simultaneously. And Drury would constantly be reminded by the press of Morrison's suspicions and of his much-publicized promise never to approve further coalitions involving the UFO.[64] Less than a fortnight before voters went to the polls Morrison conveyed some brutal truths to Crerar, who had obviously pleaded with him to moderate his views. After reviewing the UFO's effort to break down 'party fealty' and form a 'group of non-partisan intelligent voters,' he told Crerar that he and Drury, through their Broadening Out schemes and overtures to other parties, had done 'more to destroy the power to do good that lay at our door than any other cause. I can compare it only to the action of a cow that gives a fine pail of milk then kicks it over.'[65] So much for the truce.

Morrison's stand would appear to have ruled out even the possibility of continuing the liaison with Labour, one which had helped to buttress the government for over three years. However, there were sufficient straws in the wind to indicate to the premier that the ILP, like the UFO clubs, was in decline anyway, having lost the spontaneity and zeal that had propelled its emergence on the political stage in 1919. To complicate matters for Drury, progressively disposed citizens who favoured his government's programs were alienated by the radicalism of some of the Labour candidates nominated in 1923, particularly those in Toronto. Others such as George Keen had no great respect for ILP candidates generally and was convinced that in the Brantford area specifically a UFO standard-bearer with urban connections would stand a better chance.[66]

Not only this, vocal anti-prohibitionists in the labour movement were rallying around George Halcrow, who had never made a secret of his dislike for the righteous zeal of Drury and Raney. So visible was his souring on the coalition with the Farmers that an aggrieved ILP executive refused to renominate him in Hamilton East. But Halcrow's exclusion could not hide the fact that he had been expressing the view of a good many urban voters distressed by the determination to take away the 'workingman's beer.' The prohibition campaign was also linked with other unwelcome Drury initiatives, such as the one that denied the city man the convenience of Sir Adam Beck's radials. All of this doubtless prompted John Hamm at the *Sun* to write town voters off as potential supporters of a genuine progressive movement.[67] Even Atkinson of the *Star*, the only metropolitan paper that unreservedly backed the government, wrote gloomily that the average urban resident did not realize that his future would be better safeguarded if Drury were returned.

At any rate, armed with his conviction that his record and a stout defence of the temperance act would carry the day, the premier stepped up the pitch of his campaigning. The month of June turned into a bake-oven and Drury had to swelter through it along with the other candidates. He did not spare himself and, hoarse of voice, visited most of the ridings to provide the 'personal touch.' As usual he appeared to enjoy himself on the stump, energetically addressing the prohibition question, clarifying other items in his legislative package, and seeking, of course, to ridicule Ferguson and his cronies. One of Drury's assistants, who like critics in the past, unflatteringly described him as an egotist, none the less caught the essence of his platform ability. 'He is a wonderful campaigner,' he told a friend just days before the election, 'and speaks oftener and longer than either of the opposition leaders, there is no place where he shines so well as on his feet ... he is convincing and has an air of sincerity that ... takes well.'[68] All of these strengths Drury put to use. On the subject of mother's allowances he claimed at Harriston – using a kind of measurement then popular – that 'stretched out, two yards apart, mothers and children ... benefited by this legislation ... would reach seventeen miles down the road.' In Owen Sound, while in full throttle on prohibition, he denounced Ferguson as the 'political chameleon of the province,' a charge that he, the supposedly changeable premier, usually had to field. A few days later in Hamilton, Drury was in his usual good form responding to outclassed hecklers and, once they were squelched, defending his 'clean record' and extolling the contributions of his Labour ally, Walter Rollo.[69] The *Hamilton Spectator* castigated him for his 'meddling, manoeuvring ways' in blocking the radials and, along with the *Globe*, another Beck supporter, hailed the Hydro chairman's dramatic entry into the race as a Conservative candidate in London. This decision rekindled on the hustings the long-smouldering fight between Drury and Beck over Hydro's responsibility. The premier insisted, as he always had, that that responsibility ultimately belonged to the province, which paid the bills; Beck, with Ferguson's approval, argued that it was to the municipalities which constituted the heart of the system.

Drury also had to contend with W.F. Nickle, a one-time sympathizer who was now serving as the Conservatives' financial critic. The Kingston lawyer, put off by the government's handling of the university question and the college of education, also lashed out at the supposed extravagance and misapplication of revenues that had trebled the provincial debt to over $240 million by 1922. In a campaign booklet, 'Financial Squandering and Bogus Deficit,' Nickle labelled Drury's minority administration a ghastly failure and an affront to democracy because of its unrepresentative character.[70] Raney responded to these changes with what friends immodestly called the 'finest piece of campaign literature ever published.' Happily, Raney's statement effectively encapsulated the government's major undertakings. Among the items highlighted, apart from such flagship ones as its social legislation, were the rejuvenation of the north country, the rural credits program, the provincial savings bank, the lifting of the British cattle embargo, the 'constrictive policy of select immigration' of British farm hands, and the financial support offered the province's universities.[71]

Fortified by Raney's rebuttal, Drury added some messages of his own that sought to counter the charges of extravagance. He tried to show that the marked spending increases were not in the nature of public expenditures at all. Rather they were sums which the government had collected and handed back to the people to assist them in carrying on the vital activities that a and demanding society had generated, among them Biggs's roads and Beck's Hydro. He stressed that expenditures always came from general revenue, which had been augmented by increased succession duties and by taxes on luxuries such as race tracks and other 'amusements.' No special property or income taxes, he assured the voters, were planned by the government.

While fending off the scoffers, Drury had difficulty dealing with some of the petty though telling charges made by Ferguson and his supporters. Thus the premier was accused of having squandered one hundred dollars of the taxpayers' money on a gold coal scuttle for his office, a species of extravagance, the Conservatives gloated, that should not be tolerated in a farmer premier committed to retrenchment. The truth was more prosaic: Drury had spent much less than the publicized sum on the refurbishing of his office fireplace with a highly polished brass facility. All the same, the smear stuck.

When election day, 25 June, finally arrived the premier may have nervously contrasted it with the October one nearly four years before when he and Ella had voted for their UFO candidate in North Simcoe. Then crisp but bright fall weather had ushered in the proceedings. In 1923 they were greeted with the most torrid weather of that month of June. And it would be climaxed by a horrendous electrical storm in the early evening that wrecked the wire services in Hamilton and forced local newspapers to use the largely untried medium of radio to transmit the returns. The thunderheads and lightning that accompanied the last few minutes of balloting proved an unhappy augury for the government.

When the votes were counted the pessimists' worst fears were confirmed. Not only was the administration not returned, even as a minority one, but its forces were rudely swept away by what one paper called a 'political cyclone.'

Drury's own fate put the finishing touches to the story of the débâcle. In every municipality in Halton he trailed his Tory opponent by as much as three to one, a clear enough indication that the town voter wanted no part of a UFO government.[72] When the total vote was tabulated Drury fared better overall, having garnered 4,440 votes to the Conservatives' 5,251. And it was clear too that had the transferable vote been in place, as many had urged, Drury might have won, for the trailing Liberal piled up some 1,800 votes. The same result might have come if the Liberals had heeded the premier's entreaties and declined to contest the seat.

Province-wide, the Tories captured an impressive 50 percent of the vote, winning seventy-five seats, while the Liberal contingent in the House was reduced by more than half to a mere fourteen. The UFO would emerge with seventeen seats – three more than the Liberals – but they suffered the more devastating loss, and this embraced every cabinet minister except Raney, Biggs, Doherty, and Bowman. As for Labour, their following had plummeted from eleven to a handful of four.

Biggs's success in Wentworth doubtless reminded the outgoing premier of what he had been criticized for at his nomination meeting in Milton just two weeks before – of failing to deliver in Halton the kind of solid benefits the high-profiled Biggs had conferred on neighbouring Wentworth. Even if Biggs and Doherty, by supposedly 'going too far and too fast,' had alienated some of the farm vote in their ridings, they had clearly appealed to other species of electors.

Some weeks after the outcome, by which time the worst of the dust had settled Drury responded to a commiserative letter from Crerar and drew up a short list of the factors that he thought had brought down his government. They were reduced to three: the Ontario Temperance Act, Morrison, and the *Globe* in that order. He concentrated, first, on Ferguson's 'clever bit of political juggling' on prohibition. Then out of the air Drury snatched the statistic that the anti-prohibition vote was roughly one-third of the whole and that it swung solidly behind the Conservatives and ensured their victory. He remained convinced that the province was still overwhelmingly in favour of prohibition and, further, that a party should be formed to defend it. Most of his well-wishers were not so sanguine and concluded that if the election demonstrated anything, it was that the temperance vote was untrustworthy.[73] 'The prohibitionist,' a newspaper in Drury's part of the country had flatly stated years earlier, 'will always find some excuse to vote party and let his pet hobby horse take care of itself.'[74] Another possible determinant that Drury chose to ignore was the much-publicized success, only two days before the Ontario election, of the effort to end prohibition in neighbouring Manitoba.

Drury then returned to the dissension that had rocked the UFO camp and the divisive role played by Morrison. The supposed bewilderment and apathy that Drury blamed on the internecine squabbling had in his view been responsible for keeping many farmers from the polling places and many first-class candidates from seeking office. This point Good also stressed in his post-election correspondence.[75] Others, however, would plausibly challenge the argument, claiming that many farmers were more perceptive than Drury and Good gave them credit for, and interpreted the divergence as nothing more than a 'political fiction devised by Liberals and Conservative newspapermen to destroy the Farmer Government.'[76] And, some observers asked, what about the possibility that, dissension or no at the upper levels of the farm movement, a good many rural voters had simply made up their minds on their own to reject a goverment that seemed neither attuned to their basic aspirations nor capable of governing effectively?

Finally, Drury scolded the *Globe* for the 'sensational' way it had handled the reconciliation with Morrison. He insisted that it had not really involved the scuttling of Broadening Out at all but had merely guaranteed that any future coalitions would be subject to closer scrutiny. He complained to Crerar that as a result of the paper's 'exaggerations,' his government had been presented to the electors as nothing more than an instrument of class rule.[77] In all this the defeated premier was treading on some very thin ice. Clearly any form of rapprochement with the unyielding Morrison signalled a retreat of sorts from Broadening Out.

So much for what Drury incorporated in his own post-mortem. Equally significant is what he left out. He made no reference to what had been manifest throughout the campaign, that the rural fervour and working-class zeal for social reform and political rehabilitation, a marked feature of the unsettled postwar months, could not be indefinitely sustained and were all but dissipated by 1923. The return to the normal and the disintegration of wartime idealism and postwar enthusiasms dealt a crippling blow to the virulent anti-party mood of 1919. Joseph Flavelle, the Toronto businessman, had shrewdly prophesied this outcome within weeks of the Farmers' victory. 'The group system .. which is so clearly with us,' he wrote, 'will probably remain for a number of years, until ... disappointments and anxieties determine a new alignment into Conservative and Liberal parties.'[78] A person close to Drury's administration was inclined to agree, and hazarded a guess that many Conservative farmers would desert him and take refuge with Ferguson's brand of leadership.[79]

Nor did Drury take into account his failure to revoke Regulation 17 and the impact this may have had on the Franco-Ontarian response to his re-election bid. And English-speaking Catholics could also have been alienated by the government's reluctance to offer more aid to the province's separate schools. Ironically, this alleged betrayal of francophone and Catholic interests did not endear the Drury administration to those directing the Orange revival in Ontario, even if some influential Orangemen in the beginning had been grudgingly prepared to give the fledgling UFO a chance. But their tolerance had been short-lived. The premier and others in his entourage, including Sissons, had had the temerity to question Regulation 17 even if they had not been able to destroy it. Sissons had further angered the Orange Order by lamenting its political influence at a convention of the Ontario Educational Association, where ratepayers and school trustees had 'enthusiastically' voted down the teaching of French and grants to separate schools.[80]

Furthermore, the *Sentinel*, the Orange Order's official mouthpiece, suspected Drury of unduly favouring Franco-Ontarian interests in his plans for the north. Nor did the paper warm to what Sissons called a great speech by the premier on the eve of the campaign. Calling for the strengthening of relations between Ontario and Quebec, Drury had received a warm reception, particularly when he stressed that the French Canadian was 'not racially a distinct type from our own English population.'[81]

Drury also came under attack from a strong Orange element in his own riding, presumably for his aberrant political experiment at Queen's Park and for his having challenged the Conservative orthodoxy of Arthur Meighen in 1921.[82] This volatile factor, like the furor over Regulation 17, went unmentioned in the election analysis he sent off to Crerar. So did the Hydro question. Undoubtedly Drury's successful war on the radials was shrewdly misrepresented by the Tories as a repudiation of the principle of public power itself and a denial of cheap transportation to the workingman. Like the image of the gold coal scuttle, the charge was difficult to erase. Meanwhile, in other quarters it was believed that the government's management of the Backus affair had 'knocked their whole set of principles on the head and destroyed public confidence completely.'[83]

It was left to Sissons to have one of the last words on the subject. 'The Farmer[s] ... appear to have succumbed,' he wrote in the *Canadian Forum*, 'to the combined hostility of a series of minorities, which were skilfully arrayed against them by Mr. Ferguson – notably the anti-prohibitionists, Beck's friends, and Orangeism.' Interestingly, he downplayed Morrison's role, arguing that it had no bearing on the result. What really mattered for Sissons was the decline of the UFO clubs, 'the feeding roots of the farm movement ... [When] they atrophied,' he concluded sadly, 'the tree became sickly and its fruit – political activity – fell to the ground.' In a final tribute to his friend, reminiscent of Good's at the time, he added that the situation 'had been too much for a party whose vitality depended mainly on the eloquence and ability of one man.'[84] Sissons struck close to the heart of the matter. Apart from Raney and Doherty, Drury throughout had been the only compelling spokesman on the government side. He alone had been able to preserve the semblance of a respectable front in the presence of the enemy. The rank and file had counted for comparatively little on the hustings.

If people expected to see a totally chastened Drury on the election's morrow they were in for a disappointment. Though comforted by the touching plaudits that came his way, he would have had to put a jaunty face on his defeat anyway. The *Sun*, however, detected a sense of relief mingled with dejection when Drury appeared at Queen's Park the day after the voting. The editor assumed, quite rightly, that his family, especially Ella, were pleased that he was liberated from the demands of government and allowed to return to the pastoral calm of Crown Hill. If his unpublished novel is any guide, Ella Drury had made no attempt to enlarge her social circle since the events of 1919, and had shunned Toronto's fancier shops and continued to buy her clothes in Barrie.[85] The children, of whom much had been expected by teachers and others because they were a premier's offspring, also welcomed the respite from publicity.[86] For his part, Drury was never quite certain that the recognition and flattery they had received had been good for them at that susceptible age, though they warmly recalled their father's unstinting affection during even his most hectic days in the premiership.[87] As for his immediate future, Drury characteristically refused to look upon the political situation as a lost cause and defiantly concluded in his letter to Crerar that 'while I naturally hope for a year or two in private life, yet I can assure you when the fight is on you will find me in my place.'[88]

Drury may well have been amused by some of the critical commentaries on his administration. A New York newspaper, for example, was happy that the Ontario election had seen a 'complete swing of the pendulum from an extreme experiment in radicalism to ... saner and broader tenets.'[89] On the other hand, he may not have smiled over a Canadian farm journal's judgment that 'Ontario has returned from her little run into strange, new paths of progress.' He could, however, readily concur in the opinion expressed in the *Canadian Forum* that the 'hard faced men' around Ferguson 'see in the result not only a defeat for forces they discerned as perilous for their blessed fetish of stability, but a rising tide of sentiment for old-fashioned Toryism.'[90] But there was more to it than that. There was also a rising tide for an Ontario version of American normalcy, and if it had to be ushered in on the coattails of a Conservative resurgence then the voters were plainly prepared to take that chance.

The pain and poignancy of defeat had been eased somewhat for Drury when he learned that the cabinet, during his absence on the campaign trail, had accepted the offer of a highly reputed Toronto portrait painter to do his likeness for the premiers' gallery in the Parliament Buildings. J.W.L. Forster, who had done portraits of many public men, including two of Drury's predecessors, invited the former premier to his studios the day after the election 'for a preliminary sitting at his earliest convenience.'[91] Drury duly sat (or stood) and had his portrait painted, and it was hung at Queen's Park as the cabinet had wished. Forster, however, made no reference to the episode in his memoirs a few years later.[92] Perhaps the omission reflected the public's consignment to near oblivion of a comparatively short-lived government and a political leader whose career was reduced to the inconsequential by victorious foes and hostile newspapers. Even so, the portraitist may have spoken for many of his fellow citizens when he told Raney immediately after the election that men like Drury 'are often honoured by the enemies they make.'[93]

14

Life after Queen's Park

'And so,' Drury wrote whimsically in his memoirs, 'Howard Ferguson became premier of Ontario and I returned to my farm.' On the face of it, the change of scene could have afforded an idyllic substitute for the long-endured urban frenzy of Toronto. But the idyll was clouded by the disarray into which his farm business had fallen during the protracted absences at Queen's Park. Nor had he been fortunate in the manager he had hired to look after the place. Yet when Drury set about to catch up on the backlog of work at Crown Hill he knew he would sorely miss the exhilarating jousts and debates in the political arena. Suddenly, from helping to shape the future he was rudely reduced to the much less exciting task of rehabilitating his farm. In these circumstances the restlessness, despondency, and frustration that sometimes marked his behaviour in the fall of 1923 are easily explained.

All the same, he was comforted by the thought that there were still important political chores to complete. Evidently, in spite of June's setback, he had not abandoned his long-cherished hope that a successful progressive or people's party could be organized. Indeed, he believed there was good reason to think that the setback, perceived as a repudiation of group government, might even improve the chances for Broadening Out and the creation of a new party embracing political elements across Ontario. Shortly after the election, stories circulated that the former premier had actually been offered the leadership of the UFO rump in the legislature and that he had accepted provided he be given a free hand with his plans.[1] The proviso, which predictably drew Morrison's ire, and the difficulty of finding a seat for him, supposedly wrecked the scheme, and for the time being Manning Doherty, who had won re-election, was picked to lead the Farmer contingent in the House. And that contingent, in spite of being larger than the Liberal one, was passed over as the official opposition thanks to the efforts of Howard Ferguson and the insistence of Morrison and the UFO executive.

The future of the Farmer group and the fate of the UFO as a political force was a subject of heated discussions at the organization's annual meeting in December 1923. Drury, who would never forget or forgive the treatment he had received at Ferguson's hands, spoke feelingly to a resolution calling upon the Conservatives to either substantiate or withdraw the serious charges they had made, among other things, about the Backus deal. Apart from complaining of the treatment Drury had received at Ferguson's hands, the convention offered some significant resolutions on political action. Many delegates were agreed that political activities had seriously eroded the 'social, educational and economic features' of the Ontario farm movement. They had also seen some members of the Farmer caucus and cabinet as so many opportunists whose sole concern had been to cling to office and power. The names of Biggs and Smith readily sprang to their lips when this matter was discussed.

Yet the feeling survived that as an 'occupational organization' the UFO ought to stay in a 'position at all times to appeal to or criticize any government ... on matters of policy affecting the [farm] industry or the common good.' To implement that procedure some delegates urged that a distinctive 'agrarian' contingent be maintained in the legislature. But ranged against them were those like Drury who were anxious to promote a broadened out 'progressive party.' Out of these conflicting approaches came a compromise resolution: that the UFO take no political action as a party and confine itself to the objects set out in its constitution, but that it not oppose the formation of a political party embodying the principles of the farm movement, since 'political action was necessary to the full attainment of the [movement's] ideals and aspirations.'[2] Attempts to defer discussion of the resolution were defeated, so it was past midnight, on 13 December, before it was finally voted on and carried.

Much of the time had been taken up with speeches invited from Drury and former cabinet ministers. Drury appeared to have shaken off the worst of his post-election despondency, and in a burst of good humour congratulated the resolutions committee on its 'exceedingly wise' contribution to the convention's proceedings. He had every reason to be gratified; what the resolution proposed was essentially what he had been advocating all along. Unaccountably to some, Morrison appeared to be in general agreement on the question, a factor that may well have swayed the vote in the resolution's favour.

Some time later, however, the UFO secretary took pains to point out that in fact he had not unequivocally recommended the resolution simply because it would 'leave us just where we were, to do as we liked.' So why, some asked, had he appeared to go along with Drury and favour the resolution? As he later tried to explain to Good, he had taken it easy on the matter because 'anger and excitement' brought on supposedly by Drury's promotion of Broadening Out, had 'set him back medically,'[3] a problem that had bothered him on at least one other crucial occasion. At any rate, a seemingly self-assured Drury made the point crystal clear to Morrison and everyone else that he had not abandoned his political career; interrupted it perhaps, but only for a time. Besides, he was convinced that the 'present Tory ascendency [*sic*] in Toronto is [nothing] to worry about ... Ferguson ... is doing very badly,' he added with a certainty that others would have challenged, 'and is making many enemies.'[4]

Morrison's reflections on the convention's work were in part a reaction to two Drury letters that the *Sun* printed early in 1924. They in turn had been a critical response to letters that Good had written, questioning the whole process of Broadening Out. Good made the argument that a people's party was unfeasible given the unlikely prospect of co-operation among all the varied groups that made up the electorate. He recommended for the political process not 'secret diplomacy' but the 'open discussion' and sound political education that group representation would make possible. In reply Drury praised his friend for his idealism, but, drawing on his own recent experiences, asked him to to be more pragmatic and resign himself to the reality that 'Parliament was not a debating society' where points were awarded the winners but a place where hard decisions had to be made. In effect, Good was told, action and not mere words, however eloquent and impassioned, was needed to resolve the problems of the postwar years.[5]

Good's attempt to challenge Drury's position produced some private correspondence. 'I still think you are wrong,' the former premier wrote Good. 'I frankly see no chance of a distinctly Farmers' Group getting anywhere at least in this generation. We can, however, provide the basis of a great political movement which may in the very near future bring great good to the country.' His optimism never seemed to sag. He had convinced himself that the time had arrived to found a new progessive party with strong urban backing. It would be formed, he prophesied, out of the 'national necessity of a prosperous and contented Canadian countryside' and not, as the National Policy party had been, on the 'supposed need for smoking factory chimneys.'[6]

This esoteric discussion was abruptly shouldered aside in 1924 by a major political scandal involving the previous administration. It began when Aemilius Jarvis, a prominent Toronto broker, financier, and sportsman, was charged with financial conspiracy. That was remarkable enough. But what followed was a thunderbolt: Peter Smith, Drury's former provincial treasurer, was sentenced along with Jarvis on the same charge. Jolted out of the present, an anxious Drury was obliged to review the circumstances that had culminated in this event.[7]

Until recently his published accounts of it have virtually ruled the field. In a series of *Maclean's* articles in 1933 and later in *Farmer Premier* he called upon his own recollections in an effort to 'set the record straight.'[8] He recalled for his readers that early in 1920 Smith had brought Jarvis to see him, saying he had a matter to discuss with the government. Having made the introductions, Smith supposedly excused himself and decamped to catch a train. Jarvis had a proposition that revolved around a decision taken by the previous government to purchase and retire provincial bonds held in Britain 'when conditions were right.' The broker believed that that time had arrived because of the favourable rate of exchange on the pound. Apparently he suggested that the Drury government use his services to purchase the bonds and then recompense him with an appropriate commission and underwrite his expenses. The premier claimed that as a virtual stranger to the mysteries of high finance he took refuge in the counsel of those who were more expert, particularly Sir Edmund Walker, whom he was then meeting regularly on university matters. That financier purportedly suggested an alternative arrangement whereby Jarvis would undertake all the risks and the expense by buying the bonds in his own name and selling them to the government at an agreed-upon price that would net him a reasonable profit. This advice a relieved Drury followed. Ultimately Jarvis swallowed his objections and accepted the government's terms. The upshot was that the broker proceeded to Britain and completed a successful deal that yielded the province a tidy profit of approximately four million dollars and a handsome return to himself of over half a million. Drury claimed at the time that Smith had less to do with the matter than other members of the cabinet, even though as the minister responsible he had officially sanctioned all the arrangements.

Doubtless Drury was convinced that his rendition of the proceedings was the correct one but information that subsequently came to light during Smith's trial calls it sharply into question. When summoned to testify, the former premier was subjected to a withering and unsettling cross-examination during which he was made to admit that when the scheme was first discussed Smith suggested that Jarvis, not Walker, be called upon to advise the government on its feasibility. Not only this, Drury appeared not to have approached Walker at all though the banker was named by Jarvis as a possible consultant. And as for Drury's later claim that Smith's role was a largely nominal one, it seemed plain enough, again according to Drury's responses in court, that Smith had been present throughout the discussions.

In any case, Drury claimed that Smith had alerted him to yet another bond matter. Smith's predecessor in the treasury portfolio, Thomas McGarry, had apparently sold a bond issue to the Home Bank in what were described as suspicious circumstances. McGarry, dismissed by his enemies as a Ferguson crony and an unsavoury representative of the old school of Ontario politics, was thought perfectly capable of arranging such a dubious transaction. But after being directed to act on his suspicions, Smith reported to Drury that the loan, though a 'piece of bad business,' had been neither illegal nor corrupt. McGarry would have been in perfect agreement about its propriety. Indeed, he later claimed publicly that his dealings with the Home Bank were totally above board and that if he had been disposed to favour it at all it was only because it was a 'Catholic institution.' In any event, Smith's supposed disposition of the McGarry business appeared to end the matter.

Appearances, however, were deceiving. In the fall of 1923, some months after the defeat of the Drury government, the same Home Bank startled the financial world by collapsing without warning. Because it had had dealings with government, its affairs came under the immediate scrutiny of the Public Accounts Committee. Some interesting facts came to light. Among the more sensational was the discovery that some time before the 1919 election, large numbers of 'legals' (bills of $1,000 or more) had shown up in a minister's office, the same kind of legal tender reportedly used for the Tory war chest in the election. Everything seemed to be shaping up for a full-scale indictment of the Conservative party, this within a year of its convincing return to power.

And then the committee's review took an unexpected twist. Drury later recalled how shocked he had been by the disclosure that on 13 December 1919 a cheque had been made out to Smith for $15,000 – an apparent rebate to the province on the Home Bank loan transaction – and that no such sum had found its way into the treasury. And even though the cheque had been cashed, an equal amount of money had been paid out a few days before. Without a moment's hesitation the committee, off on a new tack, sent to Stratford for Smith's bank account. They offered the assurance, reported the local paper, that while essential details would be scrutinized there would be 'no unnecessary prying into [Smith's] personal business.' One essential detail revealed that on 22 December 1919 Smith had deposited $7,500 in 'legals' in his account. In addition, subsequent investigations discovered that at regular intervals throughout the following year he had deposited coupons from the provincial bonds held by Aemilius Jarvis, to the tune of some $6,500. At once the outcry over the Home Bank affair and possible Tory wrong-doing was deflected to this 'mysterious' transaction and to the business that Jarvis had done on behalf of the Drury government. What Drury understatedly called a 'breath of scandal' immediately threatened the reputation of that government, a state of affairs that properly alarmed the former premier and outraged farm spokesmen such as Good and Morrison, whose opinion of Smith had never been flattering.[9] The bon vivant who had allegedly orchestrated the unspeakable 'last awful night' enjoyed little credit in their moral bank.

Drury's first reaction had been to collect the equally distressed Doherty and Raney, the leaders of the Farmer rump in the House, and arrange a meeting with the former treasurer. Inexplicably, the seemingly untroubled Smith declined to tell all either to his erstwhile colleagues or to the Public Accounts Committee. As a result of his silence he was arrested, as was Jarvis in due course, and both charged with theft, bribery, and conspiracy. Still anxious, in spite of Smith's baffling optimism. Drury sought out Jarvis and received the categorical assurance that he had not rewarded Smith in any way for the part that he had played in the overseas bond purchase. Then, according to Drury's account, the aggrieved broker divulged that a former business associate of Smith's, William H. Pepall, had advised him there was a good deal to be had in arranging the bond transaction. It turned out that it was Jarvis's action on Pepall's tip that had brought him and Smith to Drury's office early in 1920. What this version of the story does not disclose, however, is that Pepall subsequently accompanied Jarvis to Britain ostensibly in order to protect the province's interests. This curious arrangement, which had come to light in 1921, must have been known to Drury, but it received no attention in his reconstruction of the episode. At any rate, Jarvis finished his discussion with the former premier by revealing that after the consummation of the bond deal he had paid Pepall a commission in bonds held by his firm.

When the case went to trial in October 1924, Smith's jauntiness was swiftly shattered and Drury's worst fears confirmed. Smith ended up pleading guilty to receiving $15,000 and, though acquitted on the bribery and theft charges, he and Jarvis were convicted on the conspiracy one. Meanwhile Pepall, who had started the ball rolling four years before, had repaired to California and refused to return voluntarily to give evidence. When extradition efforts failed to dislodge him, Drury smelled a conspiracy and later alleged that Pepall had been deliberately detained in the United States by 'baseless' criminal charges brought on by the perjured testimony of an official in the attorney general's office.[10] But it so happened that the decision to detain Pepall arose from obscure American regulations and not from the alleged skulduggery of provincial officials. What also became clear was that Jarvis had rewarded Pepall rather lavishly for his efforts as intermediary. Moreover, payment had been made in such a roundabout and unconventional fashion that it cast a good deal of suspicion on Jarvis's way of doing business. None of this was reported by Drury at the time or later in his account of the episode.

A year after Smith and Jarvis were sentenced and with the case disposed of, the American red tape was finally cut and the way cleared for Pepall's extradition to Canada. Like the other two, he was charged with conspiracy. But at his trial a new piece was added to the puzzle. A loan that Pepall had made to friend Smith had taken the form of coupons on the very bonds he had received as a commission from Jarvis. Drury later asserted that a mortgage securing the loan and signed by Smith was produced in evidence and led to Pepall's acquittal. But that acquittal came about in spite of the fact that no such hard evidence materialized at the trial. Nevertheless, Drury stayed convinced that had this information been produced at the earlier trial Smith and Jarvis – certainly Jarvis – would also be free men. What he seemed to overlook was that the Pepall loan accounted for only a fraction of the funds that had mysteriously come Smith's way.

One question that plagued the former premier was why Smith had adamantly refused to submit the crucial mortgage, or something like it, as evidence in his favour. Another was why it had been impossible to have Pepall attend and testify when Smith and Jarvis had been put on trial. These developments, coupled with Howard Ferguson's flat rejection of Doherty's repeated requests for a royal commission to investigate the matter, convinced the suspicious Drury that every effort was being made to hound the 'innocent' Jarvis and impugn the reputation of his government. He was not alone. The *Canadian Forum* noted that Smith and Jarvis were imprisoned at a time when the 'present Government ... of Ontario is investigating the former administration with all the viciousness usually attendant upon a political trial of this nature.' It told its readers that much of that viciousness stemmed from the Tories' desire to seek revenge for Drury's relentless probe of their timber policy. Ferguson seemed to add substance to the argument when he refused to consider the re-trial of Jarvis that a number of political and business heavyweights, headed by Sir John Willison and Sir Joseph Flavelle, repeatedly requested after 1925. Those friendly to Drury and the former government understandably accused the Conservative leader of acting solely out of a desire to enhance his own party's advantage and to divert attention from past Tory lapses.

In the meantime Drury had been obliged to set aside the Jarvis episode and address his own political prospects. In spite of Good's objections and the scepticism of political observers and the *Sun*, a modest provincial progressive party was organized in 1925 and local associations formed. In view of his recent pronouncements, many of the newly recruited Progressives understandably wanted Drury for the leadership. But he put off giving them a definite answer because he was already toying with bigger game.

After turning the problem over in his mind, he made the decision to withdraw from the provincial scene and venture into federal politics, the course he had considered and discarded four years before. Only there, he told the disappointed provincial Progressives, could he hope to do battle on behalf of free trade. But there may well have been other considerations. Might not a federal win provide him with a passport to Mackenzie King's cabinet circle, a prospect he had long cherished? Was there also a possibility that Good's arguments against a 'broadened' people's party in Ontario had finally struck home? At any rate, on 1 October 1925 Drury allowed himself to be nominated by the Progressives to contest the federal riding of North Simcoe.[11] The move was warmly welcomed by those who had long felt that his talents would be wasted on any more 'excursions' at Queen's Park. For them the only significant political stage was Ottawa. 'Without success [there],' a Good confidant wrote even before the 1923 election had been called, 'our economic advance will be but slight; even legislative developments in the provinces can do comparatively little for us. I would like to see Drury in Ottawa.'[12]

Other more dispassionate observers had believed at the close of 1923 that Drury stood a good chance of being taken into King's cabinet as the spokesman for Ontario's Progressives.[13] But the belief was ill-founded. Certainly in *Farmer*

Premier Drury mentioned that he received at this time a tempting offer from King which he claimed to have turned down because of Ottawa's foot-dragging on the tariff.[14] King, however, made no reference to such an arrangement in his voluminous diary entries or equally voluminous correspondence. Yet the offer might have been made when the prime minister visited his sister in Barrie in the summer of 1923, a sojourn that was extended to include a post-election meeting with Drury.[15] At any rate, it seems fairly clear that the old links with King were never entirely severed after Drury declined to join him in 1921. Throughout the remainder of his term at Queen's Park, Drury had kept in touch with the Liberal leader on possible alignments that could affect the provincial scene and his own political future. Drury could also appreciate the fact that King had remained at arm's length from the 1923 election and refused Hay's requests for aid for fear of alienating the Progressives and 'work[ing] an injury ... where healing is most needed.'[16] When Drury was unanimously endorsed by the Progressives in North Simcoe, to his relief he was offered support from the riding Liberals who had obviously picked up their cue from Ottawa. But Drury realized that even with their real or tacit backing, which a local Tory paper claimed he did not deserve, he would have a stiff fight on his hands. The Tory candidate, W.A. Boys, a Barrie native, a popular lawyer, and a highly regarded mayor of the town, was about to embark on a well-funded and aggressive campaign to make up for an unsuccessful showing in the 1921 election. Boys's standing and presence combined with local disenchantment with the King government to make heavy inroads on Drury's chances. Nevertheless, Drury campaigned with his customary eloquence on a straight free trade platform. He reminded his audiences that even in the Barrie area productive industries, financed by townspeople and 'prosperous farmers' – the magical combination of Broadening Out – had been born without the need for the midwife of protection.

Though Drury preferred to think that the electorate saw it purely as an ideological debate between him and Boys, an out-and-out protectionist, his wartime setback in the area may have come back to cloud his image there eight years later. As well, the belief that he had been an anti-conscriptionist lingered in some veterans' quarters and worked against him.[17] Apart from these factors, he told King that the 'influence of the [UFO] head office' and a 'strong Orange element' in the riding also handicapped his chances.[18]

His foreboding was justified. When the votes were counted he emerged the loser by some 800 votes. All the same, he might have ruefully thought, so much for King's pious hope that a popular front of Liberals and Progressives would carry the day. For that matter, the Liberal leader had gone down to defeat in a battle that nearly restored the two-party system at the federal level. The formidable contingent that the Progressives had put together in 1921 was slashed by nearly two-thirds and the Conservatives emerged with the largest tally, 116 to 101 for the Liberals. Desperately hoping that he could survive with the 'cross bench' support of the Progressive rump, King decided to cling to office and meet Parliament. The scheme worked and he managed to carry on until the following summer.

In the interval Drury and King exchanged condolences and observations. After complaining about the Tory penchant for 'dirty tricks,' Drury waxed eloquent on the tariff question. He tried to reassure King, who may not have entertained this possibility at all, that the election's outcome did not mean that the 'people of Canada are content with a protective tariff.' Their proper indoctrination in free trade principles, Drury continued sanguinely, would bring them around to an understanding of the question. But in the meantime he urged King to eschew a 'half way course' designed to placate wavering Progressives and hard-line Conservatives in Liberal clothing. That course, he argued, would fail to appease the 'beneficiaries of Protection' and arouse 'no enthusiasm among its opponents.'

In the cause of educating the electorate, Drury fell back on the time-honoured practice of his own administration and urged King to name a commission to investigate the tariff. With obvious relish, as if indeed he were assembling another Sutherland Commission, he envisaged the appointment to such a body of an economist (not the 'defeatist' Leacock, he stressed), a farmer, a labourite, a professor (Sissons, a kindred soul on the issue?), and a manufacturer, even a high protectionist. Then he asked what King by this time must have been waiting for – that he, Drury, be considered for the farmer's place on such a commission. All he really wanted, he claimed, was to do '*real* service for *real* Liberalism.'[19] In view of his prospects at the time, he may have been less than candid when he assured the prime minister that he was not merely job-seeking.

For his pains he received a characteristic King rebuff. What the prime ministerial response amounted to was 'free trade if necessary but not necessarily free trade.' And although King promised to give the commission idea some thought, he did not wish to do more at this time for fear of 'challenging the fates.' Drury was then chided for having refused to join his cabinet in 1921. A month after this exchange King appeared to settle for a small tariff advisory board but made no mention of considering Drury for an appointment to it.[20]

For the time being the former premier and luckless candidate was obliged to shelve his political ambitions and tend to less stirring chores. These included not only the farm at Crown Hill but the directorship of a farmers' mutual insurance company and the management of a co-operative packing house he had helped organize in Barrie. 'It has been very badly managed,' he said of the co-operative early in 1924, 'and has nothing co-operative about it but the name. We are trying to abandon all speculative lines and introduce [genuine] co-operation.'[21] Drury also continued to attend, though not on a regular basis, the shareholders' meetings of the United Farmers Co-operative Company, and periodically he allowed his name to stand for a directorship.[22] Though time-consuming, these varied activities were a poor substitute for the compelling tasks of politics and he readily responded when another call to arms was sounded within a year of the 1925 election.

King's precarious minority government became unstuck over a scandal in the Customs Department and a constitutional crisis the prime minister engineered over the governor general's refusal to grant him a dissolution.[23] King abruptly resigned in June 1926 and Arthur Meighen, his arch foe, was called upon to form a government. If, as was then the parliamentary practice, Meighen appointed his followers to the cabinet as salaried officers under the crown, they would have to vacate their places and seek re-election. This would leave the Conservative rank and file without leadership, an unpalatable option that led Meighen to form a temporary government of acting ministers without portfolio to serve for the remainder of the session. This device, on the face of it constitutionally acceptable, was seized upon by King as an unprecedented and arrogant assumption of power. He immediately brought in a resolution so worded as to persuade some 'muddled and gullible' Progressives to vote against the Meighen government and bring it down. Meighen then sought and received a dissolution, and another general election was in the offing. In this contest, scheduled for September 1926, Drury would try his luck and stamina again.

In the course of the recent contretemps in the House of Commons, Drury may have been as 'muddled' as the Progressives were supposed to be on the constitutional issue King had raised. 'The time has come,' Drury wrote the prime minister after the imperial conference of 1926, 'as evidenced by the constitutional crisis of last Summer, when in the history of Canada it is absolutely necessary to define our position' on such matters.[24] On the other hand, Meighen's haughtiness and condescension during the 1921 election shaped much of Drury's personal distaste for the Conservative leader and his fears for the country's future under his tutelage. Better King's Liberals, he may have reasoned, than that kind of insensitive Tory rule.

This time out, Drury shed the Progressive label and for all intents and purposes returned to the two-party fold as a 'free trade liberal.' His move symbolized the disintegration of the Progressive cause as electoral reverses and disenchantment robbed it of the zeal and momentum that had carried it to success earlier in the decade. In 1926 Drury thought his chances much better anyway. Reports were coming in that local Conservatives, made complacent by the previous year's victory, would have difficulty getting out the vote for Boys. To bolster Drury's chances even more, his supporters conducted an enthusiastic door-to-door canvass in Barrie and Collingwood and put a paid organizer to work throughout the riding. For a time the issue was in doubt when the predominantly rural vote cut heavily into Boys's majority. At one point before all the returns were in, Drury's aides organized a victory procession, complete with band, from the Barrie town hall to their rallying place. But their reports proved premature. Boys was re-elected, albeit with a sharply reduced majority of some 200 votes.

That result provided small comfort for Drury and he could easily guess at the factors that had shaped this defeat. He probably placed Morrison and the Orange element once again at the top of the list of culprits, along with his growing reputation for being a political loser. Some months after the election, however, he attributed the setback to the opposition's tactics on the tariff question. 'During the campaign,' he wrote in an unpublished article, 'much breath was expended in trying to convince the farmer that he should become part of the system of Protection. It is useless, and dishonest, to quote impressive figures showing the totals of agricultural imports into Canada, and to infer that the ... farmers would be benefited by a protective tariff on these ...'[25] This was the final shot he fired in the post-mortem on the 1926 campaign. Now he had to turn his attention to considering a life outside the political arena and to preserving his farm at Crown Hill.

After two costly elections Drury had his own financial well-being to consider. Although his farm was free and clear, falling farm prices and the rising cost of implements (thanks, as he put it, to the 'plutocrats gorged with prosperity'), had made imperative some lucrative employment beyond his line fences. He looked to King, his original political benefactor, for help. One letter he composed for the prime minister early in 1927 had an equal mixture of supplication and self-pity. 'I have been defeated twice in succession,' he wrote after scoring out 'three times' 'largely because I was foolish enough to run in an impossible constituency, because I happened to be a native of it ... I have to a certain extent lost prestige because of being defeated.' What he required, he bluntly told King, was some form of 'public service, to restore [his] situation ... in short, a job.'[26]

One that he coveted was the recently vacated chairmanship of the International Waterways Commission. Because it oversaw power development on the St Lawrence, a matter of vital interest to Ontario. Drury felt that the province should have the lion's share of representation on the commission. Armed with what he called his 'four years' intensive course on Ontario,' he thought he would make a suitable chairman and, moreover, be acceptable to the Americans because of the stand he had taken against Beck's radials. Stressing that this was the 'first time [he had] ever asked the Liberal party for anything for [him]self,' he pleaded that the position would restore his prestige and enable him to re-enter public life. King was politely unmoved, however, and the job did not materialize in spite of the quiet diplomacy on his behalf by, among others, Colonel Maclean.[27] In all this Drury seemed totally unaware of how his search for public employment could be seen as inconsistent with his earlier strictures on the evils of patronage.

After his setback on the job front, Drury spent many hours on fine-tuning his views on free trade and the place of agriculture in modern society. He also pondered the peculiar plight of farming in Ontario:

When we compare the farms of [this province] with those of Quebec and the Maritimes, we find a fertility of soil, a generosity of climate, and a variety of production that cannot be approached by the latter. When we make a comparison with the Western Provinces we find that, while the latter have greater areas of easily cultivated land, this advantage is more than offset by an unreliable rainfall and greater distances from the seaboard, involving higher freight rates. All things considered then, we might expect to find the farmers of Ontario the most prosperous in the Dominion.[28]

But the reverse was seen to be the case and this gave Drury the opportunity to blacklist once more the conditions that produced this anomaly: rural depopulation, misguided urban and industrial growth, and the protective tariff. On the subject of rural depopulation he struck a strong nativistic note. He feared the day when 'foreigners' and immigrant 'peasants' who knew nothing of the Ontario rural ethic would come to work the farms abandoned by the native-born and in the process destroy the 'fine Canadianism of our countryside.'[29]

Such reflections gave way in the fall of 1927 to a full-scale row with the UFO executive. Drury brought it on by supporting the Liberals in a federal by-election in North Huron. Angered by the creation of a UFO political committee to 'muzzle' Farmer candidates, he set out to clear the air. 'The dominant clique in the UFO,' he charged in the *Sun*'s columns, 'are pursuing an unworkable and unrealizable policy ... Strings are attached to the [Farmer] candidates.' Using a term snatched from the dark past of Tory rule, he branded the political committee a 'pretty tight family compact.'[30] He told his friends that Morrison and his clique were all but working for the Conservatives and that their policy 'is the greatest help they could have.'[31] His suspicions were fuelled by reports that Morrison privately applauded Ferguson's supposedly sensitive treatment of the UFO.[32] The gauntlet Drury threw down in 1927 was immediately picked up; Morrison and the executive of the farm organization predictably denounced the former premier's charges as fabrications.

The main bout, however, was scheduled for the annual UFO convention at the end of the year. Those in the know reported that it would be asked to consider a resolution that would remove any vestige of a political association from the organization. Drury also received the unwelcome word that should he wish to speak at the convention he would be subjected to 'organized rowdyism.' The executive, anxious to curb the acrimony that had scarred previous meetings, were determined to bar all discussion of Broadening Out. At the same time they also felt obliged to censure Drury for attacking the Farmer nominee in North Huron 'as well as UFO officials and speakers from Liberal platforms.'[33] In order to give himself a free hand at the convention and not entangle others in his private fight, Drury had resigned the presidency of the provincial Progressive Association, to which he had been elected in 1924.

As always, Drury responded feelingly to any attack on his own political conduct, and he quickly put together a counter-assault. As a member of the salary committee of the co-operative company, he raised a matter already prominently aired in the press – that Morrison had found lucrative places on the firm's payroll for members of his family. The charge had first been made by a young, unruly UFO member from West Elgin, Mitchell F. Hepburn, who in 1926 had been elected as a Liberal to the House of Commons. Hepburn had also echoed Drury's criticisms of UFO manipulation of candidates, only to be raked over the coals for his pains. When the former premier renewed Hepburn's charges of nepotism at the convention, the secretary was upheld even though the company's general manager admitted that Morrison's decision to hire his son, daughter, and son-in-law had perhaps not been 'good business.'[34] Drury and Hepburn were, however, only briefly thrown together. Before long Drury grew disappointed with the younger man's tactics, which probably reminded him too much of his nemesis, Howard Ferguson.

The flare-up over Morrison had essentially been a sideshow to the convention's main event – the fielding of Drury's accusation that the political committee was acting like a tight family compact. The resolution that eventually carried seemed to bear him out, for it stated that the committee did 'not represent the opinion of the UFO clubs in that it forbids freedom of thought and action on the part of constituencies and candidates.' Official authorization was then given for Farmers to co-operate 'politically with individuals or parties who may think along similar lines.'[35] Drury should have been equally gratified when the resolution buried the formula of group government and reaffirmed the UFO as a class organization committed to its original aim of educating farm citizens in the economic facts of life. On the face of it, Drury appeared to be totally vindicated but it was something of a hollow victory for it came eight years too late.

The affairs of the UFO were not the only ones that drew Drury's anger in 1927. If Morrison was still seen as the serpent within the fold, Howard Ferguson continued to play that role outside it. The latest excuse for reviling the Conservative administration was their alleged packing of the Mothers' Allowance Commission with political favourites. Mrs Adam Shortt, who had long served as the commission's vice-chairman, resigned in protest over the issue. 'I regret more than I can say,' she wrote a friend, 'that conditions at Head Office became so bad that I felt in honour bound to [do so] ... At first I [remonstrated] privately and at length to the premier [Ferguson] but nothing effective being done I sent in my resignation and protest.' Another major problem she cited was the political influence being exerted to include 'ineligible beneficiaries' in the program. A few years later she put the blame not so much on the premier as on Forbes Godfrey, the minister responsible for the commission.[36]

Drury soon received a personal word from the aggrieved Mrs Shortt. 'The occasion of your letter,' he replied in the fall of 1927, 'is one that fills me with great regret, not only because of your resignation ... which I regard as a real loss, but more particularly because of the cause.' One of Mrs Shortt's colleagues also complained that no employees had been sent to the commission's staff through the Civil Service Commission after the defeat of the Drury government.[37]

The year 1927 would bring another disappointment, and again Ferguson could be blamed. The enactment that year of the Ontario Liquor Control Act dealt a lethal blow to the cause to which Drury had passionately committed his government in the 1923 election. In the interval there had been indications that disaster might overtake the Ontario Temperance Act and its displaced defenders. Within a year of the election, Ferguson's administration cautiously called for a plebiscite on the question, the results of which dramatically reduced the impressive prohibitionist majorities of 1919 and 1921. Then, having fought and won an election in 1926 largely on bringing back liquor sales under government control, long the goal of anti-prohibitionists, Ferguson introduced the necessary legislation. Its passage, like the erosion of the outrage and moral fervour that had produced an agrarian revolt and anti-partyism just a few years before, reflected society's desire to return to the certainty and comfort that only normality could provide. In any case, what Drury had graphically warned the community about in 1923 had come to pass under the aegis of the Conservatives.

From the hours he spent fuming over Morrison and the exploits of Ferguson, Drury had to wrench some time to pursue his personal interests. And these it seems had to go beyond his farm at Crown Hill, which, he claimed, could not stand the strain of sustaining him and his family. A project floated in Collingwood stood out among the several he considered at this time. For years he had been fascinated by the commercial and navigational possibilities of the upper lakes and by the prospect of capitalizing on the ever-swelling grain trade from the prairies. Now, with the wholehearted support of Collingwood's town fathers, he explored the feasibility of harbour improvements there for accommodating grain carriers, and the vital next step, the putting up of a large elevator.

But before Drury and Collingwood could make any move they would have to spell out the situation to the federal government which would have the final say on such a public work. In a lengthy memorandum Drury told Mackenzie King that in spite of Ottawa's past investment in Collingwood harbour the returns had been unsatisfactory because the port could not handle modern grain boats. He urged the improvement as a means of arresting Collingwood's decline into a 'mere market town.'

In the fall of 1927, much to Drury's satisfaction, the minister of public works responded and, after inspecting the harbour, stated that he would support the necessary dredging program if the town showed 'its good faith by ... [erecting] an elevator.'[38] Collingwood took him at his word and, with Drury's encouragement, sought out the necessary financing from, among others, the Willison-Neeley Corporation. Founded by Sir John Willison and T.A. Neeley, it included on its directorate the president of Canadian Terminal System Limited, and a former Ontario premier, Sir William Hearst.[39]

Ironies abounded in the proposed arrangement. Willison's stand on the tariff had long been anathema to Drury. 'We live in a protectionist world,' Willison had written during his administration. 'Even if it were otherwise at this stage of our national existence ... I would be in favour of protection for Canada.' He had also accused the country's free traders, Drury included, of insincerity, and declared the tariff controversy an 'imposter.'[40] There is nothing to indicate that he had changed his mind on the question by 1927. And although Drury had been grateful to Hearst for courtesies extended in 1919, he had only recently dismissed him as a 'Tory, first, last and all the time.'[41] Drury's pursuit of private income, as distinct from ideological goals, promised to produce improbable bedfellows. The town fathers of Collingwood, however, were sensibly unconcerned with such ironies and early in 1928 proceeded to conclude an agreement with Canadian Terminal System, acting on Willison-Neeley's behalf, for the construction of the elevator. The task of supervising the operation was entrusted to a new venture, Collingwood Terminals Limited, set up by the Willison-Neeley firm and to be presided over by Drury himself. The actual construction work was assigned to C.D. Howe and Company of Port Arthur, a well-regarded firm known to the former premier.

So far, so good. But then Ottawa, pleading financial problems, began to drag its feet on the dredging program. In April 1928 Drury wrote an urgent letter to King and, in a mixture of statesmanlike observations and appeals to local political considerations, stressed the 'advisability of the expenditure from a national stand-point' and how it might improve the Liberals' political situation in North Simcoe. Drury waited weeks for a reply and then it came in the form of King's thin apology for having been unable to look into the matter.[42] Shorn temporarily of Ottawa's help, Drury and his associates were obliged to mark time.

In the interval, apart from supervising farm work at Crown Hill, Drury did some serious magazine writing. Indeed, in the fall of 1927 he had intimated that he would fancy this kind of employment, once suggested to him by Colonel Maclean. The upshot was that the publisher commissioned him to prepare a series of articles for the *Financial Post* on the state of the nation's farm movement, particularly on the prairies. As well as satisfying his writing ambitions, Drury might have seen the project as a way of scouting western support for his plans in Collingwood. At any rate, most of January 1928 he was away from home busily interviewing farm leaders, provincial politicians, and urban businessmen on the prairies. Drury's long-standing critics read sinister political motives into the junket. The *Telegram*, for example, accused him of trying to mobilize western farmers behind the banner of the Liberal party, a charge *Maclean's* heatedly denied.[43]

Out west Drury was in his element, eagerly collecting information and opinion for his series. In the course of his odyssey he attended the United Farmers of Alberta convention in Calgary and had an opportunity to watch the redoubtable Henry Wise Wood in action. He came away impressed with Wood's ability to dominate the proceedings, though the author of the 'Alberta scheme' of group government did not invite the former Ontario premier to address the gathering. But Drury did savour that experience elsewhere on his western expedition and, generally speaking, his views on Broadening Out and his past contributions to the farm movement were applauded.[44] It was like old times, reminiscent of his mission years before helping to organize the CCA. There was, however, one jarring note that spoiled the prairie melody. Drury did not welcome what he perceived to be 'Bolshevist' tendencies among those militant farm leaders who were demanding more state intervention in the economy. After his return from the west he had nine articles accepted for publication in the *Financial Post*, four of which dealt critically with the wheat pools, the prairies' favourite form of grain marketing.[45] He followed this up in the spring of 1928 with a less technical three-part series for *Maclean's*.

By this time he was gratified by something more momentous than having his ideas put into print. After stalling for so many weeks on the Collingwood scheme, Ottawa finally decided to go ahead with Drury's harbour improvement plan. At the same time there was talk that no less a person than Thomas Crerar of the prestigious United Grain Growers Company would be recruited for Collingwood Terminals. If he was, he would bring to the firm a name and reputation that would appeal not only to prairie producers but to otherwise cautious eastern investors. But Drury had no way of knowing that Crerar was concerned about the former premier's inexperience with the grain trade and thought that he should seek help from 'skilled Winnipeg people' before he went any further. Crerar also queried the feasibility of routing grain through Collingwood in spite of the company's glowing assertion that the port was 'ideally situated and ... [its] harbour is of the best.'[46] In the end a sceptical Crerar turned down Drury's offer of a directorship when his own private qualms were not allayed by what others said in defence of the undertaking, but this factor he kept from its president. Crerar gave as his public reason the UGG directors' fear that he would lose contact and credibility with western graingrowers if he joined an eastern firm. He confessed to Drury the absurdity of their concern but even so he would have to accommodate it. The crestfallen Drury was then urged to seek the advice of 'old grain hands' before he took any further steps, a point that had weighed heavily with Crerar from the outset.[47]

Crerar's decision to steer clear of the Collingwood scene and the tentative nature of the enterprise drove Drury in the fall of 1928 to take refuge, as he invariably did in times of disappointment, at his writing desk. Late in the year he again accepted an invitation to do a series of *Maclean's* articles on a subject which had first caught his fancy when premier – the St Lawrence waterway.[48] Over a six-month period, ending in July 1929, he wrote as many pieces on the virtues of the inland seaway, which for some years had been the subject of chequered negotiations between Canada and the United States. By 1928 the scheme had foundered on Canadian opposition to the internationalization of the St Lawrence.

Howard Ferguson's flatly stated opposition to the project may have been sufficient reason for Drury to accept *Maclean's* invitation. Taking a strong nationalistic line, Ferguson had been urging Ottawa to retain 'complete sovereignty of navigation to the sea,' and not to 'sell a proprietary interest in [our] biggest national asset.'[49] The Conservative premier's position was one that Drury briefly considered and then brusquely discarded in his first article for the series. An all-Canadian enterprise, he argued, would be a prohibitively costly reprise of the radials scheme he had combatted as premier and whose only dividend would be an appeal to 'our supersensitive national pride.' He also feared that if Canada did not co-operate on a joint undertaking, the United States might proceed unilaterally with the building of an all-American route from Lake Ontario to the Hudson River, and ultimately to New York City. The results, Drury warned, would be deplorable for Canada. Much of the west's traffic would be drawn away from the St Lawrence and Canadian shipping on the projected American waterway would be subjected to discriminatory tolls. The result would be a blow to the Canadian shipping industry and the possible extinction of shipyards like those at Collingwood in which his own business plans were wrapped up. On the other hand, if international canalization went forward Montreal would stand to gain from increased shipments of western commodities, and her position as head of navigation would be assured.[50] All of these arguments were incorporated in the persuasive and straightforward prose that Colonel Maclean always admired, and they accompanied an impressive array of maps, charts, and tables.

Drury may well have been moved to his almost lyrical description of the St Lawrence and its benefits by the welcome improvements then going forward at Collingwood. By July 1929 construction of the grain elevator was well under way and the word was out that it would be fully operational by the following month. But the affairs of the future seaway and events at Collingwood were abruptly forced to yield to another call to political arms and what turned out to be Drury's fifth and last election campaign. In the closing weeks of 1929 a federal general election seemed to be in the offing. The dramatic stock market crash and the beginning of a crippling depression suggested that governments everywhere might have to seek fresh mandates for coping with this full-scale catastrophe. On a visit to Ottawa early in the new year Drury had what he described as a pleasant talk with King in which he again ritualistically advised tariff changes and expressed his regrets at not having joined Ottawa's ranks in 1921.[51] He also urged the prime minister to go to the country no later than the following year. Whether or not King thought Drury's advice was right, he was so badgered by opposition criticism that in mid-summer 1930 he decided to teach them a lesson and call a general election.

Drury's decision to enter the contest suggests that Collingwood Terminals was turning out to be less stimulating and profitable than anticipated. On the other hand, he may have thrown himself into that business not only to make a living but to gather the funding he would need for a renewal of political combat, perhaps the only kind of life that really mattered to him now. Whatever the motive, Drury allowed his name to stand in North Simcoe, and he was unanimously nominated by an alliance of Liberals and Progressives.

In one sense the 1930 campaign would be 1921 all over again. Drury went out of his way, as he had then, to draw a distinction between high and low species of tariffs. Indeed, he went beyond even this. He seemed anxious to assure the King government and Charles Dunning, the author of its moderate tariff program, that he would not dogmatically oppose it. 'I am not blind to the fact,' he was reported to have said on his nomination day by a paper not his friend, 'that there is a necessity for some tariffs in Canada for protection from the tariff barriers of other countries ... We must protect our own people and our own industries.' If this was an accurate transcript of his remarks, then his unswerving free trade friends must have listened with disbelief. Apparently he also urged countervailing duties against the rigorously protectionist ones of the United States, all the while astutely praising Dunning's efforts to open up increased trade with the United Kingdom and the empire. Holding out the 'hand of good fellowship to Great Britain, our biggest market,' was a goal that the farm movement had been setting for Ottawa for over a generation. Even so, Drury's reported utterances, which he did not appear to deny, hardly square with the categorical statement in *Farmer Premier* that he ran in 1930 'on the same free trade platform as before.'[52] As might have been expected, his nomination and his speeches elicited warm congratulations from King who shared his conviction that the 'prospects in North Simcoe look exceedingly bright.'[53]

Early on in the campaign Drury was brought up short by a questionnaire prominently displayed in Barrie's Conservative paper. First of all, he was asked if he was chairman of the executive committee of Canadian Terminal System, the firm that had a controlling interest in Collingwood Terminals. And if so, the query continued, was he receiving an anual salary of $12,000, and had he been given 1,250 shares of common stock 'for which he never paid a copper'? Finally, was the company the beneficiary of a grant of some $80,000 from the Liquor Control Board for having agreed to store spirits in their Toronto warehouse for sale in Ontario?[54] According to the paper's reporter, Drury refused to respond to the questionnaire during a prepared speech at the Barrie Armouries, claiming that the matter was a private one and had no connection with the election campaign.[55] These and other opposition tactics, described later by C.B. Sissons as particularly despicable, caused Drury much discomfiture. But it was eased by the comforting presence in Barrie of King himself, who had acted on Drury's request to lend his prestige to the occasion. King later exulted in his diary that it had been a 'good day' in Barrie and that he had been given a 'fine hearing.'[56]

Yet if King and Drury thought that such efforts would clinch the local contest, they were both in for a surprise. Drury again ended up, in a straight two-party fight, on the losing side. And this time he had not been forced to challenge the formidable Boys, who had retired, but a comparatively unknown farmer serving as Simcoe County's clerk. When the final tally was completed Drury learned that he had lost by a margin of some 800 votes out of a total of 14,000 cast, not exactly a total humiliation but not a triumph either. The jubilant Tory press had little difficulty putting his latest rejection down to a lack of candour on the tariff question. Drury in turn blamed his defeat on a 'strong Tory bias of inherited sentiment,' the ravages of a depression that threatened every government, and not least the Conservative 'appeal to local and sectional interest.' The Conservatives' argument that high protection could benefit farmers as well as workingmen, and the promise made by their leader, R.B. Bennett, to 'blast his way into world markets' with his tariff artillery, probably swung many rural votes their way. Crerar also tasted defeat at the hands of a victorious Conservative in Brandon. While Drury characteristically put a brave face on this, his fourth consecutive electoral rebuff, and urged King to continue the fight for a Liberal-Progressive alliance, a disenchanted Crerar threw cold water on such talk. He prophesied instead the imminent emergence of a new and more militant farmer-labour combination, a 'sort of call to the Proletariat.'[57]

Drury did not pause to contemplate that or any other political possibility. What he had to do in the immediate future was to take stock of his financial state after this, the most costly campaign of all. To answer newspaper questionnaires and fend off charges he had been compelled to spend considerable sums on explanatory advertisements – five hundred dollars to one paper alone. Innocent as usual of a war chest, he was obliged to dig deep into his own pocket. It may have been a fairly ample one, however, if he was actually being paid by Canadian Terminal anything like the presidential salary the hostile press claimed he was. Although company records, where they exist, are silent on the point, Collingwood Terminals' general manager, by way of possible comparison, enjoyed an annual salary of some three thousand dollars. Whatever the circumstances, the net result was that Drury was reduced to a state of financial embarrassment. He was also resigning himself to a life outside politics and, to quote a remark made later by Sissons, the 'flinging away of ambition.'[58] But worse was to come, something infinitely more devastating than electoral reverses and bad political investments.

15

Turning Point

In the early fall of 1931, Ella Drury underwent a preventive operation on the advice of the family physician. Drury knew the doctor and trusted him implicitly. Assured there was nothing dangerous but that trouble might develop should surgery be postponed, Drury and his wife had readily assented to the operation. Following it, he was told that it had been a success and that a speedy recovery was fully expected. 'That was on Monday,' Drury recalled in his autobiographical novel. 'The terrible week that followed ... [he] was to remember in minutest detail ... so etched with fire was it upon his very soul ... A time of heart-wringing and impotent regret, and cruel fear, and false hopes, no less cruel.'[1] What Drury tersely called 'unanticipated surgical developments' led at the week's close to Ella's death. The widower's desolation was complete. The childhood sweetheart, partner, confidante, comrade, and homemaker who had helped to sustain him in what had not been an easy life had abruptly been snatched away.

The bereavement that followed sorely tested Drury's 'simple Christian faith' that had come to his rescue in lesser disappointments and drove him into a renewed contemplation of the after-life. Although Ella and he had never accepted the concept of physical resurrection, they had believed in a life beyond this one. Years later when he comforted the widow of C.B. Sissons he recalled for her an experience he had with Ella's 'spiritual resurrection,' no less real for him than a corporeal manifestation might have been. He confessed that he and his wife had been 'telepaths,' a fact he had never told anyone before, not even Mackenzie King, who for different reasons would have been intrigued. As a result of this telepathy, Drury had strongly felt Ella's presence several times. 'The room, the dawn, the trees outside,' he remarked, 'everything was unfolded in a beauty such as I had never seen before ... I got a message just as plainly as though it had been spoken.'[2] Whatever comfort Sissons's widow derived from Drury's experiences, there is no question that they helped to sustain him in the worst times of his bereavement. Certainly thoughts of remarriage never entered his head. 'Ella,' he typically wrote his old friend, H.B. Cowan, 'was too won- derful and we were too close for that.'[3]

Even so, an enervating sleeplessness plagued him for months. Sometimes he would wake up the family in the small hours by showering, dressing, and then banging the door behind him as he left the house.[4] Shunning sleeping pills – a despised narcotic – he came to live with his insomnia by rising and working at his writing desk, the place to which he had often repaired in times of boredom and disappointment. Articles and essays, published and unpublished, had been the outpouring of those earlier spells of enforced literary activity; in the months after his wife's death he put together something more ambitious to take his mind off his problems – the makings of a 'little book.'[5] It colourfully distilled his thinking on a wide range of themes, from major preoccupations like protection through the depression's effects on agriculture to the state of Canada's political parties. Familiar with his agrarian journalism and his *Maclean's* pieces, Ryerson Press agreed to publish his manuscript after it was favourably assessed by Gilbert Murray, the economist. Entitled *Forts of Folly* after some lines he had come across by Matthew Arnold, the book was mainly a therapeutic exercise for filling the void of bereavement. None the less he was gratified by a notice of it in the *Globe*, and a year later, following the creation of the Young Farmer's movement, he confided his wish to Good that the book be used as part of their course of study. 'I wrote it with the hope,' he told his friend, 'that it might bring some light to a question [protection] that I still regard as one of the most important economic questions.'[6]

Another diversion in the months following Ella's death was speaking to school children on such subjects as farm life, patriotism, his own political experiences, and, increasingly, local history and historical personalities. The stories he had heard at his father's knee – the legacy of Kenilworth in Warwickshire – he would supplement with homely Ontario chronicles. Not surprisingly, he preferred vis- iting small rural schools like the one-roomed facility in Trafalgar, in his old Halton riding, where he spoke early in 1934. He could, recalled one admirer, hold pupils 'spellbound with the history of Simcoe County while [his] big white bull-dog sat beside him on the platform.'[7]

It was at about this time that he embarked on another kind of literary therapy, the novel that has already been mentioned in these pages. Based on his own life and experiences, it featured John and Alice Brooks who farmed near Cedarvale, a town that bore an unmistakable resemblance to Barrie. The vicissitudes of farming, commentaries on small-town life, family joys and tribulations, spiritual reflections, and, above all, agrarian politics, dominate its pages. Written in a sprightly and at times moving style, it betrays throughout his predilection for federal politics, the only arena in which the battle for free trade could be effec- tively fought. Thus he sends his protagonist, John Brooks, not to Queen's Park but to Ottawa to combat the 'interests,' a device inspired in part by the parliamentary career of his friend, W.C. Good. Drury's distaste for group government and its western apostle, Henry Wise Wood, surged out in his depiction of the Alberta leader as a dangerous political force and in his naming him, in comic strip fashion, Clutterbrane. The charges that Drury once levelled at Stephen Leacock, that he 'disguised his characters so thinly that they couldn't help but be identified,' applied equally in his own case.[8] The preparation of the novel, which runs to some five hundred pages of typescript, consumed many hours of writing and polishing.

Work on the exercise was interrupted in the summer of 1933 by an invitation from the owner of *Maclean's*. Colonel Maclean wanted the former premier to 'rethrash' the Jarvis case that had agitated the mid-1920s and threatened to blacken the reputation of his government. Concerned individuals and groups, Drury included, had for some years been seeking a re-trial for Aemilius Jarvis. Indeed, after the federal change of government in 1930 Drury and Manning Doherty had decided to give it another try and, at Jarvis's urging, went up to Ottawa in the hope of reopening the question. But the hope soon died.

Now, armed with Maclean's commission to review the matter, Drury went in search of some answers, this with Jarvis's full backing, a condition stipulated by the publisher. But Drury also required a willing Peter Smith, the other party to the episode. Though sickly and distinctly unenthusiastic, the former provincial treasurer agreed to tell more than he had when the scandal had broken a decade before. After talking about his meeting with Thomas McGarry, Smith revealed something new, at least for Drury – that J. Cooper Mason, the Home Bank president who had subsequently committed suicide, had offered to pay Smith $15,000 for the part he had played in the government loan arrangement. Smith, who now assured Drury that he was 'not of that nature,'[9] claimed that he refused the offer. Then he stated that a few days later he found some $7,500 on his desk accompanied by an unsigned note saying that it was for his bank account. When supposedly queried by Smith, Mason denied any responsibility for it. Convinced of this, Smith then banked the funds, the same ones uncovered by the Public Accounts Committee. After digesting all this, Drury could still come up with no plausible explanation for Smith's summary appropriation of the controversial $7,500, nor any reason for his stubborn silence in the 1920s. All the same, in the *Maclean's* series the former premier reiterated the argument that Smith and Jarvis, in the light of the Pepall disclosures, should have been acquitted of the charges that had sent them to prison in 1924.

Drury's series, theatrically entitled 'Is There a Canadian Dreyfus?', came as something of a bombshell and understandably commanded much attention, not only for the articles' plausibility but for their scathing indictment of Ferguson's alleged foot-dragging and attempts to conceal Tory wrong-doing during the Hearst administration. 'Everything I said in the articles,' Drury assured Good, 'was absolutely and unshakably true,' and they raised, he scornfully added, 'not a peep from the bunch in Queen's Park.'[10] As recent research has demonstrated, however, there was much that was decidedly shakable in Drury's reconstruction of the Smith-Jarvis case.[11] At any rate, in spite of the publicity and the pressure brought to bear by what Drury and others wrote, the decision taken by the minister of justice in 1933 to refuse Jarvis a re-trial was allowed to stand. The so-called outstanding political episode of 1924 was not about to unravel.

The work on the *Maclean's* series and his other literary exercises took Drury out of the worst of his bereavement and provided some income to boot. But no distraction, however stimulating, could hide the serious financial crisis that faced him. For reasons that remain obscure he was by this time no longer president of, or even associated with, Collingwood Terminals. The depression's impact on the grain trade, his unsuccessful flirtation with federal politics, or differences of opinion with business associates, all these might have dictated his departure from the company.[12] Whatever the reasons, the fact is that he now had no real source of income beyond the returns from the Crown Hill farm. And a suggestion that he be put on *Maclean's* permanent payroll was summarily vetoed by a senior editor on the grounds that the magazine's readers were only occasionally interested in the 'heavy stuff' that Drury contributed.[13]

Selling the farm, Drury realized, would be no solution even if a tidy profit materialized, which was very doubtful in the circumstances. The fact of the matter was that two of his sons, Carl and Harold, wanted to work it. A third son, Varley, who like his father was an OAC graduate, was married and employed by the co-operative packing plant his father had helped put on its feet in Barrie. Beth, the older daughter, who had followed in Varley's footsteps to the OAC and graduated as a dietitian, was at home where the rest of the family needed her help and counsel. The younger daughter, Mabel, had just completed normal school and was employed as a teacher at a nearby rural school for the usual depression salary of four hundred dollars a year.

Meanwhile, with no pension and few savings, Drury took out an expensive life insurance policy to meet possible contingencies. He then cast about for additional sources of income. One came readily to mind though he did not fancy it: the possibility of recovering all or part of the salary arrears he had denied himself while premier. Shortly after his defeat in 1923, the unfriendly *Northern Advance* had accused him of ordering that a cheque be issued in his favour for financial arrears dating from the fall of 1922. 'Having been rejected by the people,' the editor sneered, 'he decided to banish his economy idea and take all he could while the getting was good.' Drury did not deny the allegation, but pointed out that he had not requested reimbursement for the earlier span in office, which covered the better part of three years.

A well-placed intermediary and friend of Drury's, C.H. Carlisle, president of Goodyear Tire and Rubber Company, called upon the premier, George S. Henry, to consider the reimbursement, which amounted to some $8,800. Henry complied and a special warrant was issued to expedite the arrangement, a move inspired by what a grateful Drury called the premier's 'liberal view of my claim.' He may have thought differently, however, had he known that the matter may have been clinched for Henry by Carlisle's supposed assurances that Drury was through with provincial politics.[14] At this time there was concern in Tory ranks about the possible revival of some sort of farmers' party, and Henry was warned that Conservative farmers were 'restless and [that] anything [could] happen,' particularly if the depression's impact on agricultural prices deepened.[15] In these circumstances the premier would have been well advised to encourage the departure from the political scene of a rallying figure such as Drury. Yet there is no evidence that Henry advised his predecessor that an act of political renunciation was the price for meeting his financial request.

The depression that stirred Drury to act on his salary arrears also reactivated his pen and his political instincts. Once again *Maclean's* offered a forum for his views on what had precipitated the world's worst economic crisis. Drury's devotion to a laissez-faire economy and the notion that the jobless were often the victims of their own shortcomings were challenged by what he saw for himself in the 1930s. 'I drive home every evening,' he wrote in his private reflections at the time,

and nearly always I pick up a hitch-hiker ... And almost invariably my passenger is a transient unemployed. They're mostly young ... and not such a bad lot ... They're not tramps, or dirty, slovenly, shiftless, lazy, debauched [but] clean ... making the most of their thread-bare clothes ... They want work, they say – and I believe them ... There's tragedy on the highways these days – the tragedy of the Unwanted Man, homeless and hopeless.[16]

Yet in his *Maclean's* articles, three in all, published in the spring of 1933, Drury touched on those familiar and homely correctives that had already been aired by local farmers' organizations: the need to combat selfishness, to promote 'more brotherhood among mankind,' and to have rural people take a more active interest in economic and social problems.[17] However he might have been appalled by the social consequences of the depression, he was not prepared to embrace the fundamental reforms the newly organized Co-operative Commonwealth Federation was promoting. They smacked too much of the Bolshevist tendencies he had detected on the prairies a few years before. A liberal of the old school, Drury set his face against any blatant form of socialism or economic planning that did violence to the 'individualism and the freedom that we have.' Socialism, he firmly told Barrie's pleased Kiwanian businessmen, leads to bureaucratic tyranny and the abuse of power.[18]

Drury's distaste for the sort of expansionist government the CCF was threatening to put in place made him agonize briefly over what he himself had done during his premiership. The 'first Minimum Wage Act, the first Mothers' Allowance Act, the first Provincial Highway policy in Canada,' he recited. 'I do wonder about the whole thing taken collectively – the whole trend.'[19] But he did not agonize for long. His reforms, he assured himself, though undertaken in the name of the state, had either sought to entrench traditional virtues in a bewilderingly changing society or to confer the benefits of a Christian humanitarianism upon that society's unfortunates. After all, he reasoned, the distant parentage of his legislation had been the liberation movements of the nineteenth century that had abolished slavery and blunted the hard edge of industrialization, and certainly not the doctrines of Marx or the social democracy of western Europe. Having satisfied himself on this score, he strongly questioned the various efforts to cure the depression through a planned economy, regulated production, or 'spend yourself into prosperity programs.' In the spring of 1934, when he wrote to congratulate Mackenzie King on a Liberal by-election victory, he looked forward to a triumph of 'real liberalism' over the 'twin dangers of Toryism and Socialism, and I don't know which is worse.'[20]

Meanwhile other farm leaders such as W.C. Good were becoming more concerned with another 'ism' raising its head in central Europe. Good may have been influenced in his thinking by Reinhold Niebuhr, the American theologian and philosopher who was already sounding the alarm about the rise of fascism. In a commentary on a manuscript that Good had asked him to assess, Niebuhr wrote: 'The only suggestion I would have would be that it ought to include a chapter describing the efforts to maintain the old Social Order against the pressure of the new. I mean by that the general tendency toward Fascism. Though we will never have German Fascism on this continent there will be analogous movements and the farmers will be tempted to support them if they do not get clear instruction.'[21] The possibility that Ontario farmers, out of their revulsion for socialism and their suspicion of the old-line parties, might opt for a dangerous right-wing alternative may have occurred to Good already.

But not, it would appear, to Drury. Like many others on the concession lines, he began to pay closer attention to the revival of the provincial Liberal party. That revival was engineered by the same Mitchell Hepburn who had made for lively UFO meetings in the late 1920s. The farm boy from Yarmouth, made leader of Ontario's Liberals after a stint in the House of Commons, bade fair to inter the Conservative government at Queen's Park. Encouraged by that prospect, Drury and other former Liberals in the UFO, much to the disgust of hard-liners, swallowed their personal misgivings about Hepburn's flamboyant tactics and his notorious reputation as a 'wet,' and came out in his support. The Progressive remnant in the legislature, led by Harry Nixon, entered into an open alliance with the new Liberal leader, an alignment that one Conservative strategist correctly predicted would spoil the 'recrudescence of [a] Farmers' Party.'[22] But this was now small comfort to a harassed George Henry who on the eve of a general election in the spring of 1934 had to contend with a rejuvenated Liberalism in league with provincial Progressives.

Drury's interest in the contest brought a visit from Hepburn and Nixon, who arrived on his Crown Hill doorstep to sound him out on possible tactics to use against the Conservatives.[23] But whatever suggestions Drury offered probably counted for little in the campaign. Hepburn's dynamism, stump humour, and telling charges of government incompetence and corruption paid handsome dividends in their own right. The Tories under Henry took a drubbing as the Liberals stormed to victory in June 1934. Drury would probably have agreed with the defeated premier that Ontario was in for interesting times.

Genuinely delighted by Hepburn's victory for its own sake, Drury soon saw in it a means to achieve that gainful return to public service he had often discussed with King. Barely a week after the election Drury dashed off a letter to Ottawa urging King to use his influence with Hepburn on his behalf.[24] While he anxiously awaited an answer he composed a letter for his would-be benefactor at Queen's Park. After congratulating Hepburn on his splendid victory, Drury dispensed some blood-thirsty views on what the fate of the Conservative party should be. 'I hope ... you will not make the mistake I did,' he cautioned Hepburn, 'of being too generous and merciful toward them. Part of your work during the next two years must be to shoot them to pieces so they cannot come back, a new opposition party must be created.'[25]

Having released his barbs against old political foes, Drury turned to the matter of a job. As he had with King, he put himself forward as a possible member of the Hydro Commission. He assumed that his one-time colleague, Harry Nixon, victorious along with Hepburn and slated for a cabinet post, would endorse his application. 'Even my worst enemies,' Drury claimed, 'admit my ability and integrity, and besides, I know Hydro matters as well as any man in the Province ... and saved the Hydro by ... beating Beck on the radial issue.'[26] He left Hepburn in little doubt that if anyone deserved an appointment he did. Once again he seemed to be forgetting what he himself had once said so critically about this very sort of job-seeking.

In the meantime he received some bleak news from Ottawa. King, he learned, would not intercede with Hepburn because 'it would prove embarrassing to him as well as to me, and ... to the party were it thought that I was having anything to do with appointments.'[27] This drove Drury to one final personal appeal to Hepburn. In the circumstances he felt that all he could legitimately do was ask for 'some position which I could fill with a certain amount of dignity and where the salary would enable me to carry on.' Prominent Liberals in Drury's riding supplemented his appeal with remonstrances of their own, warning Hepburn of a bad reaction if something were not done for the former premier.[28] This kind of intervention may have helped to produce the appointment that Drury had long been seeking.

But he failed to end up with a position of provincial scope. What Hepburn offered was the combined offices of sheriff, county court clerk, and local registrar of the Supreme Court of the County of Simcoe. Given his circumstances, however, Drury was happy enough with it, even if the county shrievalty had been dismissed for years as a dying office. The annual salary that accompanied the position, though not as munificent as a Hydro commissioner's, was none the less set at $3,750, which was decidedly above the average in the depression year of 1934. Shortly after the appointment was made Drury received warm congratulations from W.D. Gregory, who may well have had a hand in it. 'I have already heard people say,' Gregory added in a fitting burst of gallows humour, 'that if they are to be hanged, they would like you to do the job.'[29] Moreover, the office Drury now entered was in a sense all in the family, his father and grandfather having held it – a consideration Hepburn may have weighed when he made the appointment.

Entrusted with a full-time job, Drury had to come to an arrangement about the farm. In the end, though with some misgivings, because Harold had barely turned seventeen, he divided it between him and his older brother, Carl, reserving to himself only a life interest in the house.[30] With that matter settled, he could thankfully turn to his new responsibilities.

New Careers and Old Reflections

There were distinct advantages that went with Drury's new position. For one thing, he could function out of Barrie, in his own home county, and continue to live at Crown Hill. For another, the work was not overly taxing for a fifty-six-year-old, and promised him the kind of rewarding public service, albeit highly regionalized, that he had long sought. As clerk and registrar Drury served in a kind of rubber-stamping capacity, overseeing records and ensuring that the proper documents were signed. As registrar he was required to countersign judgments nisi in divorce cases. Years later he wrote W.C. Good that of the hundreds of divorces that had gone through his office 'only two of them ... affected farm homes,' a statistic he predictably expanded on to show the disintegrative effects of modern urban life.[1] His growing pessimism about declining city standards and the accompanying spread of vices such as alcoholism was obviously reinforced by what he saw at first hand in the courts.[2]

When he donned his sheriff's hat he enjoyed more latitude than he did as clerk-registrar. 'Frequently,' he wrote, 'a sheriff can temper the wind to the shorn lamb,' particularly when he dealt with the enforcement of writs of *fieri facias*, designed to cover arrears from judgment debtors. The least complicated device for achieving this was the so-called sheriff's sale of goods and chattels and lands and tenements. Apart from the unpleasant publicity it fostered, Drury had another reason for avoiding it. 'In one of my early experiences,' he recollected, 'the debtor was a village merchant whose goods were put on sale. After the local demand was satisfied, it soon became clear that three outside bidders had agreed not to bid against each other, and the goods went at scandalously low prices.' The alternative he much preferred was to seize the debtor's goods and secure a bond requiring the debtor to produce them on demand.[3] The problem of indebtedness in a society that condoned, indeed encouraged, easy credit and instalment buying, frequently distressed him. One visitor to his court house office heard him grumble about the unthriftiness of such practices and how some of the victims 'didn't even own their own beds.'[4]

Even more unpleasant was his obligation to make arrangements for the execution of convicted murderers. In one case, his impatience with petty sectarianism burst out of his recollections. The night before the execution,

I did not sleep. I got up before five o'clock, drove to the jail through the star-bright winter morning, and there met the official witnesses: the jail surgeon and the sergeant of the Provincial Police. The boy's spiritual advisor, a member of one of the splinter sects, refused to accompany him to the gallows and had left him some hours before the execution. He explained that he did not want to make a mockery of the Lord's Prayer. I think it was simple cowardice. The boy walked to the gallows alone ... Then there followed, so quickly that I hardly knew what was happening, the strapping of his hands and feet, the drop through the trap door. And the thud.[5]

An incident like this raised for Drury some fundamental questions. Although he had always considered justice an impersonal matter, the death penalty was something special because it unleashed 'highly emotional elements which judge and jury, [not least himself] being human, cannot disregard.' Then there was always the possibility that the innocent could receive the maximum punishment. 'Further,' he added, 'there is the [brutalizing] effect on the public mind: I cannot forget that eager crowd gathering outside the jail, to peek, after the late movies.'[6]

In the early years of office Drury's day normally commenced at ten and ended at four in the afternoon, though sometimes he waited impatiently, 'with everything done up,' for the closing hour to arrive. Consequently he had considerable time at his disposal for indulging his penchant for tractarianism. This invariably took precedence over letter-writing (and the biographer is the poorer for that); he had 'no faculty for writing a satisfactory letter to a friend,' he apologized to Good on one occasion, 'business letters yes, but the other, no.'[7]

His writings at this time reveal that his fervour for reforestation and conservation had not abated over the years. Following his government's establishment of the Hendrie Forest, he was gratified that Simcoe County had undertaken other ventures, notably the reforestation plant at Orr Lake first mooted in 1927. Ten years later, with the Orr Lake Forest a thriving concern, steps were taken to commemorate the Drury government's initiative when a special Forestry Field Day was staged on the site. Peter Heenan, the durable spokesman for northwestern Ontario who was serving as Hepburn's minister of lands and forests, was there to unveil an appropriate cairn.

The main event, however, was the dinner speech that Drury had been invited to make. And he gave it with all the oratorical flourishes and humorous asides that had illuminated his speech-making during the days of power. Without being egotistic (a trait he was often accused of), he claimed to have had 'as great a part in inaugurating and establishing the policy of reforestation in Ontario as anyone in the Province.'[8] E.J. Zavitz, who was in the audience that evening, would doubtless have agreed. Drury drew the forester into his speech when he went on to reminisce how together they had driven by horse and buggy over the plains of Simcoe County.

Throughout his speech, as in past ones, biblical allusions abounded. While dealing with reforestation's impact on the water supply, for example, he talked alliteratively of the 'children of Israel wandering in a waterless wilderness, encouraged by the vision of the land that was to be theirs.' This kind of oratory, still more or less acceptable in the days of his premiership, was much less so in an Ontario struggling through the depression and confronting the grim prospect of another world war. However, Drury characteristically refused to tailor what he thought was still proper to dubious changes in the popular mood.

While going over a draft of his Orr Lake speech Drury made some deletions. One of them was highly revealing because it alluded to his assumption of the premiership. 'In 1919', the excised passage began, 'in an evil hour for myself, and much against my will, I was pitchforked into [power]' a bitter reference that, after all those years, betrays the sting of his defeat in 1923 and his subsequent setbacks at the polls. But he kept these loaded remarks to himself and went on with his discourse on reforestation.

Drury's much publicized address may have had something to do with a local revival of interest in his political career. The *Barrie Advance* (a change-of-tune successor to the hostile *Northern Advance*) thought the time had arrived to inform other communities in the province of what this Simcoe County native had accomplished. In the fall of 1938 it complained that the 'Canadian Press organization, which issues biographies of prominent persons and keeps adding facts to bring the sketches up to date, has sent out no biographical material on [Drury] since 1922. He's in the "Who's Who in Canada," but the last sixteen years are covered in one sentence.'[9]

However, the Hendrie commemoration in 1937 probably inspired an educational program shortly undertaken in Simcoe County. School children's plots and a School Reforestation Day were inaugurated in the summer of 1938 in the hope of putting the county on the map and mobilizing the younger generation's interest in forestry. Encouraged by the response in his birthplace, Drury eagerly accepted invitations to speak on the theme in neighbouring communities. At a Goderich luncheon in 1939, in what the local paper called the best Druryesque fashion, he urged Huron County to emulate what had been done in his own. Memories must have come surging back on this occasion. At the head table sat the same Nelson Monteith who had served with him long ago on the forestry committee of the OAC's Experimental Union.

Then in 1943, as a kind of capping stone to the structure of conservation he had been trying to build over the years, Simcoe County named an extension of its reforested lands in Oro Township the E.C. Drury Forest. A ministry official at the ceremony lauded the former premier for having 'so guarded his idea that it was sheltered from the confusion of the many and protected from the cabals of the few.' Drury properly appreciated the event as a tribute to his efforts, and reminded those in attendance of his own attachment to the place. Joseph Drury, his great-grandfather, he noted proudly, had settled on a lot adjacent to the designated forest nearly a century and a quarter before.[10]

The pleasure of the Oro commemoration may have helped to blot out any reaction to another symbolic event in 1943. The demise of the UFO, the organization that Drury had helped found nearly thirty years before, went unnoticed in his reflections. For many years he had had little to do with the farm movement he had once nurtured and directed. As it happened, the UFO's work and mission had been progressively assumed by its ultimate successor, the Ontario Federation of Agriculture, formed in 1935. Similarly, the OFA's national counterpart, the Canadian Federation of Agriculture, had taken over from the old and ailing CCA, which expired shortly after the depression took hold of the country.[11]

By that time local and provincial events had been forced to share space and attention with the Second World War. The role that European dictators had played in bringing it about and the threat posed by their totalitarian ideologies had periodically pushed Drury to his writing desk. He had been trotting out his views on Bolshevism for more than a decade but the excesses of Nazi Germany sickened him far more and reactivated the Germanophobia that had seized him during the First World War. 'Personally, I think Communism is a million times better than Fasism [sic],' he wrote in the late 1930s, 'but I don't like either.' 'The path of Nazism,' he announced with flourishes that would have made a Churchill sit up and take notice, 'leads back to the jungle, to a foul morass where lurk ... tyranny, oppression ... cruelty, and injusice – creatures of the primordial slime that we thought had been left behind forever.' He concluded with a statement that a Niebuhr might have challenged: 'Nazism ... could never have come forth from peoples ... soundly and healthily rooted in the land.'[12]

The war expanded Drury's duties at the court house in Barrie when his office was directed to help administer such wartime devices as rent controls and to regulate the Landlord and Tenant Act. In the midst of his labours he must have been touched when he learned that J.B. Maclean was touting him as a possible replacement for James Gardiner, Mackenzie King's minister of agriculture.[13] Though flattered by the attention, Drury realized that his economic views would carry little weight in wartime Ottawa. In any event, nothing came of the suggestion. Perhaps for Drury that was just as well. For some time he had been grumpily complaining about the decline of political morality at every level, and he wished to distance himself from that state of affairs.

Drury's musings on such themes, which coloured his writing in the postwar years as well, may have been triggered by the rare accounts that appeared on the fate of his premiership. In 1948, for example, after years of silence on the subject, a contributor to the *Canadian Forum* marked the twenty-fifth anniversary of that event with an essay on the 'Drury Débâcle.' The author approvingly quoted an American observer's comment that Drury's progressive administration had done much for the 'maladjusted members of the society.' He then alluded to the major factors that had probably precipitated the fall: dissension in UFO ranks, the woeful lack of any kind of effective party organization, and the charges of waste and extravagance so shrewdly exploited by the opposition.[14] Drury however, gave no sign that he even saw the piece.

Drury did respond, however, to a series of *Saturday Night* articles which appeared in 1952, and which his friends considered possibly harmful to his reputation. Their author, R.A. Farquharson, claimed he had once been asked to help publish J.J. Morrison's memoirs, a move forestalled apparently by the UFO secretary's declining health.[15] Copies of Farquharson's articles, which dealt with the 'Farmer Government's Rise and Fall' and with the alleged attempt to make Adam Beck leader of the UFO, were despatched to Crown Hill by an anxious Good. This information a grateful Drury conveyed to H.B. Cowan, who in turn disclosed that he had allowed Farquharson an interview. But Cowan assured Drury that he had been at pains to recount 'faithfully' as a 'neutral bystander' what he remembered of those early events. Drury hastened to advise his well-wishers that Farquharson had had the courtesy to give him a preview of what he planned to write, and that he had responded by 'setting him straight on some points [Beck's supposed machinations for one] on which he appeared misinformed.' In any case, when the articles appeared the former premier seemed satisfied enough, deeming them very fair and to have done him 'more justice than had before been done.'[16]

This enforced return to his days in power opened up unhappy memories of how Morrison had tried to hobble him and how Ferguson had helped to obliterate his premiership in the public memory. Although he claimed thirty years after the event to harbour no bitterness for either man, Drury could still describe the former Conservative leader in quaintly severe biblical language. 'I think Ferguson,' he solemnly told Cowan, 'was the wickedest man ever to be in Canadian politics. He deliberately sold Ontario to the liquor interests, and tricked the people into accepting it. The evil that he did lives after him [but] in Christian charity I hope he is not where he ought to be.'[17] As for Morrison, Drury would not have quarrelled with M.H. Staples's assessment of the man in 1958: 'He was a lonesome and a lonely [figure], and for that very reason was prone to lend a ready ear to doubtful advice ... By dalying [*sic*] with gossipers and tale-bearers a brake was put on his steam for going forward ... [and] his gifts for real leadership were severely circumscribed.'[18] To all this Drury would have added a comment on Morrison's 'overweening ambition.'

While recalling ancient battles and mourning the passage of political morality, it is not surprising perhaps that Drury should take refuge in the past and recon-struct it with the aid of his long-held views on what commanded so little respect in the present. Anyway, as far back as he could remember, history, particularly the local variety, had never failed to fascinate him. Now, as he entered his seventies, he decided to compose some contributions of his own to it. He was eager to combine writing with his court house duties in any case and, as he put it to Cowan, to see 'if I cannot do a stroke or two more with my pen before the six o'clock whistle blows.'[19]

When Drury turned his hand to writing local history he sensibly confined his efforts to the area he knew best – Simcoe County. One of his first attempts was a paper he prepared in 1948 for the annual meeting of the Ontario Historical Society. It dealt with the 'Negro Settlement in Oro Township' and gave him an opportunity to discourse on Abraham Lincoln, and on Victorian humanitarians generally, one of his favourite subjects.[20] A few years later, after he wrote an anecdotal history of the county at the request of its tourist committee, he admitted to Good that he had been rather foolish to do it because his office regimen in the mid 1950s was more onerous than usual. To do justice to his position and his writing he was now obliged to retire earlier so that he could rise before dawn and put in 'an hour or two at his desk before breakfast.'[21]

The little promotional tract on the county, written in his usual lively fashion, gave some promise of the more substantial book that Drury already had in mind. For some years he had been telling his friends that he was unhappy with the work brought out a half-century earlier by the county's first chronicler, Andrew F. Hunter. He conceded that it was comprehensive but he complained of its dryness, a flaw that ensured that few would read it even after it was republished in 1948.[22] Drury also challenged Hunter's view that local history, by its very nature, had to be dull. He warmly endorsed a comment, printed in a magazine preserved among his papers, that 'local history has too long been left in the hands of pedants puttering about with trivia.'[23]

Drury wanted to break away from the heavy political accents and ancestral eulogies that characterized early Canadian historical writing and address what he regarded as larger issues. This was understandable given his passion for economic and social questions and in line with the preoccupations of a new breed of professional historians in Canada. This led him to concentrate on what seemed to be the much livelier French and Indian period of Simcoe County's history and to forgo a full-scale treatment. The legendary fur trade, the exploits of those who had travelled the ancient route of the Toronto Carrying Place, and the culture of the local Huron Indians – the stuff of his youthful reading – came back to excite him in his old age. 'The period is so intriguing,' he told Good with pardonable enthusiasm, 'that it developed into a small book,' one that took the name of *All For a Beaver Hat*.[24]

Drury was also eager to challenge the condescending view of the Indian that

Hunter had shared with his generation of historians. Although Hunter had published a well-received ethnography,[25] his references to the Hurons' filthy domestic habits and their strange mode of burial struck a raw nerve in Drury. So did the earlier works of Francis Parkman, the Victorian American who had produced the first 'heroic' history of the French regime. Whatever Parkman's virtues as an historian, the unpardonable sin in Drury's eyes were his strictures on 'naked savages' and their 'barbarous' behaviour. He was even more disturbed when a contemporary, Thomas B. Costain, could write much the same sort of thing. In a letter to Good, Drury angrily dismissed as 'that latest monstrosity' Costain's *The White and the Gold*, published in 1954, and stated that the Indians' supposed 'barbarities were not as great as [those] ... of the White Race then and since, and they were not sunk in licentiousness and superstition.'[26] In other writings Drury went further and condemned the varied ways the Indian had been exploited by the white man: 'We ... cheated them in trade, debauched them with bad whisky, infected them with the white man's diseases, and cooped them up finally, the wards of the paternalistic state, on reservations.'[27] His son recalled that as sheriff Drury had been so moved by the mental plight of a convicted Indian murderer on whose behalf he had unsuccessfully interceded with Ottawa that he could not bring himself to witness his execution.[28]

Drury's thoughts on the Indian's place in history had been taking shape for some twenty years. 'These primitive people,' he had written in one of his many unpublished essays in the 1930s, 'aren't fools by any means ... [and] they know a good idea when they see one.' One such – that murder was not punishable by death in the Huron community – matched his own feelings about capital punishment. He also showed his fondness for the ethic of individualism when he stressed that those ancient societies of hunters and fishermen, while they might have lived communally for 'sociability and protection,' were none the less 'all economically independent of each other. [Theirs] is an individualist economy, in the strictest sense.' Drury, who had condemned first Canadian radicals and later the CCF as dangerous to freedom, seemed to be imposing a Cobdenite brand of liberalism on his reconstruction of ancient Indian society. Interestingly enough, some anthropologists were disposed to take a similar line, arguing that Indian land was not in every instance communally held but reserved for families and even individuals.[29]

Although presentism coloured much of Drury's approach to his subject, he combined it at times with a brave attempt to understand an older society in terms of how it might have perceived itself. He sought help on the prehistoric period from Kenneth E. Kidd of the Royal Ontario Museum, who was just then completing the excavation of a Jesuit mission site at nearby Midland.[30] In the spring of 1948 Drury received a warm response from Kidd whose father had known the former premier through their membership in the UFO. Along with a reading list, the archaeologist sent him the information he had been seeking on the

Huron's clothing, diet, hunting practices, and trading skills. Drury supplemented his reading with at least one visit to his mentor's excavation at a Huron ossuary.[31] Two years later he had enough of his manuscript in hand to send it off for an assessment. Kidd's response was encouraging. He welcomed Drury's defence of the Huron, remarking that 'it can only redound to our honour to do so.'[32] Having said this, Kidd felt bound to add that on a few occasions Drury had made slighting remarks on his own. These were deleted before the work was published.

In other instances Drury did not follow his learned informant's advice, notably when he came to polish up a section on the Five Nations Iroquois Confederacy, traditionally regarded as the Huron's mortal enemy. He depicted the Mohawks and their kinsmen as so many seventeenth-century forerunners of those modern totalitarians who had so recently plunged the world into total war. By contrast, Drury extolled the Huron's 'forest democracy' (similar in his mind to that of the ancient English?) and virtually made them out to be the aboriginal counterparts of the UFO. This was present-mindedness with a vengeance, a manipulative approach that did not sit well with Kidd, who all along argued that the Five Nations were just as 'democratic' as the Huron.[33] All the same, a quarter-century later the archaeologist could write the following:

Looking back over the years ... I can still say that I feel the book was a useful one, but not necessarily a scholarly one ... I think [Drury] did a good job of bringing together a set of facts that it was important to bring to the attention of the popular reader ... The book appeared [at] ... precisely the time when [the] official treatment of Canadian Indians began to come into question. Drury's book must have given at least a little impetus to the then novel sympathetic attitude to their condition and I think he deserves much credit for having had ... the courage to present it to the public.[34]

Drury's preoccupation with the problems of the twentieth-century world intruded throughout the book. He likened the administrators of New France, for example, to a 'businessman's government, probably the most dangerous of all governments, short of dictatorship.' 'The business interests, myopic as always,' he added for good measure, 'dictated governmental policy.'[35] A friendly academic reviewer addressed this point after the book was published in 1959, and was gratified to see the 'spirit of the erstwhile leader of the UFO still shine through.' Drury was also commended for his 'markedly good treatment of Huronia' and for 'utilizing old information in a fresh and vivid way.'[36]

By the time Drury was receiving these plaudits he had already retired from one of the public positions he had been filling for nearly a quarter of a century. In 1957, in his eightieth year, he vacated the sheriff's office while retaining those of registrar and clerk. Although he claimed in his memoirs that he had been a rather strict disciplinarian, his former staff recalled the lightness of the office regimen and their superior's understanding ways. A reprimand for an egregious typing error usually took the form of a mock stern lecture prefaced by the full name of the culprit. When office gaffes were made that inadvertently spoofed the pomp of a judicial procedure he was reduced to helpless laughter.[37]

He could also go out of his way to help lawyers with problems, sometimes getting up in the middle of the night to search out documents they had either mislaid or failed to produce for court. On the other hand, he had little patience with sham and cant in the legal profession, whether it was displayed by a lawyer defending a client or by a judge deciding a case. On one occasion, when he was wrongly accused by a peremptory assizes judge of producing irrelevant documentation, he was defended by an attending lawyer who may have been in the sheriff's debt for past favours.[38] In several instances, however, Drury was called upon to review lawyers' bills and reduce them to more plausible proportions, and twice he remembered 'cutting a bill of costs squarely in two.'[39] In his presence he was invariably addressed by members of the profession as simply Mr Drury; out of earshot as the Honourable E.C.

Between assizes and court appearances and in breaks from his office routine he was often sought out for conversation and story-telling by lawyers and others who shared his love of country lore and political reflection.[40] Such diversions and Good's recently published memoir, *Farmer Citizen*, made him responsive to a suggestion made by historian Arthur Lower that he compose his own autobiography for publication. Drury took the suggestion seriously. 'My present intention,' he told Good in the spring of 1959, 'is to retire at the end of the year, and write what I remember of a long and not uneventful life.'

That life and its contributions to society had already been honoured some months before at the University of Western Ontario. It chose to remember that the Drury government, to quote the laudatory editorial in the local paper, had 'set [that] pattern of provincial ... aid to Western' which had been so important to the university. In the fall of 1958 one of the residences to be built for the expanding campus was named after him. The convocation statement announcing the decision read:

For generations the largest single group of students attending Western have come from rural homes. Even in the face of major industrialization in Ontario this situation still holds. It is a tribute to the abilities ... of those great citizens who live on our farms and in our small villages. Their interest in education has always been great. Mr. E.C. Drury was typical. And in addition his initiative, and his own work in sponsoring Conservation was a forerunner to the extensive conservation projects presently supported in this province. The establishment by Mr. Drury in 1920 of a Royal Commission to study the financial problems faced by Western, Queen's, and Toronto Universities had a profound effect upon Western's future.[41]

The statement was deserved and did belated public justice to Drury and his administration. What a forgetful society had done to his record and reputation was partially repaired at Western nearly forty years later when in addition to naming Drury House, the university conferred on him an honorary degree, one that joined the LL.D. received from the University of Toronto during his premiership.

These honours were awarded while Drury was still in harness. But as he had intimated he would do, a little over a year later, at the close of 1959, he retired from his remaining duties as registrar and clerk and formally bade farewell to his lengthy career as a Simcoe County public servant. In retirement he resolved to settle down to the task of preparing the account of his life.

17

The Last Days

The writing that ultimately led to *Farmer Premier* was summarily disrupted by a mild stroke shortly after Drury took his retirement. This reverse, which confined him for long periods to a wheelchair, was followed by bleeding stomach ulcers brought on over the years by a wholesale consumption of aspirin to combat the pain of an arthritic knee.[1] Previously Drury had been able to cope with the ulcer problem, but on a Sunday early in 1962 he appeared shaky and weak after attending church. His family conveyed the sombre news to W.C. Good that he was 'just slipping away right there in front of them.' After a series of blood transfusions he rallied though he seemed resigned to dying, a mood the family called uncharacteristic because 'he had always fought back with everything he ever had.'[2] In the end he rallied and did return to something like a normal life. And that included spending a month or so every winter in Barrie with Beth, his daughter, even though he confided to a friend that 'I would very much rather be here in my home.'[3]

His recovery may have been helped along by the Archaeological and Historic Sites Board of Ontario, the body entrusted with memorializing places and people prominent in the province's history. 'I see,' Drury laconically wrote Good early in 1962, 'you already know of the decision of the Historic Sites Board to erect a plaque [to me] while I am still alive. That is all very gratifying, of course, though not too important.' He then philosophized on this and other recent honours: 'When I was in the thick of it, I got nothing but brick-bats from all sides. Now, when I am out of it, I am getting bouquets, perhaps more than I deserve.'[4] The main object of his writing Good was to invite him to the ceremony, which was scheduled to unfold in front of the farm property on a June afternoon in 1962. Much to Drury's regret, his old friend could not attend the event. Good's own infirmities, which shortly consigned him to a nursing home, ruled out an opportunity for the two old comrades-in-arms to swap reminiscences.

Whatever satisfaction Drury derived from his recent honours was rudely blotted out in the fall of 1962 by the death of his eldest son, Carl. For Harold, the other son at home, it meant taking over his brother's farm, that came complete with a dairy herd of some twenty cattle, and this at a time when the 'plowing [was] only partly finished.' But friends and neighbours pitched in to help. They organized a bee and finished the chore, exhibiting a generosity that Drury lauded as typical of farm communities all over the province.

By this time Drury's recollections, written up in bits and pieces for over a quarter of a century, were being culled for his autobiography. He also appears to have solicited help in jogging his memory of events and persons. One informant urged him to consult newspaper files whenever he could, adding correctly that there must be a 'terrific file on yourself.'[5] At first Drury had contemplated nothing more ambitious than a long article, or a series of articles, for *Maclean's*, the monthly magazine that had earlier found room for his views on public questions. But neither *Maclean's* nor the once friendly Toronto *Star*, which was also approached, showed any substantial interest and the discussions came to a close.[6] Obviously he was no longer deemed a sufficiently compelling political subject.

That was not, however, the end of the matter. After he narrated his story to Pete McGarvey, a broadcaster with CFOR in Orillia, McGarvey took the completed manuscript to Jack McClelland, the publisher, who agreed to read it and offer an assessment. To Drury's delight he reported favourably and, after a publication grant was received from the Social Science Research Council, he arranged to bring it out. An outside reader, James A. Gibson, then serving as president of the newly established Brock University, also gave the memoir a favourable review.[7] It would appear, however, that Drury had written (or narrated) far more than what finally appeared in *Farmer Premier*, and unfortunately those earlier drafts did not survive. His position on higher education and his dealings with Arthur Meighen, for example, receive little or no mention in the final version. As well, some reviewers complained about inaccuracies and omissions, and accused Drury's editor of laxity and overpruning.

But when the book appeared in 1966 it was, on the whole, warmly received by historians, students, old friends, politicians, active and retired, and veterans of the farm movement.[8] A member of the parliamentary press gallery spoke for many when he congratulated Drury on the 'delightful pen pictures' that illuminated the book's 'charmingly written' pages.[9] Former premier Leslie Frost paid tribute to his 'high assessment ... both of his colleagues and of those ... in opposition.' 'One marvels,' he continued, 'at his generous treatment of a political opponent, Adam Beck, whom he kept in office.'[10] Perhaps it was not so marvellous, as Frost probably appreciated in private. Old age may have inclined Drury to embellish the record with a generosity and forgiveness that an earlier assessment would have denied.

While basking in the glow of *Farmer Premier* Drury learned that he was to be further commemorated by the so-called Drury Appreciation Committee, whose members were drawn from a 'variety of walks of life in [Simcoe] county.'[11] But at that point, in the fall of 1967, his health again began to fail and he was swiftly despatched to Barrie's Royal Victoria Hospital. He had already been saddened by the death of Good and the passing of an ancient comradeship. Given the precarious state of Drury's own health, steps were taken to speed up the 'Appreciation' proceedings. They included the setting aside of Drury Appreciation Days in the local schools, the planting of commemorative trees on a Drury Memorial Day, and appropriate addresses by the premier and assorted cabinet ministers.

But before any of these ambitious programs matured the man for whom they had been planned took a turn for the worse. On Saturday, 17 February 1968, Drury died, at the start of his ninety-first year. The following Tuesday a funeral service was held in the small United Church in Crown Hill where the family had traditionally worshipped. As expected there was a good turn out, particularly of provincial politicians – among them, Robert F. Nixon, Harry's son, appropriately representing the Ontario Liberals, and Donald MacDonald of the New Democratic Party. MacDonald was moved to say that Drury had been the first to promote social democratic legislation in the province, a precedent the man being eulogized might not have relished given his critical views of the CCF, the NDP's predecessor. After the service Drury's remains were buried in Crown Hill's Union Cemetery, not far from the grave of his pioneer great-grandfather.

Those who eulogized Drury and commended his legacy invariably spoke of his decency, courage, and humanity when he had dealt with the stricken and the needy of his times. There were those who lauded his work on behalf of the farm movement and saw how, like some enlightened arcadian patrician, he had bent every effort to educate, encourage, and raise the morale of those condemned to lower levels of achievement in Ontario's less than monolithic rural community. Still others stressed his deep commitment to the functional Christianity that had governed his public as well as private conduct.[12] All these plaudits were solidly based and not mere graveside rhetoric. Drury, like W.C. Good and other farm activists, often went that extra mile and performed acts of selflessness on behalf of public order and social improvement that helped to make their world a better place in which to live.

Throughout, Drury had taken a broad moral view of his government's mandate and sought to entrench those fundamental obligations that Ontario society had supposedly set so much store by in his boyhood, particularly by his family legislation, designed to strengthen that basic social unit in a time of bewildering change and loss of direction. He had also addressed the future when he embarked on his campaign for conservation and implemented his varied plans to replenish the province's timber resources before they were devoured by a seemingly insatiable society. He had clearly welcomed, too, the technological revolution of his day and appreciated the enormous potential of the internal combustion engine and the engineering marvels that would unfold on a revitalized St Lawrence waterway.

But Drury also had his detractors who seldom hesitated to pull their punches, and sometimes they landed solid ones. They frequently and with some justification dwelt on his egotism, his self-righteousness, his political naïveté, not to mention the aberrant nature of his government. Nor did Drury endear himself to those who thought that Ontario's problem in the 1920s deserved more imaginative approaches than the supposedly outworn ones of yesteryear. This sort of criticism anticipated the strictures heaped on Populism and other forms of American agrarianism by historians such as Richard Hofstadter.[13] Once considered a healthy reaction to industrialism, that agrarianism was denigrated as an otherworldly idealization of the past, an escape into some 'lost rural Eden' that blinded it to the realities and concrete problems of its own generation. In spite of his substantial attempts to meet some of the very real difficulties that beset his times, Drury was similarly accused of all too often permitting the past to distort his view of the present and its challenges.

Yet they may all, friends and foes, contemporary and later observers alike, have missed a point that Drury's most abusive enemy seized upon to blacken him in the eyes of the public and posterity. In one of his jibes Howard Ferguson had dismissed Drury as an 'idealist,' a species he plainly thought unsuited to the rough and tumble of politics. Not as wounding as 'Bolshevik' or 'Prussian' perhaps, the term none the less conveyed to many in the hardened 1920s a picture of hopeless ingenuousness and impracticality. But inadvertently the Conservative leader may have isolated a factor that played a dominant role in shaping Drury's approach to public service and social engineering.

For a generation of late-Victorian intellectuals on both sides of the Atlantic, 'idealism' had been more than a word. It represented a new philosophical, literary, and moral force for challenging the utilitarian and mechanistic order that had transformed the western world in the nineteenth century. Inspired by German transcendentalism, the creed of Idealism that took root in Britain and spread to North America called for the exaltation of the spirit and the repudiation of the material values spawned by the modern industrial age.[14]

The kind of hero-worship that Drury sometimes indulged in when he held forth on the place in history occupied by the Mills, the Wilberforces, and the Lincolns was considered by the Idealist as a way of cutting down to size the commercial spirit that strangled an appreciation of what broad-minded and large-hearted persons had contributed to human progress. Again, the unsympathetic 'interests' that Drury often railed against fitted the category of selfishness the Idealists condemned. Indeed, much of what they said about the heartlessness of the industrial order would have found comfortable quarters in the gospel of the rural ethic that Drury and other farm leaders so feelingly preached throughout their lives. In the realm of the spirit, Drury's rejection of personal salvation as an unseemly denial of the Christian's obligation to the larger community owed something to the Idealist challenge to late-Victorian insensitivity. Drury's impatience with self-serving clergymen and narrow theological doctrines that remained blind to larger social responsibilities formed part of the same response.

Whatever the inspiration of Drury's outlook on the duties and obligations of a citizen or public servant, his administration may have represented not so much an aberration as a kind of apotheosis. Imbued with the spirit of Victorian humanitarianism, he had placed on Ontario's statute books what amounted to a concrete expression of the views of those Idealist thinkers and doers who had aimed at creating a political and social order of conscience in the nineteenth century.

Notes

ABBREVIATIONS

CAR *Canadian Annual Review*
CCA Canadian Council of Agriculture
CUC Canadian Union of Co-operatives
DFP Drury Family Papers
FP *Farmer Premier*
OA Archives of Ontario
OAEU Ontario Agricultural Experimental Union
OHA Ontario Hydro Archives
OPL Orillia Public Library
PAC Public Archives of Canada
QUA Queen's University Archives
SCA Simcoe County Archives
UCO Library, United Co-operatives of Ontario
UFO United Farmers of Ontario
UGL University of Guelph Library
UTA University of Toronto Archives
UWL University of Waterloo Library
UWO Regional Collection, University of Western Ontario

CHAPTER I: THE ROAD FROM KENILWORTH

1 *Guide to Kenilworth and Its Neighbourhood* (London 1858), 10–11. Sometimes Kenilworth – 'farm of a woman named Cynehild' – was rendered 'Killingworth,' the name that appears on Joseph Drury's petition for land in Upper Canada. (PAC, RG 1, L3, Upper Canada Land Book K, vol. 155, 112). See J.E.B. Grover, A. Mawer, and F.M. Stenton, *The Place Names of Warwickshire* (Cambridge 1936), 172.

2 It is likely that he is the one entered in the parish lists as the son of Joseph and Hannah Drury and as having been baptized on 29 June 1773. Warwickshire County Record Office, DRO 101, 4, Parish Lists, Registers and Baptisms, A Register belonging to the Parish Church of Kenilworth, 1763. No birthdate appears on his gravestone in Crown Hill's Union Cemetery though his age is given as fifty-three years. This could well be an error. There is no record in Warwick of any Joseph Drury having been born in 1770. It may not be coincidental that Hannah, his mother's name, was handed down at least twice to his descendants.

3 OA, Drury Papers, MU 955, Literary Works III, Ch. 3: Personal Credentials, 8

4 Adam Murray, *General View of the Agriculture of the County of Warwick, 1813* (abridgement, n.p.)

5 J.M. Martin, 'Warwickshire and the Parliamentary Enclosure Movement' (PH D thesis, University of Birmingham 1965), 85, 87

6 PAC, RG 1, L3, Upper Canada Land Book K, vol. 155, 112

7 Drury Papers, MU 955, Literary Works, ms. article

8 SCA, E.C. Drury interviews, Grace Chappell (1965), 14–15

9 See G.E. French, *Men of Colour: An Historical Account of the Black Settlement on Wilberforce Street in Oro Township, Simcoe County, Ontario, 1819–1949* (Orillia 1978), 43.

10 Drury interviews, Chappell, 34

11 *FP*, 23

12 C.B. S[issons], 'The Crown Hill School: A Study in Rural Education,' *Canadian Forum* III (Feb. 1923), 135–6

13 Drury Papers, MU 955, Personal Credentials, 22

14 *Historical Sketch of the Town of Barrie, prepared for the Occasion of Laying the Memorial Stone of the New Post Office ... 8 October 1884* (Barrie 1884), 3

15 Owen Scott, 'The Changing Rural Landscape in Southern Ontario,' *Third Annual Agricultural History Seminar: Proceedings 1978* (Guelph 1979), 32

16 *The British Farmer and Farm Labourer's Guide to Ontario, the Premier Province of the Dominion of Canada* (Toronto 1880), 25, 26. See D.A. Lawr, 'The Development of Ontario Farming, 1870–1914: Patterns of Growth and Change,' *Ontario History* 64 (1972), 239–51.

17 S[issons], 'The Crown Hill School,' 135

18 Gerald A. Hallowell, *Prohibition in Ontario* (Ottawa 1972), 14–15

19 *FP*, 18; SCA, A.F. Hunter Papers, Box 6, Row 3P, Envelope 3, Section 7

20 UGA, Reynolds Papers, Autobiography, 'The Village' [2]

21 *Ontario: Premier Province of Canada* (Toronto 1897)

CHAPTER 2: GROWING UP IN SIMCOE COUNTY

1 *FP*, 22

2 SCA, E.C. Drury interviews, Grace Chappell (1965), 6

3 Alan Skeoch, 'The Ontario Agricultural Implement Industry, 1850–1891,' *Third Annual Agricultural History of Ontario Seminar: Proceedings 1978* (Guelph 1979), 4
4 *FP*, 37
5 C.B. Sissons, *Nil Alienum: Memoirs* (Toronto 1964), ch. 2, and 'The Crown Hill School,' *Canadian Forum* III (Feb. 1923), 136
6 OPL, Ironside Collection, interview
7 SCA, Mrs Morley Black tape, 31 July 1973
8 R.D. Gidney and W.J.P. Millar, 'Rural Schools and the Decline of Community Control in Nineteenth Century Ontario,' *Fourth Annual Agricultural History of Ontario Seminar: Proceedings 1979* (Guelph 1980), 80–1
9 OA, Drury Papers, MU 950, II, Speeches, 1921–57; E.C. Drury, 'What We Can Expect of Our Schools' (1945), 25–7
10 *FP*, 39
11 Ironside Collection, Fred. Partridge tape (15 Feb. 1968)
12 *FP*, 41
13 F.M. Chapman, quoted in Sissons, *Memoirs*, 195–6. One recollection that he shone in mathematics would have brought a hoot from him; Ironside Collection, interview.
14 SCA, Laura Young Papers, Collection of Examination Papers from Barrie Collegiate Institute
15 Sissons, *Memoirs*, 194; Ironside Collection, Partridge tape (1968)
16 Chapman, quoted in Sissons, *Memoirs*, 195
17 PAC, Sissons Papers, II, D, 1878–1965, C.B. Sissons to E.C. Drury, 7 Oct. 1949. See also Sissons, *Memoirs*, ch. 2.
18 See J.W. Burrow, *A Liberal Descent: Victorian Historians and the English Past* (Cambridge University Press 1983, new ed.), 108, 109, 287; Drury Papers, MU 952, The Way Out, Lesson VII.
19 Interview with Harold Drury (Crown Hill), 23 July 1981
20 SCA, Lower tape, no. 23, 23 June 1973
21 Drury Papers, MU 955, Literary Works, Article IV, 12
22 Sissons, *Memoirs*, 192
23 Drury Papers, MU 955, Historical and other articles
24 Brock University Library, E.W. Bowslaugh Diaries, 1895, 26, 30 Sept.
25 For the background, see L.A. Wood, *A History of Farmers' Movements in Canada: The Origins and Development of Agrarian Protest, 1872–1924* (Toronto 1924), chs. V, X, XII.
26 See S.E.D. Shortt, 'Social Change and Political Crisis in Rural Ontario: the Patrons of Industry, 1889–1896,' *Oliver Mowat's Ontario* (Toronto 1972), 211–35; and Ramsay Cook, 'Tillers and Toilers: The Rise and Fall of Populism in Canada, 1892–1896,' *Historical Papers, 1984* (Ottawa 1985).
27 *FP*, 36

28 Drury Papers, MU 955, Literary Works, Article IV, 14
29 A.M. Ross, *The College on the Hill: A History of the Ontario Agricultural College, 1874–1974* (Toronto 1974), 41, 47
30 J.F. Clark, 'A Student's Personal Experience at the Ontario Agricultural College,' *Farming World* XIV, 4 (Dec. 1896), 239–41
31 'The Social Position of the Farmer,' *OAC Review* XI, 4 (Jan. 1900), 11–13; 'The Townward Movement,' ibid., 7 (Apr. 1900), 8–10
32 See W.D. Gregory, 'A Word of Farewell,' *Farmers' Sun*, 2 Apr. 1919, 1.
33 QUA, Gregory Papers, Correspondence, 1904, Herbert Bowles to Goldwin Smith, 17 Aug. 1904
34 *FP*, 44–5
35 For the details of the Partridge family tree, see SCA, Genealogical Record of a Simcoe County Settler – John Partridge; L. Wagar to K.W. Tingley, 26 Jan. 1977; and A.F. Hunter, *A History of Simcoe County*, II, *The Pioneers* (Barrie 1948), 104, 300, 301. Mrs S. Murdoch of the Simcoe County Archives kindly furnished the documentary material.

CHAPTER 3: RURAL ACTIVIST

1 UGL, Reynolds Papers, Addresses and Writings, Apologia ..., 3
2 *FP*, 46
3 UGL, *Twenty-Sixth Annual Report, OAEU, 1904* (Toronto 1905), 45
4 C.B. Sissons, *Nil Alienum: Memoirs* (Toronto 1964), 69
5 E.C. Drury, 'President's Address,' *Twenty-Fourth Annual Report, OAEU, 1902* (Toronto 1903), 53
6 *FP*, 47–8
7 SCA, E.C. Drury's Speech for Reforestation Meeting [11 Aug. 1937], 5
8 R.D. Craig, 'Report of the Committee on Forestry,' *Twenty-Fourth Annual Report, OAEU, 1902*, 34
9 PAC, Good Papers, Correspondence, XXXI, 1953, E.C. Drury to W.C. Good, 28 Feb. 1953
10 E.J. Zavitz, *Recollections of the First Provincial Forester in Ontario, 1875–1964* (Toronto [1965]), 3
11 *Twenty-Fourth Annual Report, OAEU, 1902*, 62
12 *Twenty-Fifth Annual Report, OAEU, 1903* (Toronto 1904), 36
13 Ibid., 38
14 See E.J. Zavitz, 'Report of Investigations regarding Farm Forestry in Ontario,' *Twenty-Seventh Annual Report, OAEU, 1905* (Toronto 1906), 42–6.
15 *FP*, 54–5. See also *Midland Free Press*, 9 June 1972.
16 G.C. Creelman, 'Have Farmers Institutes Come to Stay?' *OAC Review* XVII, 1 (Oct. 1904), 2
17 See J.W. Thompson and D.H. Hart, 'Rural Social Organizations' (BSA thesis, OAC

1922), 39–40. For a different view, consult C.L. Legg, 'Rural Progress in Old Ontario' (MA thesis, McMaster University 1915), 13. On the question of general rural dissatisfaction with government programs for the farmer, see M. Jean MacLeod, 'Agriculture and Politics in Ontario since 1867' (PH D thesis, University of London 1961), ch. 2.

18 Novel, ch. v, 5

19 J.F. Snell, *Macdonald College of McGill University: A History from 1904–1955* (Montreal 1963), chs. 4, 6

20 For the details, see *FP*, 51–2

21 Snell, *Macdonald College*, 237

22 See Jean MacLeod, 'The United Farmers Movement in Ontario, 1914–43' (MA thesis, Queen's University 1958); and L.A. Wood, *A History of Farmers' Movements in Canada* (Toronto 1924), ch. vii.

23 W.B. Hillman, 'J.J. Morrison: A Farmer Politician in an Era of Social Change' (MA thesis, University of Western Ontario 1974), 18ff

24 QUA, Gregory Papers, Letters, 1930–40, W.D. Gregory to J.J. Morrison, 2 Nov. 1933

25 PAC, Morrison Papers, Memoirs, 8

26 *Globe*, 14 Nov. 1905

27 E.C. Drury, 'The Farmer and the Tariff,' *Canadian Magazine* XXVI, 6 (1906), 506

28 E.C. Drury, 'A Canadian Farmer on the Tariff,' *Proceedings of the Canadian Club, Toronto, for the Year 1905–1906*, III (Toronto [1906]), 100

29 Good Papers, Subject Files 13–15, Political Matters, 1905–34, 'City and Country' (n.d.)

30 For a treatment of the events leading up to the Fielding tariff, see R.C. Brown and Ramsay Cook, *Canada, 1896–1921: A Nation Transformed* (Toronto 1974), 156–9.

31 *FP*, 54

32 Ibid., 57

33 Gregory Papers, Letters 1900–9, Correspondence, 1903, Morrison to Gregory, 9 March 1903

34 *FP*, 57–8

35 DFP, Helen Fraser Campbell to Drury, n.d., 1966

36 *FP*, 59

37 SCA, A.F. Hunter Papers, Box 4, Correspondence, 1906, A.F. Hunter to Mabel Smith, 14 Apr. 1906. A local paper would later deplore the 'rural depopulation' this emigration produced in Simcoe County; *Northern Advance*, 4 Sept. 1911.

38 Good Papers, Correspondence, III, 1916–17, H.B. Cowan to Good, 12 June 1917

39 *Northern Advance*, 16 Sept. 1909

40 QUA, Canadian Council of Agriculture Papers [hereafter CCA], Constitution of the CCA (microfilm)

41 PAC, Willison Papers, vol. 12, file 101, Drury to J.S. Willison, 6 Oct. 1910
42 PAC, Co-operative Union of Canada Papers, vol. 6, 1910, Good to Keen, 14 Jan. [?] 1910
43 Drury Papers, MU 950, Box 1, Drury to D. McKee, 20 July 1945; Hillman, 'Morrison,' 24
44 Gregory Papers, Correspondence, 1910, W.L. Smith to Gregory, 22 Nov. 1910
45 *Globe*, 16 Dec. 1910
46 G.F. Chipman, ed., *The Siege of Ottawa* (Winnipeg 1910), 7
47 *Globe*, 17 Dec. 1910
48 Years later Drury revised this picture, and claimed that Laurier had dealt with them 'roughly'; Drury Papers, MU 950, Box 1, Drury to McKee, 20 July 1945.
49 Gregory Papers, Letter Books, 1909–11, Gregory to John Pollard, 23 Aug. 1911
50 *FP*, 65. See Novel, ch. XIX, for an extended discussion of reciprocity.
51 See Carl Berger, *The Sense of Power: Studies in the Ideas of Canadian Imperialism* (Toronto 1970), ch. X.
52 Good Papers, Correspondence, 1905–15, Good to Wilfrid Laurier, Oct. [?] 1909
53 PAC, Laurier Papers, Series A Correspondence, vol. 458, W. Noble to Lord Elgin, 9 Apr. 1907 (copy)
54 Sissons, *Memoirs*, 197
55 *Northern Advance*, 27 July 1911; 17 Aug. 1911, and 27 July 1911
56 Gregory Papers, Correspondence, 1911, Laurier to Gregory, 30 Sept. 1911
57 *FP*, 68
58 Arthur Meighen, *Unrevised and Unrepented: Debating Speeches and Others* (Toronto 1949), 5. Although an active supporter of protection, Meighen had urged, in a speech embodying this phrase, that import duties be substantially reduced on agricultural implements.
59 M.H. Staples, ed., *The Challenge of Agriculture: The Story of the United Farmers of Ontario* (Toronto 1921), 35

CHAPTER 4: A FARMER IN WARTIME

1 Beth Good Latzer, *Myrtleville: A Canadian Farm and Family, 1837–1967* (Canadian ed., 1980), 267–8. See also J.E. Marshall, *Half Century of Farming in Dufferin* (n.p., n.d.), 10.
2 *FP*, 70–1
3 R.G. Tugwell, 'Henry George,' *Encyclopedia of the Social Sciences* VI (New York 1931), 630–1
4 C.A. Barker, 'Henry George, *Encyclopedia of the Social Sciences* V (New York 1968), 152
5 W.C. Good, *Farmer Citizen* (Toronto 1958), 91
6 PAC, Morrison Memoirs, 14

7 M.H. Staples, ed., *The Challenge of Agriculture* (Toronto 1921), 39
8 The beer story, recorded in *Farmer Premier* (p. 72), did not form part of Drury's more staid account prepared for Staples's compilation some forty years earlier. Good made no reference at all to the Kirby House meeting in *Farmer Citizen*.
9 Good, *Farmer Citizen*, 93–100. Significantly, Good's account makes no reference to Morrison's part in the proceedings.
10 QUA, Crerar Papers, Series III, Box 125, Correspondence, J.J. Morrison file, 1913–16, J.J. Morrison to T.A. Crerar, 29 Nov. 1913
11 Ibid., Morrison to Crerar, 24 Jan. 1914
12 Crerar Papers, Correspondence, Morrison file, Morrison to Crerar, 29 Nov. 1913
13 PAC, Co-operative Union of Canada Papers [hereinafter CUC], vol. 13, M file, George Keen to Humfrey Michell, 17 Oct. 1914
14 For an account of the proceedings, see Richard Allen, *The Social Passion: Religion and Social Reform* (Toronto 1971), ch. 2.
15 OA, Drury Papers, MU 953, III, Literary Works, Treatise on Economics and Politics (5), xxxiii, 216, 218
16 *Social Service Congress, Ottawa, 1914: Report of Addresses and Proceedings* (Toronto [1914]), 145–6
17 CUC, vol. 13, 1914, Michell to Keen, 2 Dec. 1914
18 Staples, *Challenge of Agriculture*, 42
19 See Ian Macpherson, 'The Co-operative Union of Canada and Politics, 1909–31,' *Canadian Historical Review* LIV, 2 (June 1973), 152–7; CUC, Keen to Morrison, 2 March 1914.
20 Good, *Farmer Citizen*, 100–1, and Staples, *Challenge of Agriculture*, 69ff
21 The UFO record states this (UCO, UFO Minute Book, 1914–17, p. 15) but in *Farmer Premier* he claims he was not elected until the following April.
22 See Carl Berger, *The Sense of Power* (Toronto 1970), 191–3.
23 E.C. Drury, *All for a Beaver Hat: A History of Early Simcoe County* (Toronto 1959), 30
24 Latzer, *Myrtleville*, 260
25 UTA, Walker Papers, Box 21, E.B. Osler, A.K. George, H.J. Cody to Edmund Walker, 20 Oct. 1914
26 PAC, Good Papers, Correspondence, III, 1916, Drury to Good, 23 Dec. 1916
27 *Canadian Champion* (Milton), 19 Feb. 1920
28 Good Papers, Correspondence, 1916, Drury to Good, 20 June 1916
29 Drury Papers, MU 954, Literary Works, Farming articles, 3–4
30 Macpherson, *Each for All*, 56. See also Good, *Farmer Citizen*, 101–2.
31 Good Papers, Correspondence, II, 1904–15, Drury to Good, 18 May 1915
32 For example, Morrison's memoirs are silent on the subject. See UFO Minute Book, 1914–17, 4 Feb. 1916, p. 50.

33 Good Papers, Correspondence, 1916, Good to W. Toole, 21 Jan. 1917; *FP*, 75. See also W.B. Hillman, 'J.J. Morrison: A Farmer Politician in an Era of Social Change' (MA thesis, University of Western Ontario 1974), 44.

34 Good Papers, Correspondence, 1916, Good to Morrison, 17 Apr. 1916; Morrison to Good, 28 Apr. 1916

35 Ibid., Morrison to Good, 7 Nov. 1916; H.B. Cowan to Good, 21 Mar. 1917

36 Ibid., 1917, Good to Drury, 1 Apr. 1917; Drury to Good, 15 Apr. 1917

37 See R.W. Trowbridge, 'War-time Discontent and the Rise of the UFO, 1914–19' (MA thesis, University of Waterloo 1967), 65.

38 Good Papers, Correspondence, 1916, Drury to Good, 20 June 1916. See also Good, *Farmer Citizen*, 101.

39 In their memoirs Drury and Good paid scant attention to this crisis in 1916. Perhaps their far busier political careers in the following decade trivialized these earlier contretemps when they sat down to capture their recollections.

40 For a full discussion of this problem, see W.R. Young, 'Conscription, Rural Depopulation, and the Farmers of Ontario, 1917–19,' *Canadian Historical Review* LIII, 3 (Sept. 1972), 289–320.

41 Good Papers, Correspondence, 1916, Good to S.F. Tilden, 12 Mar. 1916

42 Novel, ch. XXV, 10

43 Morrison Memoirs, 28

44 Good Papers, Correspondence, 1916, Drury to Good, n.d.

45 Peter Oliver, *G. Howard Ferguson* (Toronto, OHSS 1977), 91

46 Good Papers, Correspondence, IV, 1917, Good to A. Maclaren, 27 Jan. 1917

47 Under this formula, voters made their choices, when faced with three or more candidates in a riding, in order of preference on the same ballot. Further, to quote one authority, 'the quota of votes necessary for an election is determined, and as soon as that number of first preferences is counted for particular candidates, they are declared elected and the remaining ballots for those candidates for first choice are transferred to the second choice and so on. When all surplus ballots have thus been transferred, the candidate with the smallest total is eliminated and all his ballots transferred to the candidate who is the next choice on each. This process of transferring surpluses and eliminating the weaker candidates proceeds until the quota has been reached by as many candidates as there are seats to be filled.' J.A. Corry, *Democratic Government and Politics* 2nd ed. (Toronto 1952), 274. Compare this description of the transferable vote to Drury's in *Farmer Premier* (p. 77).

48 *FP*, 77

49 *Canadian Champion*, 26 Feb. 1920

50 UFO Minute Book, 1914–17, pp. 87–8

51 The phrase he would later use in *Forts of Folly* (p. 7).

52 *FP*, 78

257 Notes to pages 51–6

53 See *Northern Advance*, 3 May 1923, and OA, 'An Interview with Mr. Ernest C. Drury ... conducted by Mr. Fred Schindeler and Mrs. Jean James' (19 Mar. 1965), 24.

CHAPTER 5: WITH THE UFO IN POLITICS

1 QUA, Gregory Papers, Correspondence, 1916–19, W.F.W. Fisher to W.D. Gregory, 24 Apr. 1918
2 PAC, Morrison Memoirs, 30; M.H. Staples, ed. *The Challenge of Agriculture* (Toronto 1921), 143
3 *FP*, 81
4 PAC, Good Papers, Correspondence, IV, 1917–22, O.D. Skelton to W.C. Good, 10 Jan. 1919
5 UCO, UFO Minute Book, 1920–3, 15 Dec. 1921, p. 75
6 Staples, *Challenge of Agriculture*, 184
7 R.W. Trowbridge, 'War-time Discontent and the Rise of the UFO, 1914–19' (MA thesis, University of Waterloo 1967), 143–4
8 CCA Minutes and Proceedings, 11 Nov. 1919, p. 7
9 J.Z. Fraser, 'A Word of Greeting,' *Farmers' Sun*, 2 Apr. 1919, p. 1
10 Morrison Memoirs, 46
11 UFO Minute Book, 1920–3, p. 154 (J.J. Morrison's Report, 15 Dec. 1922, Appended to Minutes of Annual Convention of 1922)
12 See Peter Oliver, 'Sir William Hearst and the Collapse of the Ontario Conservative Party,' *Canadian Historical Review* LIII, 1 (Mar. 1972), 35–6. For the background of Bowman's triumph, see F.J.K. Griezic, ' "Power to the People": The Beginning of Agrarian Revolt in Ontario; the Manitoulin By-Election, 24 October 1918,' *Ontario History*, 69 (1977), 33–54.
13 M. Jean MacLeod, 'The United Farmers Movement in Ontario, 1914–43' (MA thesis, Queen's University 1958), 34
14 Staples, *Challenge of Agriculture*, 147–50; *FP*, 83–4
15 *Globe*, 9 Sept. 1919
16 UWO, Minutes of the East Lambton UFO, 1919–32, 24 July, 24 Sept. 1919
17 SCA, Aubrey Giffen Papers, Minutes and Accounts of Edenvale UFO (#721), 1919–42, 8 Oct. 1919
18 *Farmers' Sun*, 3 Sept. 1919
19 See T.G.T. Stortz, 'Ontario Labour and the First World War' (MA thesis, University of Waterloo 1976), 106ff; and M. Robin, 'Registration, Conscription, and Independent Labour Politics, 1916–17,' *Canadian Historical Review* XLVII (1966).
20 CCA Minutes and Proceedings, 18 December 1913 (microfilm)
21 *Hamilton Herald*, 11 Aug. 1919. See also *Globe*, 2 Sept. 1919.

22 See *Canadian Forum* II (July 1922), 678–80.
23 *Globe*, 29 Sept. 1919, *Hamilton Herald*, 4 Oct. 1919
24 PAC, Rowell Papers, vol. 5, N.W. Rowell to Robert Borden, 28 Oct. 1918. See also Ramsay Cook, *John W. Dafoe* (Toronto 1966), 97.
25 Jean Graham, 'Ontario's New Leader,' *Canadian Magazine of Politics, Science, Art and Literature* 54 (1919–20), 226
26 QUA, Dunning Papers, Box 1, Folio 2, J.A. Calder to C.A. Dunning, 14 Jan. 1919
27 *Farmers' Sun*, 17 Sept. 1919
28 *Collingwood Enterprise*, 3 July 1919
29 *FP*, 84
30 OA, Hearst Collection, Correspondence, General Election, 1919, R. Davison to Hearst, 2 Sept. 1919. See also Morrison Memoirs, 60.
31 For a useful account of the varied factors that affected the election's outcome, see Brian D. Tennyson, 'The Ontario General Election of 1919: The Beginnings of Agrarian Revolt,' *Journal of Canadian Studies*, 4 (1969), 26–36.
32 *Maclean's* Dec. 1919, 28ff
33 Bodleian Library, Lionel Curtis Papers, C. 796, J.W. Flavelle to Robert Brand, 11 Nov. 1919. This reference was kindly furnished by Dr James G. Greenlee, who is preparing a biography of Sir Robert Falconer.
34 *Canadian Countryman*, 15 Nov. 1919; quoted in Trowbridge, 'War-time Discontent and the UFO,' 173; interview with Mrs Alice Nixon (St George), 11 Nov. 1981
35 *FP*, 85
36 *Globe*, 9 Sept. 1919
37 CCA Minutes and Proceedings, 19 Nov. 1919, p. 7. Similar concerns were expressed by the *Canadian Forum* II (April 1922), 585.
38 Good Papers, Correspondence, V, 1923, Good to Drury, 16 Apr. 1923
39 Crerar Papers, Series III, Box 139, Correspondence, UFO, 1923 file, Resolution – 1919
40 *Hamilton Herald*, 21 Oct. 1919
41 W.R. Plewman, *Adam Beck and the Ontario Hydro* (Toronto 1947), 235–6
42 Morrison Memoirs, 62. See also R.A. Farquharson, 'When Sir Adam Beck Tried to be Premier,' *Saturday Night* LXVII, 36 (14 June 1952). This article is based almost wholly on Morrison's memoirs.
43 Farquharson, 'Sir Adam Beck,' 2
44 C.B. Sissons, *Nil Alienum: Memoirs* (Toronto 1964), 198
45 Farquharson, 'Sir Adam Beck,' 3. Then a young reporter from the country who had supposedly gained Morrison's confidence, Farquharson spread the 'fire escape' story and claimed that he was the only reporter 'who knew [Beck] was upstairs'; *FP*, 86.
46 Morrison Memoirs, 70–1
47 See *Farmers' Sun*, 5 Nov. 1919 for a laudatory assessment.

CHAPTER 6: PONDERING THE OPTIONS

1 *FP*, 86; *Northern Advance*, 14 Dec. 1939, Xmas supplement, 15
2 PAC, Morrison Memoirs, 75. The same point was raised in the recollections of Mr Justice Campbell Grant who met Drury when he was a law student; interview with C. Grant (Toronto), 20 June 1973.
3 William Irvine, *The Farmers in Politics* (Toronto: Carleton Library 1976), 101–2
4 OA, Drury Papers, MU 954, Literary Works, 'Protection and the Farmer'
5 See Reginald Whitaker, 'Introduction,' *The Farmers in Politics* xxii–iii.
6 OA, 'An Interview with Mr. Ernest C. Drury ... conducted by Mr. Fred Schindeler and Mrs. Jean James' (19 Mar. 1965), 5
7 Novel, ch. xx, 7–8
8 On this point, see M. Jean MacLeod, 'Agriculture and Politics in Ontario Since 1867' (PH D thesis, University of London 1961), 215–16.
9 See David Gagan, *Hopeful Travellers: Families, Land, and Social Change in Mid-Victorian Peel County, Canada West* (Toronto 1981).
10 Drury Papers, MU 955, Literary Works, ch. 3: Personal Credentials
11 Novel, ch. XIX, 28
12 C.B. Sissons, *Nil Alienum: Memoirs* (Toronto 1964), 199
13 *Family Herald*, 29 Oct. 1919; *Hamilton Herald*, 30 Oct. 1919
14 *Maclean's*, Dec. 1919, 28 ff; OA, Maclean-Hunter Records, Col. J.B. Maclean Papers, Correspondence, Box 51, E.C. Drury file, J.B. Maclean to G.E. Pearson, 20 Jan. 1920
15 *Hamilton Times*, 30 Oct. 1919
16 UWO, Minutes of the East Lambton UFO, 1919–23, p. 21–2
17 Morrison Memoirs, 74

CHAPTER 7: TAKING CHARGE

1 QUA, Gregory Papers, Correspondence, 1921, E.C. Drury to W.D. Gregory, 23 Feb. 1921; interview with Mrs Elizabeth Partridge and Mrs Mabel Dunsmore (Crown Hill), 14 Oct. 1983
2 PAC, Morrison Memoirs, 76–7
3 Bodleian Library, Lionel Curtis Papers, c. 796, Flavelle to Brand, 11 Nov. 1919
4 Letter from Robert F. Nixon, 21 Nov. 1983
5 W.C. Good, *Farmer Citizen* (Toronto 1958), 122
6 C.B. Sissons, *Nil Alienum: Memoirs* (Toronto 1974), 199
7 See *Hamilton Spectator*, 30 Mar. 1942; W.R. Young, 'Conscription, Rural Depopulation, and the Farmers of Ontario, 1917–19,' *Canadian Historical Review*, LIII, 3 (1972), 298
8 Sissons, *Memoirs*, 200

9 *Stratford Beacon-Herald*, 12 Nov. 1919

10 *Hamilton Herald*, 21 Nov. 1919

11 PAC, Rowell Papers, vol. 12, N.W. Rowell to Wm. Hearst, 16 Feb. 1917. See also Margaret Prang, *N.W. Rowell: Ontario Nationalist* (Toronto 1975), 186, 221.

12 *Hamilton Herald*, 24 Jan. 1920; *Hamilton Times*, 30 Oct., 5 Nov. 1919

13 G.S. Henry, a member of the Hearst government, was the principal critic. He made his views known in a letter to the *Haldimand Advocate* (11 Sept. 1919). See OA, Henry Papers, 1912–13, MU 1322, 1919.

14 *CAR, 1920* (Toronto 1921), 521

15 *Globe*, 15 Jan. 1920

16 Interview with Mrs Alice Nixon, 11 Nov. 1981; *Globe*, 21 Oct. 1919

17 K.M. Nicholson, 'Policies of the Ontario Department of Education during the Administration of Premier E.C. Drury, 1919–23' (MA thesis, University of Toronto 1972), 21

18 For an account of Wood's career, which incidentally makes no reference to his difficulties at Western, see F.J.K. Griezic's Introduction to the 1975 reprint of *A History of the Farmers' Movements in Canada* (University of Toronto).

19 Sissons, *Memoirs*, 161

20 Morrison Memoirs, 78

21 N.D. Farrow, 'Political Aspects of the United Farmers Movement in Ontario' (MA thesis, University of Western Ontario 1938), 381n

22 *FP*, 90

23 OA, Schindeler-James tape, 3. See *Farmers' Sun*, 12 Nov. 1919

24 OA, RG 3, Drury Papers, Box 23, W.J. Duncan to Drury, 12 Dec. 1919

25 Morrison Memoirs, 83

26 OPL, Ironside Collection, Drury to Cowan, 15 Aug. 1952

27 Morrison Memoirs, 79

28 *Canadian Forum* II (July 1922), 679

29 Interview with Harold Drury (Crown Hill), 23 July 1981

30 *Hamilton Herald*, 24 Dec. 1919

31 PAC, Dafoe Papers, M–73, 1920, J.A. Stevenson to Dafoe, 23 Jan. 1920

32 See W.B. Hillman, 'J.J. Morrison: A Farmer Politician in an Era of Social Change' (MA thesis, University of Western Ontario 1974), 60–1.

33 *Farmers' Sun*, 6 Aug., 3 Sept. 1919

34 *Globe*, 10 Jan. 1920

35 *Hamilton Herald*, 13 Dec. 1919

36 Jean Graham, 'Ontario's New Leader,' *Canadian Magazine*, 54 (1919–20), 225

37 Morrison Memoirs, 43. On the UFWO, see Margaret Kechnie, 'The United Farm Women of Ontario: Developing a Political Consciousness,' *Ontario History* 77, 4 (1985), 267–80.

38 *Hamilton Herald*, 19 Dec. 1919

39 *Globe*, 25 Sept. 1922

40 *Globe*, 21 Oct. 1919
41 QUA, Crerar Papers, Series III, Box 125, Correspondence, J.J. Morrison file, Morrison to Crerar, 21 Nov. 1921
42 *Orillia Packet*, 6 Nov. 1919
43 W.A. Craik, *A History of Canadian Journalism*, II (Toronto 1959), 171. P.F.W. Rutherford, 'The People's Press: The Emergence of the New Journalism in Canada, 1869–99,' *Canadian Historical Review* LVI, 2 (1975), 169–91
44 *FP*, 93
45 PAC, Dafoe Papers, M–73, 1921, Stevenson to Dafoe, 1 Feb. 1921
46 OA, RG 35, Hydro Electric Power Commission, Carmichael Papers, General Correspondence, 1920–3, F.J.D. Spofford to D. Carmichael, 31 Mar. 1920
47 *Hamilton Herald*, 29 Nov. 1919
48 PAC, Sifton Papers, vol. 207, Sifton to Dafoe, 16 Dec. 1919
49 Morrison Memoirs, 85
50 Ibid., 90
51 See Drury Papers, Box 20, Drury to Elliott Brothers, 20 Jan. 1920. See *Oakville Star and Independent*, 23 Jan. 1920.
52 Good Papers, Correspondence, XXXI, 1958, M.H. Staples to Good, 2 Apr. 1958
53 *FP*, 94
54 Ironside Collection, Drury to Cowan, 15 Aug. 1952
55 *Hamilton Herald*, 22 Jan. 1920
56 *Canadian Champion*, 26 Feb. 1920
57 Interview with C. Grant (Toronto), 20 June 1973; see Novel, ch. XIX, 21.
58 *Hamilton Herald*, 29 Dec. 1919. Other examples cropped up in QUA, Gregory Papers, Correspondence, 1920, Gregory to W.F.W. Fisher, 11 May 1920; Carmichael Papers, Correspondence, 1922, D. Carmichael to W.E. Raney, 19 Dec. 1922.
59 He polled 4,419 votes to Stevenson's 2,111; Drury Papers RG 3, Box 38, Statement by Returning Officer ... of Halton, 16 Feb. 1920. See also *Burlington Gazette*, 18 Feb. 1920.
60 *Canadian Champion*, 26 Feb. 1920
61 Sissons, *Memoirs*, 199
62 Drury Papers RG 3, Box 20, Combines file
63 Interview with Mrs Alice Nixon, 11 Nov. 1981
64 *CAR*, *1920*, 551–2
65 Dafoe Papers, M73–1921, Stevenson to Dafoe, 1 Feb. 1921

CHAPTER 8: TACKLING EDUCATION

1 G.L. Woltz, 'Secondary Agricultural Education in Ontario' (BSA thesis, OAC 1914), 48–57
2 See, for example, the theses by R.E. Cummings (1915), R.A. Finn (1915), A.F.S.

Gilbert (1920), A.F. Hansuld (1920), and S.B. McCready (1917). The last-named went on to become director of elementary education for Ontario and brought out a textbook for rural schools entitled *The School and Country Life*. See Robert M. Stamp, *The Schools of Ontario, 1876–1976* (Toronto: OHSS 1982), 127.

3 *Globe*, 25 Sept. 1922
4 *Hamilton Herald*, 9 Dec. 1919. See also A.E. Springstead, 'Study of Rural Problems from the Viewpoint of the Agricultural Representatives' (BSA thesis, OAC 1922), 34–5.
5 *Globe*, 7 Jan. 1920. See also *CAR, 1920*, 593.
6 UGL, McConkey Papers, Box 1, Correspondence (General), 1923–52
7 *Globe*, 7 Jan. 1920. See also R.L. Vining, 'Some Phases of Ontario's Rural Problem' (BSA thesis, OAC 1914), 20–1.
8 *Canadian Forum* II (Feb. 1923), 137
9 J.W. Thompson and D.H. Hart, 'Rural Social Organizations' (BSA thesis, OAC 1922), 10, 13
10 OA, RG 3, Drury Papers, Box 36, G.H. Locke to E.C. Drury, 28 Nov. 1922
11 J.W. Edwards, 'Effect of Different Types of Farming on Communities' (BSA thesis, OAC 1922), 8–9, 12, 17. On this lack of rural homogeneity and its effects on education, see Chad Gaffield, 'Schooling, the Economy and Rural Society in Nineteenth Century Ontario,' *Childhood and Family in Canadian History*, ed. Joy Parr (Toronto 1982), 69–92. See also D.A. Lawr, 'The Development of Ontario Farming: Patterns of Growth and Change,' *Ontario History*, 64 (1972), 239–51.
12 *Farmers' Sun*, 14 Nov. 1919
13 *Hamilton Herald*, 22 Nov. 1919; OA, Belcher Papers, ms. 93, R.E. Kingsford to A.E. Belcher, 16 Mar. 1920
14 On this theme, see Carl Berger, 'The True North Strong and Free,' *Nationalism in Canada*, ed. Peter Russell (Toronto 1966), 4–5.
15 Novel, ch. VI, 12
16 *Hamilton Herald*, 19 Dec. 1919; see also Woltz, 'Secondary Agricultural Education,' 14.
17 Drury Papers, Box 20, Drury's statement, 2 Feb. 1920
18 Ibid., H.E. Smallpeice to Drury, 4 Mar. 1920; J.W. Buckley to Drury, 29 Feb. 1920
19 C.B. Sissons, *Nil Alienum: Memoirs* (Toronto 1964), 203
20 PAC, Morrison Memoirs, 117
21 Drury Papers, Box 20, R.H. Grant to V. Massey, 3 Feb. 1920
22 Claude Bissell, *The Young Vincent Massey* (Toronto 1981), 83
23 OA, 'An Interview with Mr. Ernest C. Drury ... conducted by Mr. Fred Schindeler and Mrs. Jean James (19 March 1965),' 2–3. See K.M. Nicholson, 'Policies of the Ontario Department of Education during the Administration of Premier E.C. Drury, 1919–1923' (MA thesis, University of Toronto 1972), 112.
24 *Canadian Forum*, II (July 1922), 679

25 QUA, Nickle Papers, Box 1 file 32, W.E. McNeill to W.F. Nickle, 29 May 1922. Box 2, File 45, Nickle to R.B. Taylor, 16 Jan. 1923
26 For a comprehensive treatment of the problem, see Peter Oliver, 'The Resolution of the Ontario Bilingual Schools Crisis, 119–1929,' *Journal of Canadian Studies*, VII (1971).
27 UCO, UFO Minute Book, Book 3, 1920–3, F, p. 27; Oliver, 'Bilingual Schools Crisis,' 29
28 PAC, Sissons Papers, I, Belcourt Correspondence, Belcourt to C.B. Sissons, 3 Nov. 1920
29 Oliver, 'Bilingual Schools Crisis,' 29, 30
30 Thompson and Hart, 'Rural Social Organizations,' 28
31 *CAR, 1923* (Toronto 1924), 527; see also *Northern Advance*, 29 Mar. and 5 Apr. 1923.
32 Drury Papers, Box 20, A.N. Myer to R.H. Grant, 2 Dec. 1919
33 Robert M. Stamp, 'Technical Education, the National Policy, and Federal-Provincial Relations in Canadian Education, 1899–1912,' *Canadian Historical Review*, LII (1971), 405
34 OA, RG 35, Hydro Electric Power Commission, Carmichael Papers, General Correspondence, 1921, Albert Hellyer to W.E. Raney, 26 Feb. 1921 (copy)
35 UWO, Dean of Arts, 1919–27, Correspondence, Box 7, Drury to W.S. Fox, 21 Mar. 1922
36 *Maclean's* (December 1919)
37 Dean of Arts, 1919–27, Correspondence, Fox to R.A. Falconer, 15 Mar. 1920. See *Globe*, 4 Sept., 29 Oct. 1920.
38 OA, RG 18, Royal Commission on University Finances, Box 1, Package II/[UFO submission]
39 *Farmers' Sun*, 22 Jan. 1921
40 UTA, Walker Papers, Box 24, Falconer to B.E. Walker, 27 July 1920
41 Information supplied by Dr James G. Greenlee
42 J.G. Greenlee, 'The Highroad of Intellectual Commerce: Sir Robert Falconer and the British Universities,' *Ontario History*, 74, 3 (1982), 188. See *Globe*, 8 Sept. 1921.
43 *CAR, 1922* (Toronto 1923), 584
44 Sissons, *Memoirs*, 202
45 Walker Papers, Box 24, Falconer to Walker, 27 July 1920
46 Ibid., Box 35, Walker to Falconer, 3 Sept. 1920; Greenlee, 'Falconer and the British Universities,' 186
47 UTA, Board of Governors, 20 Sept. 1920. Grant's letter, dated 14 Sept. 1920, was read out at a board meeting.
48 Royal Commission on University Finances, Box 2, Package VII, Minutes of Organizational Meeting, 11 Nov. 1920
49 *Report of the Royal Commission on University Finances* (Toronto 1921), 11–14

50 Dean of Arts, Correspondence, Box 4, J.S. Willison to Fox, 7 Apr. 1921
51 Nickle Papers, General Correspondence, Box 1, file 3, W.F. Nickle to E.W. Beatty, 23 Apr. 1921; Beatty to Nickle, 1 May 1921. See *Report of the Royal Commission on University Finances*, II, Appendix VII: Statement of Western University, 128–43.
52 Nickle Papers, General Correspondence, Box 1, file 5, O.D. Skelton to Nickle, 30 Mar. 1922; Dean of Arts, Correspondence, Box 5, R.O. Jolliffe to Fox, 9 Feb. 1922; Fox to Jolliffe, 11 Feb. 1922
53 Walker Papers, Box 35, Walker to Falconer, 15 July 1921; Box 24, Falconer to Walker, 3 Aug. 1921
54 PAC, Good Papers, VI, Good to L.A. Wood, 21 May 1923; Beth Good Latzer, *Myrtleville: A Canadian Farm and Family, 1837–1967* (Canadian ed., 1980), 247–8

CHAPTER 9: CONFRONTING ADAM BECK

1 OA, RG 35, Hydro Electric Power Commission, Carmichael Papers, General Correspondence, 1921, E.C. Drury to A.C. Lewis, 19 Jan. 1921
2 For a useful analysis of Adam Beck's policies, see H.V. Nelles, *The Politics of Development: Forests, Mines and Hydro-Electric Power in Ontario, 1849–1941* (Toronto 1974), especially chs. 7 and 10.
3 *CAR, 1920* (Toronto 1921), 567–8
4 OA, RG 3, Drury Papers, Box 40, 'Premier Drury's Address at Chippawa Development Opening, Dec. 28th, 1921'
5 W.R. Plewman, *Adam Beck and the Ontario Hydro* (Toronto 1947), 249
6 OHA, Beck Papers, file 135, Notes on the Relations between Adam Beck and E.C. Drury, T.A. Crerar to W.F. Maclean, 27 Feb. 1922
7 Drury Papers, Box 18, J.W. Kennedy to Drury, 10 Dec. 1919; A.B. Hellyer to Drury, 27 Nov. 1919; D. Richardson to Drury, 24 Nov. 1919
8 See Keith Fleming, 'The Uniform Rate and Rural Electrification Issues in Ontario Politics, 1919–1923,' *Canadian Historical Review*, LXIV, 4 (Dec. 1983), 494–518.
9 Carmichael Papers, General Correspondence, 1921, W.S. Bowden to Drury, 28 Nov. 1919 (copy)
10 *Report of a Committee of the Legislative Assembly of Ontario on a More Equitable System of Distribution of Hydro-Electric Power and a More Uniform Price, 30 November 1920* (Toronto 1920), 3
11 Fleming, 'The Uniform Rate,' 512, 514
12 Drury Papers, Box 24, Drury to Bowden, 30 July 1920
13 *Globe*, 7 May 1921
14 Drury Papers, Box 44, 'Address by Hon. E.C. Drury at Glencoe, August 24, 1921,' 1

15 Brian Tennyson, 'The Political Career of Sir William H. Hearst' (MA thesis, University of Toronto 1963), 178
16 Beck Papers, file 7, Drury to Beck, 18 Mar. 1920
17 *FP*, 136. Plewman, in *Beck and Hydro* (p. 272), put the figure at $2 million a month.
18 *Farmers' Sun*, 16 Nov. 1921; Toronto *Star*, 17 Nov. 1921; *Financial Post*, 18 Nov. 1921; OA, Maclean-Hunter Records, Col. J.B. Maclean Papers, Correspondence, Box 51, E.C. Drury file, J.B. Maclean to Drury, 24 Jan. 1946, 18 Nov. 1948
19 Drury Papers, Box 40, Drury to Carmichael, 10 Nov. 1921; Drury to Beck, 8 Dec. 1921; Beck to Drury, 12 Dec. 1921; and Box 39, J.W. Gilmour to H. Wallis, 17 Dec. 1921
20 Drury Papers, Box 40, 'Drury's Chippawa Address,' 2–4
21 *FP*, 137–8
22 Drury Papers, Box 40, Drury to Beck, 8 Feb. 1922; Beck to Drury, 10 Feb. 1922
23 Carmichael Papers, General Correspondence, 1920–3, T.H. Binnie to Carmichael, 13 Mar. 1922
24 *Hamilton Herald*, 5 July, 26 Nov., 12, 16 Dec. 1919 (emphasis added)
25 UCO, UFO Minute Book, Book 3, 14 Dec. 1919
26 *FP*, 116
27 SCA, Drury interview, Grace Chappell (1965)
28 UFO Minute Book, 1920–3, pp. 120–2
29 *Hamilton Herald*, 24 Dec. 1919
30 *Hamilton Spectator*, 14 Feb. 1920 ('Ship by Truck' section); see Stratford-Perth Archives, Highways, Good Roads Correspondence, 1917–34, file 5.
31 Drury Papers, Box 33, Report of the Hotel Committee to Board of Directors, Commercial Travellers' Association of Canada [n.d.]
32 Ibid., Box 22, R.T. Kelley to Drury, 17 Dec. 1919. See C.M. Johnston, *The Head of the Lake: A History of Wentworth County* (Hamilton 1967, 2nd ed.), 248
33 Drury Papers, Box 37, President, Canadian Automobile Association, to Drury, 22 Jan. 1922
34 E.C. Drury, *Forts of Folly* (Toronto 1932), 108–9. See also Drury Papers, Box 27, A.S.G. Clarke to Drury, 14 Sept. 1920.
35 *FP*, 113–14
36 M. Jean MacLeod, 'Agriculture and Politics in Ontario Since 1867' (PH D thesis, University of London 1961), 236–7
37 Interview with R.O. Biggs (Waterloo), 30 July 1981
38 Drury Papers, Box 22, C.A. Wartman to Drury, 24 Feb. 1920
39 Carmichael Papers, General Correspondence, 1920–3, Hellyer to W.E. Raney, 26 Feb. 1921 (copy)
40 Ibid., Box 5, F.C. Biggs to Carmichael, 27 Oct. 1922

41 *Mail and Empire*, 22 Jan. 1920; *Northern Advance*, 5 Apr. 1923; *Hamilton Herald*, 12, 13 Jan. 1920

42 *Canadian Forum*, I (July 1921), 291

43 C.B. Sissons, *Nil Alienum: Memoirs* (Toronto 1964), 200

44 OA, 'An Interview with Mr. Ernest C. Drury ... conducted by Mr. Fred Schindeler and Mrs. Jean James' (19 Mar. 1965), 10

45 *FP*, 119

46 *Globe*, 9 July 1920

47 Beck Papers, file 38, Radials, General #1, Beck to Drury, 13 July 1920

48 *FP*, 119

49 Novel, ch. IX, I

50 *Globe*, 13, 14 Jan. 1920; Toronto *Star*, 14 Jan. 1920 and *Farmers' Sun*, 3 Dec. 1919

51 OA, RG 24, Lieutenant-Governor's Office, L.H. Clarke, Series 12-a, Drury to L.H. Clarke, 14 Jan. 1920; Clarke to Drury, 15 Jan. 1920

52 PAC, Meighen Papers, vol. 70, file 54, Howard Ferguson to Meighen, 7 Dec. 1922

53 PAC, Dafoe Papers, M 73, 1921, Stevenson to Dafoe, I Feb. 1921

54 Ibid., A.H.U. Colquhoun to Dafoe, 29 Dec. 1921. For other critical comments, see *Globe*, 15 Sept. 1919

55 *CAR, 1920*, 502

56 F.F. Schindeler, *Responsible Government in Ontario* (Toronto 1973), 179

57 Drury Papers, Box 40, Radials Inquiry file, Appendix 2: Outline of the Course of the Commission

58 Ibid., W.A. Amos to R.F. Sutherland, 20 May 1921

59 See *Report of the Royal Commission Appointed to Enquire into Hydro-Electric Railways* (Toronto 1921).

60 *Globe*, 7 Sept. 1921

61 See *Statement Respecting the Findings and Other Statements contained in the Majority Report of the Commission appointed to enquire into the Subject of Hydro-Electric Railways* (Toronto 1922)

62 Drury, 'Glencoe Address,' 15

63 *Globe*, 30 Sept. 1921

64 Beck Papers, file 38, Canadian Club Address, 11 Nov. 1921

65 Meighen Papers, vol. 33, Series 2, Lake of the Woods, vol. 2, H. Dewart to Meighen, 18 Sept. 1921

66 Drury, 'Glencoe Address,' 7, 9–10

67 *CAR, 1920*, 580; Carmichael Papers, General Correspondence, 1921, H.B. Cowan to Carmichael, 22 Sept. 1921

68 Drury Papers, Box 35, E.S. Glassco to Drury, 27 Dec. 1922; Drury to Glassco, 19 Jan. 1923

69 Plewman, *Beck and Hydro*, 288. Drury used virtually the same wording in *Farmer*

Premier (p. 122). Plewman probably interviewed him on the subject some twenty years earlier.

70 *FP*, 121

71 Denison, *The People's Power*, 148

72 Drury Papers, Box 40, Drury to Beck, 11 Sept. 1922. Beck Papers, file 33, Drury to Beck, 12 Sept. 1922

73 Drury Papers, Box 40, C.A. Maguire to Drury, 21 Sept. 1922

74 *FP*, 123

75 Carmichael Papers, General Correspondence, 1920–3, R. Home Smith to Drury, 15 Aug. 1922

76 OA, RG 15, Department of Public Works, A-3, Correspondence files, 1919–23, E.C. Drury file, Memorandum for E.C. Drury, 4 Jan. 1923

77 Dafoe Papers, M 74, 1922, W.F. Maclean to Dafoe, 4 Oct. 1922

78 Drury Papers, Box 33, Drury to E.W. Oliver, 23 Feb. 1923. See *Globe*, 4 Nov. 1922.

79 Plewman, *Beck and Hydro*, 272

80 PAC, King Papers, vol. 42, Drury to W.L.M. King, 4 Oct. 1927

81 *Hamilton Herald*, 19 June 1923

82 Sissons, *Memoirs*, 201–2

83 *FP*, 119, 122

84 Drury, 'Glencoe Address,' 16, 19

CHAPTER 10: POLITICAL HOPES AND FEARS

1 For an examination of Sissons's role, see A.G. Mills, 'The *Canadian Forum*, 1920–1934: A Study in the Development of English-Canadian Socialist Thought' (PH D thesis, University of Western Ontario 1976), ch. 1.

2 *Canadian Forum*, II (Nov. 1921), 427–8

3 See H.V. Nelles, *The Politics of Development* (Toronto 1974), 399–400, and *CAR, 1921* (Toronto 1922), 614.

4 PAC, Dafoe Papers, M 73, 1921, J.A. Stevenson to J.W. Dafoe, 1 Feb. 1921. See also Ramsay Cook, *The Politics of John W. Dafoe and the Free Press* (Toronto 1963), 112–13.

5 *Canadian Forum*, II (Nov. 1921), 427–8

6 PAC, King Papers, Diaries, 1921, 16 Dec. 1921, pp. 159–60

7 Ibid., 13 Jan. 1921, p. 7. For the origins of the Progressives, see W.L. Morton, *The Progressive Party in Canada* (Toronto 1950), ch. III.

8 M. Jean MacLeod, 'The United Farmers' Movement in Ontario, 1914–1943' (MA thesis, Queen's University 1958), 102

9 QUA, Crerar Papers, T.A. Crerar to J.J. Morrison, 23 Sept. 1920

10 Crerar Papers, H.B. Cowan to G.F. Chipman, 20 Dec. 1920

11 UCO, UFO Minute Book, 1920–3, 15 Dec. 1920, F. For the major ramifications of the problem, see W.C. Brown, 'The Broadening Out Controversy: E.C. Drury, J.J. Morrison, and the United Farmers of Ontario' (MA thesis, University of Guelph 1979).

12 *CAR, 1920,* 543; UFO Minute Book, 1920–3, 16 Dec. 1920, H

13 On this point, see David Hoffman, 'Intra-Party Democracy: A Case Study,' *Canadian Journal of Economics and Political Science*, XXVII (1961), 223–35.

14 *Globe*, 17 Jan. 1921

15 *Farmers' Sun*, 30 June 1920; *Globe*, 9 Sept. 1921. See also W.B. Hillman, 'J.J. Morrison: A Farmer Politician in an Era of Social Change' (MA thesis, University of Western Ontario 1974), 84ff.

16 *FP*, 112. See also Drury Papers, Box 38, Special Series, Civil Service Superannuation file, 'Defence of Superannuation Bill in Drury's hand.'

17 Ibid., Morrison to secretaries of UFO locals, 5 May 1920

18 OA, RG 35, Hydro Electric Power Commission, Carmichael Papers, General Correspondence, 1920, J.E. Craven to Dougall Carmichael, 14 May 1920. UWO, Minutes, East Lambton UFO, 1919–23, 22 May 1920

19 OA, Morrison Scrapbook, R.W.E. Burnaby to E.C. Drury, 10 May 1920, PAC Morrison Memoirs, 116, 117

20 Crerar Papers, Gordon Waldron to Crerar, 3 June 1920

21 Dafoe Papers, M 73, 1921, Stevenson to Dafoe, 1 Feb. 1921

22 Apparently there was more than one such debate. The one referred to here presumably took place before Victoria's literary society early in 1920 (*FP*, 94). Or Drury may have confused it with another conducted in the fall of 1921 at a reunion of student farmers who had taken a special course at the University of Toronto (see *Globe*, 8 Sept. 1921).

23 *FP*, 94–5. See also MacLeod, 'The United Farmers' Movement,' 60.

24 QUA, Dunning Papers, Box 1, file 8, Charles Dunning to Walter Scott, 17 July 1922

25 See C.B. Macpherson, *Democracy in Alberta: Social Credit and the Party System* (Toronto 1953), ch. 1.

26 W.K. Rolph's *Henry Wise Wood of Alberta* (Toronto 1950) makes no reference to Morrison.

27 King Papers, Diaries, 1921, 13 Jan. 1921, p. 7

28 UFO Minute Book, 1920–3, 19 Jan. 1921, p. 11

29 King Papers, Diaries, 1921, 17 Jan. 1921, pp. 8–9

30 *Farmers' Sun*, 19 Jan. 1921, 18 Dec. 1920

31 PAC, Good Papers, Correspondence, XXXI, 1959, Drury to W.C. Good, 20 May 1959. Correspondence of this kind probably put Drury in the mood to compose his own memoirs.

32 Ibid., 1958, M.H. Staples to Good, 2 Apr. 1958

33 *Canadian Forum* II (Nov. 1921), 438, 440. M.H. Staples, ed., *The Challenge of Agriculture: The Story of the United Farmers of Ontario* (Toronto 1921), 41
34 R.W.E. Burnaby, 'The Farmers and the Forward Movement,' *Canadian Baptist*, I (Jan. 1920), 2
35 Cook, *Dafoe*, 112–13. See also Morton, *Progressive Party*, ch. III.
36 Crerar Papers, E.C. Drury file, Drury to Crerar, 30 Aug. 1921; Crerar to Drury, 7 Sept. 1921
37 Toronto *Star*, 5 Sept. 1921
38 PAC, Meighen Papers, vol. 42, file 157, Meighen to R.H. Grant, 5 Sept. 1921; Grant to Meighen, 13 Sept. 1921; Meighen to Grant, 14 Sept. 1921
39 Crerar Papers, Drury file, Crerar to Drury, 7 Sept. 1921, 1 Oct. 1921
40 Crerar Papers, Series III, Box 125, Correspondence, J.J. Morrison file, Crerar to Morrison, 7 Sept. 1921
41 Good Papers, Correspondence, V, 1923, Crerar to Good, 24 Feb. 1923. Over forty years later he was still despairing over the issue; see Crerar Papers, Box 136, Subject Correspondence, Senate-Retirement file, Crerar to Donald Cameron, 31 May 1966
42 Ibid., Box 125, Morrison file, Morrison to Crerar, [n.d.], 1921
43 PAC, Willison Papers, vol. 10, file 81, G.C. Creelman to J.S. Willison, 10 Mar. 1921; A.J.P. Taylor, *Beaverbrook* (New York 1972), 180–1
44 Meighen Papers, Series 3, vol. 99, C.A.C. Jennings to Meighen, 13 June 1923. The telegram was enclosed with a memo Dougall Carmichael sent to Doherty on 29 July 1922 (Carmichael Papers, Correspondence, 1922).
45 PAC, Canadian Union of Co-operatives, General Correspondence, vol. 15, 1915, M, George Keen to Humfrey Michell, 6 Mar. 1915
46 *Canadian Forum*, II (Apr. 1922), 579–80
47 UFO Minute Book, 1920–3, Executive Meeting, 27 June 1921, p. 37; see also N.D. Farrow, 'Political Aspects of the United Farmers' Movement in Ontario' (MA thesis, University of Western Ontario 1938), 275–7.
48 *Globe*, 27, 30 Sept. 1921
49 Crerar Papers, Morrison file, Morrison to Crerar, 9 Sept. 1921
50 Meighen Papers, vol. 23, file 58, R.K. Anderson to Meighen, 3 Oct. 1921; Meighen to Anderson, 15 Oct. 1921
51 UCO, file 324, United Farmers Co-operative Company (affidavit of Elmer Lick)
52 Crerar Papers, Series III, Box 105, Correspondence, Drury file, T.F. Swindle to Drury, 26 Oct. 1921; Drury to Crerar, 1 Nov. 1921
53 *Globe*, 12 Nov. 1921 (emphasis added)
54 The Southam press also assailed Meighen for his change of heart and flirtation with the 'interests.' See Charles Bruce, *News and the Southams* (Toronto 1968), 106–7.
55 *Globe*, 30 Nov. 1921. Sunny Jim has long since ceased to shine, but Dutch Cleanser and Old Chum are still hale and hearty.

56 King carried the riding with a majority of some one thousand votes. See R. MacGregor Dawson, *William Lyon Mackenzie King: A Political Biography*, I, *1874–1923* (Toronto 1958), 354ff.

57 Dafoe Papers, M 73, 1921, Sifton to Dafoe, 28 Nov. 1921

58 PAC, Sifton Papers, vol. 208, Sifton to Dafoe, 8 Dec. 1921

59 *FP*, 140

60 See *Hamilton Spectator*, 7, 8 Dec. 1921

61 *Globe*, 8, 9 Dec. 1921

62 PAC, Manion Papers, vol. I, Howard Ferguson to R.J. Manion, 7 Dec. 1921

63 QUA, Gregory Papers, Correspondence, 1921, F.F. Pardee to Gregory, 14 Dec. 1921

64 *Globe*, 18 Dec. 1921

65 Oliver's *Ferguson* makes much of this point; see ch. 7.

66 *CAR*, *1921*, 619

67 See Dawson, *King*, I, 357–8.

68 King Papers, Diaries, 1921, 8 Dec. 1921, p. 149

69 Dawson, *King*, I, 358

70 King Papers, Diaries, 1920–1, 12 Dec. 1921, p. 153. Ironically, Kennedy was named minister of railways and canals, the portfolio that might have gone to Drury had he accepted King's invitation.

71 Sifton Papers, vol. 208, Sifton to Dafoe, 12 Dec. 1921

72 *FP*, 140–1

73 King Papers, Diaries, 1920–1, 14 Dec. 1921, p. 156

74 *FP*, 141

75 Good Papers, X, XXI, Correspondence, 1961, Drury to Good, 19 Dec. 1961

76 King Papers, Diaries, 14 Dec. 1921, p. 157

77 Sifton Papers, vol. 208, Sifton to Dafoe, 14 Dec. 1921; Dafoe to Sifton, 19 Dec. 1921; Crerar Papers, Drury to Crerar, 17 Dec. 1921

78 King Papers, Diaries, 1920–1, 21 Dec. 1921, p. 165

79 *FP*, 141–2

80 Dawson, *King*, I, 367

81 W.C. Good, *Farmer Citizen* (Toronto 1958), 126. See also his letter of explanation to Crerar, written some thirty years later (Crerar Papers, Box 110, W.C. Good file, Good to Crerar, 5 July 1953).

82 Good Papers, XXXI, Correspondence, 1961, Drury to Good, 19 Dec. 1961

83 Interview with Pete McGarvey (Toronto), 4 Nov. 1983

84 Interview with R.O. Biggs (Waterloo), 7 Aug. 1981

85 Novel, ch. XXI, 7

86 King Papers, Diaries, 1922–3, 5 Nov. 1922, p. 135. See Margaret Prang, *N.W. Rowell: Ontario Nationalist* (Toronto 1975), 327, 343.

87 Dafoe Papers, M 74, 1922, Stevenson to Dafoe, 31 Aug. 1922 (emphasis added)

88 PAC, Rowell Papers, vol. 5, Federal Political file, vol. 10, N.W. Rowell to Crerar, 18 Sept. 1922

CHAPTER 11: ENTRENCHING VIRTUE

1 See *Hamilton Herald*, 12 May 1923
2 PAC, Good Papers, Correspondence, XXXI, 1958, M.H. Staples to W.C. Good, 2 Apr. 1958
3 OA 'An Interview with Mr. Ernest C. Drury ... conducted by Mr. Fred Schindeler and Mrs. Jean James,' 19 Mar. 1965, 20
4 Interview with R.O. Biggs (Waterloo), 30 July 1981
5 Peter Oliver, *G. Howard Ferguson: Ontario Tory* (Toronto: OHSS, 1977), 94
6 *FP*, 108
7 SCA, E.C. Drury's Speech for Reforestation Meeting [11 Aug. 1937], p. 3
8 UWL, Shortt Papers, file 243, Langdon Correspondence, Elizabeth Shortt to Miss Langdon, 4 Jan. 1925
9 Ibid., file 140, Drury Correspondence, E.C. Drury to Mrs. M. Cook (?), 9 Jan. 1922. *Mothers' Allowance Commission, First Annual Report, 1920–1* (Toronto 1922), 9
10 See OA, Drury Papers, MU 952, Literary Works, 'The Way Out,' Lesson XXIX, Veronica Strong-Boag, 'Wages for Housework': Mothers' Allowances and the Beginnings of Social Security in Canada,' *Journal of Canadian Studies*, XIV (1979), 24–7
11 See Veronica Strong-Boag, 'Intruders in the Nursery: Childcare Professionals Reshape the Years One to Five, 1920–1940,' in *Childhood and Family in Canadian History*, edited by Joy Parr (Toronto 1982), 160–78
12 Interview with R.O. Biggs; Shortt Papers, file 383, Rollo Correspondence, W.R. Rollo to Shortt, 22 July 1920
13 Shortt Papers, file 79, Carriere Correspondence, Eva Carriere to Peter Bryce, n.d.; file 168, Franklin Correspondence, Mildred A. Franklin to Shortt, 19 Oct. 1921
14 OA, RG 3, Drury Papers, Box 35, Mothers' Allowance Act file, Drury to W.C. Nelson, 16 Feb. 1923
15 Ibid., Mothers' Allowance Administration file, Reports [to the Honourable E.C. Drury] indicating the Value of Services being rendered by the Investigators of the ... Commission, 23 Mar. 1923
16 *Globe*, 26 Aug. 1922. See also, *Ottawa Evening Journal*, 14 Aug. 1920. For small-town opinion, see *Northern Advance*, 2 June, 27 Oct. 1921
17 *Northern Advance*, 15 Dec. 1921
18 *FP*, 108–9 and Schindeler-James tape, 5
19 What follows is drawn from a self-congratulatory statement, 'Some of the Achievements of the Drury Government during its Three and a Half Years of

Office,' [1, 3]. OA, RG 35, Hydro Electric Power Commission, Carmichael Papers, Box 6, D–7, E–8

20 Oliver, *Ferguson*, 216
21 Drury Papers, MU 952, 'The Way Out,' Lesson XXX, 2–4
22 Drury Papers, Box 27, Temperance Act Referendum file, H. Arnott to Drury, 24 Nov. 1919 (emphasis added). See Novel, ch. I, 4–5.
23 *Canadian Baptist*, 30 Oct. 1919, 8
24 Drury Papers, Box 27, Standard Hotels file, 1920
25 Ibid., Temperance Act Referendum file, James Hylands to Drury, 8 Nov. 1919
26 PAC, Sifton Papers, vol. 207, Clifford Sifton to J.W. Dafoe, 16 Jan. 1920
27 *CAR, 1920*, 612
28 This was the message he gave to an ILP banquet in Toronto on 17 May 1920. See *CAR, 1920*, 534.
29 See *FP*, 24, and *Northern Advance*, 17 Feb. 1938. On this rural 'narrowness of outlook on social and political problems,' see M. Jean MacLeod, 'Agriculture and Politics in Ontario Since 1867' (PH D thesis, University of London 1961), 216 ff.
30 *Hamilton Herald*, 9 Dec. 1919
31 Carmichael Papers, General Correspondence, 1921, Albert Hellyer to W.E. Raney, 26 Feb. 1921 (copy)
32 Drury Papers, MU 950, Box 1, Drury to D. McKee, 20 July 1945
33 Drury Papers, Box 29, Unemployment Conference file, 1920, Drury to Arthur Meighen, 16 Dec. 1920
34 Drury Papers, Box 37, Unemployment Relief file, G.W. Ross to Drury, 6 Apr. 1923. See *Globe*, 19 Oct. 1922.
35 Carmichael Papers, General Correspondence, 1922, F.A. Gaby to Carmichael, 28 Mar. 1922
36 See Gerald A. Hallowell, *Prohibition in Ontario* (Ottawa 1972), ch. V.
37 UGL, Reynolds Papers, Autobiography, 'The Village,' 7
38 Drury Papers, Box 25, Oakes Charges file, J.W. Oakes to Drury, 9 Mar. 1920
39 *Globe*, 10 Mar. 1922, *FP*, 179
40 See *Globe*, 17 Jan. 1920.
41 *FP*, 109, interview with R.O. Biggs
42 *Globe*, 13, 14 Apr. 1921
43 Margaret Prang, *N.W. Rowell: Ontario Nationalist* (Toronto 1975), 390
44 *Globe*, 11 Feb. 1921
45 See Hallowell, *Prohibition in Ontario*, 80–2
46 *Canadian Baptist*, 14 Apr. 1921
47 Richard Allen, *The Social Passion: Religion and Social Reform in Canada, 1914–28* (Toronto 1971), 274
48 Reynolds Papers, Autobiography, 'The Village,' 20
49 Strong-Boag, ' "Wages for Housework",' 24, 25, *CAR, 1921* (Toronto 1922), 554

50 Stephen Leacock, *My Discovery of England* (Toronto, New Canadian Library 1961), 134, 142. This work was originally published in 1922.
51 SCA, Mrs Morley Black tape, 31 July 1973
52 See *FP*, 126–7.
53 Before Drury came to power the dispensaries had been taken out of the hands of private vendors and placed under the operating control of the Board of License Commissioners.
54 *CAR, 1920*, 613
55 Drury Papers, Oakes Charges file, Oakes to Drury, 9 Mar. 1920 (open letter)
56 See Peter Oliver, 'W.E. Raney and the Politics of "Uplift",' *Journal of Canadian Studies*, 6 (1971), 12
57 *Globe*, 1 Mar. 1921
58 Oliver, 'Raney and the Politics of "Uplift",' 10–11, and *Hamilton Herald*, 12 May 1923
59 *Hamilton Herald*, 14 Feb. 1920
60 PAC, Meighen Papers, vol. 42, file 156, César Barranco to Meighen, 11 June 1921; Meighen to Barranco, 16 June 1921
61 Oliver, 'Raney and the Politics of "Uplift",' 14
62 Schindeler-James tape, 19
63 *CAR, 1922*, 590; Hallowell, *Prohibition in Ontario*, 115
64 *CAR, 1923* (Toronto 1924), 520. See also, *Farmers' Sun*, 14 Apr. 1922.
65 Rev. O.J.L. Spracklin, a zealous Baptist minister in charge of the special liquor squad in the Windsor area, used a government speedboat to conduct sometimes illegal searches of private property. He was also accused of taking money from bootleggers and on one occasion shot and killed a man.
66 *FP*, 126, 178
67 Hallowell, *Prohibition in Ontario*, 127–28
68 Cole Harris, 'The Myth of the Land in Canadian Nationalism,' in *Nationalism in Canada*, ed. Peter Russell (Toronto 1966), 35

CHAPTER 12: CLEANING UP THE NORTH

1 OA, RG 3, Drury Papers, Box 27, Temperance Act file, James Hylands to E.C. Drury, 25, 29 Nov. 1919
2 Ibid., Box 25, J.C. Montigue file, J.C. Montigue to Drury, 30 Dec. 1919; *CAR, 1920* (Toronto 1921), 519
3 *Globe*, 28 Sept. 29 Oct. 1921. Kipling's words in our 'Lady of the Snows' were relevant to Canada: 'Daughter am I in my mother's house / But mistress in my own.' For a treatment of this family idiom, see Ronald Hyam and Ged Martin, *Reappraisals in British Imperial History* (London 1975), 101–6.
4 For an account of the camp and the origins of the settlement, see Watson Kirkconnell, *A Slice of Canada: Memoirs* (Toronto 1967), 99–105, and *Kapuskasing: An*

Historical Sketch (Bulletin 38, Departments of History and Political Science, Queen's University, Kingston, 1921).

5 Drury Papers, Box 27, Soldiers' Settlement file, T.C. Boyce to Drury, 8 Jan. 1920 (copy)

6 H.V. Nelles, *The Politics of Development: Forests, Mines and Hydro-Electric Power in Ontario, 1849–1941* (Toronto 1975), 379–80

7 See OA, RG 18, B–50, Commission of Enquiry, Kapuskasing Colony (16 Mar. 1920); Sessional Paper, 61, 1920.

8 Drury Papers, Soldiers' Settlement file, H. McLeod to Drury, 8 Jan. 1920

9 Ibid., Drury to Rev. H.J. King, 12 Mar. 1920. See also Drury to Thomas McGrath, 26 Jan. 1920.

10 Peter Oliver, *G. Howard Ferguson: Ontario Tory* (Toronto: OHSS 1977), 96

11 Drury Papers, Soldiers' Settlement file, Drury to J.A. Gunn, 24 Apr. 1920

12 Ibid., Drury to H.E. Sheppard, 20 Apr. 1920 (copy)

13 See Margaret Paterson, *Carved from the Forest: A History of Kapuskasing* (Kapuskasing 1967), 14, 19.

14 Drury Papers, Box 27, Spruce Falls Ltd. file, Drury to W.D. McPherson, 29 May 1920

15 Ibid., Box 24, Kapuskasing Town Site, Memorandum of Agreement between ... George V and Spruce Falls Company Limited, October, 1920

16 Drury Papers, Box 24, Fire Control file, J.A. Ellis to Drury, 11 Nov. 1920

17 See *The First Fifty Years: A Golden Jubilee History of Kapuskasing* (Kapuskasing [1971], 3.

18 Drury Papers, Box 24, United Farmers' Co-operative Co. Ltd., Kapuskasing file, Hector Lemieux to Drury, 27 Feb. 1921

19 OA, 'An Interview with Mr. Ernest C. Drury ... conducted by Mr. Fred Schindeler and Mrs. Jean James,' 19 Mar. 1965, 17–18

20 The story of these transactions has been told from different vantage points in Nelles, *Politics of Development*, 385–91, and Oliver, *Ferguson*, 97–101, 110–14.

21 PAC, Sifton Papers, vol. 207, Clifford Sifton to J.W. Dafoe, 3 Nov. 1920

22 Schindeler-James tape, 21

23 Oliver, *Ferguson*, 98

24 See Nelles, *Politics of Development*, 390, 394.

25 *Mail and Empire*, 8 June 1921

26 OA, *Report of the Timber Commission, 9 March 1920* (Toronto), 35. For interestingly contrasting views on the impact of the *Report*, see Nelles, *Politics of Development*, 387 ff., and Oliver, *Ferguson*, 110–14.

27 *Canadian Forum* II (July 1922), 675–6

28 *Report of the Timber Commission*, 25–6; *Final Report*, 32

29 *CAR, 1922* (Toronto 1923), 583

30 Schindeler-James tape, 6

31 E.J. Zavitz, *Recollections of the First Provincial Forester* (Toronto 1964), 15

32 *CAR*, *1920*, 525
33 *Canadian Forum* II (July 1922), 680
34 Drury Papers, Box 33, Forestry Conference file, Charles Stewart to Drury, 9 Jan. 1923
35 He acted for the government in other cases as well. See OA, RG 35, Hydro Electric Power Commission, Carmichael Papers, Correspondence, 1921, N.W. Rowell to Raney, 7 Mar. 1921, and Margaret Prang, *N.W. Rowell: Ontario Nationalist* (Toronto 1975), 383.
36 The breakdown of indemnity claims was as follows:

Shevlin-Clarke Lumber Co.	$1,250,000.00
Marshay Lumber Co.	37,759.82
Jas. Horrigan & Co.	12,600.00
Geo. E. Farlinger	13,030.74
Russell Timber Co.	55,000.00
S.L. Lambert	4,218.76

Some of the Achievements of the Drury Government ... Carmichael Papers, Correspondence, Box 6, D–7, E–8
37 For a critical assessment of the judgment and a sympathetic treatment of Ferguson, see Oliver, *Ferguson*, 112.
38 See *Toronto Telegram*, 2 Oct. 1922.
39 See Nelles, *Politics of Development*, 392.
40 PAC, Laurier Papers, vol. 616, 167419–20, Memorial of Kenora Board of Trade (G.A. Toole, President), Feb. 1910
41 Drury Papers, Box 39, Special Series, English River Limits file, 'Facts and Figures re Government Policy in this matter,' 32. Ibid., W.E. Raney, 'Speech at Uxbridge' (1923), 3
42 Ibid., E.W. Backus to Drury, 20 Aug. 1920; Drury's response recorded 3 Sept. 1920
43 Ibid., Raney, 'Uxbridge Speech,' 5
44 Ibid.
45 *Kenora Miner and News*, 2 Oct. 1920
46 See *Globe*, and *Mail and Empire*, 1 Oct. 1920, and *Farmers' Sun*, 2 Oct. 1920.
47 Drury Papers, English River Limits file, W.J. Richards to Drury, 24 Aug. 1920; *Globe*, 23 Dec. 1920
48 OA, Heenan Papers, MU 1318, Letter and Cable file, G.A. Toole to Peter Heenan, 20 Dec. 1920; Drury Papers, Box 39, 'Facts and Figures,' 29–31
49 Ibid., 21. In addition, the government proposed to double the dues on the Lake of the Woods Limit, making them 80 cents instead of the 40 cents prescribed in the 1914 agreement.
50 *Hamilton Spectator*, 21 Dec. 1920
51 *CAR*, *1921*, 630

52 Drury's speech, 6, 8–9 [23 December 1920] (emphasis added); 'Memorandum for the Minister re Timber Estimate on English River Limit, 15 and 22 December 1920'
53 Nelles, *Politics of Development*, 393. See also *CAR, 1921*, 633, and H.E. Wilmot, *The Backus Deal* (Toronto 1923).
54 *Globe*, 23 Dec. 1920. On the other hand, the *Hamilton Spectator* (23 Dec. 1920) reported the arrangement without editorial comment.
55 Sifton Papers, vol. 207, Dafoe memorandum, 23 Dec. 1920

CHAPTER 13: DISSENSION AND DEFEAT

1 PAC, Good Papers, Correspondence, V, 1922, J.J. Morrison to W.C. Good, 25, 27 Apr. 1922
2 Ibid., Morrison to Good, 16 May 1922
3 *Farmers' Sun*, 17 Aug. 1922
4 See W.C. Brown, 'The Broadening Out Controversy: E.C. Drury, J.J. Morrison, and the United Farmers of Ontario' (MA thesis, University of Guelph 1979), 211–13.
5 Good Papers, Correspondence, VII, 1924, E.C. Drury to Good, 10 Feb. 1924
6 QUA, Crerar Papers, Series III, Box 105, Drury file, T.A. Crerar to Drury, 9 Dec. 1922. See *Farmers' Sun*, 1 June 1922.
7 *Globe*, 14 Oct. 1922
8 Crerar Papers, Box 110, W.C. Good file, Good to Crerar, 5 July 1953
9 Brown, 'The Broadening Out Controversy,' 223
10 *Canadian Forum* II (Sept. 1922), 739
11 Crerar Papers, Drury file, Crerar to M. Doherty, 17 Oct. 1922
12 Ibid., Doherty to Crerar, 20 Oct. 1922; M. Jean MacLeod, 'Agriculture and Politics in Ontario since 1867' (PH D thesis, University of London 1961), 237
13 To the Canadian Colonization Association, one of the many groups he addressed, he delivered his message, one seasoned with some of the wisdom of Henry George, about the need for a 'stiff unoccupied lands tax.' 'If I had the opportunity in Ontario,' he told his audience, 'I would not hesitate to legislate such a tax. (Applause.) It would bring down the cost of agriculture so that farmers could compete in world markets.' *Globe*, 19 Oct. 1922.
14 Ibid., 14 Nov. 1922
15 *FP*, 107
16 Crerar Papers, Series III, Box 105, M. Doherty file, 1922–3, Crerar to M. Doherty, 20 Jan. 1923; UCO, UFO Minute Book, 1920–3, p. 147
17 PAC, Macphail Papers, Correspondence, I, 1920–36
18 OPL, Ironside Collection, interview with H.B. Cowan, 19 Aug. 1969
19 Quoted in the *Globe*, 27 Oct. 1922

20 Drury Papers, Box 35, Government Loans file, A.W. Tully to Drury, 12 Mar. 1923
21 Ironside Collection, Cowan interview, 19 Aug. 1969
22 PAC, Dafoe Papers, M 74, 1922, J.A. Stevenson to Dafoe, 10 Dec. 1922
23 *FP*, 150
24 Good Papers, Correspondence, VI, 1923, Good to Morrison, 1 Feb. 1923
25 *Canadian Forum* III (Mar. 1923), 172. Sissons reckoned that the average number of voters in 73 rural ridings was over 10,000, while the average number of voters to each number in 12 selected urban ridings electing 15 members was over 28,000. It was this kind of anomaly that he wished to see wiped out.
26 *Farmers' Sun*, 10 Oct. 1922. *Globe*, 10 Oct. 1922
27 Good Papers, Correspondence, Morrison to Good, 28 Feb. 1923
28 OA, RG 35, Hydro Electric Power Commission, Carmichael Papers, Box 6, Drury to All Ministers, 28 Nov. 1922
29 For example, see the Toronto *Star*'s account (12 Apr. 1923).
30 Ibid.
31 Drury Papers, Box 32, W.H. Coon to Drury, 27 Oct. 1922. For a sample of Currie's vitriolic political language, see *Farmers' Sun*, 26 Nov. 1919.
32 Toronto *Star*, 12 Apr. 1923
33 *Canadian Champion*, 19 Apr. 1923. *Farmers' Sun*, 17 Apr. 1923 (emphasis added)
34 Good Papers, Correspondence, VI, Good to John Hamm, 9 May 1923
35 *Family Herald*, 2 May 1923
36 *FP*, 153
37 *Hamilton Herald*, 5 May 1923
38 [C.B.S.], 'The Ontario Experiment in Government,' *Canadian Forum* II (July 1922), 680
39 *Maclean's*, 1 May 1923, 46
40 Good Papers, Correspondence, Good to Drury, 24 Apr. 1923
41 UFO Minute Book, 1920–3, pp. 188–91
42 *Hamilton Herald*, 7 May 1923
43 UWO, Minutes of the East Lambton UFO, 1919–1923 (20–21 June 1923). For Drury's complaints about the *Sun*, see *FP*, 156.
44 J.W. Thompson and D.H. Hart, 'Rural Social Organizations' (BSA thesis, OAC 1922), 27
45 C.B. Sissons, *Nil Alienum: Memoirs* (Toronto 1964), 194–5
46 Drury Papers, Box 36, Roads file, M.H. Harker to Drury, 20 Feb. 1923
47 Ibid., Box 33, HEPC – Nipigon file, G.F. Doan to Drury, 5 Apr. 1923
48 Ibid., Box 32, B. Normandale to Drury, 16 May 1923; J.A. Hough to Drury, 16 May 1923; J.H. Kerr to Drury, 12 June 1923. For accounts of the Haileybury fire, see ibid., Boxes 30 and 32; *FP*, 145–7; Albert Tucker, *Steam into Wilderness: Ontario Northland Railway 1902–1962* (Toronto 1978), 77–80.

49 Drury Papers, Box 32, W.H. Coon to Drury, 27 Oct. 1922
50 Ibid., Box 31, Banting and Best file, S. Floyd to Drury, 4 Apr. 1923. For the background, see Michael Bliss, *The Discovery of Insulin* (Toronto 1982).
51 Interview with R.O. Biggs (Waterloo), 30 July 1981
52 Letter from Robert F. Nixon, 21 Nov. 1983
53 See Peter Oliver, *G. Howard Ferguson: Ontario Tory* (Toronto: OHSS 1977), 138–9.
54 Carmichael Papers, Box 7, B.H. Spence to Carmichael, 13 Jan. 1923; B.H. Spence, *Six Years Dry* (Toronto 1922)
55 See Richard Allen, *The Social Passion: Religion and Social Reform in Canada 1914–28* (Toronto 1971), 274–5.
56 Peter Oliver, 'W.E. Raney and the Politics of "Uplift",' *Journal of Canadian Studies* VI (1971), 3–18
57 *Globe*, 21 May 1923
58 *Border Cities Star*, 16 June 1923; *Hamilton Herald*, 30 May 1923
59 *Canadian Forum* III (June 1923), 260
60 *FP*, 158–9
61 UFO Minute Book, 1920–3, p. 38 (Executive Meeting, 21 June 1921)
62 Drury Papers, Box 35, Meat Inspection file, Drury to E.S. Glassco, 19 Jan. 1923. According to the less than friendly *Northern Advance*, Drury had been hesitant to try his luck in Halton again, and had only done so after making 'careful enquiries as to his chances' there (7 Dec. 1922).
63 *Border Cities Star*, 13 June 1923; *FP*, 157
64 UFO Minute Book, 1920–3, pp. 155, 204 (J.J. Morrison's Report, 7 Dec. 1925)
65 Crerar Papers, Box 125, Morrison file, Morrison to Crerar, 15 June 1923
66 Good Papers, Correspondence, J.A. Martin to Good, 30 May 1923; Ibid., Keen to Good, 11 May 1923
67 Ibid., Correspondence, V, 1922, Hamm to R. Hooper, 6 June 1922; VI, 1923, Good to Staples, 1 Feb. 1923
68 Provincial Archives of Alberta, Blair Papers, General Correspondence, C–L, 1921–3, C.H. Fullerton to W.J. Blair, 16 June 1923. Mr. Keith Stotyn of the Alberta Archives kindly made this available.
69 *Border Cities Star*, 14 June 1923. *Farmers' Sun*, 16 June 1923. *Hamilton Herald*, 16 June 1923
70 Oliver, *Ferguson*, 140
71 Carmichael Papers, Box 6, 'Some of the Achievements of the Drury Government during its Three and a Half Years of Office'
72 The returns were as follows:

George Hillmer (Cons.)		E.C. Drury (UFO)	L. Dale (Lib.)
Milton	513	183	263
Georgetown	420	138	400 (?)

| Oakville | 1117 | 481 | 92 |
| Burlington | 614 | 191 | 162 |

Oakville Star and Independent, 6 July 1923
73 Crerar Papers, Drury file, Crerar to Drury, 26 June 1923. See also *Farmers' Sun,*
27 June 1923.
74 *Collingwood Enterprise,* 23 Oct. 1919
75 Good Papers, Correspondence, VII, 1924, Good to C.A. Good, 29 Feb. 1924
76 N.D. Farrow, 'Political Aspects of the United Farmers Movement in Ontario' (MA
thesis, University of Western Ontario 1938), 315
77 Crerar Papers, Drury file, Drury to Crerar, 13 July 1923
78 Bodleian Library, Lionel Curtis Papers, C. 796, J.W. Flavelle to Robert Brand,
11 Nov. 1919. Dr James G. Greenlee kindly furnished this reference.
79 Blair Papers, General Correspondence, C–L, 1921–3, Fullerton to Blair, 16 June
1923
80 *Canadian Forum* II (May 1922), 613. See also *Globe,* 24 Oct. 1922.
81 PAC, Sissons Papers, I, Belcourt Correspondence, 1922–30, Sissons to N-A.
Belcourt, 21 Mar. 1923. The same point is made in Drury Papers, MU 955, Literary
Works, articles, p. 3.
82 See R.S. Pennefather, 'The Orange Order and the United Farmers of Ontario,
1919–1923,' *Ontario History,* 69 (1977), 169–84, especially 171–2; PAC, King
Papers, vol. 114, Drury to King, 2 Nov. 1925.
83 PAC, Sifton Papers, vol. 211, Sifton to Dafoe, 3 Oct. 1924. As for the coal scuttle,
it was removed from the premier's office by Ferguson only to be restored by one
of his Conservative successors, Leslie Frost. Frost chose to describe it as a 'very
modest brass arrangement,' and the political use made of it as phoney. Ironside
Collection, Drury Appreciation file, transcript of a taped interview with Leslie
Frost, 22 Jan. 1968, p. 4
84 [C.B.S.], 'A Reaction,' *Canadian Forum* III (July 1923), 295–6; Good Papers,
xviii, Subject files, 13–15, political matters, 1905–34
85 Novel, ch. XXI, 5–6; Ironside Collection, 'A Tribute to the Hon. E.C. Drury'
86 Interview with Mrs Mabel Dunsmore and Mrs Elizabeth Partridge (Crown Hill)
14 Oct. 1983. See Novel, ch. XXIII, 6.
87 Interview with Harold Drury (Crown Hill), 23 July 1981
88 Crerar Papers, Correspondence, Box 105, Drury file, Drury to Crerar, 13 July
1923
89 Quoted in *Hamilton Herald,* 27 June 1923
90 *Family Herald,* 4 July 1923; *Canadian Forum* III (July 1923), 294
91 Drury Papers, Box 43, Drury Portrait file, Raney to J.W.L. Forster, 12 June 1923.
The portrait was commissioned at $1,200, the price paid for Hearst's, though
done by another portraitist.

92 J.W.L. Forster, *Under the Studio Light: Leaves from a Portrait Painter's Sketch Book* (Toronto 1928)
93 Drury Papers, Drury Portrait file, J.W.L. Forster to W.E. Raney, 26 June 1923

CHAPTER 14: LIFE AFTER QUEEN'S PARK

1 *Canadian Champion*, 12 July 1923
2 UCO, UFO Minute Book, III, 1920–3, pp. 211, 238; J.N. Ponton to J.J. Morrison, 30 Aug. 1923. For an account of the UFO after 1923, see Jean MacLeod, 'The United Farmers Movement in Ontario, 1914–43' (MA thesis, Queen's University 1958), 144 ff.
3 PAC, Good Papers, Correspondence, VII, 1924, Morrison to Good, 24 Feb. 1924. Good to Morrison, 4 Mar. 1924
4 PAC, King Papers, vol. 99, Drury to W.L.M. King, 12 Mar. 1924
5 *Farmers' Sun*, 19 Jan. 1924; 9 Feb. 1924
6 Good Papers, Correspondence, Drury to Good, 10 Feb. 1924
7 Much of what follows is based on what Drury wrote about the case. See his 'Is There a Canadian Dreyfus?' *Maclean's*, 15 Sept. 1 and 15 Oct. 1933; *FP*, 102–3, 161–5.
8 Peter Oliver in his *Public and Private Persons: The Ontario Political Culture, 1914–1934* (Toronto 1975), 180–281, makes it plain, however, that he fell short of this goal.
9 Good Papers, Correspondence, Good to Drury, 16 May 1924
10 Ibid., 1925–33, Drury to Good, 13 Nov. 1933. For an authoritative rebuttal, see Oliver, *Public and Private Persons*.
11 *FP*, 168
12 Good Papers, Correspondence, Henry Moyle to Good, 15 Mar. 1923
13 PAC, Sifton Papers, vol. 210, J.W. Dafoe to Clifford Sifton, 27 Dec. 1923
14 *FP*, 167
15 King Papers, vol. 86, 1923, F.A. McGregor to Drury, 18 Aug. 1923
16 R.M. Dawson, *William Lyon Mackenzie King, 1874–1923* (Toronto 1958), 541 n
17 Drury Papers, Box 36, Soldiers' Aid Commission file, J. McNamara to Drury, 12 Feb. 1923
18 King Papers, vol 114, Drury to King, 2 Nov. 1925
19 Ibid.
20 Ibid; King to Drury, 18 Nov. 1925; King to Charles Dunning, 19 Dec. 1925
21 Good Papers, Correspondence, Drury to Good, 10 Feb. 1924
22 See UCO, Minute Book of the United Farmers Co-operative Company, III, p. 14.
23 For the details, see R. McG. Dawson, *The Government of Canada* (Toronto 1952), 166, 390, 392–3; Roger Graham, *The King-Byng Affair, 1926: A Question of Responsible Government* (Toronto 1967).
24 King Papers, vol. 131, Drury to King, 17 Dec. 1926
25 Drury Papers, MU 954, III, Literary Works, 'Can the Farmer be Protected?' [1927]

26 King Papers, vol. 142, Drury to King, 17 Jan. 1927. See also vol. 131, Drury to King, 17 Dec. 1926.
27 Ibid., Drury to King, 17 Jan. 4 Oct. 1927; King to Drury, 10 Oct. 1927; OA, Maclean-Hunter Records, Col. J.B. Maclean Papers, Correspondence, Box 51, E.C. Drury file, Drury to J.B. Maclean, 11 Oct. 1927
28 Drury Papers, 'Can the Farmer be Protected?' See also *Northern Advance*, 17 Dec. 1925.
29 *Farmers' Sun*, 16 Feb. 1924
30 Ibid., 15 Sept. 1927
31 King Papers, vol. 142, Drury to King, 4 Oct. 1927
32 W.C. Brown, 'The Broadening Out Controversy: E.C. Drury, J.J. Morrison, and the United Farmers of Ontario' (MA thesis, University of Guelph 1979), 263
33 UFO Minute Book, V, 1926–33, pp. 38–9, 41 (annual meeting, 1927)
34 Ibid., p. 39. See MacLeod, The United Farmers Movement in Ontario, 172 ff.
35 Drury Papers, MU 954, Box 6, IV, UFO Resolutions, 1927
36 UWL, Shortt Papers, 202, Annie Hasley Correspondence, Elizabeth Shortt to Annie Hasley (n.d.)., Peter Oliver, G. *Howard Ferguson: Ontario Tory* (Toronto: OHSS 1977), 473 n. 90
37 Toronto *Star*, 29 Sept. 1927
38 King Papers, vol. 142, Memo for Rt. Hon. W.L.M. King re Collingwood Harbor; Ibid., vol. 151, Drury to J.C. Elliott, 26 Apr. 1928. (Collingwood is identified as 'Pottersville Harbour' in Drury's unpublished novel, ch. XXXIII, 15.)
39 QUA, Crerar Papers, Box 105, Drury file, Memorandum re Willison-Neeley Corporation. No references to this enterprise were found in the Willison Papers at the Public Archives.
40 PAC, Manion Papers, vol. 1, J.S. Willison to R.J. Manion, 9 June 1920
41 King Papers, vol. 142, Drury to King, 17 Jan. 1927
42 Ibid., vol. 151, Drury to King, 12 Apr. 1928; Drury to King, 26 Apr. 1928; King to Drury, 14 July 1928
43 *Toronto Telegram*, 11 Jan. 1928
44 *Regina Leader*, 10 Feb. 1928; *Calgary Albertan*, 11 Jan. 1928; *Winnipeg Free Press*, 10 Jan. 1928
45 They appeared in the following issues: 3, 10, 17, 24 Feb. 2, 9, 16, 23, 30 Mar.; and 6 Apr. 1928.
46 Crerar Papers, Correspondence, Drury file, Drury to T.A. Crerar, 10 Sept. 1928; Crerar to Drury, 19 Sept. 1928
47 Ibid., A.K. Cameron to Crerar, 8 Oct. 1928; Crerar to Drury, 16 Oct. 1928; Drury to Crerar, 24 Oct. 1928
48 *Maclean's*, 1, 15 Feb.; 1 Mar.; 1, 15 Apr.; 15 July 1929. See also, E.C. Drury, *Forts of Folly* (Toronto [1932]), 67.
49 G.W. Stephens, *The St. Lawrence Waterway Project* (Montreal 1930), 233
50 *Maclean's*, 1, 15 Feb.; 1 Mar. 1929

51 In the late 1920s he had seldom hesitated to offer King gratuitous advice on a wide range of matters. See, for example, King Papers, vol. 161, Drury to King, 12 Dec. 1929.
52 *FP*, 170
53 King Papers, King to Drury, 6 June 1930; Drury to King, 23 June 1930
54 *Northern Advance*, 17 July 1930
55 Unfortunately company records, which could have possibly disclosed details of Drury's salary and shares, were destroyed when the company was recently purchased by another firm.
56 PAC, King Diaries, 1930, vol. I, 19 July 1930, pp. 166, 167
57 King Papers, vol. 173, Drury to King, 2 Aug. 1930; vol. 172, Crerar to King, 7 Nov. 1930
58 C.B. Sissons, *Nil Alienum: Memoirs* (Toronto 1964), 204

CHAPTER 15: TURNING POINT

1 Novel, ch. XXVII, 10
2 PAC, Sissons Papers, II, D; 1878–1965, E.C. Drury to Mrs C.B. Sissons, Sept. 1956. See also, Novel, ch. XXVII, 16–17.
3 OPL, Ironside Collection, Drury to H.B. Cowan, 15 Aug. 1952. He conveyed much the same sentiments to Col. J.B. Maclean. See OA, Maclean-Hunter Records, Col. J.B. Maclean Papers, Correspondence, Box 51, E.C. Drury file, Drury to J.B. Maclean, 13 Nov. 1931.
4 Interview with Harold Drury (Crown Hill), 23 July 1981
5 E.C. Drury, *Forts of Folly* (Toronto [1932])
6 PAC, Good Papers, Correspondence, IX, 1925–33, Drury to Good, 13 Nov. 1933. On the Young Farmers and related developments in the farm movement, see Ian Macpherson, 'An Authoritative Voice: The Reorientation of the Canadian Farmers' Movement, 1935–1945,' *Historical Papers 1979* (CHA) (Ottawa 1980), 164–81.
7 Ironside Collection, 'Tribute to the Honourable E.C. Drury'
8 SCA, Grace Chappell interview with E.C. Drury (Summer 1965), 24
9 OA, Drury Papers, MU 950, Evidence of Peter Smith taken at Kingston Penitentiary, 6 Apr. 1925
10 Good Papers, Correspondence, Drury to Good, 13 Nov. 1933
11 Peter Oliver, *Public and Private Persons: The Ontario Political Culture, 1914–1934* (Toronto 1975)
12 Company records provide no clues. Nor do the memories of his children. Varley Drury, for example, was 'surprised' to learn that at one time his father had been president of a company. See letter from Margaret E. Drury, 6 Sept. 1983.
13 Maclean-Hunter Records, Maclean Papers, Correspondence, H.N. Moore to Maclean, 14 Dec. 1933; H.T. Hunter to Maclean, 29 Nov. 1933
14 OA, Henry Papers, MU 1347, 1932, G.S. Henry to C.H. Carlisle, 26 Mar. 1934

15 Ibid., A.C. Pratt to Henry, 19 Jan. 1932
16 Drury Papers, MU 952, 'The Way Out,' Lesson IV
17 *Maclean's*, 15 May, 1 and 15 June 1933; UWO, Minutes of the East Lambton UFO, 6 Nov. 1932
18 *Northern Advance*, 8 Dec. 1932
19 Drury Papers, MU 952, 'The Way Out,' Lesson VI
20 PAC, King Papers, vol. 199, Drury to King, 17 Apr. 1934
21 Good Papers, Correspondence, 1933–4, Reinhold Niebuhr to Good, 21 Nov. 1934. On Niebuhr's ideas and philosophy, see William H. Dray, *Philosophy of History* (Englewood Cliffs, 1964), chs. 5 and 8.
22 Henry Papers, 1932, Pratt to Henry, 19 Jan. 1932. See Neil McKenty, *Mitch Hepburn* (Toronto 1967), 49.
23 Interview with Harold Drury; OA, RG 3 Hepburn Papers, 1934, Drury to M.F. Hepburn, 27 June 1934
24 King Papers, vol. 199, Drury to King, 26 June 1934
25 Hepburn Papers, 1934, Drury to Hepburn, 27 June 1934
26 Ibid.
27 King Papers, vol. 199, King to Drury, 7 July 1934
28 Hepburn Papers, 1934, Drury to Hepburn, 7 Aug. 1934; Ibid., Frank Hammond, D.F. McCuaig, A.J. Sergeant to Hepburn, 4 Sept. 1934; W.D. Smith to Hepburn, 6 Sept. 1934
29 QUA Gregory Papers, Letters, 1930–1940, Gregory to Drury, 24 Oct. 1934
30 Interview with Harold Drury (Crown Hill), 14 Oct. 1983; Ironside Collection, Drury to H.B. Cowan, 15 Aug. 1952

CHAPTER 16: NEW CAREERS AND OLD REFLECTIONS

1 PAC, Good Papers, Correspondence, XXXI, 1953, E.C. Drury to W.C. Good, 28 Feb. 1953
2 Over the years he clipped out and saved bits of poetry and doggerel that reflected his distaste for urban turmoil and immorality: 'Clang of machines ... / Men crawling ant-like in mud / Progress and heartbreak and blood ...' OA, Drury Papers, MU 955, Miscellaneous file.
3 *FP*, 189; interview with Harold Drury (Crown Hill), 14 Oct. 1983
4 SCA, Tape recordings, no. 23, interview with Professor A.R.M. Lower, 23 June 1973
5 *FP*, 191
6 Ibid., 192
7 Good Papers, Correspondence, Drury to Good, 28 Feb. 1953
8 SCA, E.C. Drury's Speech for Reforestation Meeting [11 Aug. 1937], 1–15
9 *Barrie Advance*, 25 Oct. 1938. This was more or less true of later editions of *Who's Who in Canada*. See, for example, the volume *1960–1* (Toronto 1960), 988.

10 *Collingwood Enterprise-Bulletin*, 20 May 1943
11 See Jean MacLeod, 'The United Farmers Movement in Ontario, 1914–43' (MA thesis, Queen's University 1958), 198–9, and Ian MacPherson, 'An Authoritative Voice: The Reorientation of the Canadian Farmers' Movement, 1935–1945,' *Historical Papers 1979* (CHA) (Ottawa 1980), 164–81.
12 OA, Drury Papers, MU 952, 'The Way Out,' Lessons X, XIV, XXI; ibid., MU 955, Literary Works, Ms. articles, p. 2
13 OA, Maclean-Hunter Records, J.B. Maclean Papers, Correspondence, Box 51, E.C. Drury file, F.S. Chalmers to J.B. Maclean, 30 Dec. 1940
14 J. Lloyd Harrington, 'The Drury Débâcle: An Inquiry into the Causes of the Farmers' Defeat of '23,' *Canadian Forum* XXXVIII (October 1948), 153–5
15 R.A. Farquharson, 'When Sir Adam Tried to be Premier,' and 'The Rise and Fall of the UFO,' *Saturday Night* LXVII (14, 21 June 1952)
16 OPL, Ironside Collection, Drury to Cowan, 15 Aug. 1952
17 Ibid.
18 Good Papers, Correspondence, 1958, M.H. Staples to Good, 2 Apr. 1958
19 Ironside Collection, Drury to Cowan, 15 Aug. 1952
20 The paper was not printed in their *Proceedings* but notice was given of his attendance at the meeting; *The Ontario Historical Society News Letter* IV (Mar. 1948), 2
21 Drury Papers, MU 954, Drury to W.C. Good, 24 May 1954
22 A.F. Hunter, *A History of Simcoe County* (Barrie 1909). See *Midland Free Press-Herald*, 4 Dec. 1946; Good Papers, Correspondence, 1959, Drury to Good, 20 May 1959.
23 *Western Ontario Historical Notes* VIII, no. 14 (Dec. 1950), title page. For a more favourable judgment of Hunter's work, see *Review of Historical Publications relating to Canada* XIV (1910), 102.
24 Drury Papers, MU 950, Drury to Good, 18 Dec. 1958
25 See *Papers and Records, Ontario Historical Society* III (1901), and Gerald Killan, *David Boyle: From Artisan to Archaeologist* (Toronto 1983), 111, 120, 135.
26 Good Papers, Correspondence, 1961, Drury to Good, 19 Dec. 1961
27 DFP, 'Red Parlour Politics, 1867–1967: Reflections by the Hon. E.C. Drury'
28 Interview with Harold Drury (Crown Hill), 23 July 1981; see *FP*, 190–1.
29 Drury Papers, MU 952, 'The Way Out,' Lesson XVII. On this point, see F.G. Speck and L.C. Eiseley, 'Significance of Hunting Territory Systems of the Algonkian in Social Theory,' *American Anthropologist*, new series, XLI (1939), 269–80; and A.G. Bailey, *The Conflict of European and Eastern Algonkian Cultures, 1504–1700: A Study in Canadian Civilization*, 2nd ed. (Toronto 1969), xx-xxii.
30 See Kenneth E. Kidd, *The Excavation of Ste. Marie I* (Toronto 1949).
31 Drury Papers, MU 950, Box 1, 1932–48; K.E. Kidd to Drury, 30 Apr. 1948; letter from Kenneth Kidd to the author
32 DFP, Kidd to Drury, 19 May 1950

33 Ibid.; for recent studies of the Huron, see Bruce Trigger, *The Children of Aataent-sic: A History of the Huron People to 1660* (Montreal 1976), and Conrad Heiden-reich, *Huronia: A History and Geography of the Huron Indians, 1600–1650* (Toronto 1971).
34 Letter from Kenneth Kidd to the author
35 E.C. Drury, *All for a Beaver Hat: A History of Early Simcoe County* (Toronto 1959), 160
36 *University of Toronto Quarterly* XXIX (1959–60), 524–5. The reviewer was J.M.S. Careless of the university history department. See also *Canadian Historical Review* XL (Dec. 1959), 352.
37 Interviews with Greta Harradine and Amelia Whalen (Barrie), 14 Oct. 1983
38 Interview with John Murphy (Barrie), 14 Oct. 1983
39 *FP*, 193
40 Interview with John Murphy
41 UWO, Presidents' Papers, G.E. Hall, 1957–8, Box 17, R.B. Willis to G.E. Hall, 21 Oct. 1958. 'Men's Residence,' Names, p. 3

CHAPTER 17: THE LAST DAYS

1 Interview with Elizabeth Partridge and Mabel Dunsmore (Crown Hill), 14 Oct. 1983
2 PAC, Good Papers, Correspondence, XXXI, 1962, Marion and Harold Drury to Good, 16 Jan. 1962
3 PAC, Sissons Papers, II, D, 1878–1965, E.C. Drury to C.B. Sissons, 22 Dec. 1964
4 Good Papers, Correspondence, Drury to Good, 17 Feb. 1962
5 OA, Drury Papers, MU 950, Box 1, 1960–7, W.E. Elliott to Drury, 12 May [1960]
6 Ibid., Robert Fulford to Stuart Brownlee, 23 Sept. 1963
7 McMaster University Archives, McClelland and Stewart Archive, Drury File, J.A. Gibson to J.G. McClelland, 10 May 1964
8 See DFP, Laura Chisholm to Drury, 7 Sept. 1966
9 Ibid., Patrick Nicholson to Drury, 29 Aug. 1966
10 OPL, Ironside Collection, Transcript of a Taped Tribute to the Hon. E.C. Drury ... Jan. 22 1968, by the Hon. Leslie Frost, Broadcast over CFOR Nite Line
11 Ibid., Drury Appreciation Committee, Pete McGarvey to Bas Mason, 13 Nov. 1967
12 See W.C. Brown. 'The Broadening Out Controversy: E.C. Drury, J.J. Morrison, and the United Farmers of Ontario' (MA thesis, University of Guelph 1979)
13 Richard Hofstadter's views in *The Age of Reform* (Chicago 1955) have been challenged in Norman Pollock's *The Populist Response to Industrial America* (New York 1966). Pollock's generous assessment of the Populist legacy has influenced writings on their Canadian counterparts, the Patrons of Industry. See Russell Hann, *Some Historical Perspectives on Canadian Agrarian Movements* (Toronto 1973).
14 See Melvin Richter, *The Politics of Conscience: T.H. Greene and His Age* (London 1964).

A Note on Sources

Those who venture to write on E.C. Drury face a mixed blessing. Alone among Ontario's premiers, he wrote his memoirs. *Farmer Premier* provides a welcome understanding of the man and his times, an exercise that is massively supplemented by his varied auto-biographical and thematic writings, mostly unpublished, which now, thanks to his family, reside in the Archives of Ontario. These include a lengthy, uncompleted novel and essays of varying substance (the ones under the rubric 'The Way Out' are among the most revealing) together with draft articles on topics close to his heart: prohibition, free trade, and agrarianism. But what makes the blessing a mixed one, especially in the case of *Farmer Premier*, is that these writings either totally ignore or only cursorily recall certain important aspects of his life and career. Sometimes they also recall major events inaccurately and tend to distort the record. But on the whole, the voluminous commentaries and reflections that Drury committed to paper over his long lifetime provided vital background information and helped to illuminate his character, personality, and strongly held views. The pieces he had published in farm journals and in such popular magazines as *Maclean's* also served this cause.

No sizable body of private correspondence exists, though some does survive in the provincial archives along with the bulky public correspondence in Record Group 3. Fortunately some of Drury's letters are preserved in the archival collections of others. Thus the literary remains of fellow activist W.C. Good, and of his life-long friend C.B. Sissons, which are available at the Public Archives of Canada, furnished insights and information vital to an understanding of Drury and his era. Much the same can be said for the papers of T.A. Crerar and J.D. Gregory in the archives of Queen's University in Kingston. Of value too were the published memoirs of both Good and Sissons, not to mention the unpublished ones of J.J. Morrison in the Public Archives, which tell the other side of the UFO's story of political involvement. An assortment of newspapers, periodicals, and magazines were also called upon for assistance. Although the *Farmer's Sun*, the *Globe*, *Maclean's*, and the *Canadian Forum* tend to predominate, other voices of the urban press, secular and denominational, were listened to along with the editorial views of small-town and rural papers.

University theses were important assets to this study. Leading the way were those of M. Jean MacLeod. Her Queen's MA thesis (1958) and 'Agriculture and Politics in Ontario since 1867' (London, PH D, 1961) included important correctives to earlier accounts and sound assessments of Ontario agrarianism. Also helpful were W.C. Brown's 'The Broadening Out Controversy: E.C. Drury, J.J. Morrison and the United Farmers of Ontario' (Guelph, MA, 1979): K.M. Nicholson, 'The Policies of the Ontario Department of Education during the Administration of Premier E.C. Drury, 1919–1923' (Toronto, MA, 1972); N.D. Farrow, 'Political Aspects of the United Farmer Movement in Ontario' (Western, MA. 1938); and R.W. Trowbridge, 'Wartime Discontent and the Rise of the UFO, 1914–1919' (Waterloo, MA, 1967). The Ontario Agricultural College, through the courtesy of the University of Guelph Library, also came to the rescue. A mine of information and analysis was uncovered there on rural themes and problems thanks to the BSA thesis program launched at the OAC in 1906.

Of the published works, L.A. Wood's *A History of the Farmers' Movements in Canada* (Toronto, 1924, 1977) and M.H. Staples's *The Challenge of Agriculture: The Story of the UFO* (Toronto 1922) assume almost the aura of primary sources now, given the authors' intimate association with the agrarian movements of their day. Other sources of a secondary nature will be found in the endnotes.

What follows is a list of the repositories visited and the documentary collections examined:

ARCHIVES OF ONTARIO

E.A. Belcher Papers
Dougall Carmichael Hydro Papers
E.C. Drury Papers (private collection, and Prime Ministers' Papers, Record Group 3)
William Hearst Collection
Peter Heenan Papers
G.S. Henry Papers
M.F. Hepburn Papers
J.B. Maclean Papers

PUBLIC ARCHIVES OF CANADA

Co-operative Union of Canada Papers
J.W. Dafoe Papers
W.C. Good Papers
George Keen Papers
W.L.M. King Papers and Diaries
Wilfrid Laurier Papers
Agnes Macphail Papers
R.J. Manion Papers

Arthur Meighen Papers
J.J. Morrison Memoirs
Charles Murphy Papers
N.W. Rowell Papers
Clifford Sifton Papers
John Willison Papers
J.S. Woodsworth Papers

ONTARIO HYDRO ARCHIVES

Adam Beck Papers: Historical Correspondence and Mementoes, 1903–1925

LIBRARY, UNITED CO-OPERATIVES OF ONTARIO

Minute Books of the United Farmers of Ontario
Minute Books of the United Farmers Co-operative Company

QUEEN'S UNIVERSITY LIBRARY

T.A. Crerar Papers
Charles Dunning Papers
W.E. Lambert Papers
W.F. Nickle Papers
R.B. Taylor Papers
Minutes and Proceedings of the Canadian Council of Agriculture

UNIVERSITY OF TORONTO ARCHIVES

R.A. Falconer Papers
Edmund Walker Papers
Minutes and Correspondence of the University Board of Governors

REGIONAL COLLECTION, UNIVERSITY OF WESTERN ONTARIO

Dean of Arts' Correspondence
Presidents' Correspondence
Fred Landon Papers
Minutes of the East Lambton UFO, 1919–1923

UNIVERSITY OF GUELPH LIBRARY

Creelman Papers
McConkey Papers
Reynolds Papers

UNIVERSITY OF WATERLOO LIBRARY

Elizabeth Shortt Papers

McMASTER UNIVERSITY ARCHIVES

McClelland and Stewart Archive

BROCK UNIVERSITY LIBRARY

Bowslaugh Diaries

SIMCOE COUNTY ARCHIVES

A.F. Hunter Papers
Kenneth Kidd Collection
Laura Young Papers
Grace Chappell Interviews with E.C. Drury
Minute Books of Simcoe County Reforestation Committee, 1925–1952

ORILLIA PUBLIC LIBRARY

Allan Ironside Collection

HAMILTON PUBLIC LIBRARY

William Hendrie Collection
Recollections of John Peebles

WARWICKSHIRE COUNTY RECORD OFFICE (UK)

Parish Lists, Registers, and Baptisms

Index

THE ONTARIO HISTORICAL STUDIES SERIES

The Ontario Historical Studies Series is a comprehensive history of Ontario from 1791 to the present, which will include several biographies of former premiers, numerous volumes on the economic, social, political, and cultural development of the province, and a general history incorporating the insights and conclusions of the other works in the series. The purpose of the series is to enable general readers and scholars to understand better the distinctive features of Ontario as one of the principal regions within Canada.

THE BIOGRAPHIES OF THE PREMIERS

J.M.S. Careless, ed., *The Pre-Confederation Premiers: Ontario Government Leaders, 1841–1867*

Charles W. Humphries, *'Honest Enough to Be Bold': The Life and Times of Sir James Pliny Whitney* (Premier, 1905–1914)

Charles M. Johnston, *E.C. Drury: Agrarian Idealist* (Premier, 1919–1923)

Peter Oliver, *G. Howard Ferguson: Ontario Tory* (Premier, 1923–1930)

A.K. McDougall, *John P. Robarts: His Life and Government* (Premier, 1961–1971)

FORTHCOMING

A. Margaret Evans, SIR OLIVER MOWAT (Premier, 1872–1896)
Robert J.D. Page, SIR GEORGE W. ROSS (Premier, 1899–1905)
John T. Saywell, HON. MITCHELL F. HEPBURN (Premier, 1934–1942)
Roger Graham, HON. LESLIE M. FROST (Premier, 1949–1961)

Milton Keynes UK
Ingram Content Group UK Ltd.
UKHW031027291024
450383UK00001B/59